CASE CLOSED™

VOLUME 78

Gosho Aoyama

Case Briefing:

Subject:
Occupation:
Special Skills:
Equipment:

Jimmy Kudo, a.k.a. Conan Edogawa
High School Student/Detective
Analytical thinking and deductive reasoning, Soccer
Bow Tie Voice Transmitter, Super Sneakers,
Homing Glasses, Stretchy Suspenders

The subject is hot on the trail of a pair of suspicious men in black when he is attacked from behind and administered a strange substance which physically transforms him into a first grader. When the subject confides in the eccentric inventor Dr. Agasa, they decide to keep the subject's true identity a secret for the safety of everyone around him. Assuming the new identity of first-grader Conan Edogawa, the subject continues to assist the police force on their most baffling cases. The only problem is that most crime-solving professionals won't take a little kid's advice!

Table of Contents

CONFIDEN

CASE CLOSED
Volume 78
Shonen Sunday Edition

Story and Art by GOSHO AOYAMA

MEITANTEI CONAN Vol. 78
by Gosho AOYAMA
© 1994 Gosho AOYAMA
All rights reserved.
Original Japanese edition published by SHOGAKUKAN.
English translation rights in the United States of America, Canada, the United Kingdom,
Ireland, Australia and New Zealand arranged with SHOGAKUKAN.

Translation
Tetsuichiro Miyaki

Touch-up & Lettering
Freeman Wong

Cover & Graphic Design
Andrea Rice

Editor
Shaenon K. Garrity

Printed in the U.S.A.

Published by VIZ Media, LLC
P.O. Box 77010
San Francisco, CA 94107

10 9 8 7 6 5 4 3 2 1
First printing, April 2021

shonensunday.com

viz.com

FILE 1: MYSTERY TRAIN (DEPARTURE)

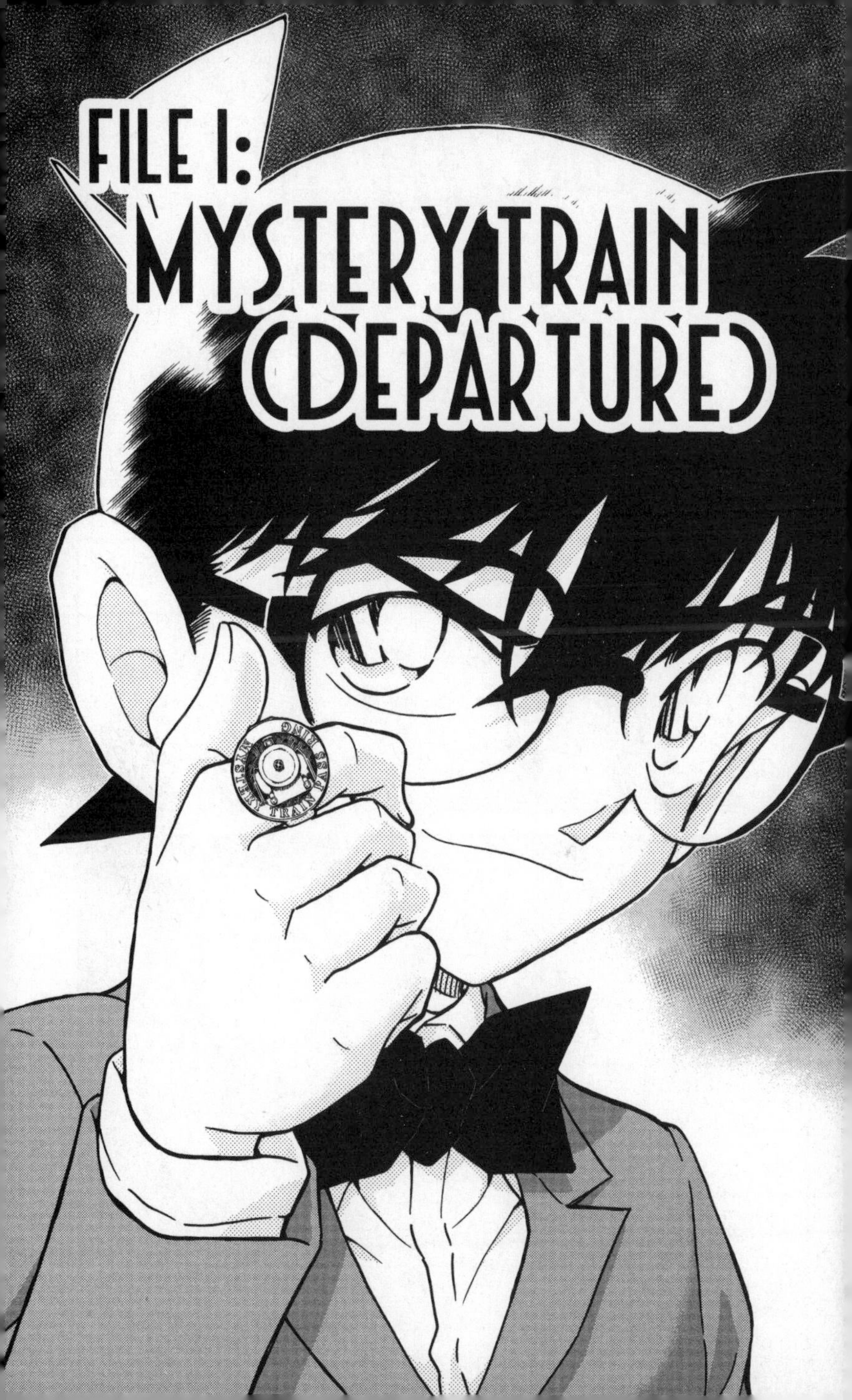

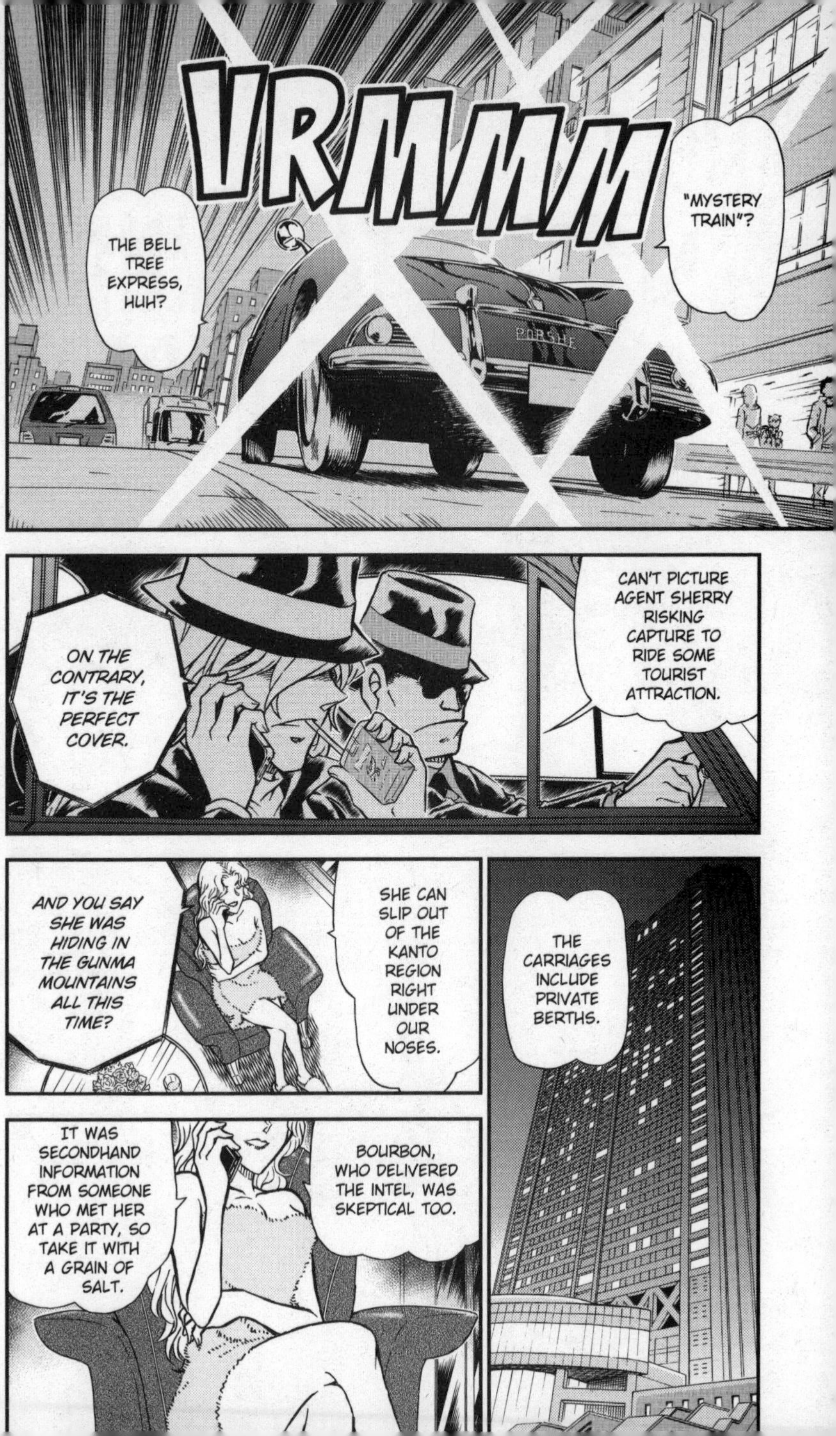
VRMMM
"MYSTERY TRAIN"?
THE BELL TREE EXPRESS, HUH?
CAN'T PICTURE AGENT SHERRY RISKING CAPTURE TO RIDE SOME TOURIST ATTRACTION.
ON THE CONTRARY, IT'S THE PERFECT COVER.
THE CARRIAGES INCLUDE PRIVATE BERTHS.
SHE CAN SLIP OUT OF THE KANTO REGION RIGHT UNDER OUR NOSES.
AND YOU SAY SHE WAS HIDING IN THE GUNMA MOUNTAINS ALL THIS TIME?
BOURBON, WHO DELIVERED THE INTEL, WAS SKEPTICAL TOO.
IT WAS SECONDHAND INFORMATION FROM SOMEONE WHO MET HER AT A PARTY, SO TAKE IT WITH A GRAIN OF SALT.

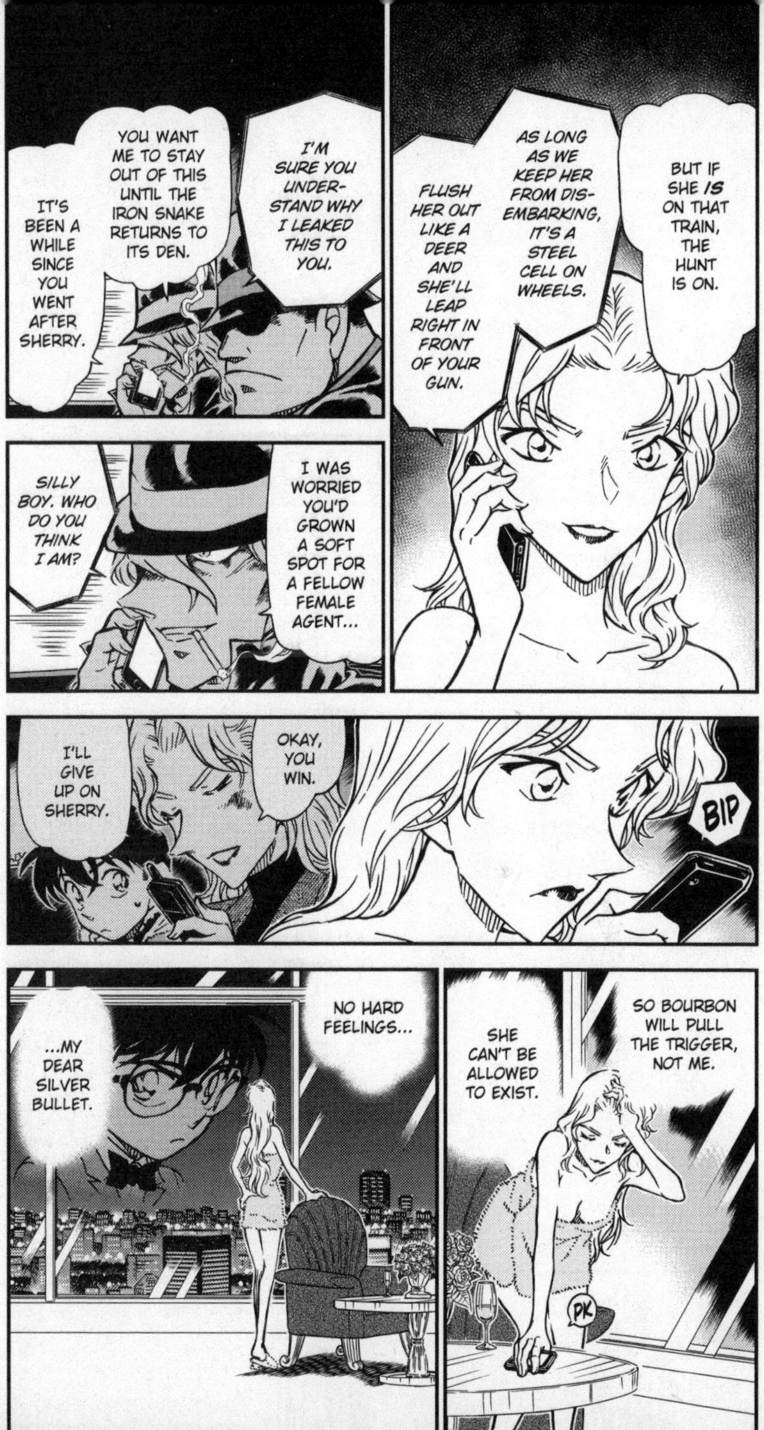
BUT IF SHE *IS* ON THAT TRAIN, THE HUNT IS ON.
AS LONG AS WE KEEP HER FROM DIS-EMBARKING, IT'S A STEEL CELL ON WHEELS.
FLUSH HER OUT LIKE A DEER AND SHE'LL LEAP RIGHT IN FRONT OF YOUR GUN.
I'M SURE YOU UNDER-STAND WHY I LEAKED THIS TO YOU.
YOU WANT ME TO STAY OUT OF THIS UNTIL THE IRON SNAKE RETURNS TO ITS DEN.
IT'S BEEN A WHILE SINCE YOU WENT AFTER SHERRY.
I WAS WORRIED YOU'D GROWN A SOFT SPOT FOR A FELLOW FEMALE AGENT...
SILLY BOY. WHO DO YOU THINK I AM?
BIP
OKAY, YOU WIN.
I'LL GIVE UP ON SHERRY.
SO BOURBON WILL PULL THE TRIGGER, NOT ME.
SHE CAN'T BE ALLOWED TO EXIST.
PK
NO HARD FEELINGS...
...MY DEAR SILVER BULLET.

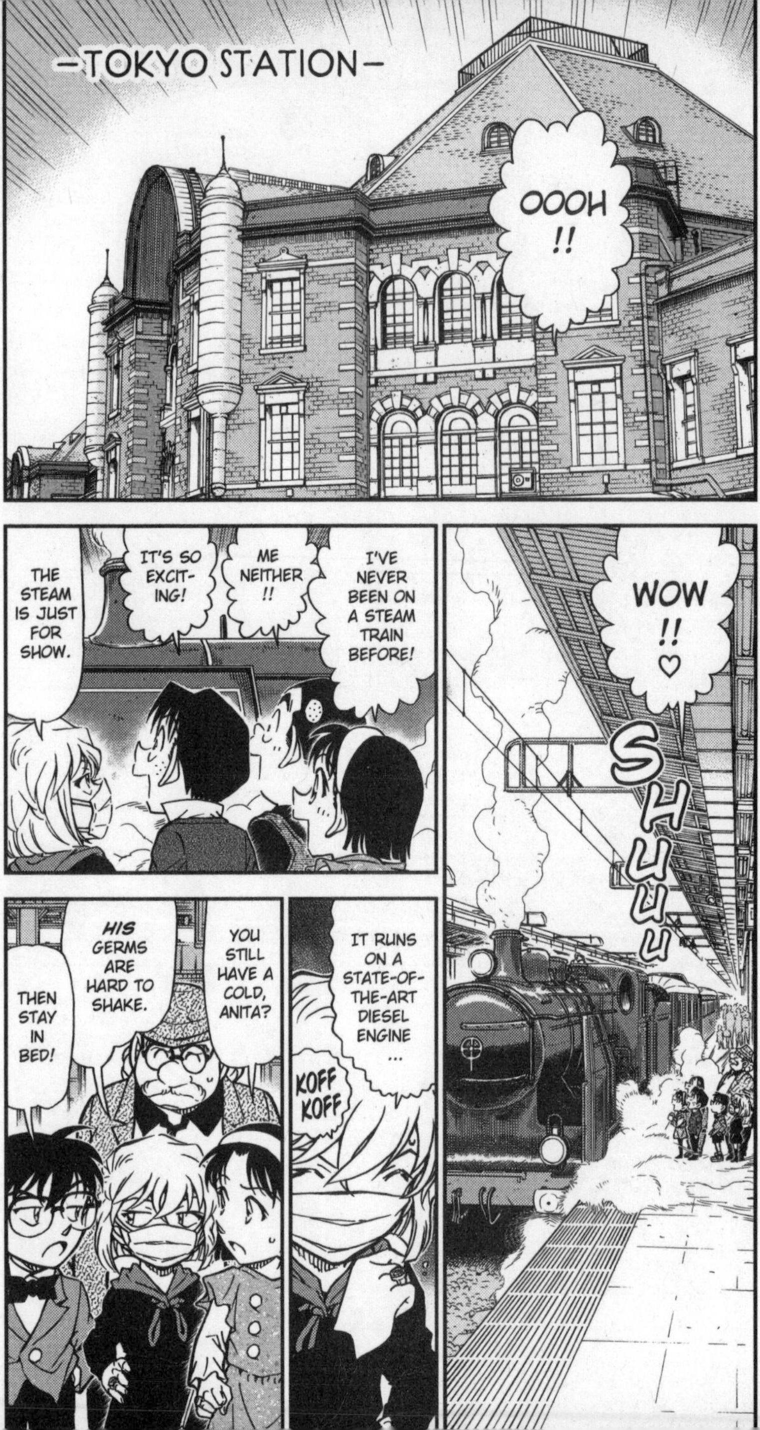
—TOKYO STATION—
OOOH !!
WOW !! ♥
SHUUUU
I'VE NEVER BEEN ON A STEAM TRAIN BEFORE!
ME NEITHER !!
IT'S SO EXCITING!
THE STEAM IS JUST FOR SHOW.
IT RUNS ON A STATE-OF-THE-ART DIESEL ENGINE ...
KOFF KOFF
YOU STILL HAVE A COLD, ANITA?
HIS GERMS ARE HARD TO SHAKE.
THEN STAY IN BED!

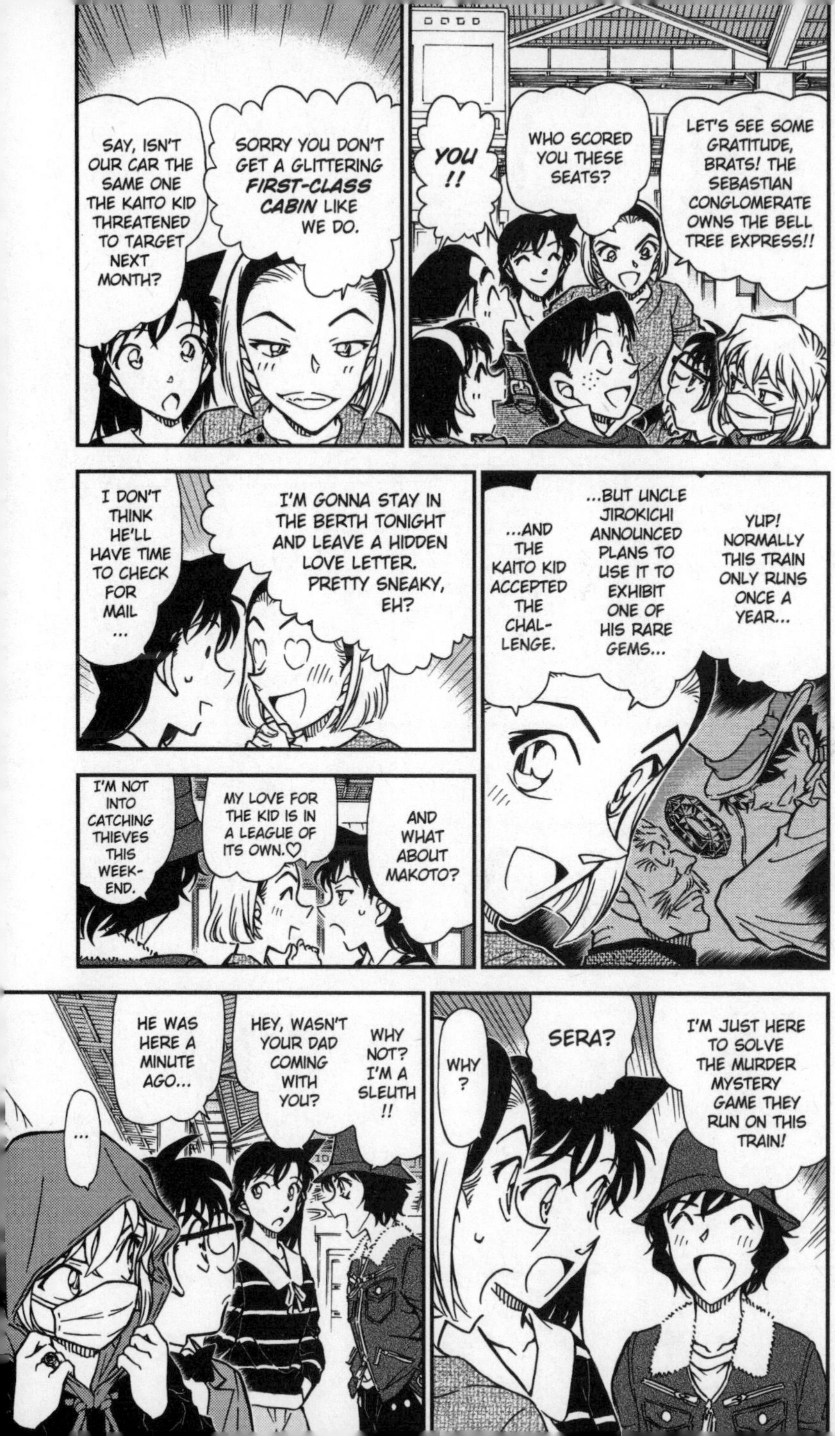
LET'S SEE SOME GRATITUDE, BRATS! THE SEBASTIAN CONGLOMERATE OWNS THE BELL TREE EXPRESS!!
WHO SCORED YOU THESE SEATS?
YOU !!
SORRY YOU DON'T GET A GLITTERING FIRST-CLASS CABIN LIKE WE DO.
SAY, ISN'T OUR CAR THE SAME ONE THE KAITO KID THREATENED TO TARGET NEXT MONTH?
YUP! NORMALLY THIS TRAIN ONLY RUNS ONCE A YEAR...
...BUT UNCLE JIROKICHI ANNOUNCED PLANS TO USE IT TO EXHIBIT ONE OF HIS RARE GEMS...
...AND THE KAITO KID ACCEPTED THE CHAL-LENGE.
I'M GONNA STAY IN THE BERTH TONIGHT AND LEAVE A HIDDEN LOVE LETTER. PRETTY SNEAKY, EH?
I DON'T THINK HE'LL HAVE TIME TO CHECK FOR MAIL ...
AND WHAT ABOUT MAKOTO?
MY LOVE FOR THE KID IS IN A LEAGUE OF ITS OWN.♡
I'M NOT INTO CATCHING THIEVES THIS WEEK-END.
I'M JUST HERE TO SOLVE THE MURDER MYSTERY GAME THEY RUN ON THIS TRAIN!
SERA?
WHY ?
WHY NOT? I'M A SLEUTH !!
HEY, WASN'T YOUR DAD COMING WITH YOU?
HE WAS HERE A MINUTE AGO...
...

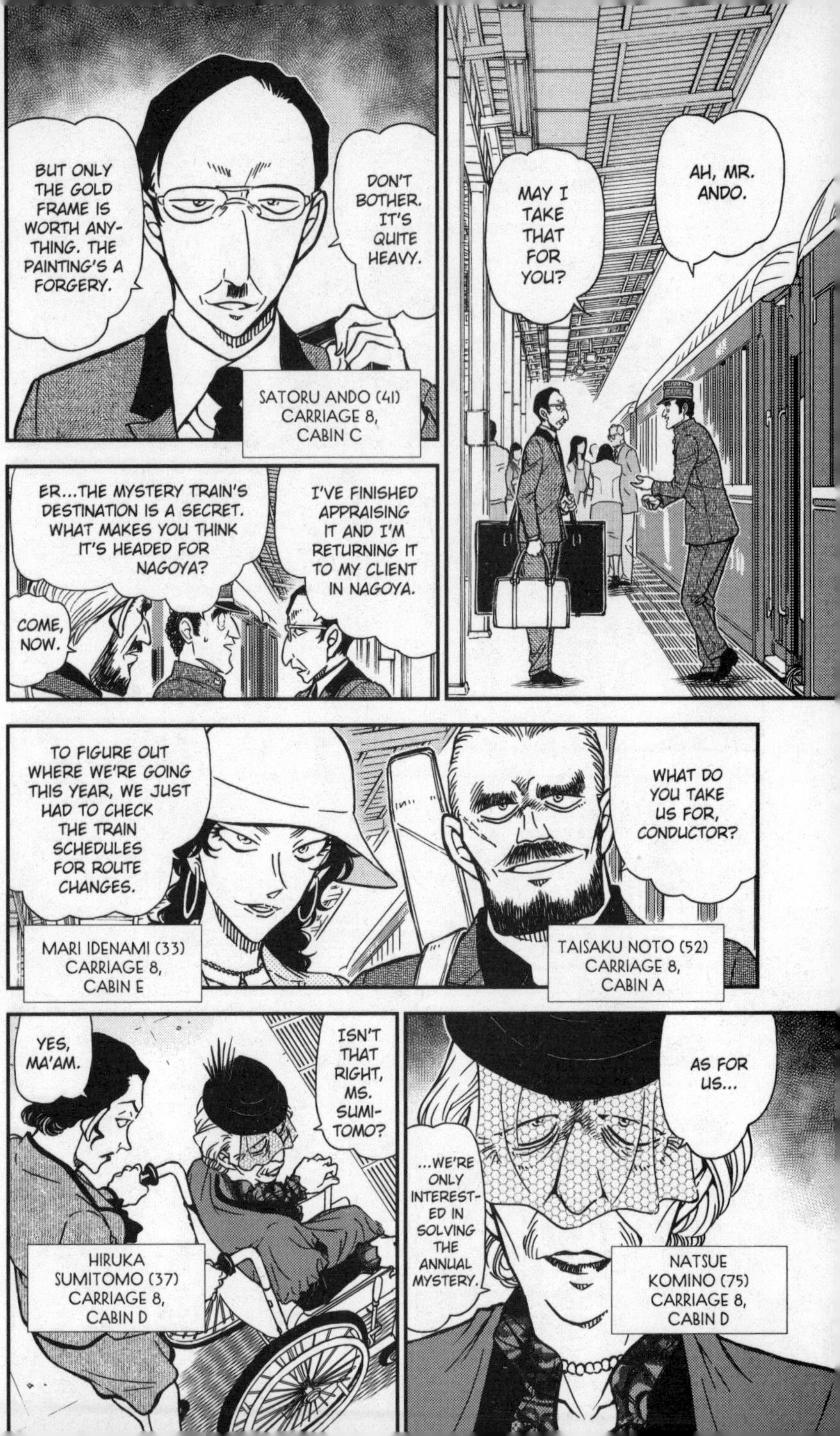
AH, MR. ANDO.
MAY I TAKE THAT FOR YOU?
DON'T BOTHER. IT'S QUITE HEAVY.
BUT ONLY THE GOLD FRAME IS WORTH ANYTHING. THE PAINTING'S A FORGERY.
SATORU ANDO (41) CARRIAGE 8, CABIN C
I'VE FINISHED APPRAISING IT AND I'M RETURNING IT TO MY CLIENT IN NAGOYA.
ER...THE MYSTERY TRAIN'S DESTINATION IS A SECRET. WHAT MAKES YOU THINK IT'S HEADED FOR NAGOYA?
COME, NOW.
WHAT DO YOU TAKE US FOR, CONDUCTOR?
TAISAKU NOTO (52) CARRIAGE 8, CABIN A
TO FIGURE OUT WHERE WE'RE GOING THIS YEAR, WE JUST HAD TO CHECK THE TRAIN SCHEDULES FOR ROUTE CHANGES.
MARI IDENAMI (33) CARRIAGE 8, CABIN E
AS FOR US...
...WE'RE ONLY INTEREST-ED IN SOLVING THE ANNUAL MYSTERY.
NATSUE KOMINO (75) CARRIAGE 8, CABIN D
ISN'T THAT RIGHT, MS. SUMI-TOMO?
YES, MA'AM.
HIRUKA SUMITOMO (37) CARRIAGE 8, CABIN D

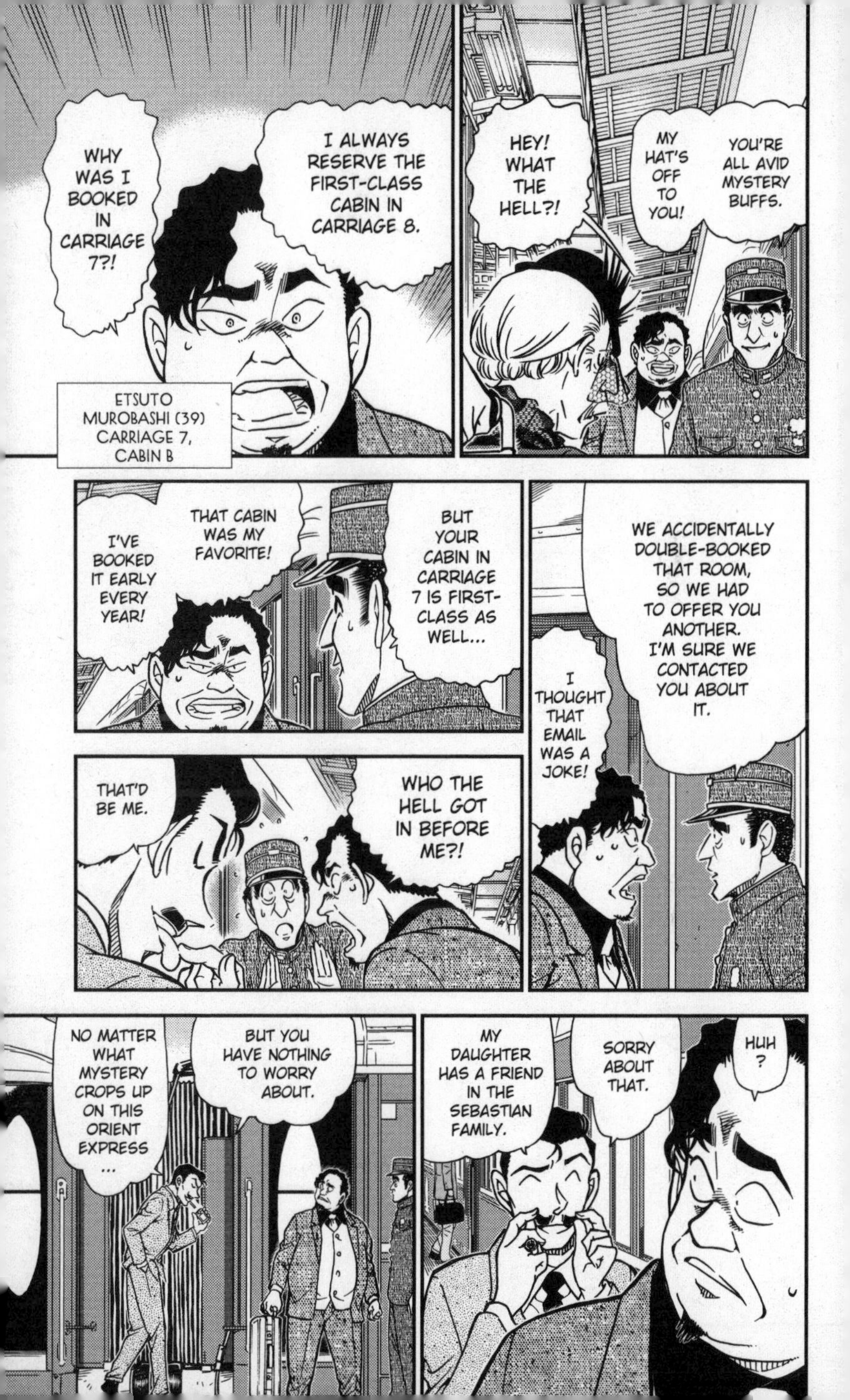
YOU'RE ALL AVID MYSTERY BUFFS.
MY HAT'S OFF TO YOU!
HEY! WHAT THE HELL?!
I ALWAYS RESERVE THE FIRST-CLASS CABIN IN CARRIAGE 8.
WHY WAS I BOOKED IN CARRIAGE 7?!
ETSUTO MUROBASHI (39) CARRIAGE 7, CABIN B
WE ACCIDENTALLY DOUBLE-BOOKED THAT ROOM, SO WE HAD TO OFFER YOU ANOTHER. I'M SURE WE CONTACTED YOU ABOUT IT.
I THOUGHT THAT EMAIL WAS A JOKE!
BUT YOUR CABIN IN CARRIAGE 7 IS FIRST-CLASS AS WELL...
THAT CABIN WAS MY FAVORITE!
I'VE BOOKED IT EARLY EVERY YEAR!
WHO THE HELL GOT IN BEFORE ME?!
THAT'D BE ME.
HUH?
SORRY ABOUT THAT.
MY DAUGHTER HAS A FRIEND IN THE SEBASTIAN FAMILY.
BUT YOU HAVE NOTHING TO WORRY ABOUT.
NO MATTER WHAT MYSTERY CROPS UP ON THIS ORIENT EXPRESS ...

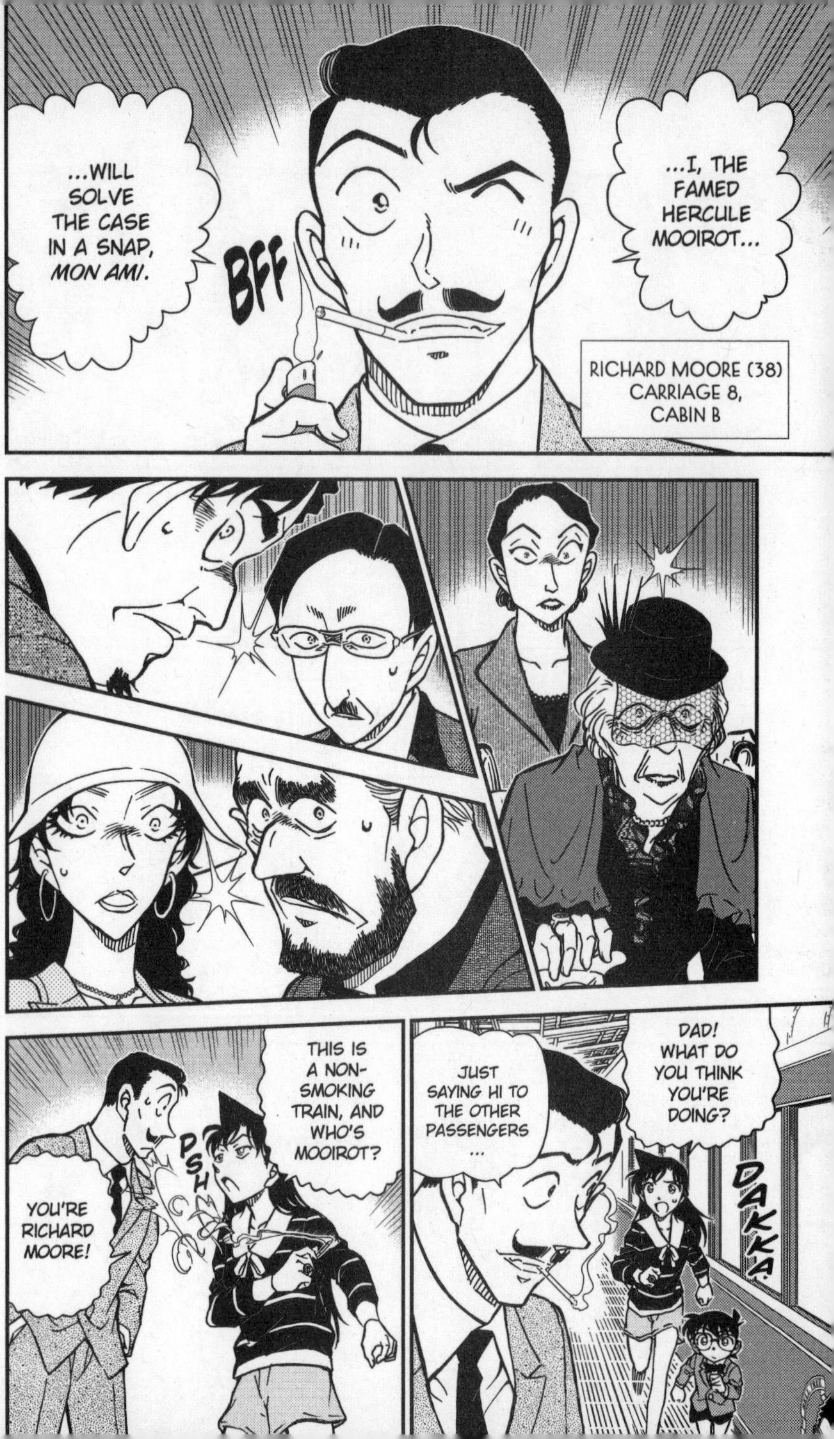
...I, THE FAMED HERCULE MOOIROT...
BFF
...WILL SOLVE THE CASE IN A SNAP, *MON AMI.*
RICHARD MOORE (38) CARRIAGE 8, CABIN B
DAD! WHAT DO YOU THINK YOU'RE DOING?
DAKKA
JUST SAYING HI TO THE OTHER PASSENGERS ...
THIS IS A NON-SMOKING TRAIN, AND WHO'S MOOIROT?
PSH
YOU'RE RICHARD MOORE!

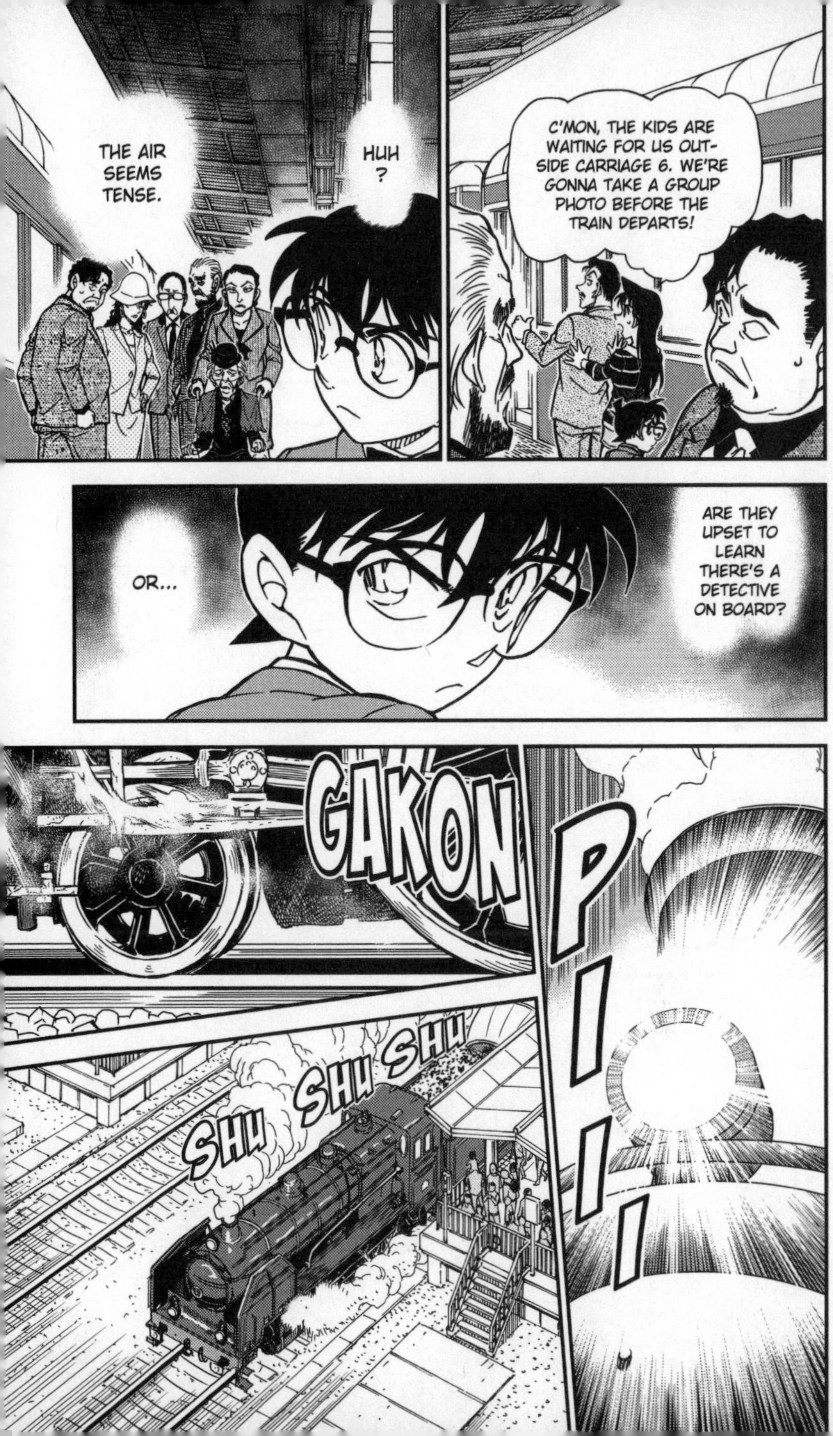
C'MON, THE KIDS ARE WAITING FOR US OUT-SIDE CARRIAGE 6. WE'RE GONNA TAKE A GROUP PHOTO BEFORE THE TRAIN DEPARTS!
HUH ?
THE AIR SEEMS TENSE.
ARE THEY UPSET TO LEARN THERE'S A DETECTIVE ON BOARD?
OR...
PIIII
GAKON
SHU SHU SHU

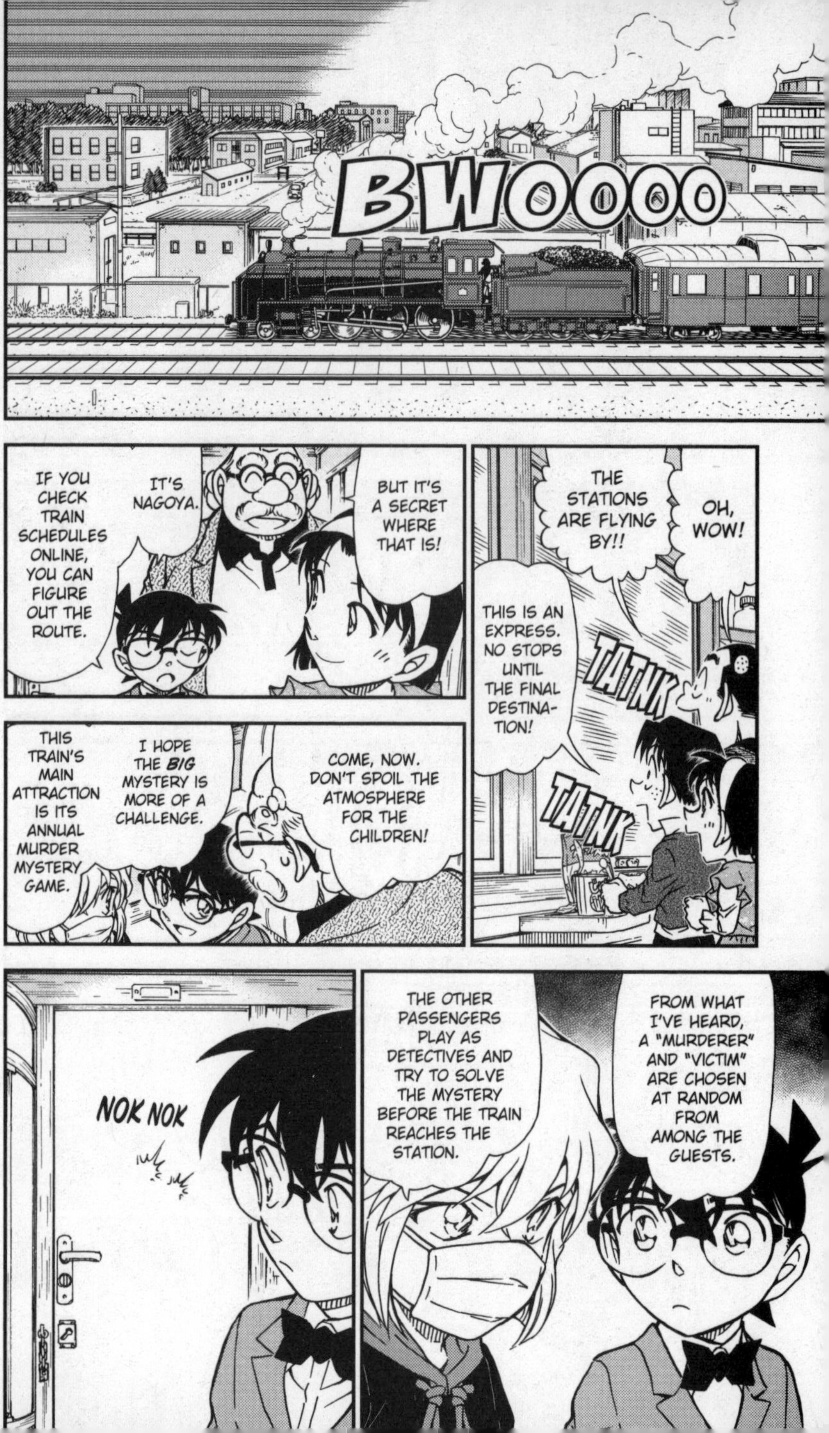
BWOOOO
OH, WOW!
THE STATIONS ARE FLYING BY!!
THIS IS AN EXPRESS. NO STOPS UNTIL THE FINAL DESTINA-TION!
TATNK
TATNK
BUT IT'S A SECRET WHERE THAT IS!
IT'S NAGOYA.
IF YOU CHECK TRAIN SCHEDULES ONLINE, YOU CAN FIGURE OUT THE ROUTE.
COME, NOW. DON'T SPOIL THE ATMOSPHERE FOR THE CHILDREN!
I HOPE THE *BIG* MYSTERY IS MORE OF A CHALLENGE.
THIS TRAIN'S MAIN ATTRACTION IS ITS ANNUAL MURDER MYSTERY GAME.
FROM WHAT I'VE HEARD, A "MURDERER" AND "VICTIM" ARE CHOSEN AT RANDOM FROM AMONG THE GUESTS.
THE OTHER PASSENGERS PLAY AS DETECTIVES AND TRY TO SOLVE THE MYSTERY BEFORE THE TRAIN REACHES THE STATION.
NOK NOK

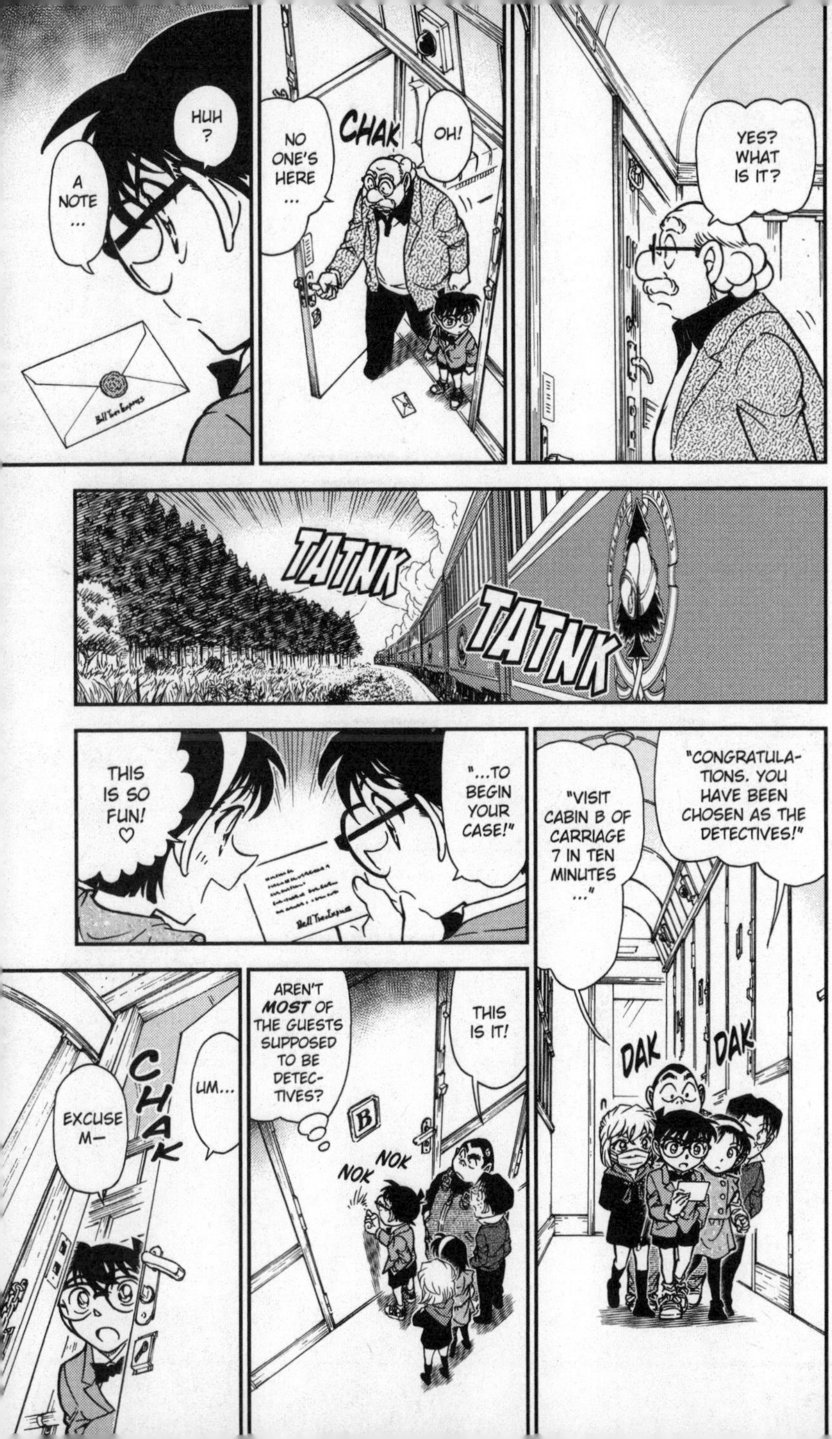
YES? WHAT IS IT?
OH!
CHAK
NO ONE'S HERE ...
HUH ?
A NOTE ...
TATNK
TATNK
"CONGRATULA-TIONS. YOU HAVE BEEN CHOSEN AS THE DETECTIVES!"
"VISIT CABIN B OF CARRIAGE 7 IN TEN MINUTES ..."
DAK
DAK
"...TO BEGIN YOUR CASE!"
THIS IS SO FUN! ♡
THIS IS IT!
AREN'T MOST OF THE GUESTS SUPPOSED TO BE DETEC-TIVES?
B
NOK
NOK
UM...
CHAK
EXCUSE M—

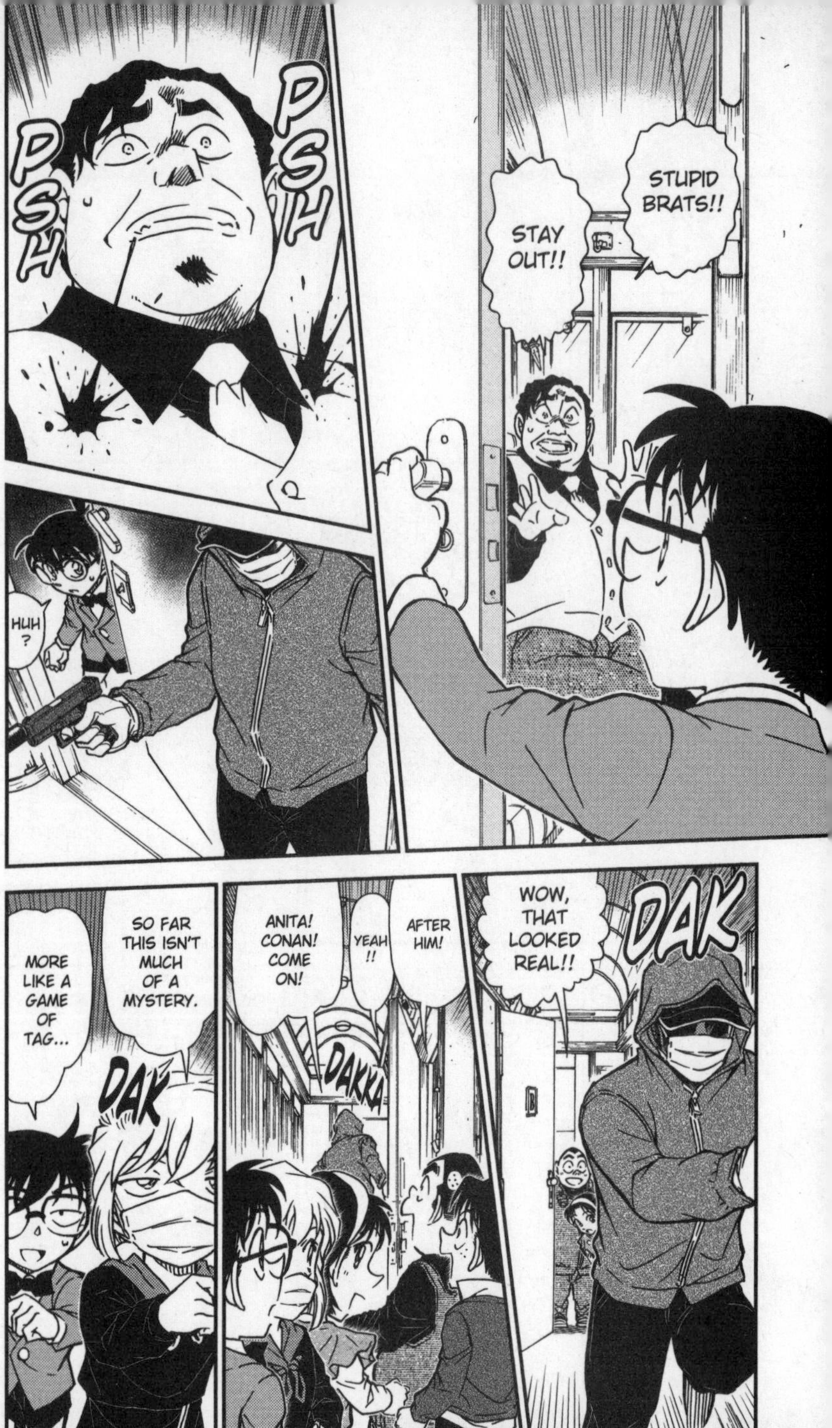
STUPID BRATS!!
STAY OUT!!
PSH
PSH
HUH?
DAK
WOW, THAT LOOKED REAL!!
AFTER HIM!
YEAH!!
ANITA! CONAN! COME ON!
DAKKA
SO FAR THIS ISN'T MUCH OF A MYSTERY.
MORE LIKE A GAME OF TAG...
DAK

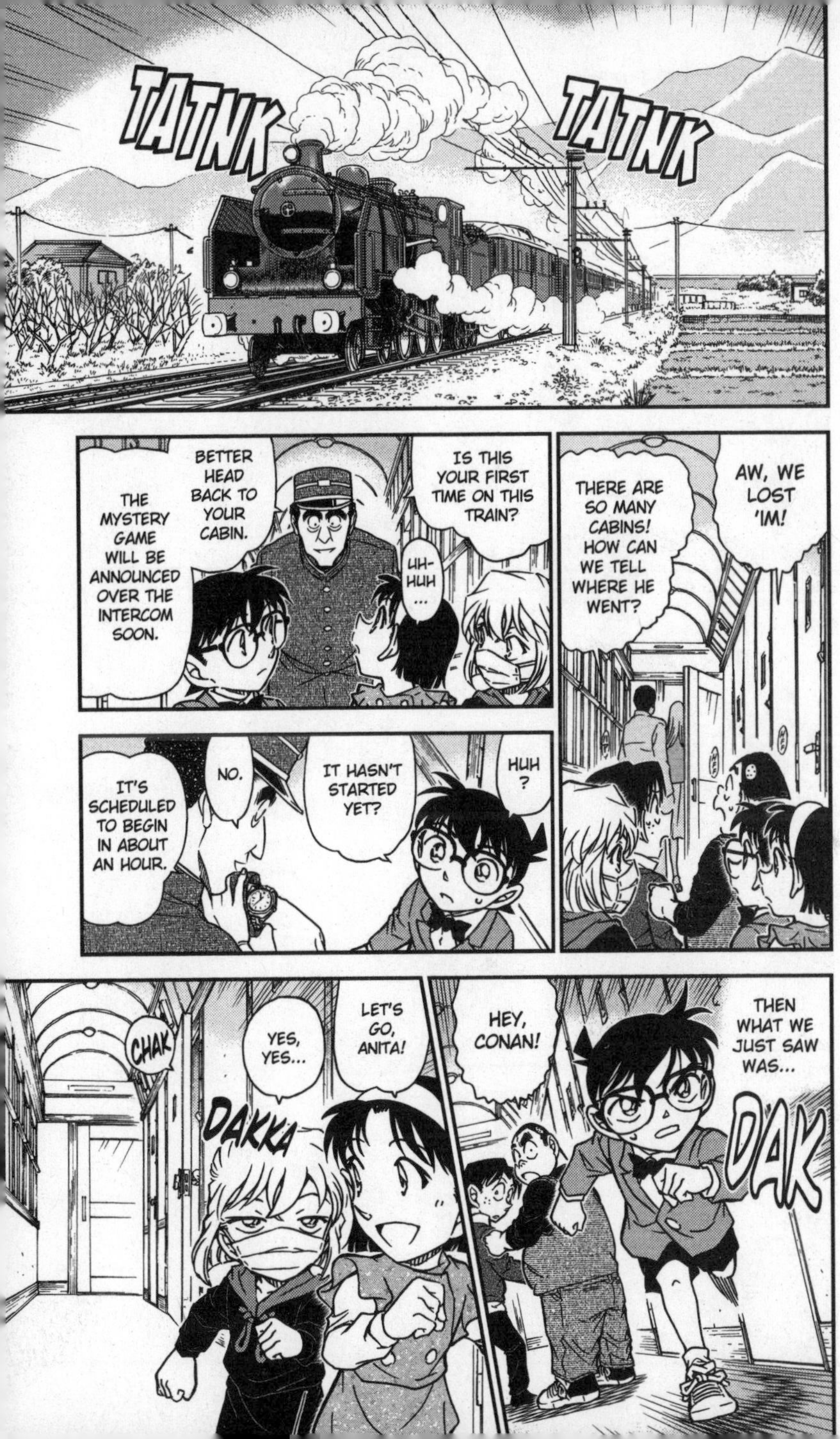
TATNK
TATNK
AW, WE LOST 'IM!
THERE ARE SO MANY CABINS! HOW CAN WE TELL WHERE HE WENT?
IS THIS YOUR FIRST TIME ON THIS TRAIN?
UH-HUH...
BETTER HEAD BACK TO YOUR CABIN.
THE MYSTERY GAME WILL BE ANNOUNCED OVER THE INTERCOM SOON.
HUH?
IT HASN'T STARTED YET?
NO.
IT'S SCHEDULED TO BEGIN IN ABOUT AN HOUR.
THEN WHAT WE JUST SAW WAS...
DAK
HEY, CONAN!
LET'S GO, ANITA!
YES, YES...
DAKKA
CHAK

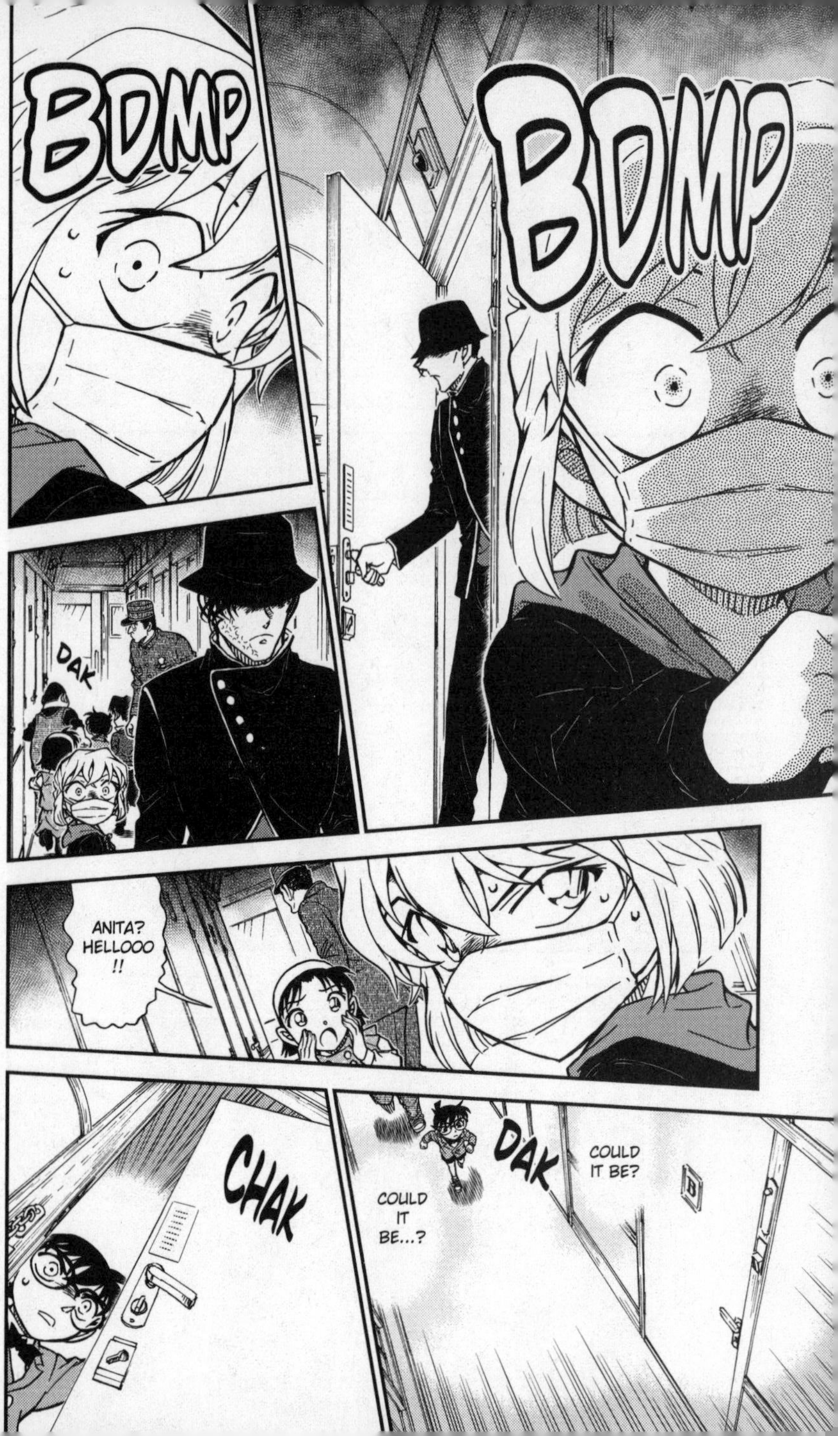
BDMP
BDMP
DAK
ANITA? HELLOOO !!
COULD IT BE?
DAK
COULD IT BE...?
CHAK

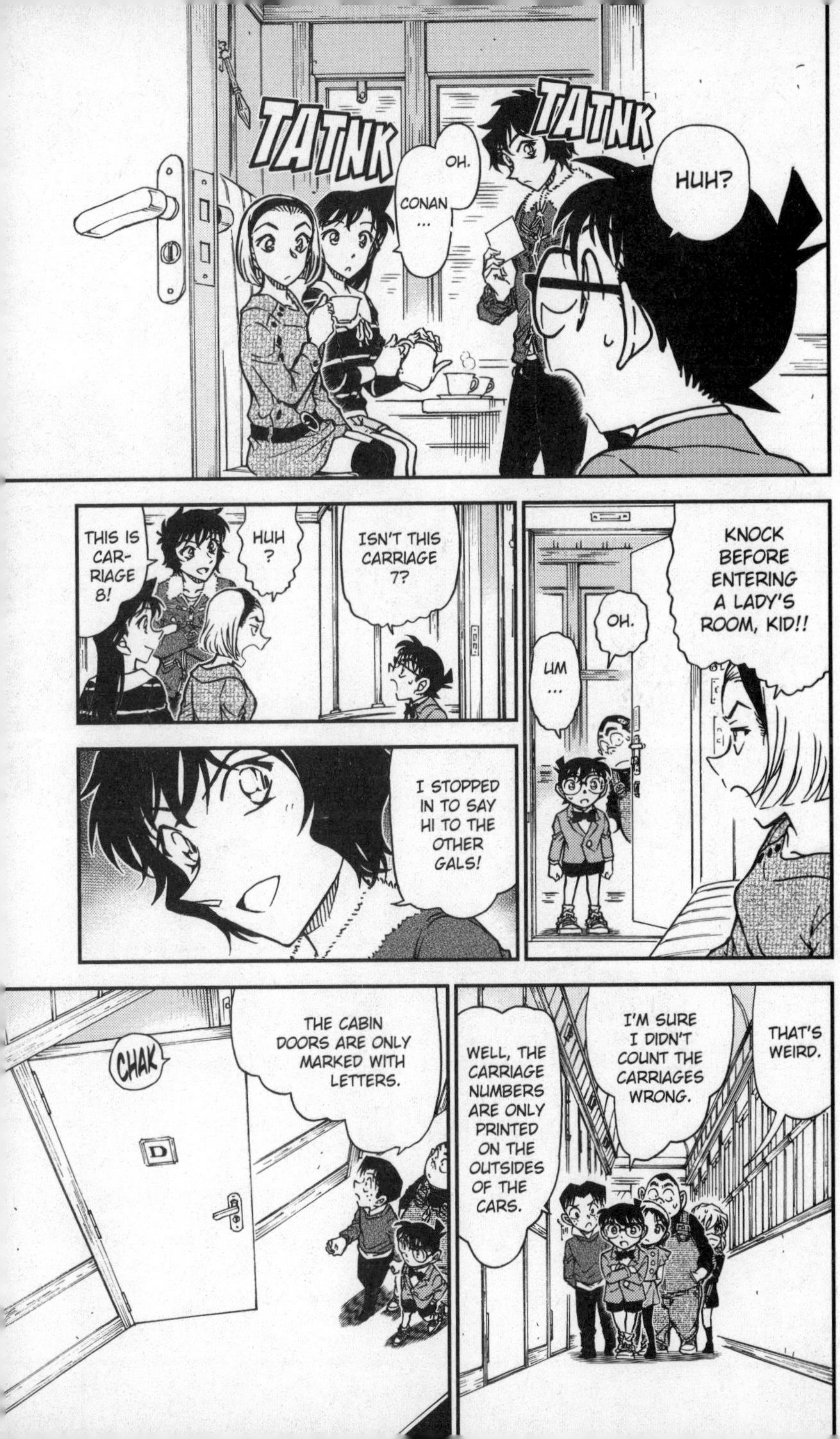
HUH?
TATNK
OH. CONAN...
TATNK
KNOCK BEFORE ENTERING A LADY'S ROOM, KID!!
OH.
UM...
ISN'T THIS CARRIAGE 7?
HUH?
THIS IS CARRIAGE 8!
I STOPPED IN TO SAY HI TO THE OTHER GALS!
THAT'S WEIRD.
I'M SURE I DIDN'T COUNT THE CARRIAGES WRONG.
WELL, THE CARRIAGE NUMBERS ARE ONLY PRINTED ON THE OUTSIDES OF THE CARS.
THE CABIN DOORS ARE ONLY MARKED WITH LETTERS.
CHAK
D

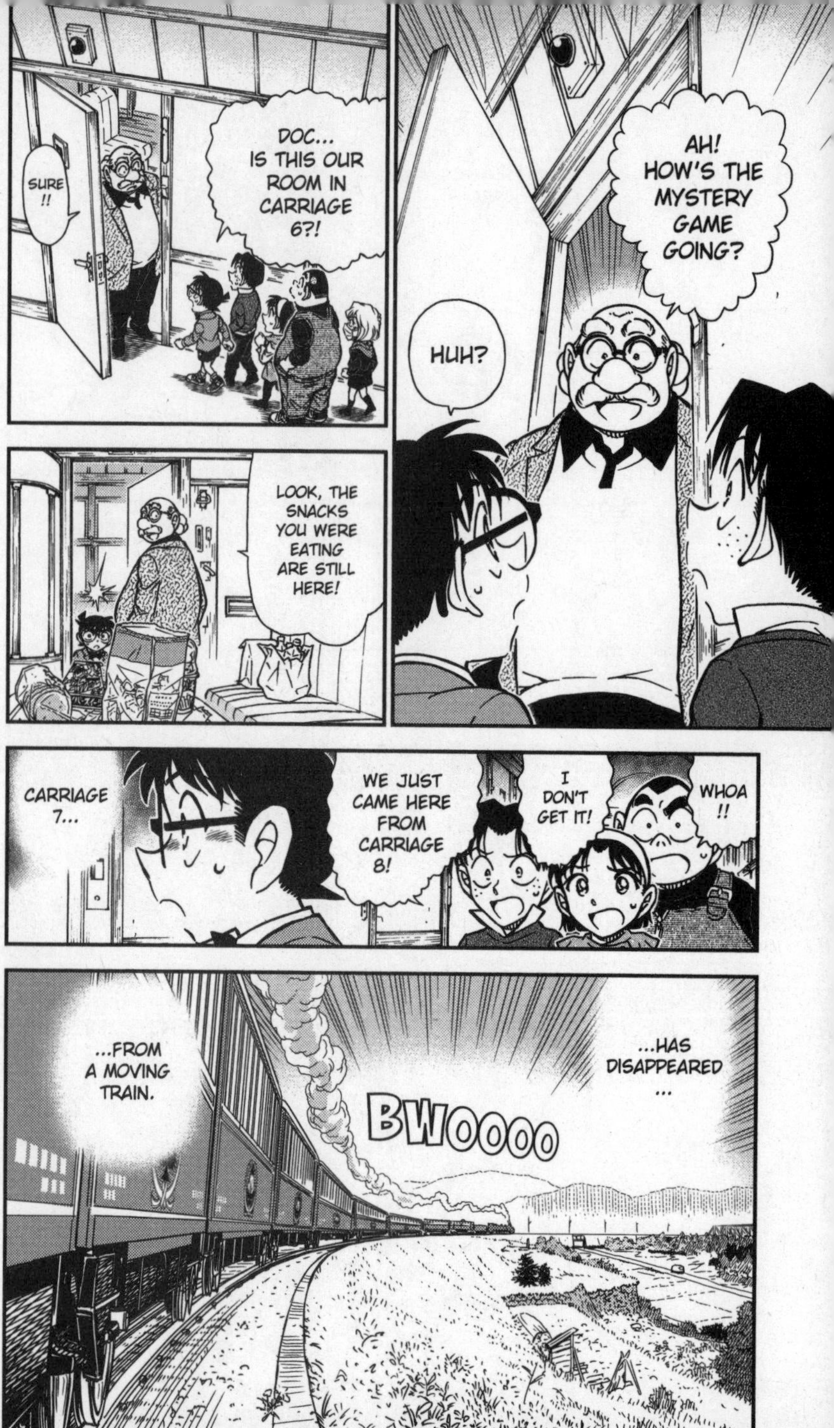
AH! HOW'S THE MYSTERY GAME GOING?
HUH?
DOC... IS THIS OUR ROOM IN CARRIAGE 6?!
SURE !!
LOOK, THE SNACKS YOU WERE EATING ARE STILL HERE!
WHOA !!
I DON'T GET IT!
WE JUST CAME HERE FROM CARRIAGE 8!
CARRIAGE 7...
...HAS DISAPPEARED ...
BWOOOO
...FROM A MOVING TRAIN.

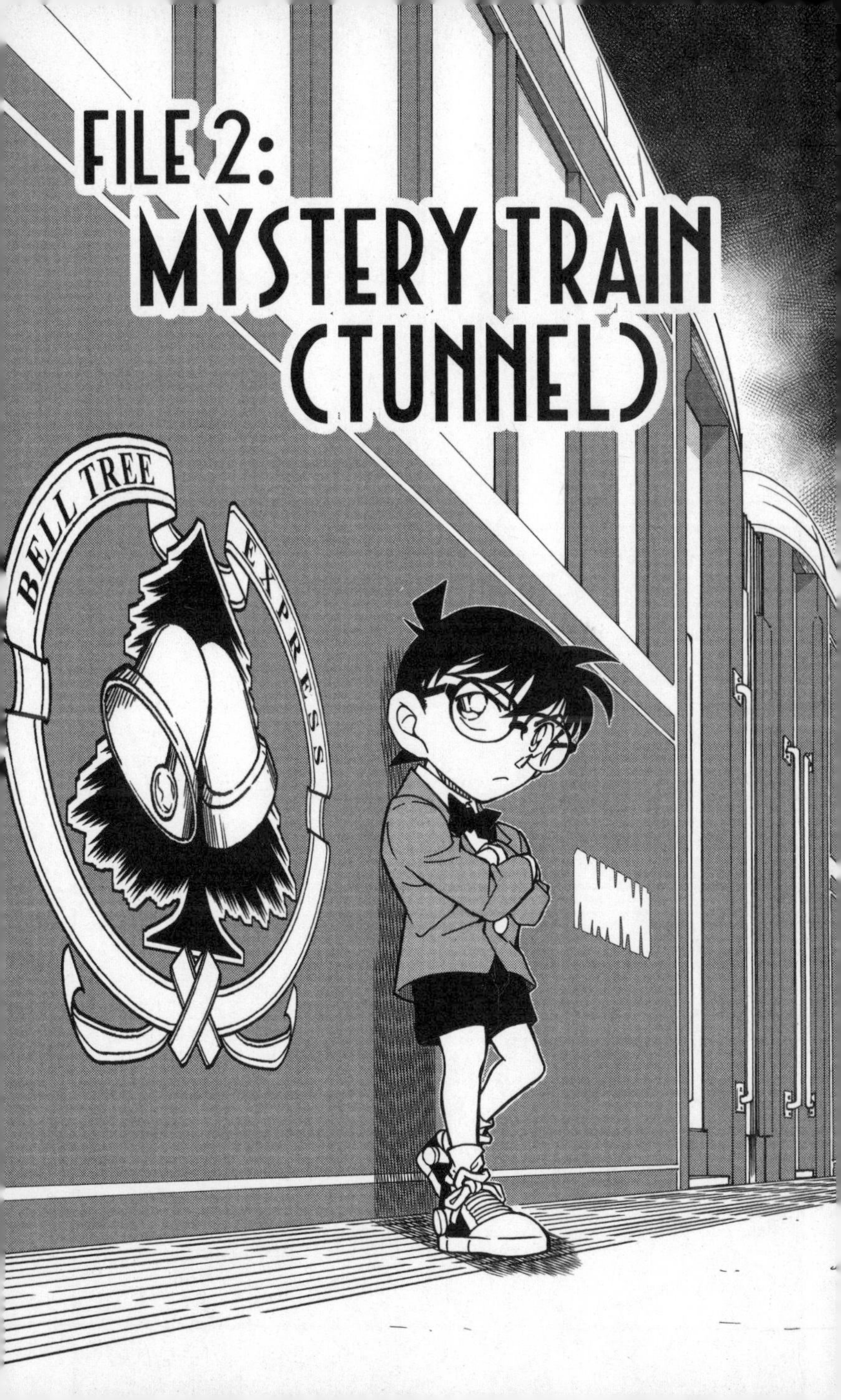
FILE 2:
MYSTERY TRAIN
(TUNNEL)
BELL TREE
EXPRESS

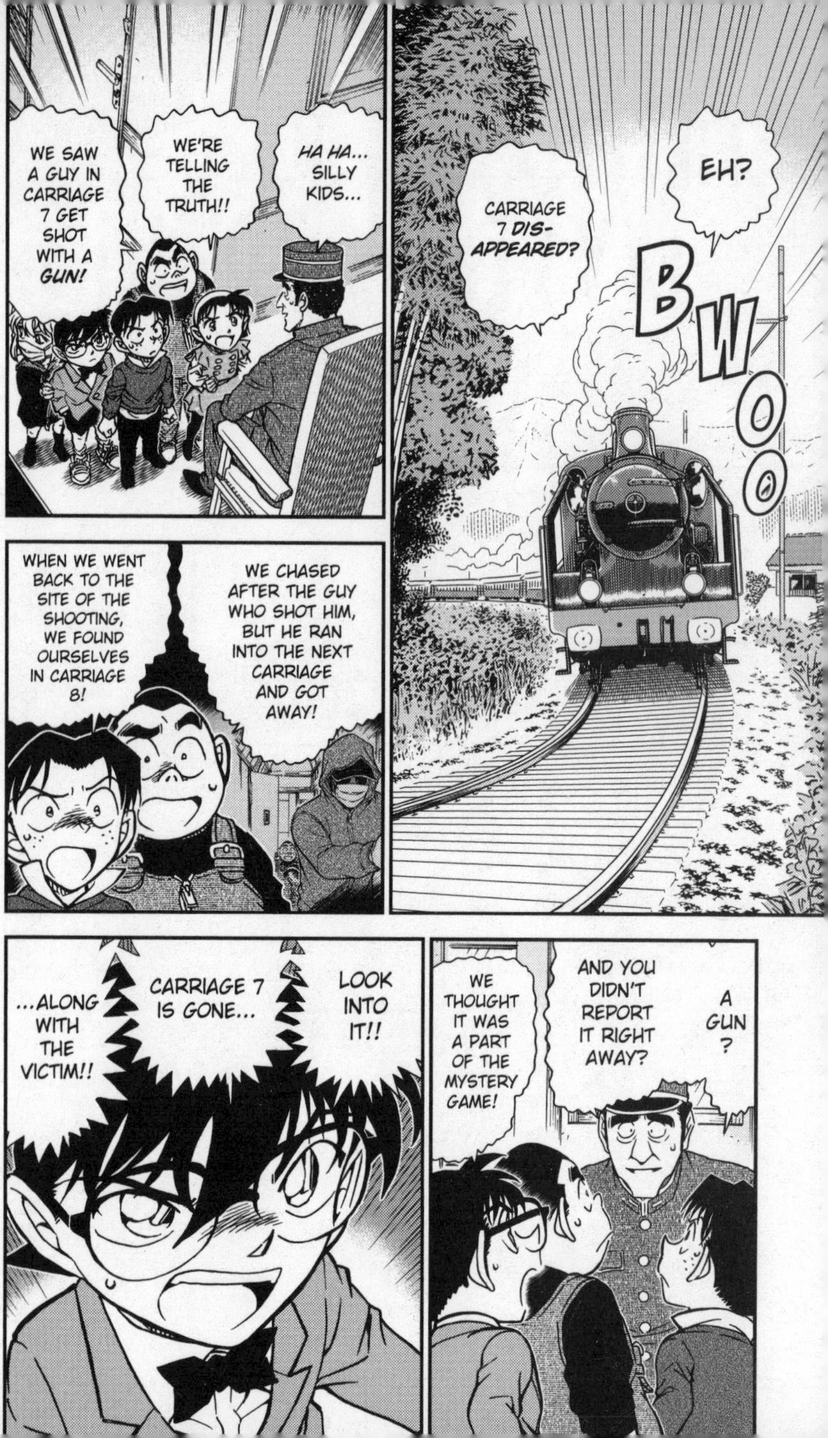
EH?
CARRIAGE 7 DIS-APPEARED?
BWOOO
HA HA... SILLY KIDS...
WE'RE TELLING THE TRUTH!!
WE SAW A GUY IN CARRIAGE 7 GET SHOT WITH A GUN!
WE CHASED AFTER THE GUY WHO SHOT HIM, BUT HE RAN INTO THE NEXT CARRIAGE AND GOT AWAY!
WHEN WE WENT BACK TO THE SITE OF THE SHOOTING, WE FOUND OURSELVES IN CARRIAGE 8!
A GUN?
AND YOU DIDN'T REPORT IT RIGHT AWAY?
WE THOUGHT IT WAS A PART OF THE MYSTERY GAME!
LOOK INTO IT!!
CARRIAGE 7 IS GONE...
...ALONG WITH THE VICTIM!!

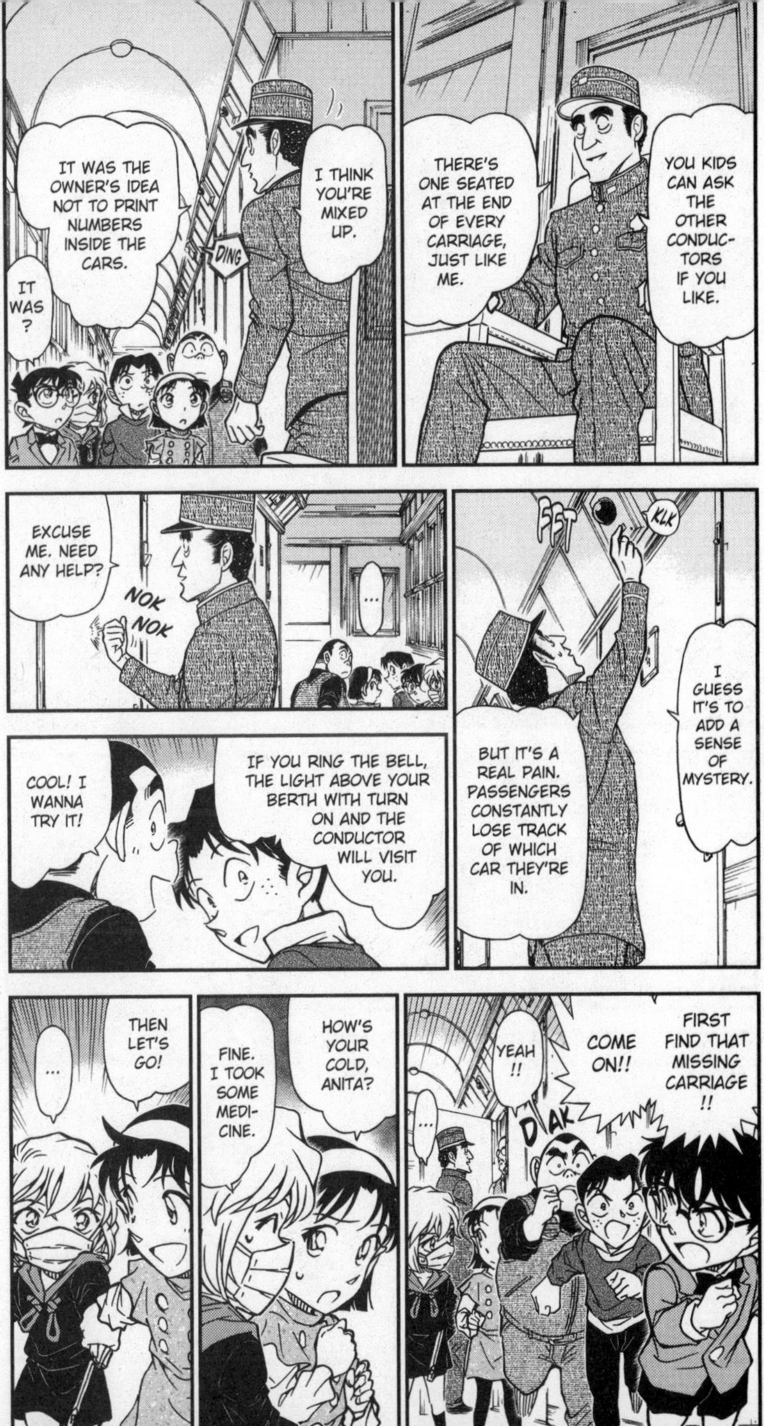
YOU KIDS CAN ASK THE OTHER CONDUC-TORS IF YOU LIKE.
THERE'S ONE SEATED AT THE END OF EVERY CARRIAGE, JUST LIKE ME.
DING
I THINK YOU'RE MIXED UP.
IT WAS THE OWNER'S IDEA NOT TO PRINT NUMBERS INSIDE THE CARS.
IT WAS ?
FST
KLK
I GUESS IT'S TO ADD A SENSE OF MYSTERY.
BUT IT'S A REAL PAIN. PASSENGERS CONSTANTLY LOSE TRACK OF WHICH CAR THEY'RE IN.
EXCUSE ME. NEED ANY HELP?
NOK NOK
...
IF YOU RING THE BELL, THE LIGHT ABOVE YOUR BERTH WITH TURN ON AND THE CONDUCTOR WILL VISIT YOU.
COOL! I WANNA TRY IT!
FIRST FIND THAT MISSING CARRIAGE !!
COME ON!!
YEAH !!
DAK
...
HOW'S YOUR COLD, ANITA?
FINE. I TOOK SOME MEDI-CINE.
THEN LET'S GO!
...

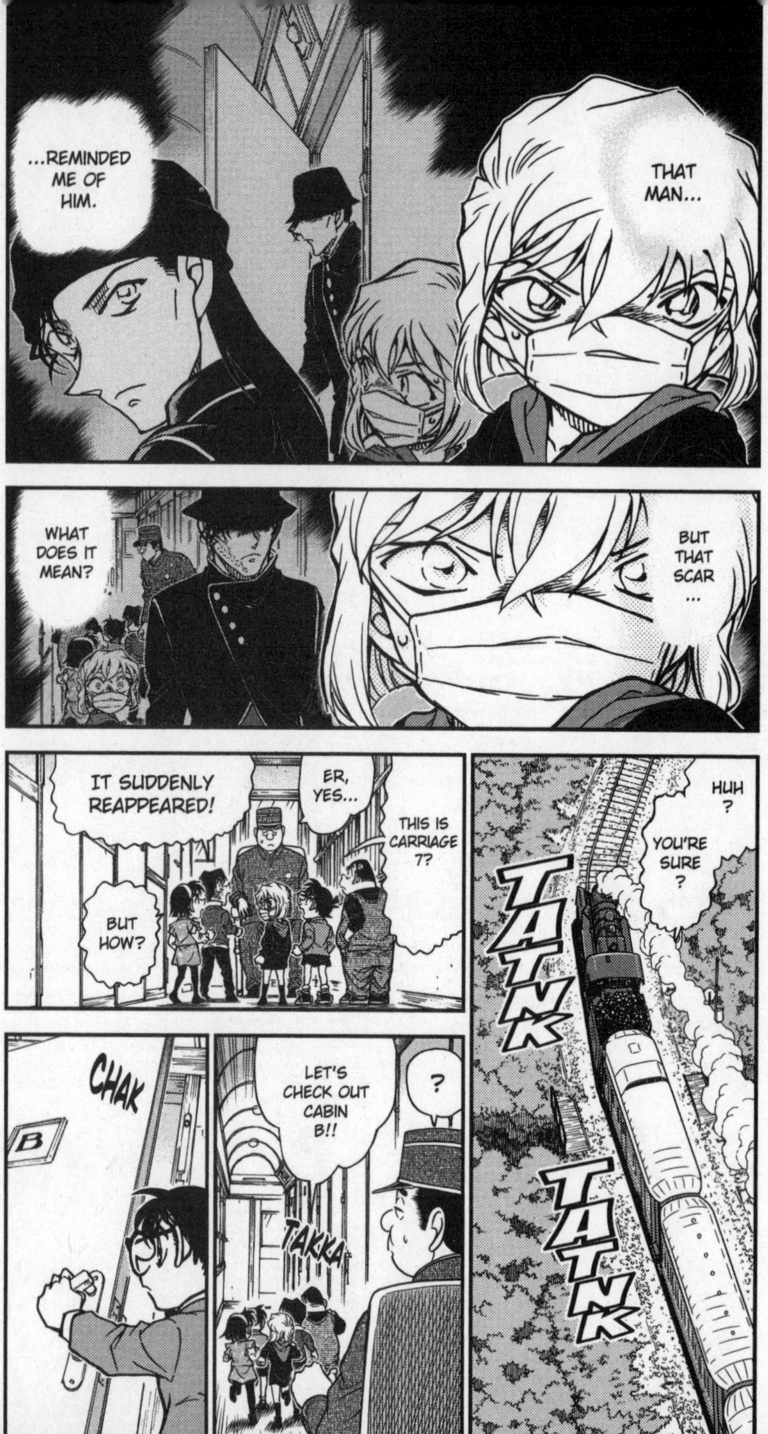
THAT MAN...
...REMINDED ME OF HIM.
BUT THAT SCAR ...
WHAT DOES IT MEAN?
HUH ?
YOU'RE SURE ?
TATNK
TATNK
THIS IS CARRIAGE 7?
ER, YES...
IT SUDDENLY REAPPEARED!
BUT HOW?
?
LET'S CHECK OUT CABIN B!!
TAKKA
CHAK
B

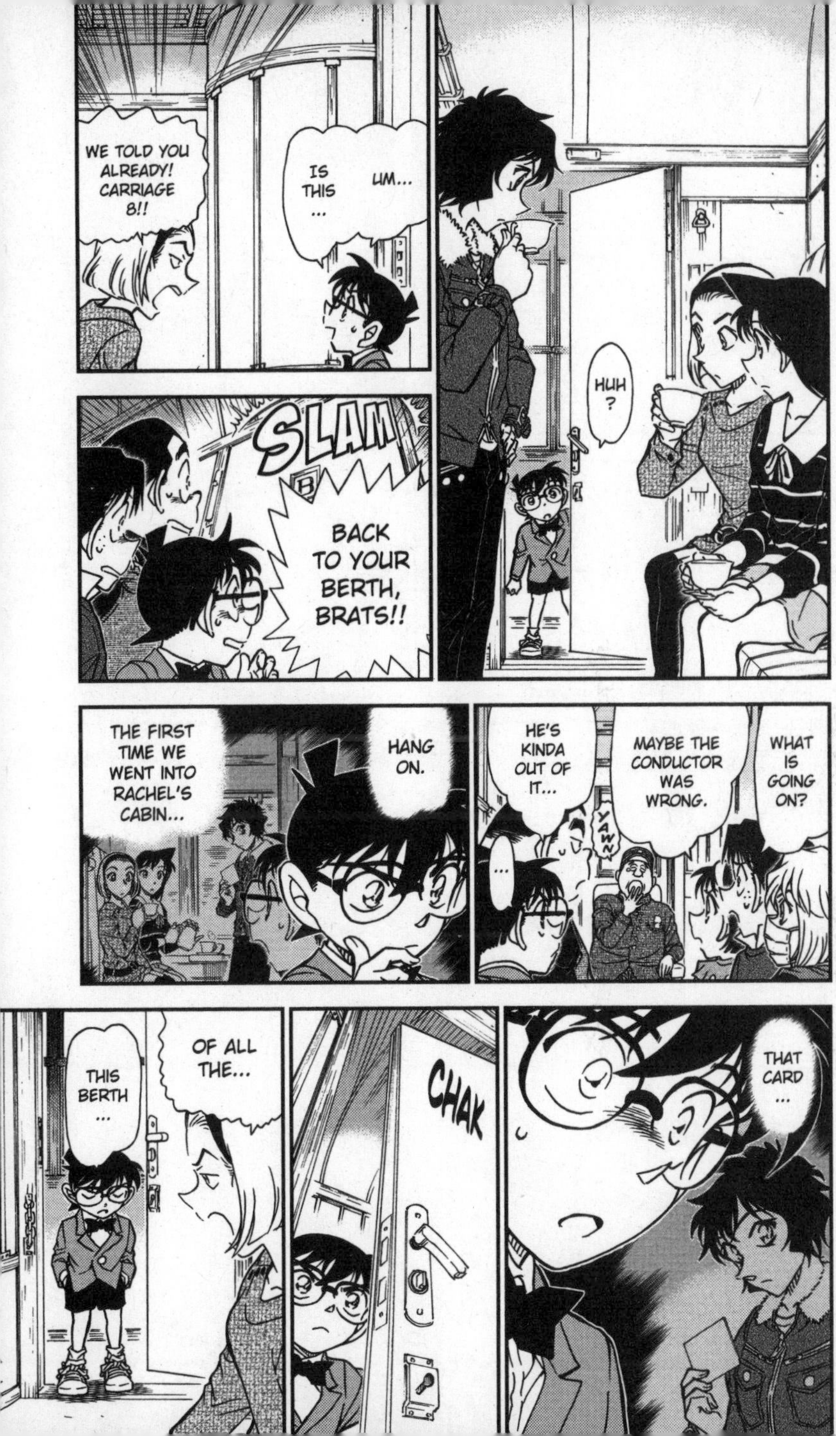
HUH?
UM...
IS THIS...
WE TOLD YOU ALREADY! CARRIAGE 8!!
SLAM
BACK TO YOUR BERTH, BRATS!!
WHAT IS GOING ON?
MAYBE THE CONDUCTOR WAS WRONG.
HE'S KINDA OUT OF IT...
YAWN
...
HANG ON.
THE FIRST TIME WE WENT INTO RACHEL'S CABIN...
THAT CARD...
CHAK
OF ALL THE...
THIS BERTH...

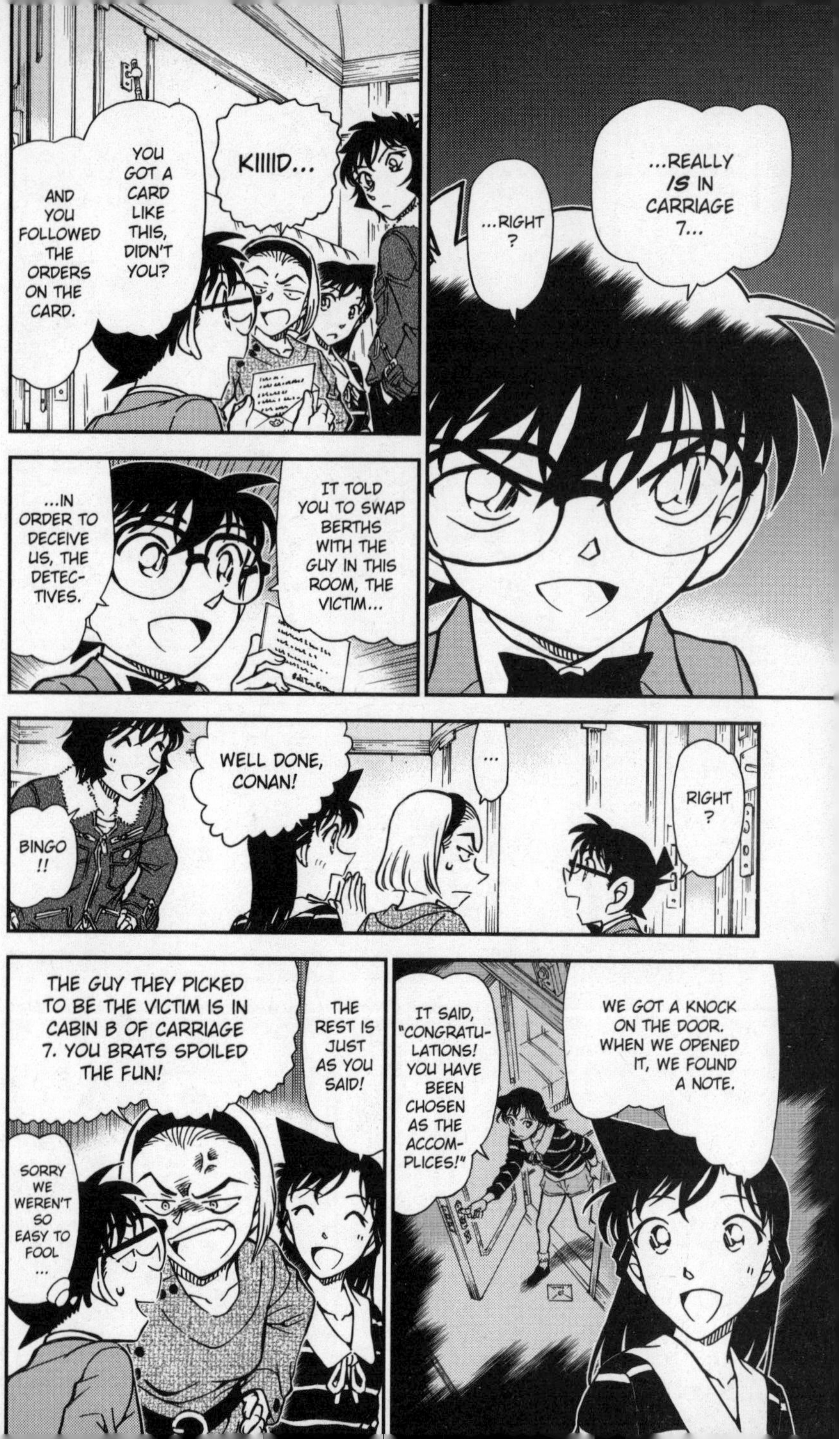
...REALLY IS IN CARRIAGE 7...
...RIGHT?
KIIIID...
YOU GOT A CARD LIKE THIS, DIDN'T YOU?
AND YOU FOLLOWED THE ORDERS ON THE CARD.
IT TOLD YOU TO SWAP BERTHS WITH THE GUY IN THIS ROOM, THE VICTIM...
...IN ORDER TO DECEIVE US, THE DETECTIVES.
RIGHT?
...
WELL DONE, CONAN!
BINGO!!
WE GOT A KNOCK ON THE DOOR. WHEN WE OPENED IT, WE FOUND A NOTE.
IT SAID, "CONGRATULATIONS! YOU HAVE BEEN CHOSEN AS THE ACCOMPLICES!"
THE REST IS JUST AS YOU SAID!
THE GUY THEY PICKED TO BE THE VICTIM IS IN CABIN B OF CARRIAGE 7. YOU BRATS SPOILED THE FUN!
SORRY WE WEREN'T SO EASY TO FOOL...

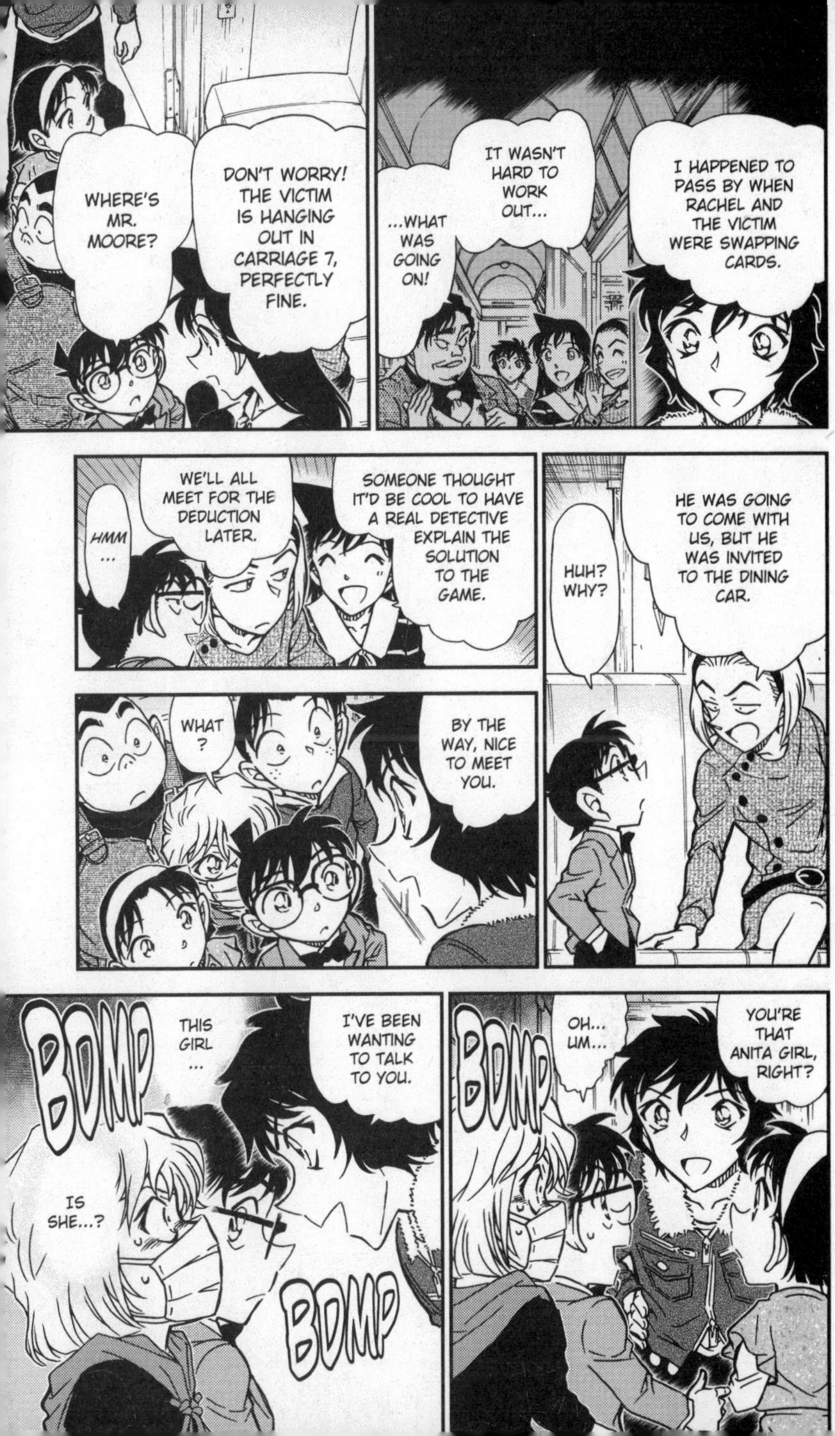

I HAPPENED TO PASS BY WHEN RACHEL AND THE VICTIM WERE SWAPPING CARDS.
IT WASN'T HARD TO WORK OUT...
...WHAT WAS GOING ON!
DON'T WORRY! THE VICTIM IS HANGING OUT IN CARRIAGE 7, PERFECTLY FINE.
WHERE'S MR. MOORE?
HE WAS GOING TO COME WITH US, BUT HE WAS INVITED TO THE DINING CAR.
HUH? WHY?
SOMEONE THOUGHT IT'D BE COOL TO HAVE A REAL DETECTIVE EXPLAIN THE SOLUTION TO THE GAME.
WE'LL ALL MEET FOR THE DEDUCTION LATER.
HMM...
BY THE WAY, NICE TO MEET YOU.
WHAT?
YOU'RE THAT ANITA GIRL, RIGHT?
OH... UM...
BDMP
I'VE BEEN WANTING TO TALK TO YOU.
THIS GIRL...
BDMP
IS SHE...?
BDMP

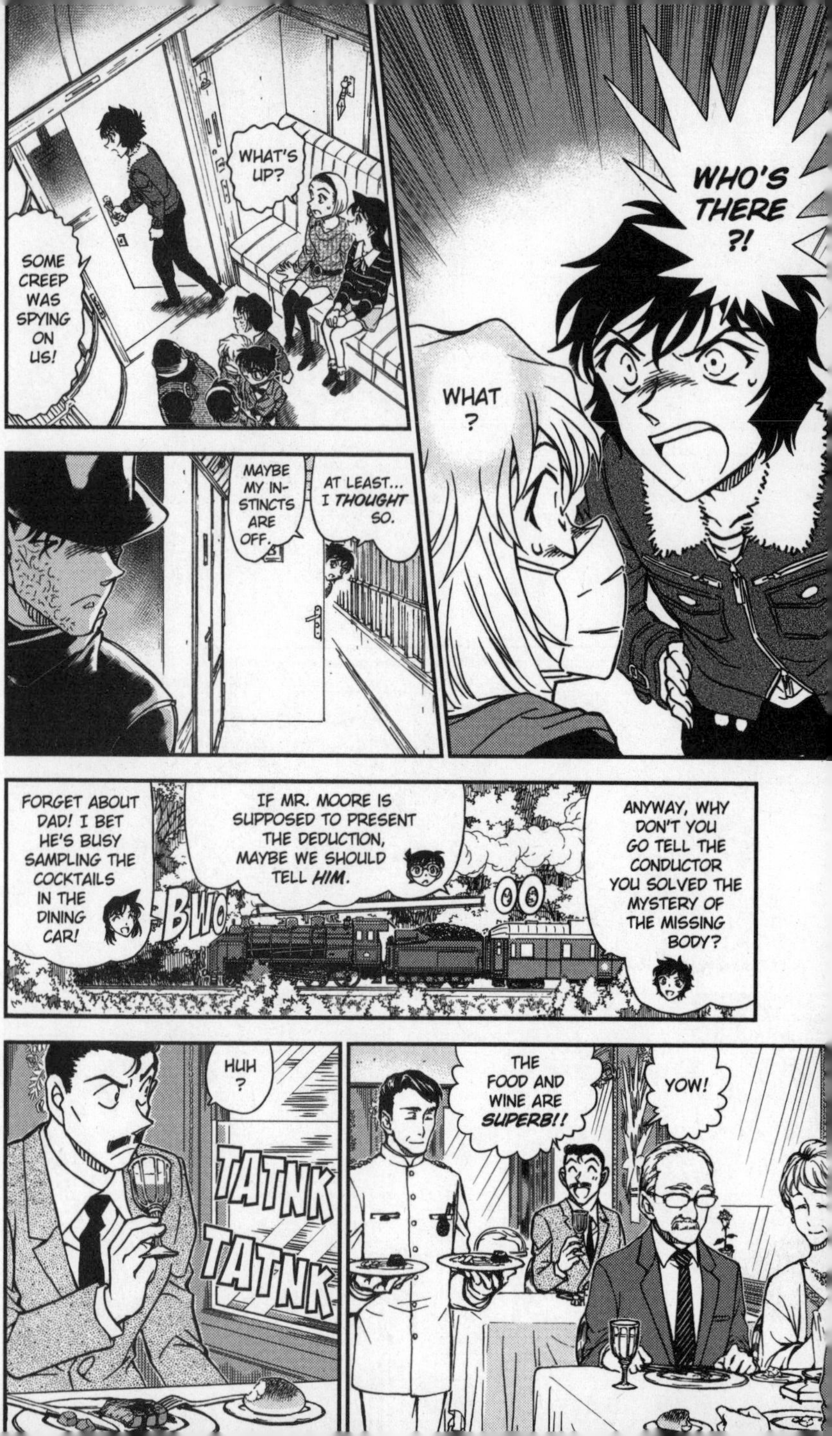
WHO'S THERE ?!
WHAT ?
WHAT'S UP?
SOME CREEP WAS SPYING ON US!
AT LEAST... I *THOUGHT* SO.
MAYBE MY INSTINCTS ARE OFF.
ANYWAY, WHY DON'T YOU GO TELL THE CONDUCTOR YOU SOLVED THE MYSTERY OF THE MISSING BODY?
IF MR. MOORE IS SUPPOSED TO PRESENT THE DEDUCTION, MAYBE WE SHOULD TELL *HIM*.
BWO
FORGET ABOUT DAD! I BET HE'S BUSY SAMPLING THE COCKTAILS IN THE DINING CAR!
YOW!
THE FOOD AND WINE ARE *SUPERB!!*
HUH ?
TATNK
TATNK

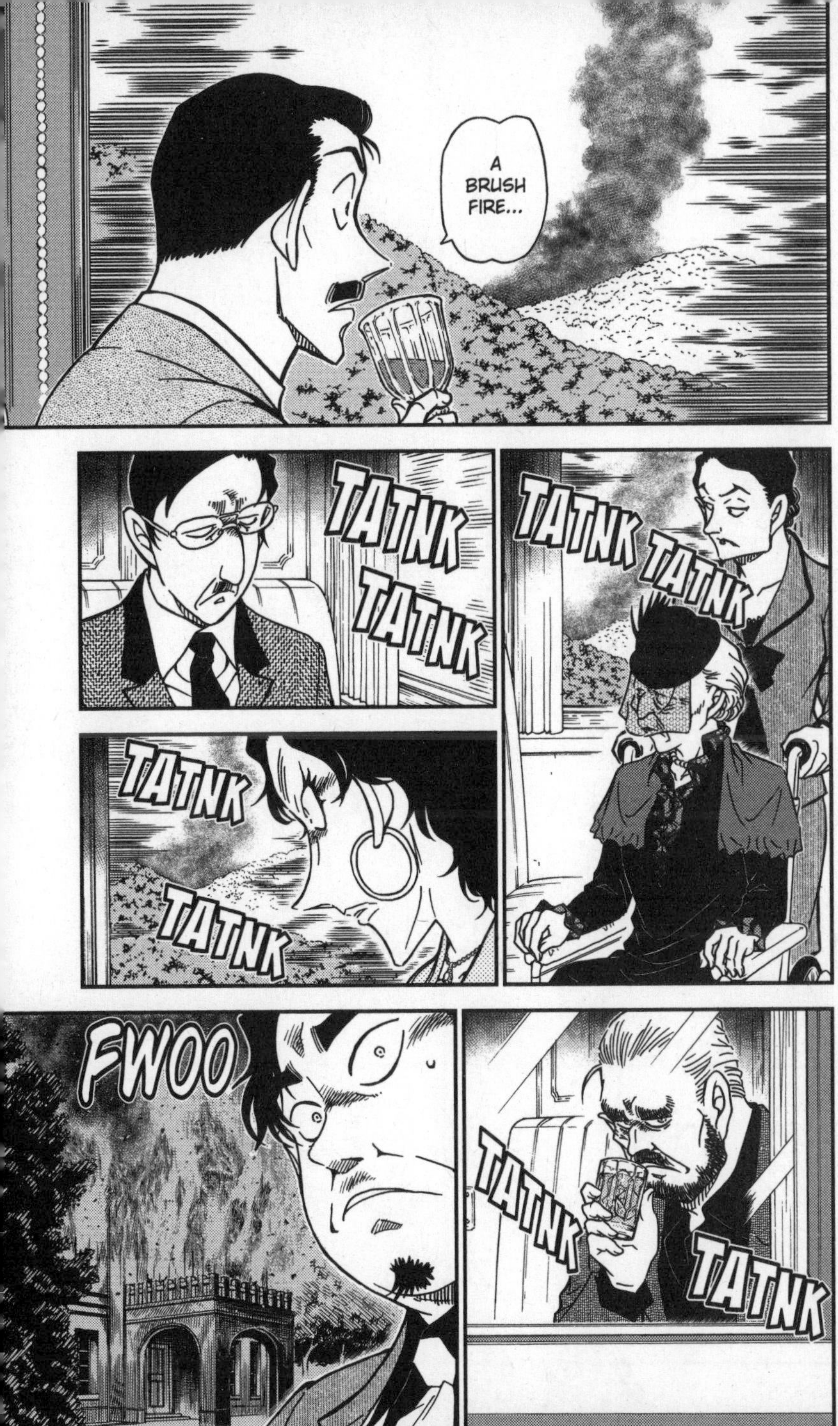
A BRUSH FIRE...
TATNK
TATNK
TATNK
TATNK
TATNK
TATNK
TATNK
TATNK
FWOO

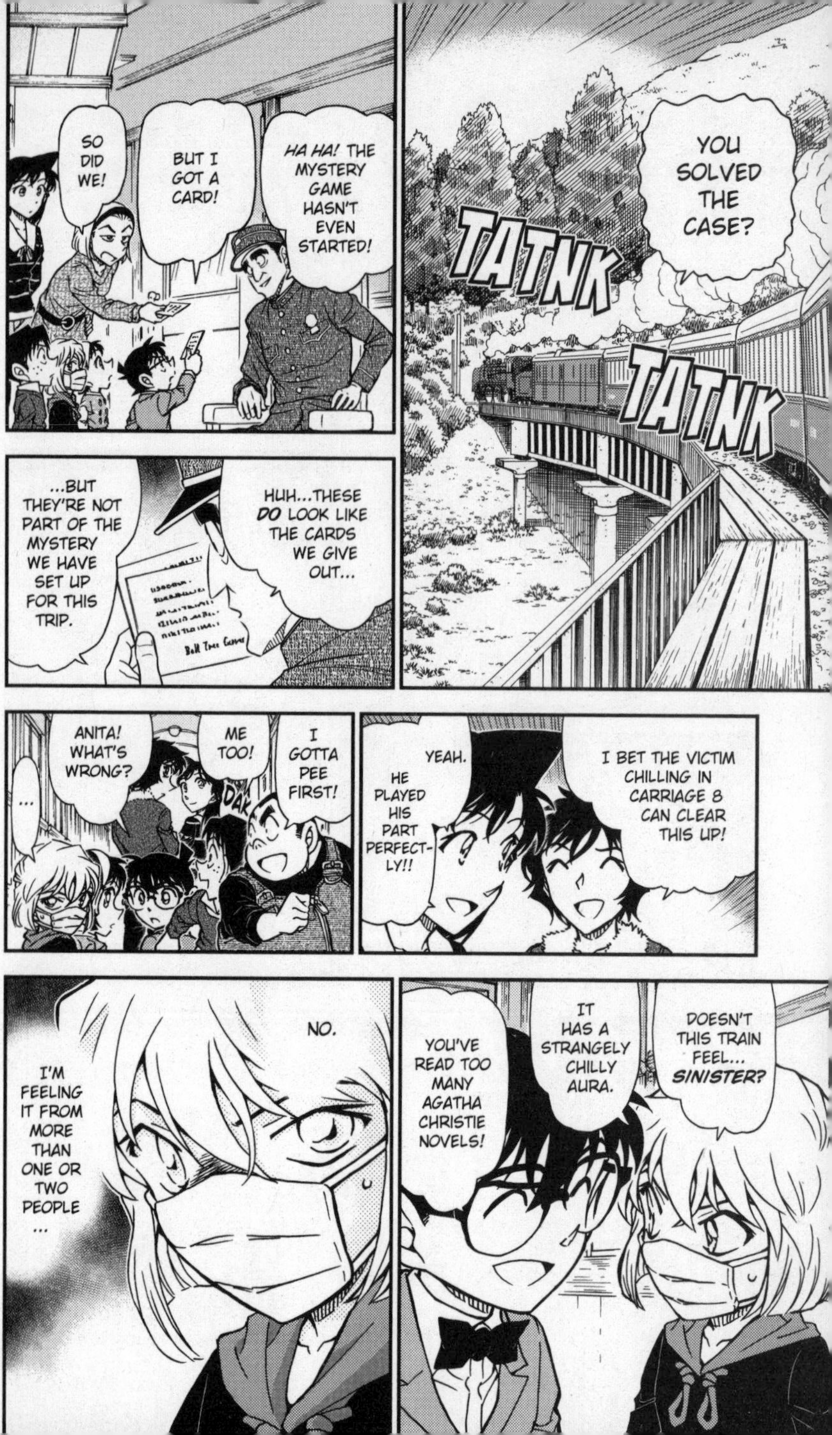
YOU SOLVED THE CASE?
TATNK
TATNK
HA HA! THE MYSTERY GAME HASN'T EVEN STARTED!
BUT I GOT A CARD!
SO DID WE!
HUH...THESE *DO* LOOK LIKE THE CARDS WE GIVE OUT...
...BUT THEY'RE NOT PART OF THE MYSTERY WE HAVE SET UP FOR THIS TRIP.
I BET THE VICTIM CHILLING IN CARRIAGE 8 CAN CLEAR THIS UP!
YEAH.
HE PLAYED HIS PART PERFECTLY!!
I GOTTA PEE FIRST!
ME TOO!
DAK
ANITA! WHAT'S WRONG?
...
DOESN'T THIS TRAIN FEEL... ***SINISTER?***
IT HAS A STRANGELY CHILLY AURA.
YOU'VE READ TOO MANY AGATHA CHRISTIE NOVELS!
NO.
I'M FEELING IT FROM MORE THAN ONE OR TWO PEOPLE...

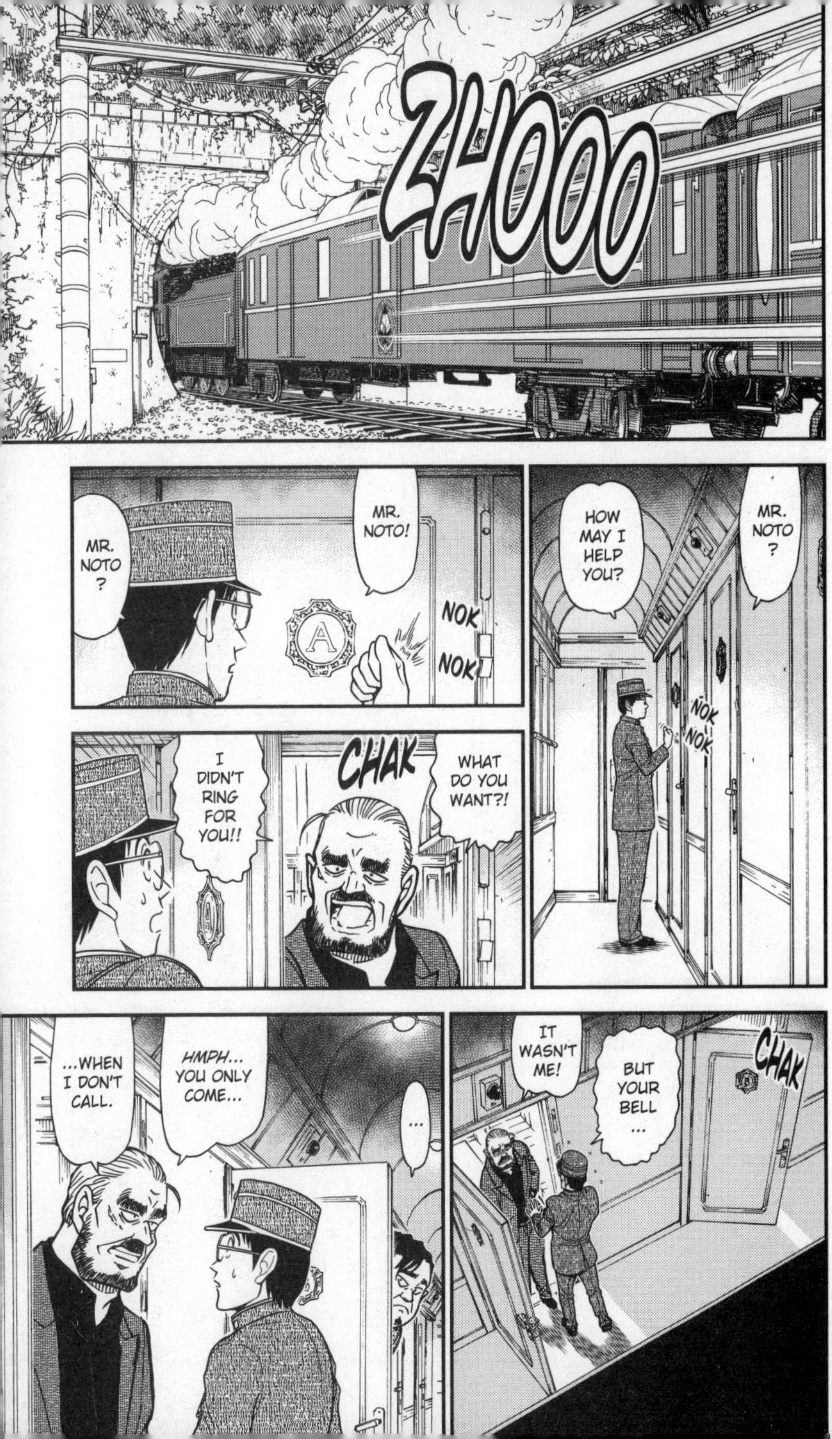
ZHOOO
MR. NOTO ?
HOW MAY I HELP YOU?
NOK NOK
MR. NOTO!
NOK NOK
MR. NOTO ?
WHAT DO YOU WANT?!
CHAK
I DIDN'T RING FOR YOU!!
CHAK
BUT YOUR BELL ...
IT WASN'T ME!
...
HMPH... YOU ONLY COME...
...WHEN I DON'T CALL.

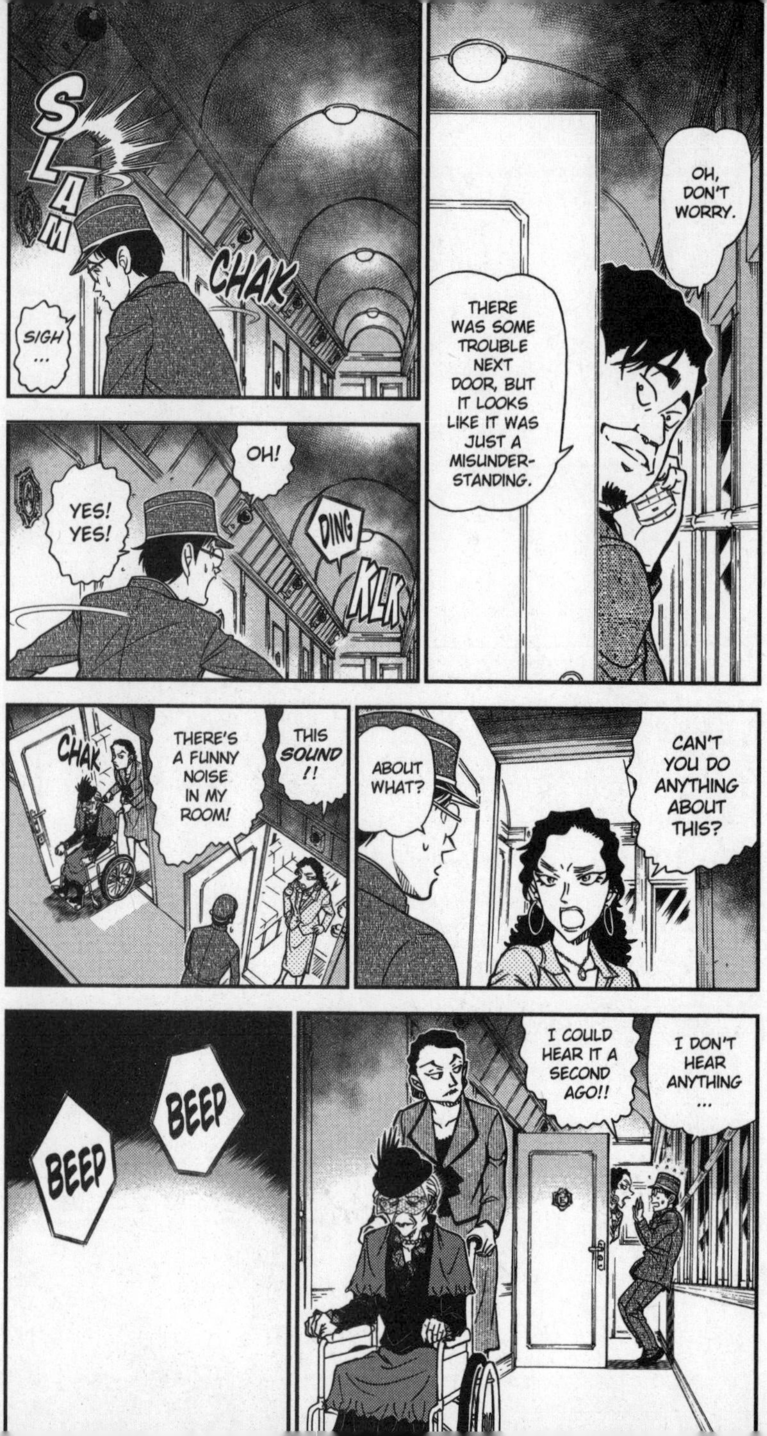
OH, DON'T WORRY.
THERE WAS SOME TROUBLE NEXT DOOR, BUT IT LOOKS LIKE IT WAS JUST A MISUNDER-STANDING.
CHAK
SLAM
SIGH ...
OH!
DING
KLK
YES! YES!
CAN'T YOU DO ANYTHING ABOUT THIS?
ABOUT WHAT?
THIS SOUND!!
THERE'S A FUNNY NOISE IN MY ROOM!
CHAK
I DON'T HEAR ANYTHING ...
I COULD HEAR IT A SECOND AGO!!
BEEP
BEEP

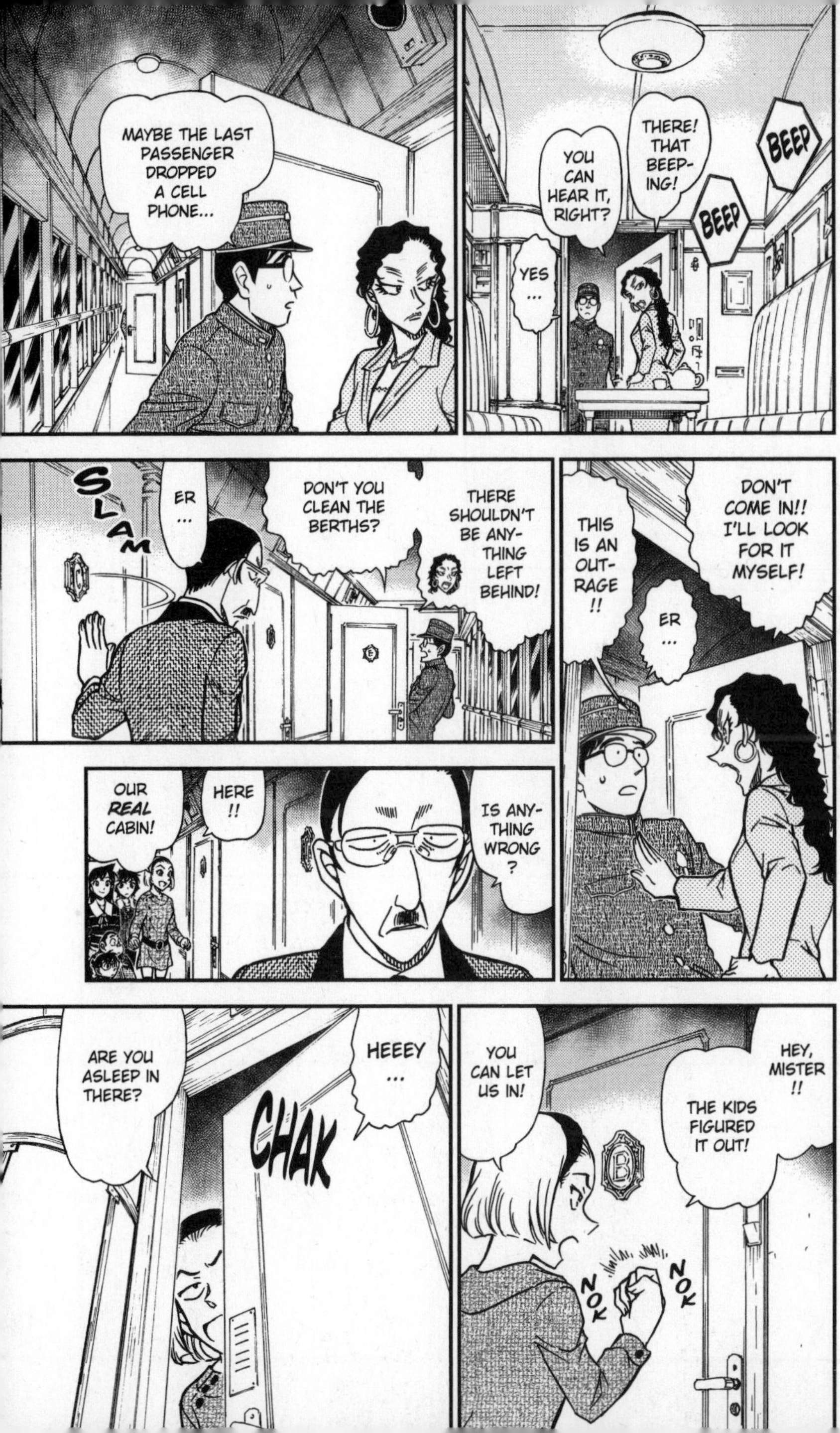
BEEP
BEEP
THERE! THAT BEEPING!
YOU CAN HEAR IT, RIGHT?
YES...
MAYBE THE LAST PASSENGER DROPPED A CELL PHONE...
DON'T COME IN!! I'LL LOOK FOR IT MYSELF!
THIS IS AN OUTRAGE!!
ER...
THERE SHOULDN'T BE ANYTHING LEFT BEHIND!
DON'T YOU CLEAN THE BERTHS?
ER...
SLAM
IS ANYTHING WRONG?
HERE!!
OUR REAL CABIN!
HEY, MISTER!!
THE KIDS FIGURED IT OUT!
YOU CAN LET US IN!
NOK NOK
HEEEY...
ARE YOU ASLEEP IN THERE?
CHAK

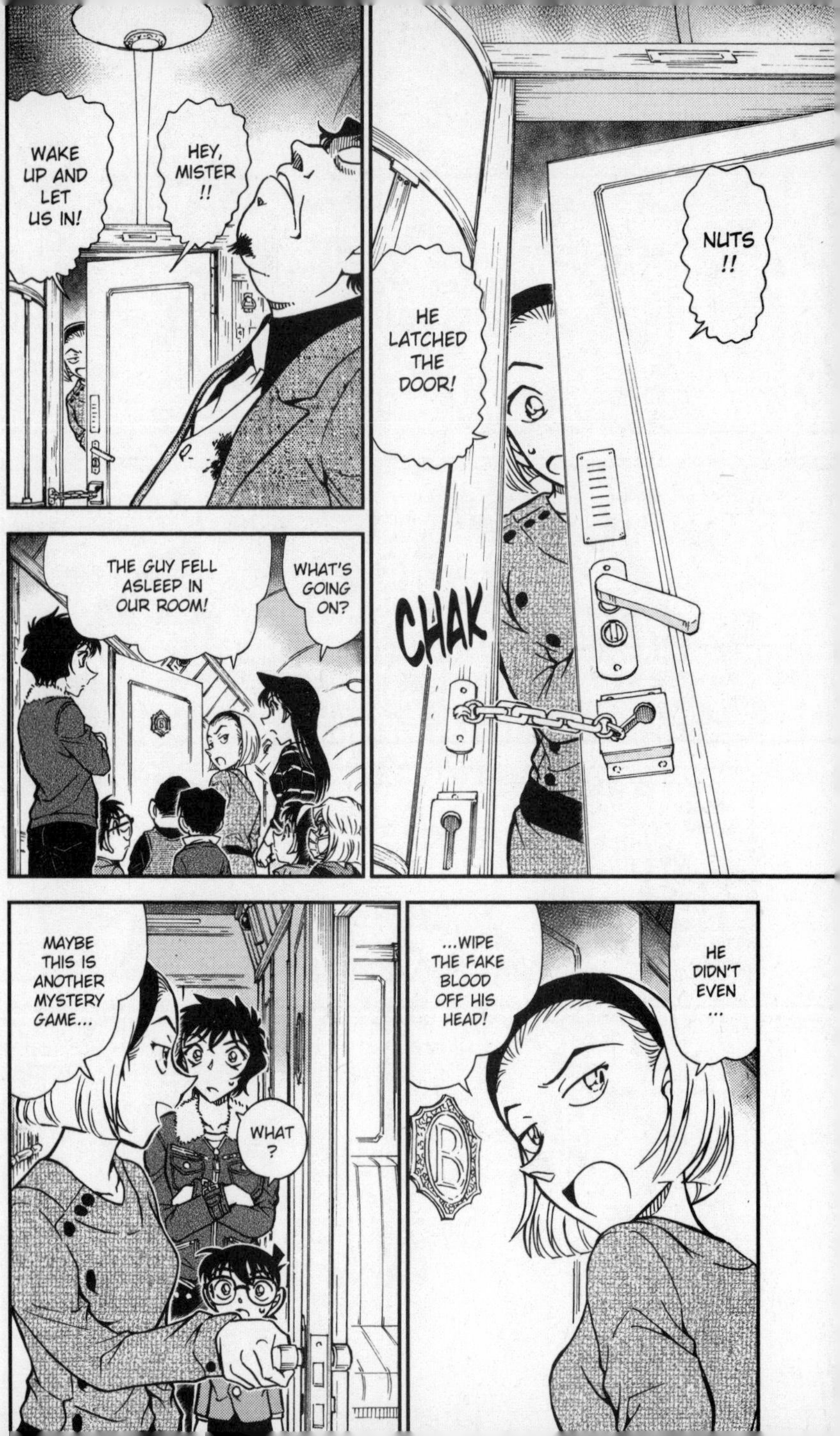
NUTS !!
HE LATCHED THE DOOR!
CHAK
HEY, MISTER !!
WAKE UP AND LET US IN!
WHAT'S GOING ON?
THE GUY FELL ASLEEP IN OUR ROOM!
HE DIDN'T EVEN ...
...WIPE THE FAKE BLOOD OFF HIS HEAD!
MAYBE THIS IS ANOTHER MYSTERY GAME...
WHAT ?

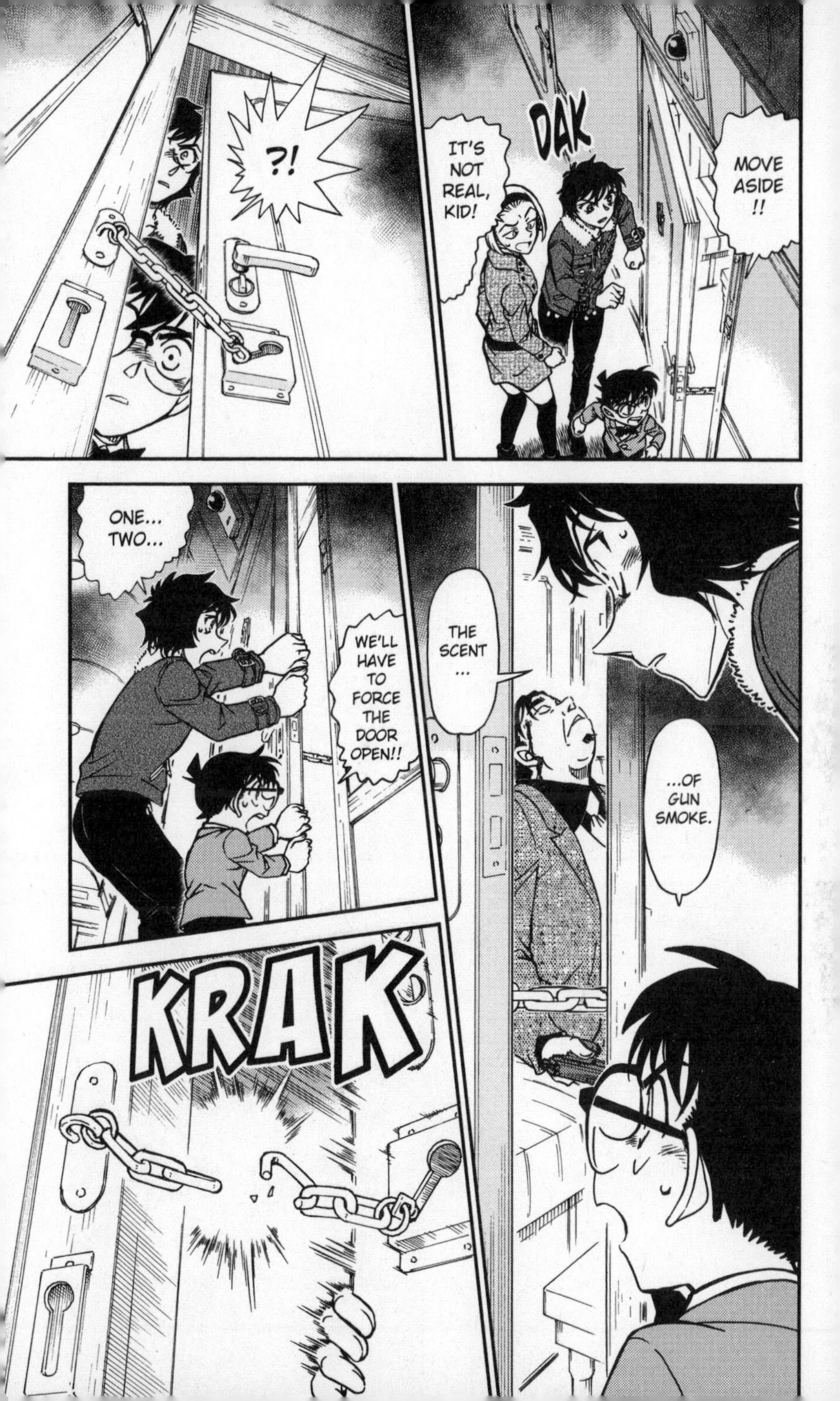
MOVE ASIDE!!
DAK
IT'S NOT REAL, KID!
?!
THE SCENT...
...OF GUN SMOKE.
WE'LL HAVE TO FORCE THE DOOR OPEN!!
ONE... TWO...
KRAK

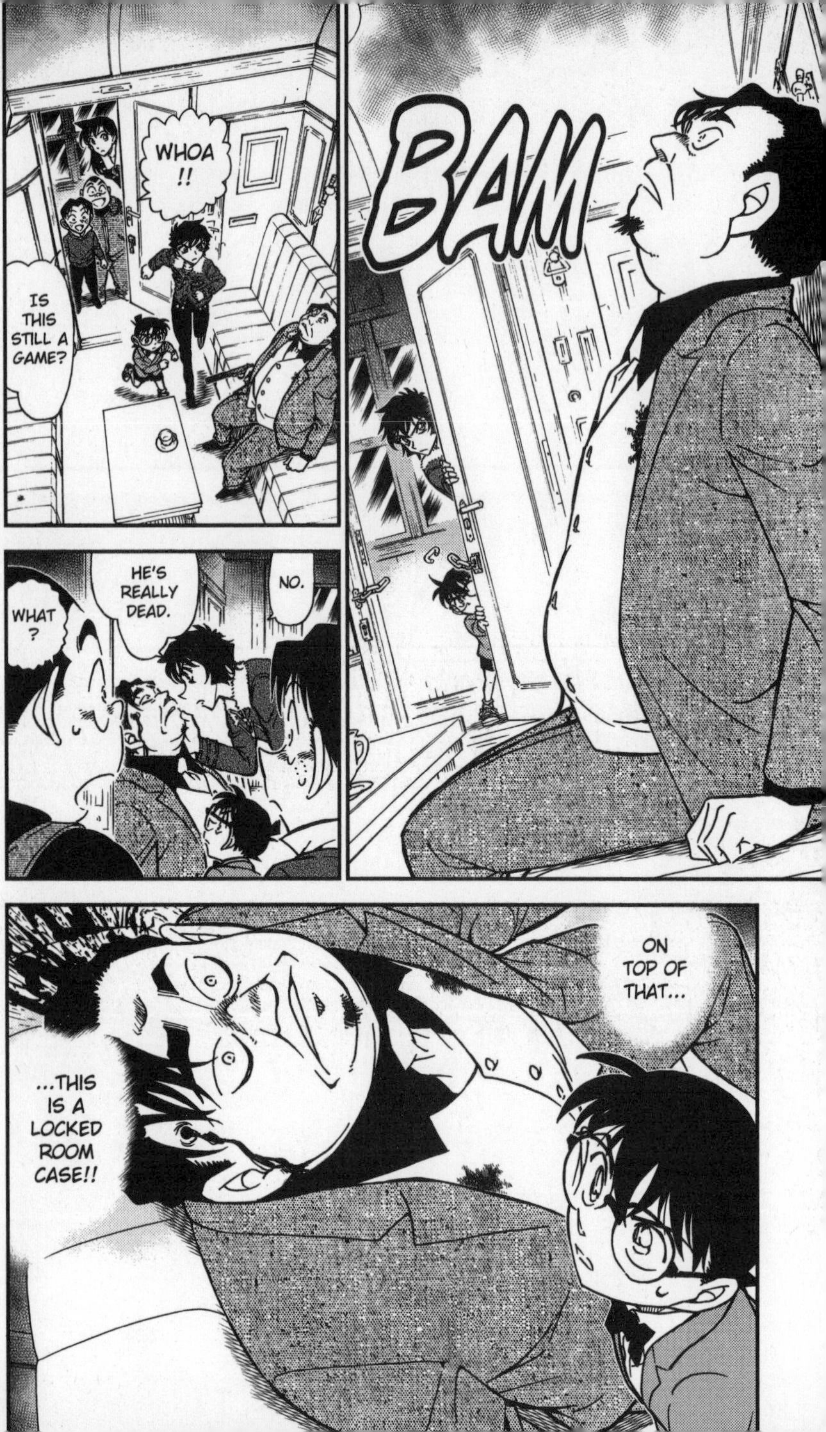
BAM
WHOA !!
IS THIS STILL A GAME?
NO.
HE'S REALLY DEAD.
WHAT ?
ON TOP OF THAT...
...THIS IS A LOCKED ROOM CASE!!

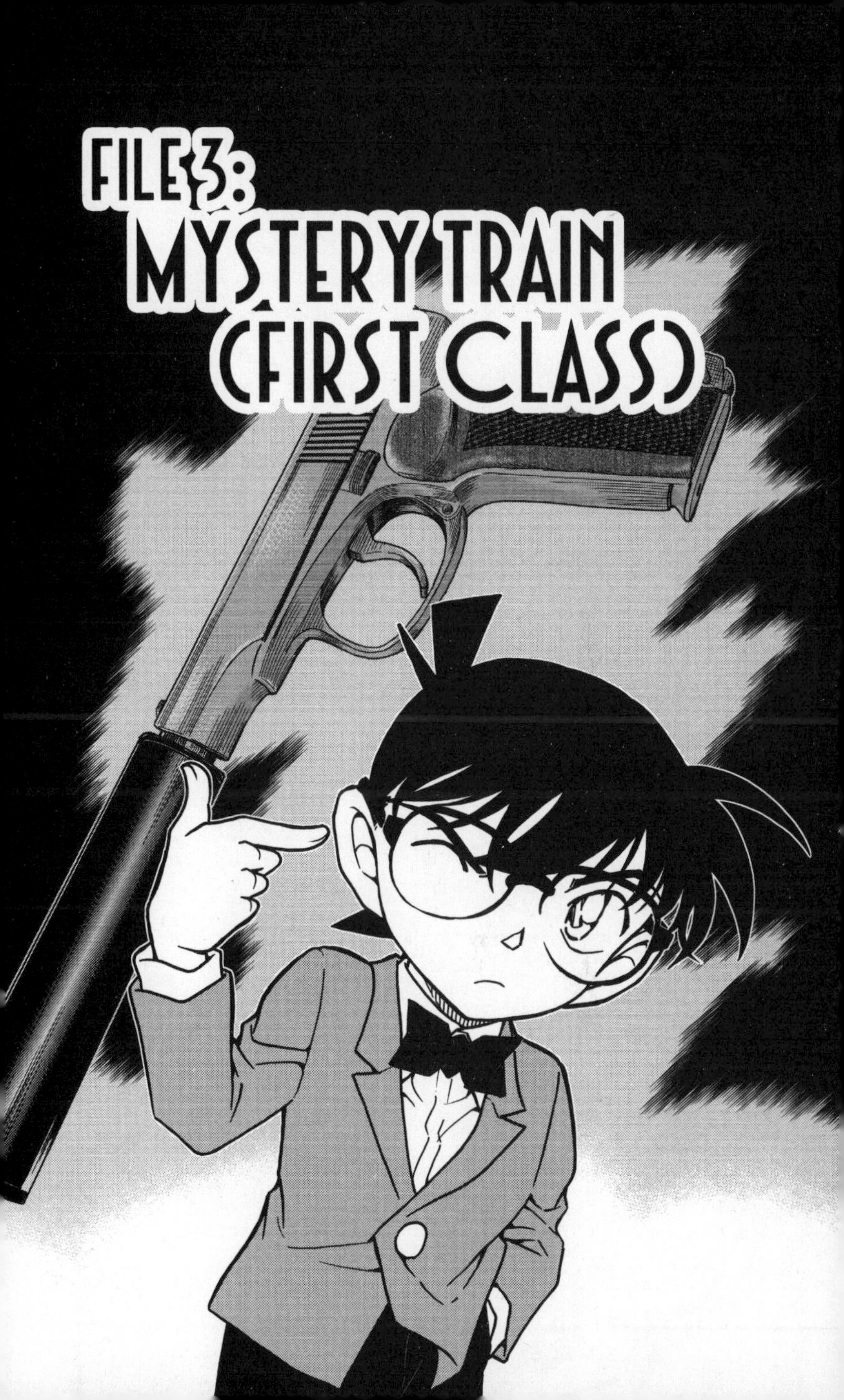
FILE 3:
MYSTERY TRAIN
(FIRST CLASS)

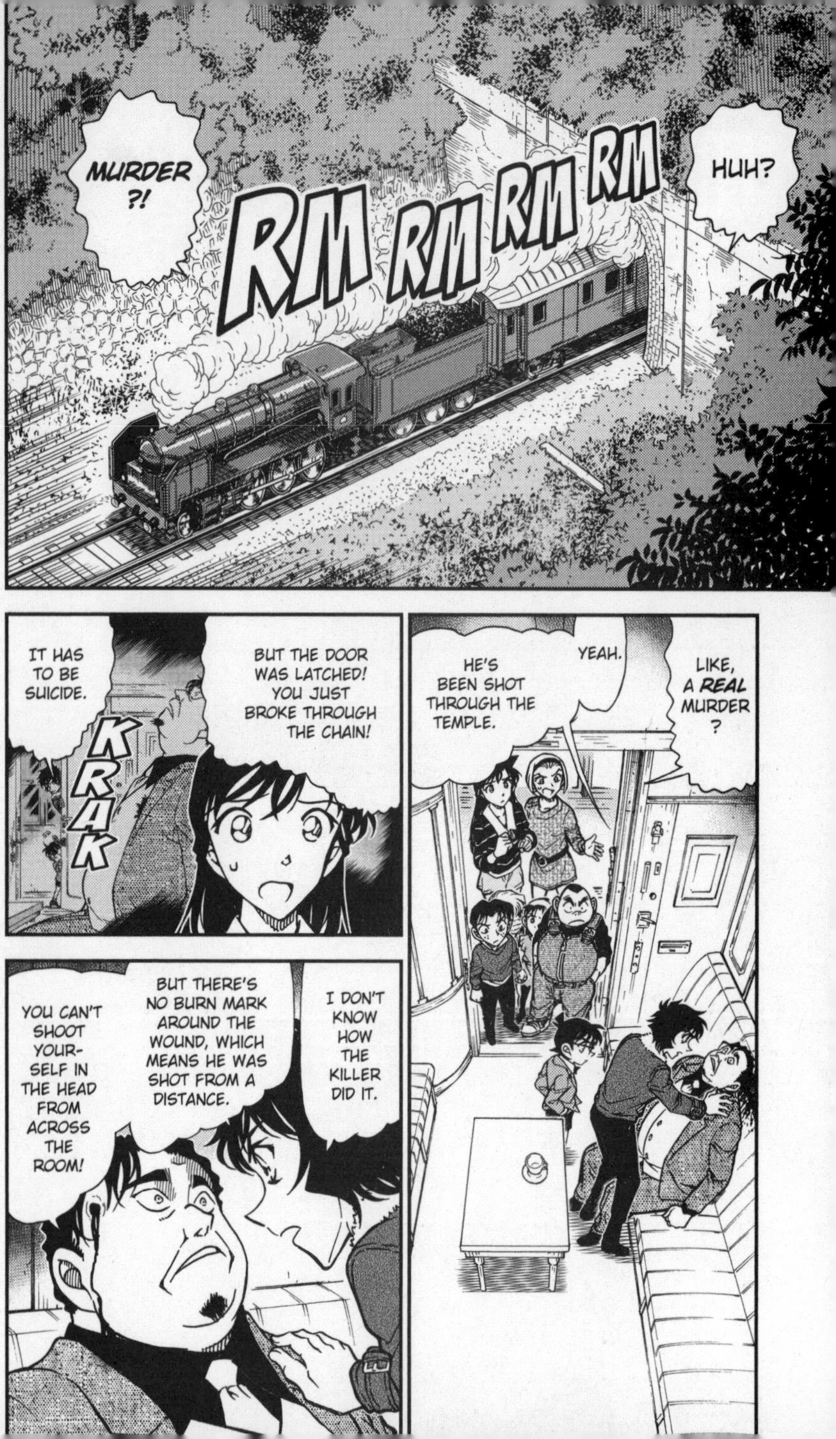
HUH?
RM RM RM RM
MURDER ?!
LIKE, A *REAL* MURDER ?
YEAH.
HE'S BEEN SHOT THROUGH THE TEMPLE.
BUT THE DOOR WAS LATCHED! YOU JUST BROKE THROUGH THE CHAIN!
KRAK
IT HAS TO BE SUICIDE.
I DON'T KNOW HOW THE KILLER DID IT.
BUT THERE'S NO BURN MARK AROUND THE WOUND, WHICH MEANS HE WAS SHOT FROM A DISTANCE.
YOU CAN'T SHOOT YOUR-SELF IN THE HEAD FROM ACROSS THE ROOM!

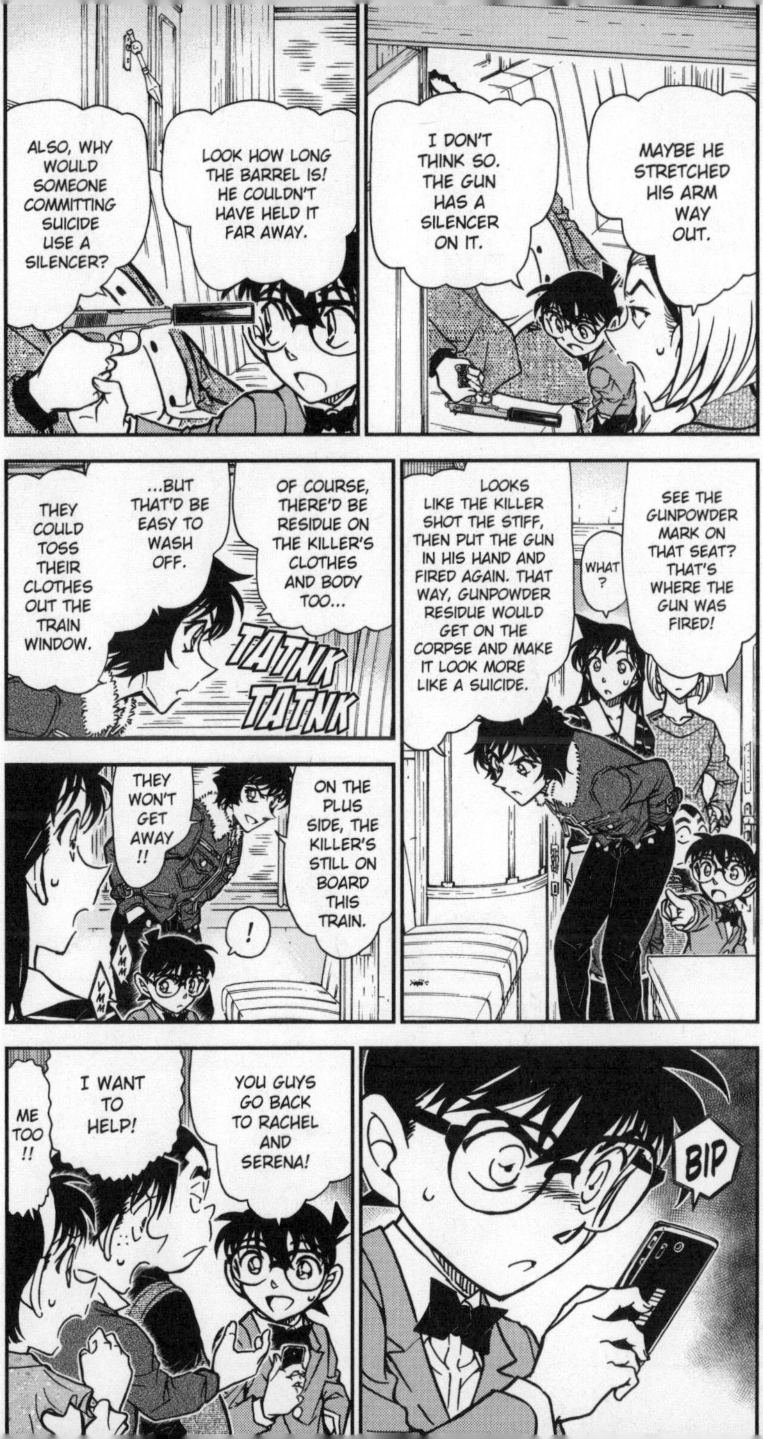
MAYBE HE STRETCHED HIS ARM WAY OUT.
I DON'T THINK SO. THE GUN HAS A SILENCER ON IT.
LOOK HOW LONG THE BARREL IS! HE COULDN'T HAVE HELD IT FAR AWAY.
ALSO, WHY WOULD SOMEONE COMMITTING SUICIDE USE A SILENCER?
SEE THE GUNPOWDER MARK ON THAT SEAT? THAT'S WHERE THE GUN WAS FIRED!
WHAT?
LOOKS LIKE THE KILLER SHOT THE STIFF, THEN PUT THE GUN IN HIS HAND AND FIRED AGAIN. THAT WAY, GUNPOWDER RESIDUE WOULD GET ON THE CORPSE AND MAKE IT LOOK MORE LIKE A SUICIDE.
OF COURSE, THERE'D BE RESIDUE ON THE KILLER'S CLOTHES AND BODY TOO...
...BUT THAT'D BE EASY TO WASH OFF.
THEY COULD TOSS THEIR CLOTHES OUT THE TRAIN WINDOW.
TATNK
TATNK
ON THE PLUS SIDE, THE KILLER'S STILL ON BOARD THIS TRAIN.
THEY WON'T GET AWAY!!
!
VMM
VMM
BIP
YOU GUYS GO BACK TO RACHEL AND SERENA!
I WANT TO HELP!
ME TOO!!

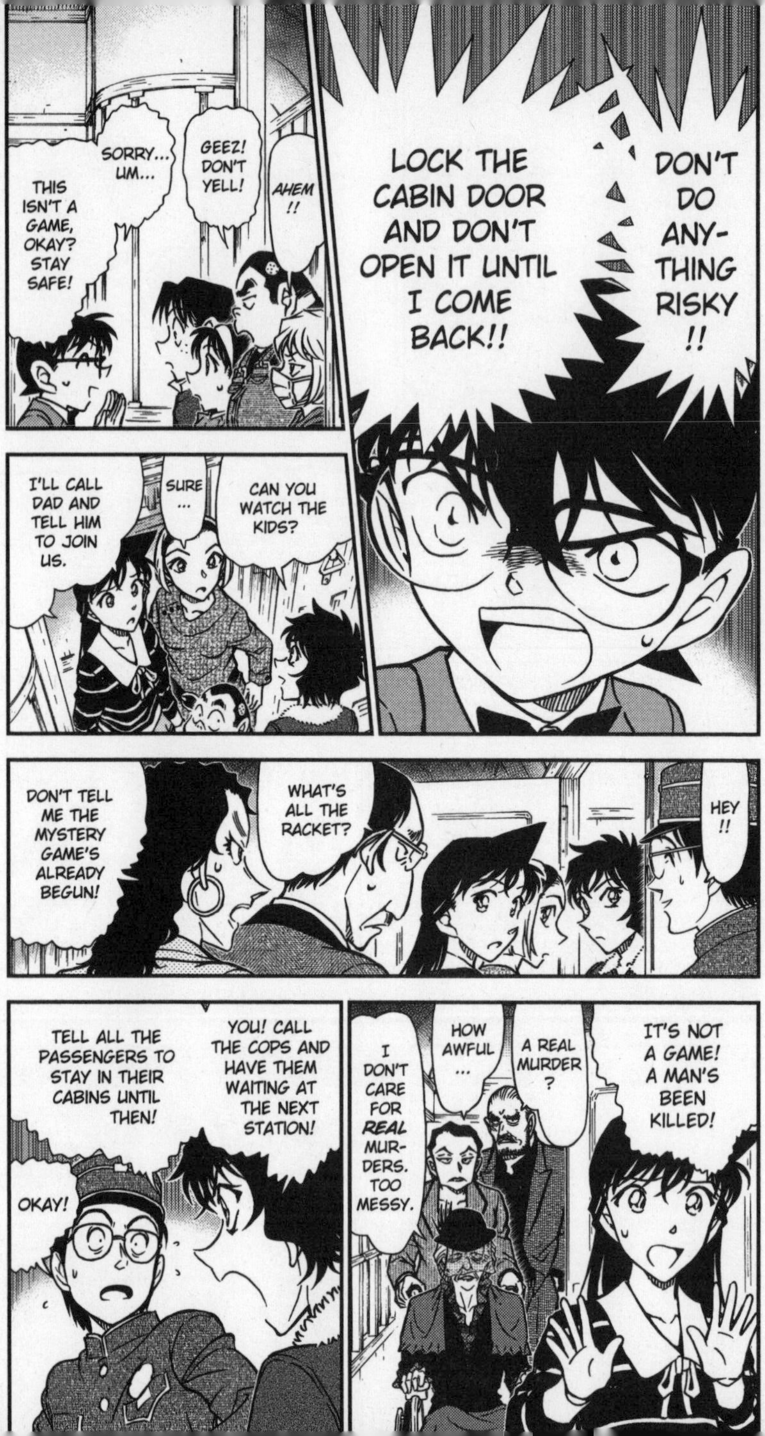
DON'T DO ANYTHING RISKY!!
LOCK THE CABIN DOOR AND DON'T OPEN IT UNTIL I COME BACK!!
AHEM!!
GEEZ! DON'T YELL!
SORRY... UM...
THIS ISN'T A GAME, OKAY? STAY SAFE!
CAN YOU WATCH THE KIDS?
SURE...
I'LL CALL DAD AND TELL HIM TO JOIN US.
HEY!!
WHAT'S ALL THE RACKET?
DON'T TELL ME THE MYSTERY GAME'S ALREADY BEGUN!
IT'S NOT A GAME! A MAN'S BEEN KILLED!
A REAL MURDER?
HOW AWFUL...
I DON'T CARE FOR *REAL* MURDERS. TOO MESSY.
YOU! CALL THE COPS AND HAVE THEM WAITING AT THE NEXT STATION!
TELL ALL THE PASSENGERS TO STAY IN THEIR CABINS UNTIL THEN!
OKAY!

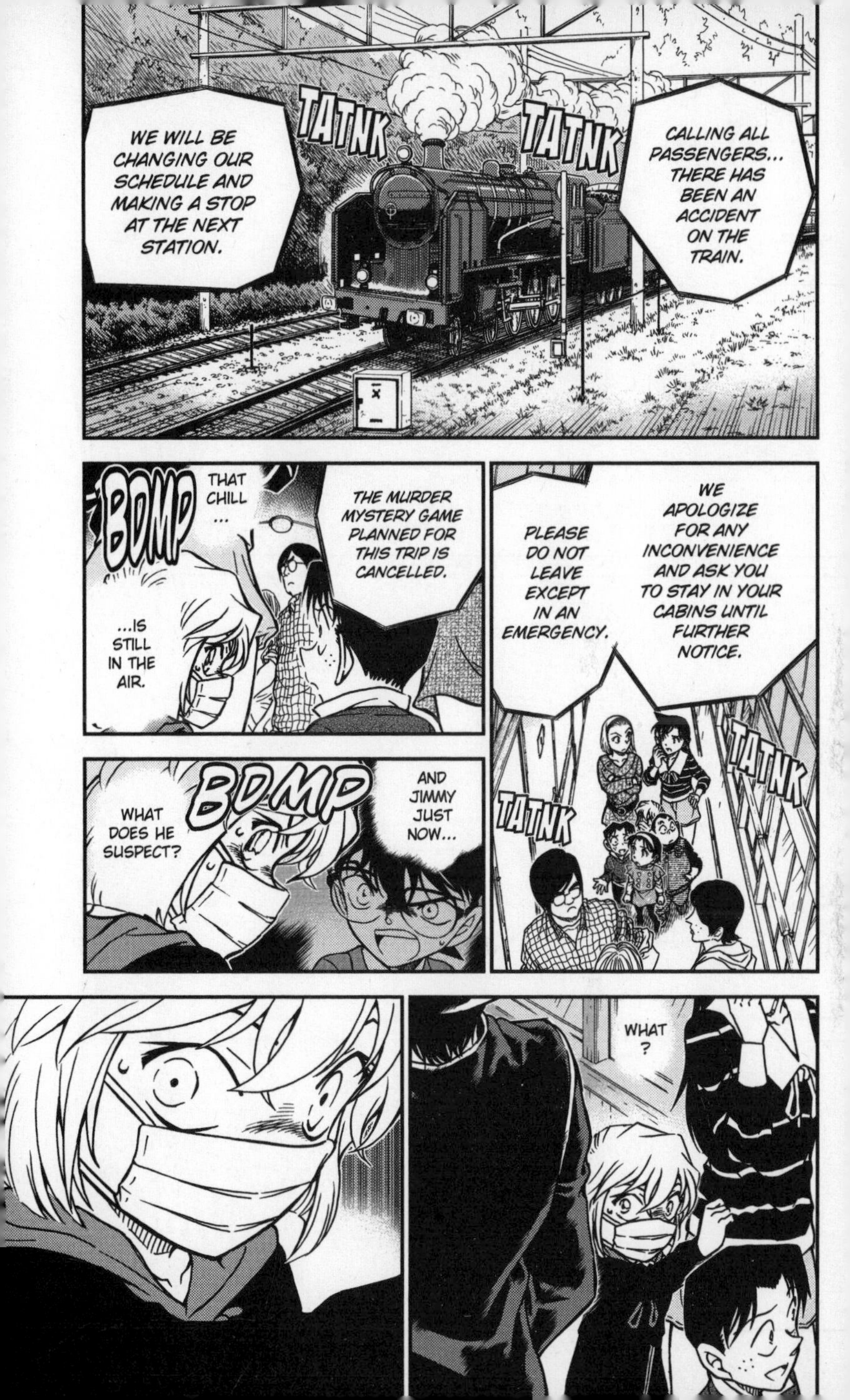
CALLING ALL PASSENGERS... THERE HAS BEEN AN ACCIDENT ON THE TRAIN.
TATNK
TATNK
WE WILL BE CHANGING OUR SCHEDULE AND MAKING A STOP AT THE NEXT STATION.
WE APOLOGIZE FOR ANY INCONVENIENCE AND ASK YOU TO STAY IN YOUR CABINS UNTIL FURTHER NOTICE.
PLEASE DO NOT LEAVE EXCEPT IN AN EMERGENCY.
TATNK
TATNK
THE MURDER MYSTERY GAME PLANNED FOR THIS TRIP IS CANCELLED.
THAT CHILL ...
BDMP
...IS STILL IN THE AIR.
AND JIMMY JUST NOW...
BDMP
WHAT DOES HE SUSPECT?
WHAT ?

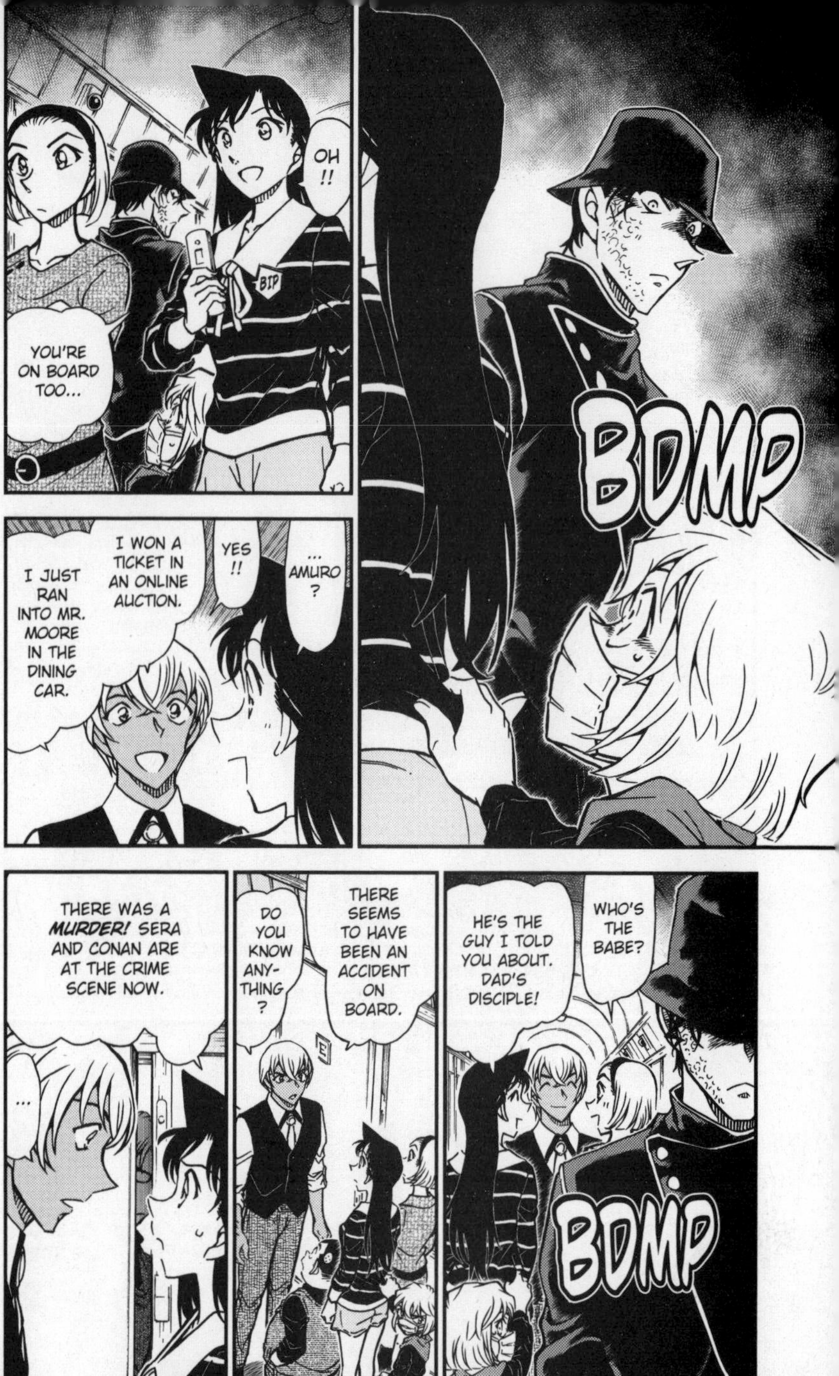
BDMP
OH !!
YOU'RE ON BOARD TOO...
... AMURO ?
YES !!
I WON A TICKET IN AN ONLINE AUCTION.
I JUST RAN INTO MR. MOORE IN THE DINING CAR.
WHO'S THE BABE?
HE'S THE GUY I TOLD YOU ABOUT. DAD'S DISCIPLE!
BDMP
THERE SEEMS TO HAVE BEEN AN ACCIDENT ON BOARD.
DO YOU KNOW ANYTHING ?
THERE WAS A MURDER! SERA AND CONAN ARE AT THE CRIME SCENE NOW.
...

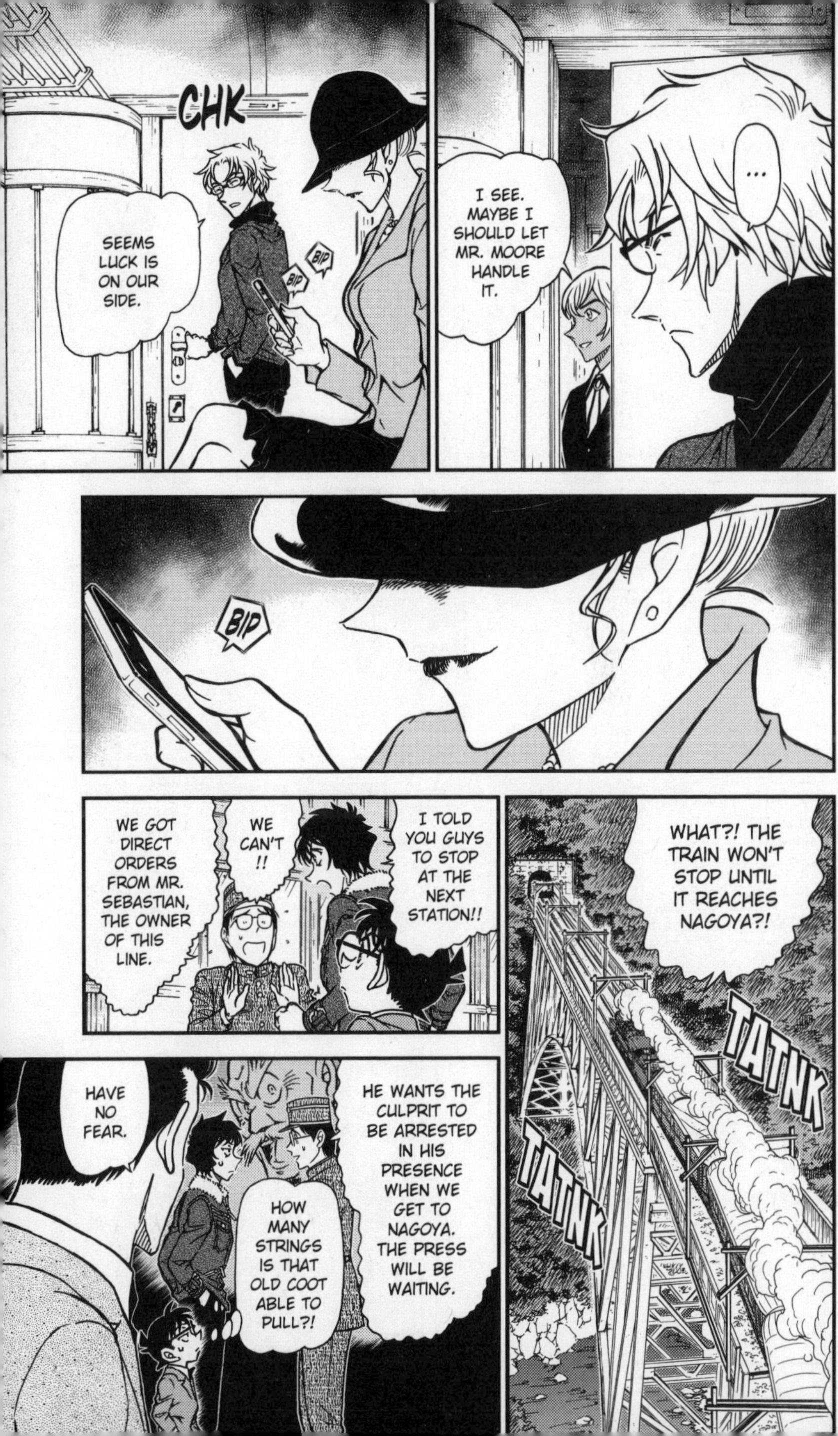
...
I SEE. MAYBE I SHOULD LET MR. MOORE HANDLE IT.
CHK
SEEMS LUCK IS ON OUR SIDE.
BIP
BIP
BIP
WHAT?! THE TRAIN WON'T STOP UNTIL IT REACHES NAGOYA?!
TATNK
TATNK
I TOLD YOU GUYS TO STOP AT THE NEXT STATION!!
WE CAN'T!!
WE GOT DIRECT ORDERS FROM MR. SEBASTIAN, THE OWNER OF THIS LINE.
HE WANTS THE CULPRIT TO BE ARRESTED IN HIS PRESENCE WHEN WE GET TO NAGOYA. THE PRESS WILL BE WAITING.
HOW MANY STRINGS IS THAT OLD COOT ABLE TO PULL?!
HAVE NO FEAR.

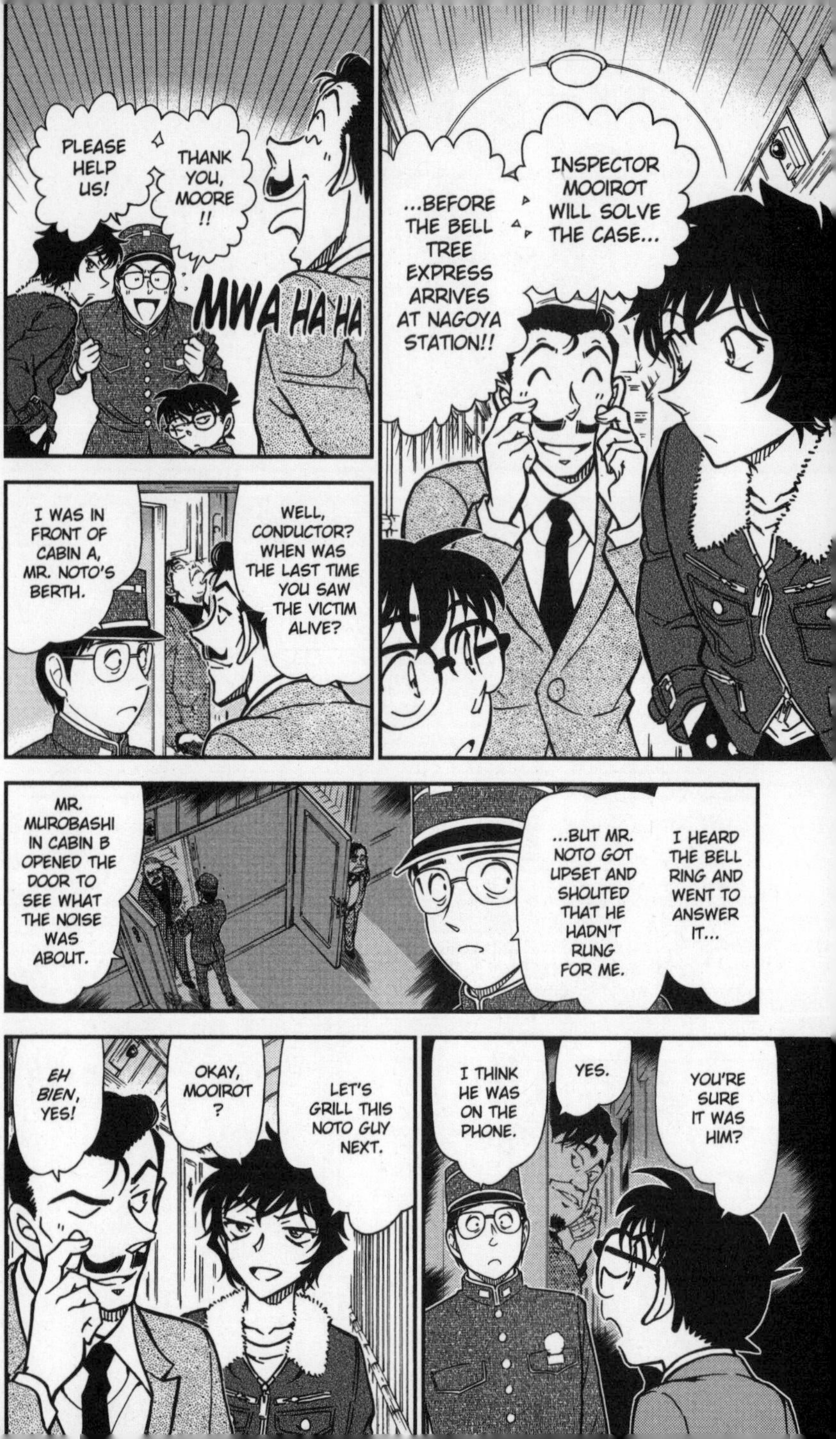
INSPECTOR MOOIROT WILL SOLVE THE CASE...
...BEFORE THE BELL TREE EXPRESS ARRIVES AT NAGOYA STATION!!
THANK YOU, MOORE!!
PLEASE HELP US!
MWA HA HA
WELL, CONDUCTOR? WHEN WAS THE LAST TIME YOU SAW THE VICTIM ALIVE?
I WAS IN FRONT OF CABIN A, MR. NOTO'S BERTH.
I HEARD THE BELL RING AND WENT TO ANSWER IT...
...BUT MR. NOTO GOT UPSET AND SHOUTED THAT HE HADN'T RUNG FOR ME.
MR. MUROBASHI IN CABIN B OPENED THE DOOR TO SEE WHAT THE NOISE WAS ABOUT.
YOU'RE SURE IT WAS HIM?
YES.
I THINK HE WAS ON THE PHONE.
LET'S GRILL THIS NOTO GUY NEXT.
OKAY, MOOIROT?
EH BIEN, YES!

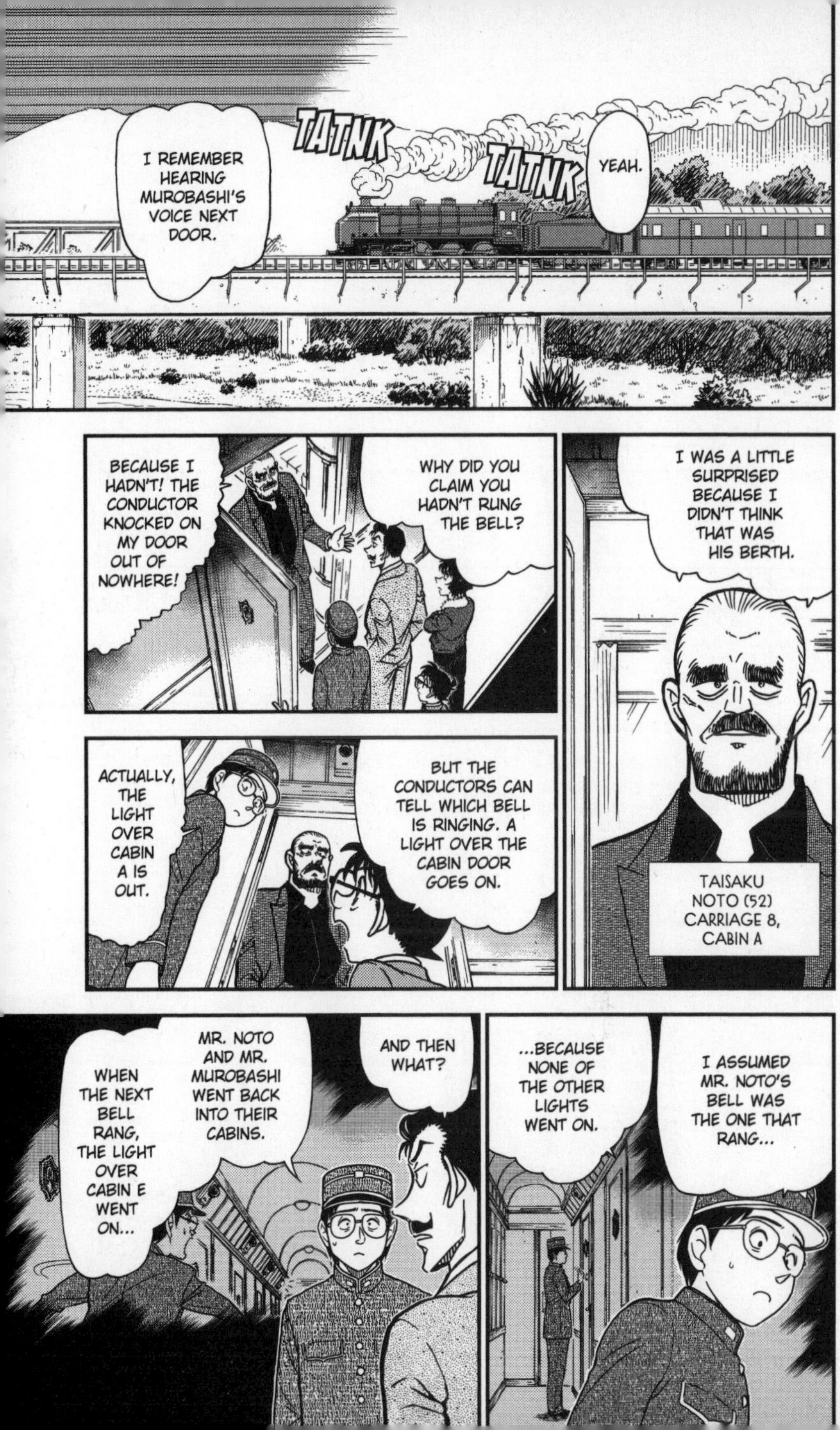
YEAH.
TATNK
TATNK
I REMEMBER HEARING MUROBASHI'S VOICE NEXT DOOR.
I WAS A LITTLE SURPRISED BECAUSE I DIDN'T THINK THAT WAS HIS BERTH.
TAISAKU NOTO (52) CARRIAGE 8, CABIN A
WHY DID YOU CLAIM YOU HADN'T RUNG THE BELL?
BECAUSE I HADN'T! THE CONDUCTOR KNOCKED ON MY DOOR OUT OF NOWHERE!
BUT THE CONDUCTORS CAN TELL WHICH BELL IS RINGING. A LIGHT OVER THE CABIN DOOR GOES ON.
ACTUALLY, THE LIGHT OVER CABIN A IS OUT.
I ASSUMED MR. NOTO'S BELL WAS THE ONE THAT RANG...
...BECAUSE NONE OF THE OTHER LIGHTS WENT ON.
AND THEN WHAT?
MR. NOTO AND MR. MUROBASHI WENT BACK INTO THEIR CABINS.
WHEN THE NEXT BELL RANG, THE LIGHT OVER CABIN E WENT ON...

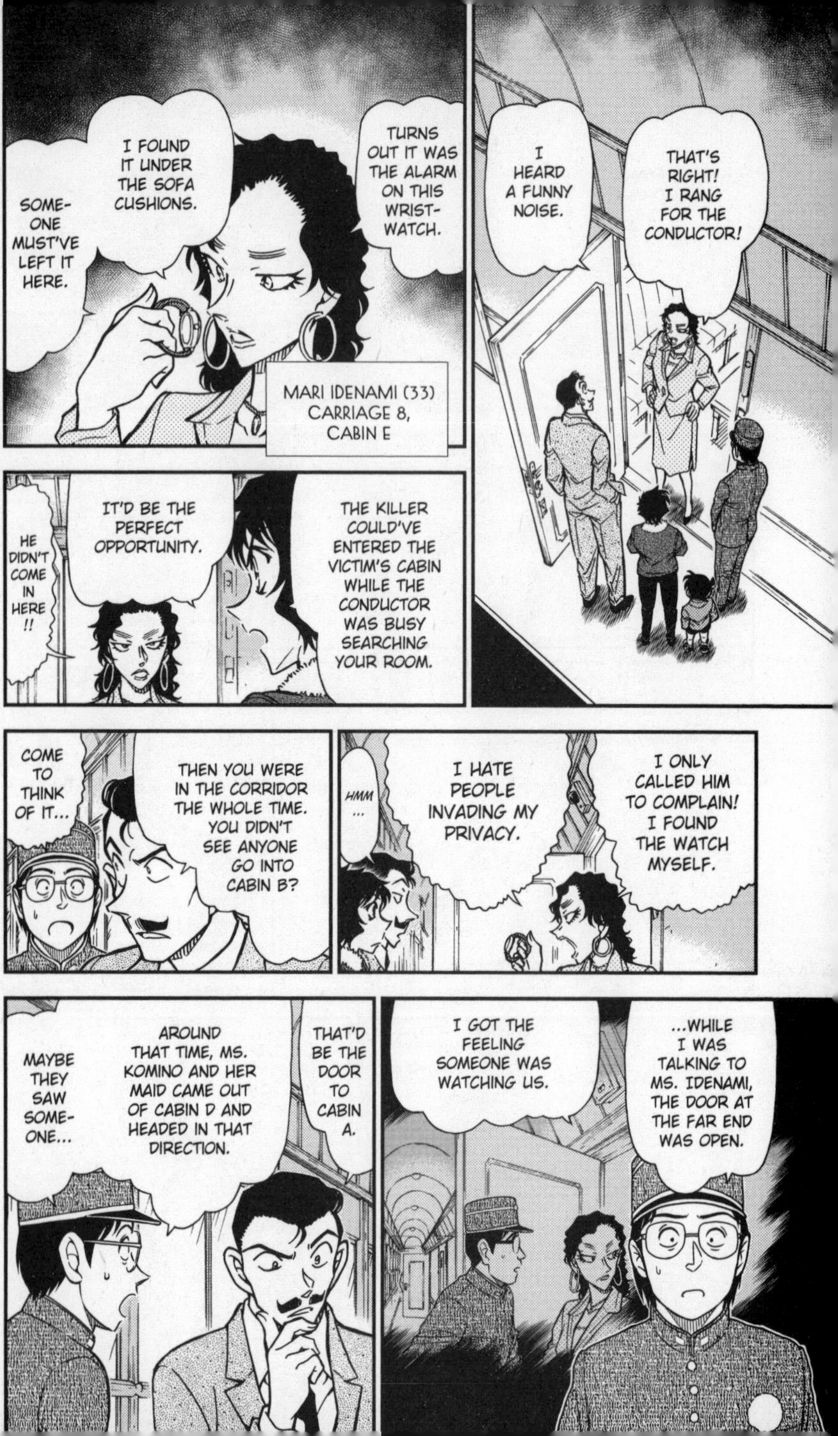
THAT'S RIGHT! I RANG FOR THE CONDUCTOR!
I HEARD A FUNNY NOISE.
TURNS OUT IT WAS THE ALARM ON THIS WRIST-WATCH.
I FOUND IT UNDER THE SOFA CUSHIONS.
SOME-ONE MUST'VE LEFT IT HERE.
MARI IDENAMI (33) CARRIAGE 8, CABIN E
THE KILLER COULD'VE ENTERED THE VICTIM'S CABIN WHILE THE CONDUCTOR WAS BUSY SEARCHING YOUR ROOM.
IT'D BE THE PERFECT OPPORTUNITY.
HE DIDN'T COME IN HERE !!
I ONLY CALLED HIM TO COMPLAIN! I FOUND THE WATCH MYSELF.
I HATE PEOPLE INVADING MY PRIVACY.
HMM ...
THEN YOU WERE IN THE CORRIDOR THE WHOLE TIME. YOU DIDN'T SEE ANYONE GO INTO CABIN B?
COME TO THINK OF IT...
...WHILE I WAS TALKING TO MS. IDENAMI, THE DOOR AT THE FAR END WAS OPEN.
I GOT THE FEELING SOMEONE WAS WATCHING US.
THAT'D BE THE DOOR TO CABIN A.
AROUND THAT TIME, MS. KOMINO AND HER MAID CAME OUT OF CABIN D AND HEADED IN THAT DIRECTION.
MAYBE THEY SAW SOME-ONE...

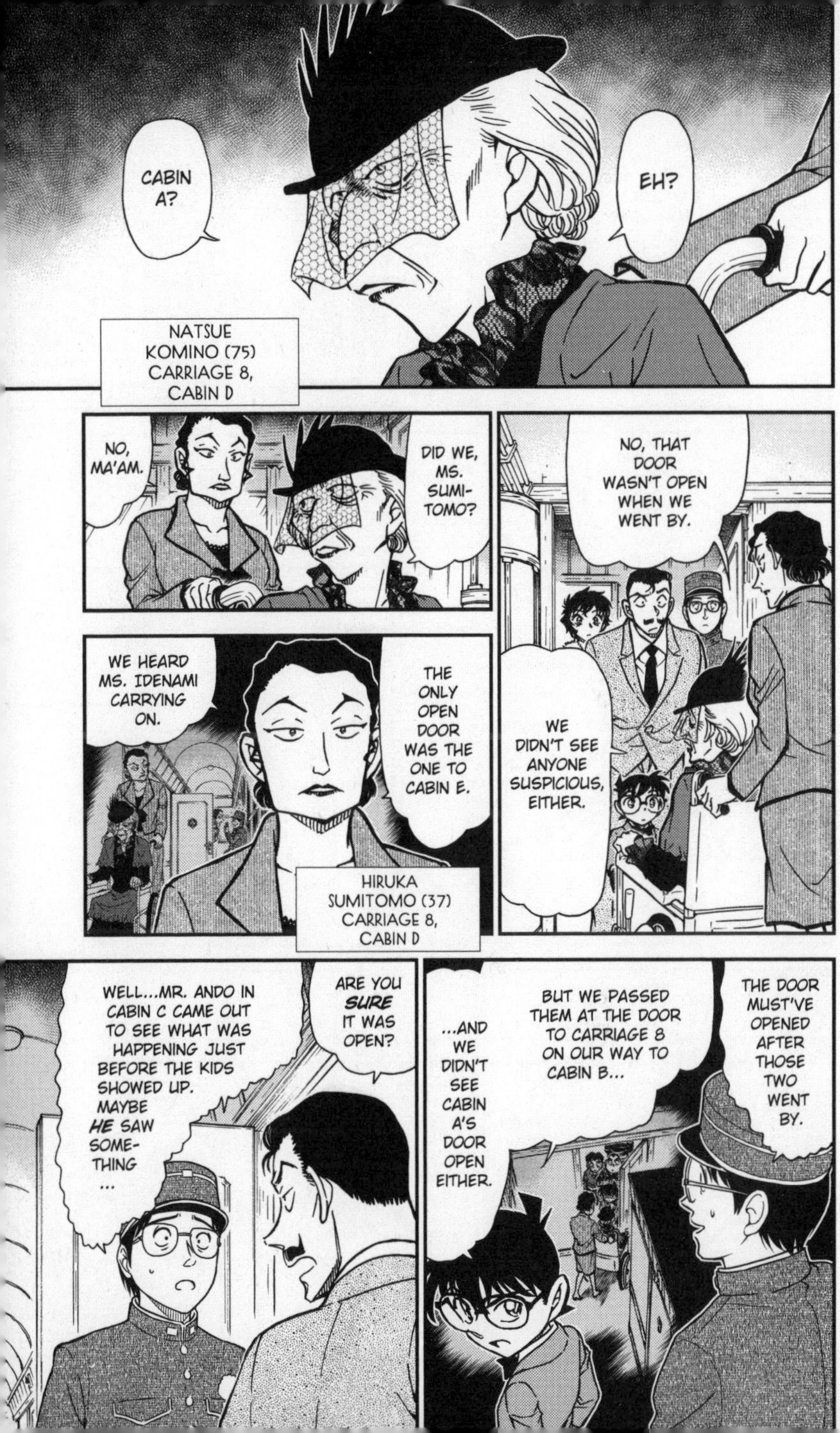
EH?
CABIN A?
NATSUE KOMINO (75) CARRIAGE 8, CABIN D
NO, THAT DOOR WASN'T OPEN WHEN WE WENT BY.
WE DIDN'T SEE ANYONE SUSPICIOUS, EITHER.
DID WE, MS. SUMITOMO?
NO, MA'AM.
THE ONLY OPEN DOOR WAS THE ONE TO CABIN E.
WE HEARD MS. IDENAMI CARRYING ON.
HIRUKA SUMITOMO (37) CARRIAGE 8, CABIN D
THE DOOR MUST'VE OPENED AFTER THOSE TWO WENT BY.
BUT WE PASSED THEM AT THE DOOR TO CARRIAGE 8 ON OUR WAY TO CABIN B...
...AND WE DIDN'T SEE CABIN A'S DOOR OPEN EITHER.
ARE YOU *SURE* IT WAS OPEN?
WELL...MR. ANDO IN CABIN C CAME OUT TO SEE WHAT WAS HAPPENING JUST BEFORE THE KIDS SHOWED UP. MAYBE *HE* SAW SOME-THING...

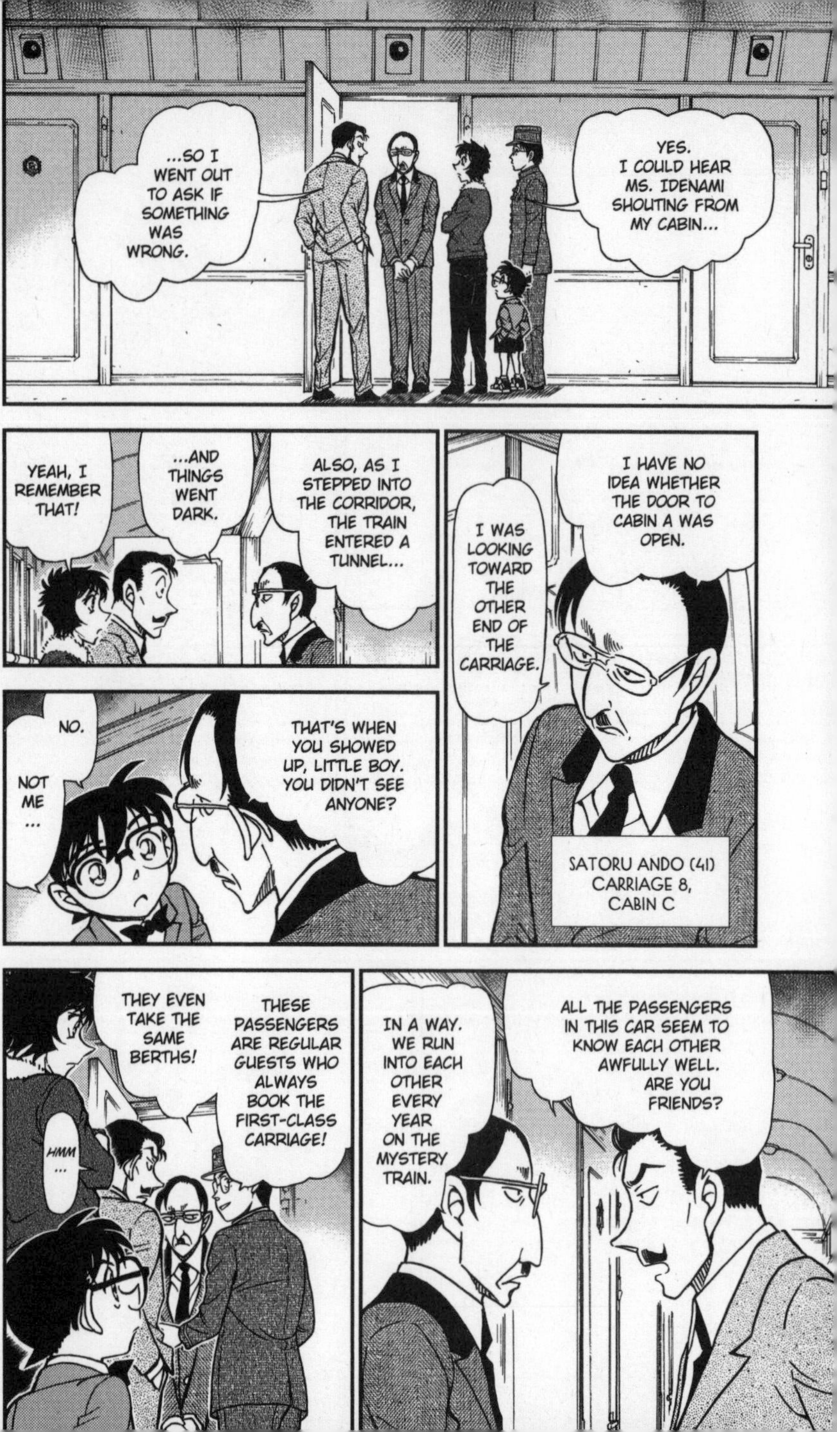
YES. I COULD HEAR MS. IDENAMI SHOUTING FROM MY CABIN...
...SO I WENT OUT TO ASK IF SOMETHING WAS WRONG.
I HAVE NO IDEA WHETHER THE DOOR TO CABIN A WAS OPEN.
I WAS LOOKING TOWARD THE OTHER END OF THE CARRIAGE.
SATORU ANDO (41) CARRIAGE 8, CABIN C
ALSO, AS I STEPPED INTO THE CORRIDOR, THE TRAIN ENTERED A TUNNEL...
...AND THINGS WENT DARK.
YEAH, I REMEMBER THAT!
THAT'S WHEN YOU SHOWED UP, LITTLE BOY. YOU DIDN'T SEE ANYONE?
NO.
NOT ME ...
ALL THE PASSENGERS IN THIS CAR SEEM TO KNOW EACH OTHER AWFULLY WELL. ARE YOU FRIENDS?
IN A WAY. WE RUN INTO EACH OTHER EVERY YEAR ON THE MYSTERY TRAIN.
THESE PASSENGERS ARE REGULAR GUESTS WHO ALWAYS BOOK THE FIRST-CLASS CARRIAGE!
THEY EVEN TAKE THE SAME BERTHS!
HMM ...

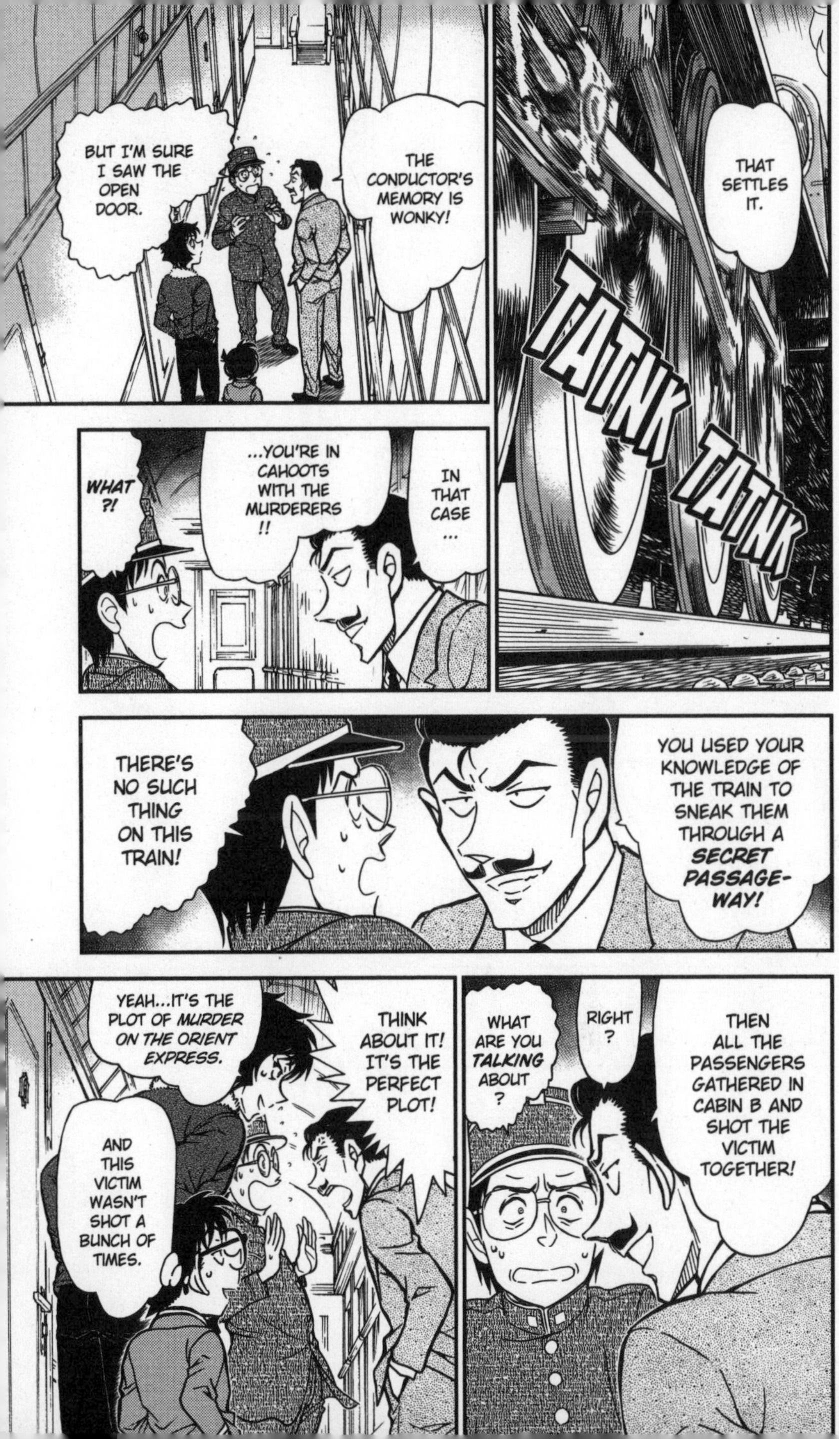
THAT SETTLES IT.
TATNK
TATNK
THE CONDUCTOR'S MEMORY IS WONKY!
BUT I'M SURE I SAW THE OPEN DOOR.
IN THAT CASE...
...YOU'RE IN CAHOOTS WITH THE MURDERERS!!
WHAT?!
YOU USED YOUR KNOWLEDGE OF THE TRAIN TO SNEAK THEM THROUGH A SECRET PASSAGEWAY!
THERE'S NO SUCH THING ON THIS TRAIN!
THEN ALL THE PASSENGERS GATHERED IN CABIN B AND SHOT THE VICTIM TOGETHER!
RIGHT?
WHAT ARE YOU TALKING ABOUT?
THINK ABOUT IT! IT'S THE PERFECT PLOT!
YEAH...IT'S THE PLOT OF MURDER ON THE ORIENT EXPRESS.
AND THIS VICTIM WASN'T SHOT A BUNCH OF TIMES.

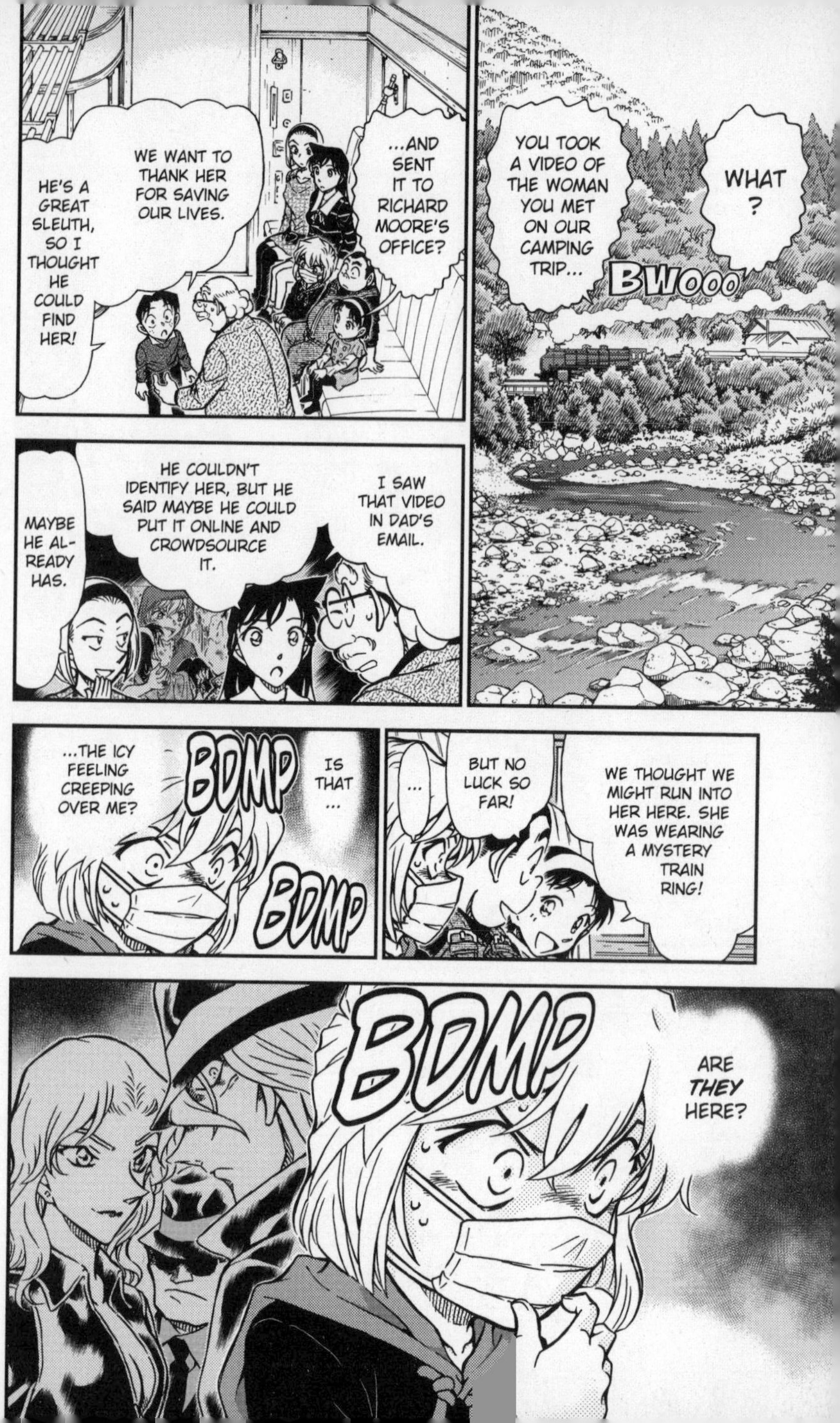
WHAT?
YOU TOOK A VIDEO OF THE WOMAN YOU MET ON OUR CAMPING TRIP...
BWOOO
...AND SENT IT TO RICHARD MOORE'S OFFICE?
WE WANT TO THANK HER FOR SAVING OUR LIVES.
HE'S A GREAT SLEUTH, SO I THOUGHT HE COULD FIND HER!
I SAW THAT VIDEO IN DAD'S EMAIL.
HE COULDN'T IDENTIFY HER, BUT HE SAID MAYBE HE COULD PUT IT ONLINE AND CROWDSOURCE IT.
MAYBE HE ALREADY HAS.
WE THOUGHT WE MIGHT RUN INTO HER HERE. SHE WAS WEARING A MYSTERY TRAIN RING!
BUT NO LUCK SO FAR!
...
IS THAT...
BDMP
...THE ICY FEELING CREEPING OVER ME?
BDMP
ARE *THEY* HERE?
BDMP

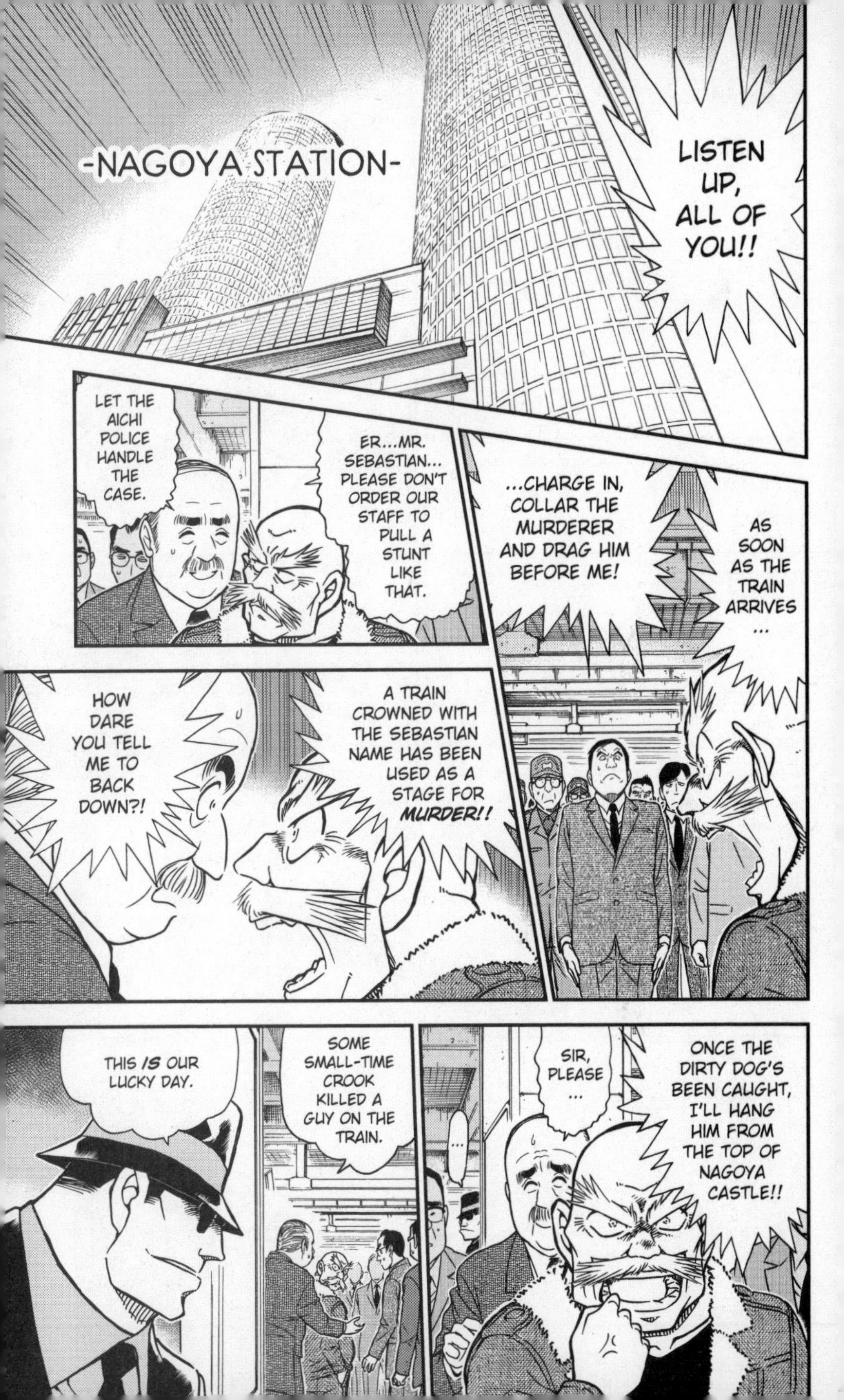

LISTEN UP, ALL OF YOU!!
-NAGOYA STATION-
AS SOON AS THE TRAIN ARRIVES...
...CHARGE IN, COLLAR THE MURDERER AND DRAG HIM BEFORE ME!
ER...MR. SEBASTIAN... PLEASE DON'T ORDER OUR STAFF TO PULL A STUNT LIKE THAT.
LET THE AICHI POLICE HANDLE THE CASE.
A TRAIN CROWNED WITH THE SEBASTIAN NAME HAS BEEN USED AS A STAGE FOR *MURDER!!*
HOW DARE YOU TELL ME TO BACK DOWN?!
ONCE THE DIRTY DOG'S BEEN CAUGHT, I'LL HANG HIM FROM THE TOP OF NAGOYA CASTLE!!
SIR, PLEASE...
...
SOME SMALL-TIME CROOK KILLED A GUY ON THE TRAIN.
THIS *IS* OUR LUCKY DAY.

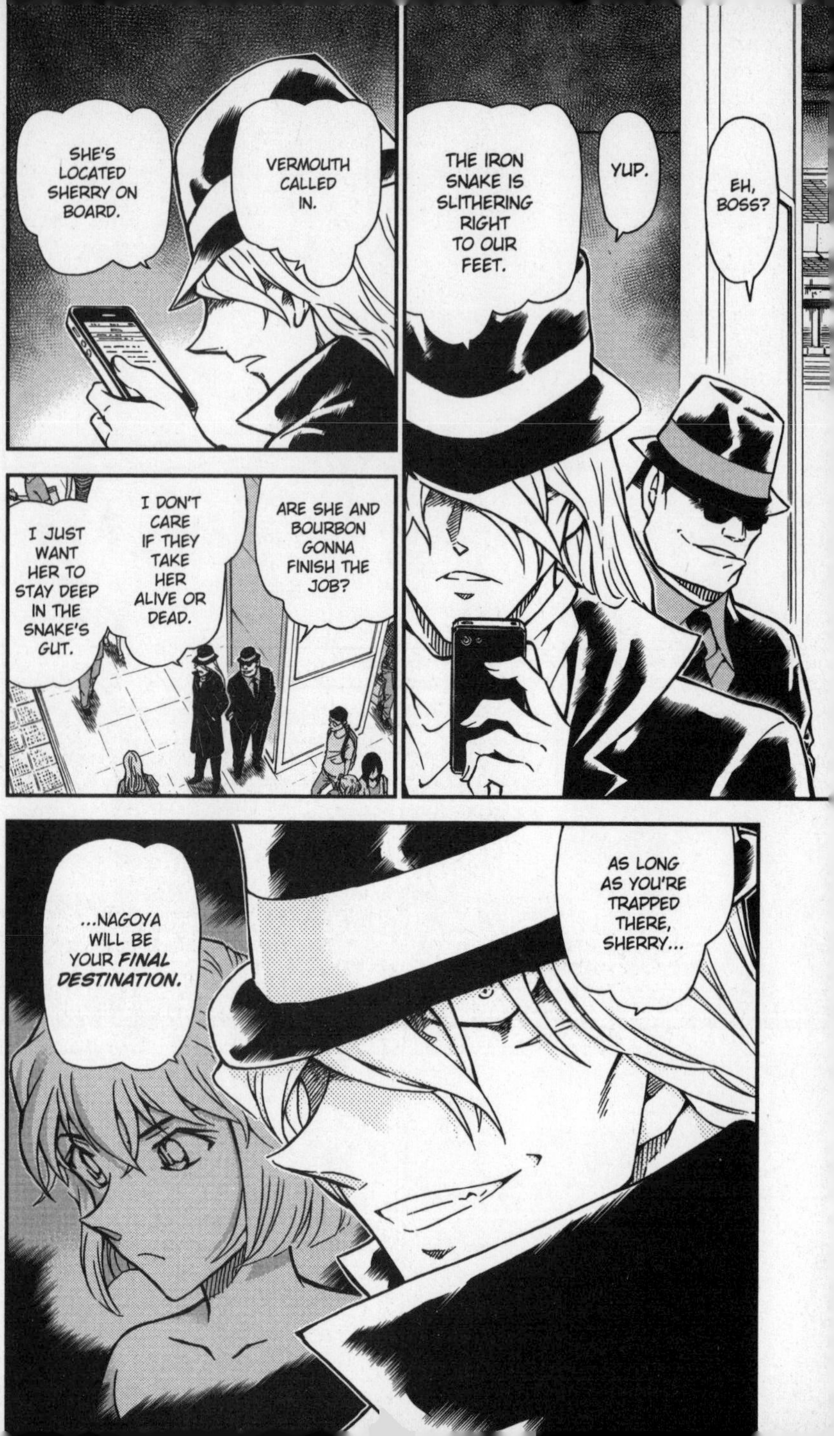
EH, BOSS?
YUP.
THE IRON SNAKE IS SLITHERING RIGHT TO OUR FEET.
VERMOUTH CALLED IN.
SHE'S LOCATED SHERRY ON BOARD.
ARE SHE AND BOURBON GONNA FINISH THE JOB?
I DON'T CARE IF THEY TAKE HER ALIVE OR DEAD.
I JUST WANT HER TO STAY DEEP IN THE SNAKE'S GUT.
AS LONG AS YOU'RE TRAPPED THERE, SHERRY...
...NAGOYA WILL BE YOUR *FINAL DESTINATION.*

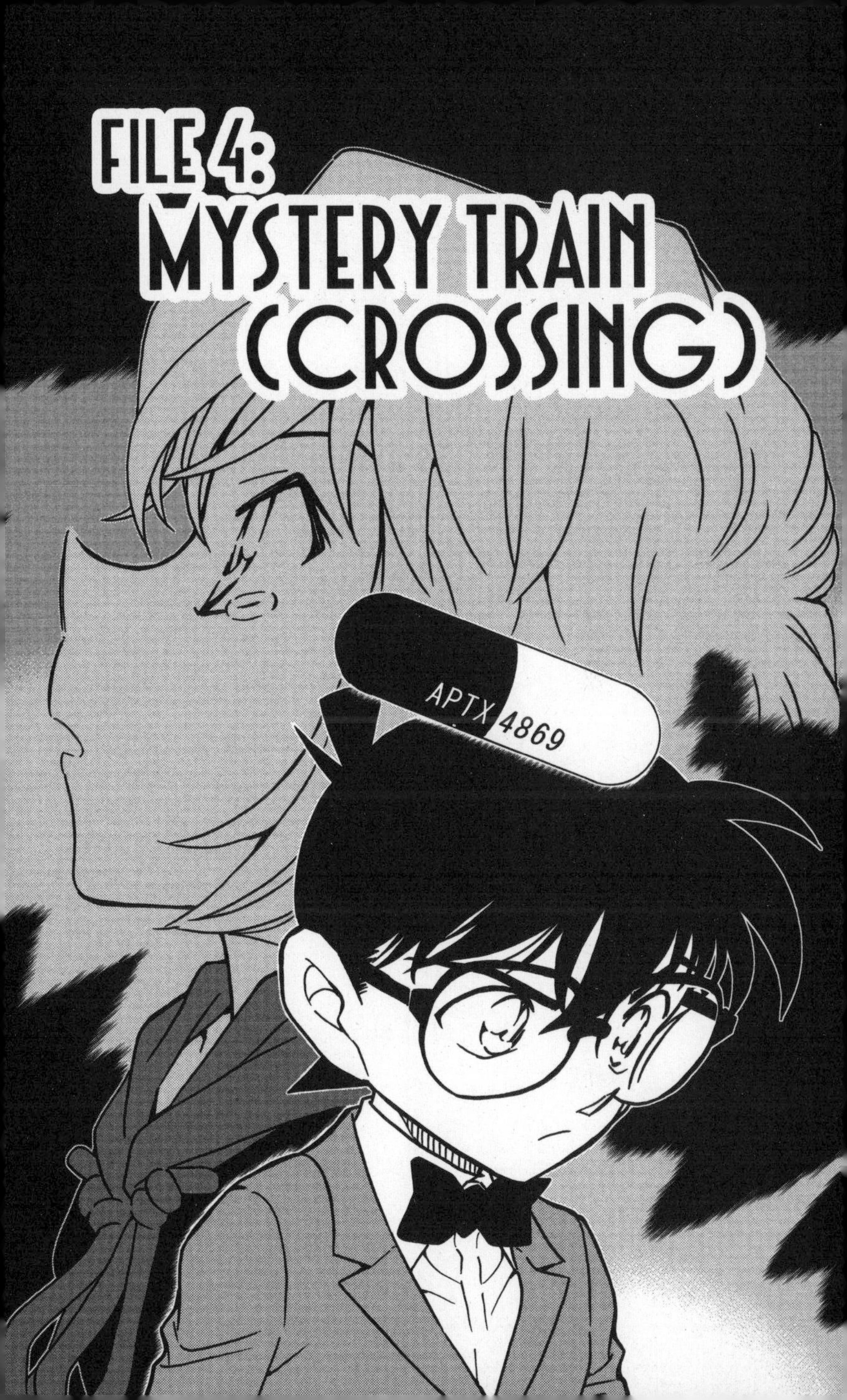
FILE 4:
MYSTERY TRAIN
(CROSSING)
APTX 4869

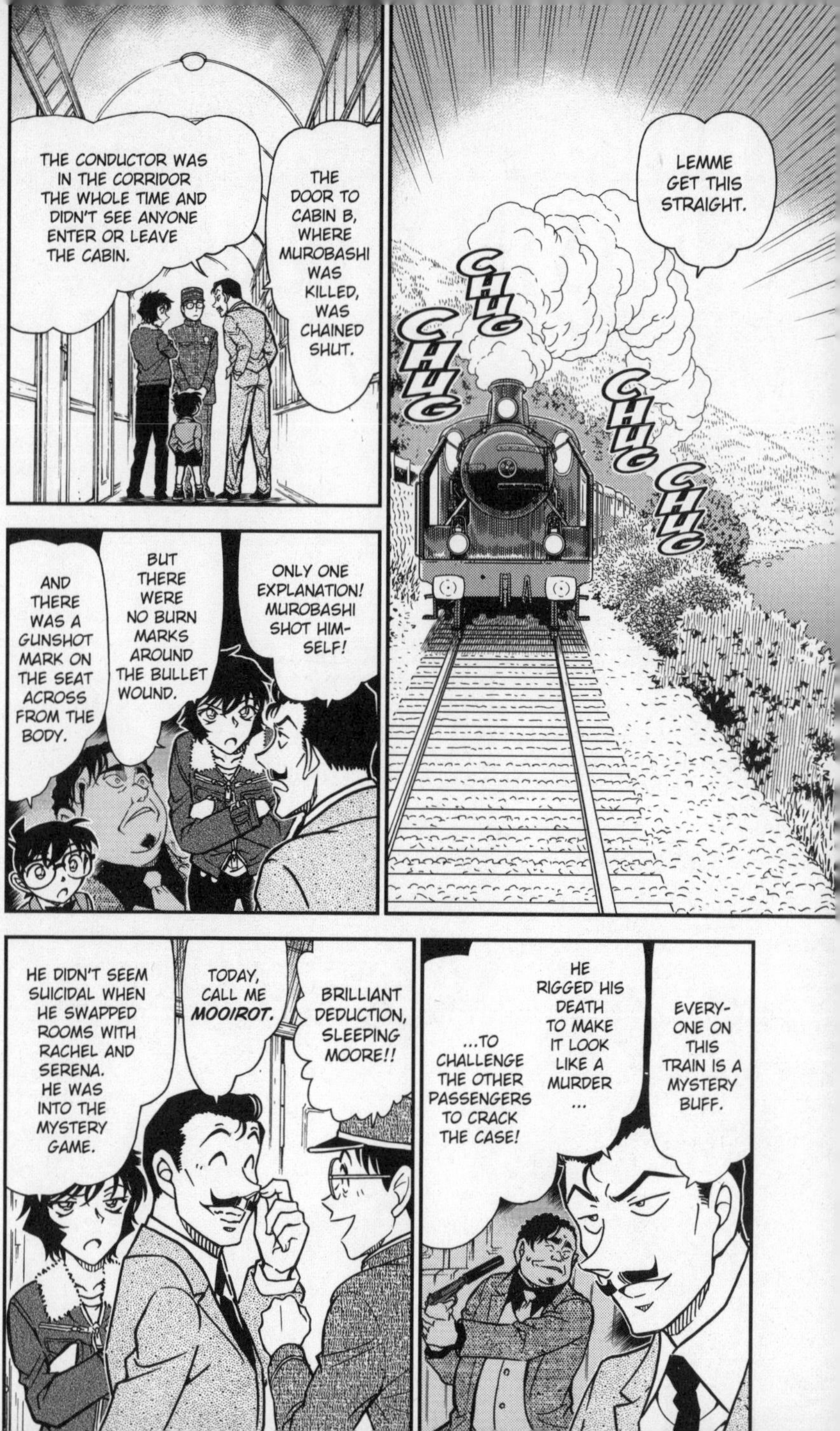
LEMME GET THIS STRAIGHT.
CHUG CHUG
CHUG CHUG
THE DOOR TO CABIN B, WHERE MUROBASHI WAS KILLED, WAS CHAINED SHUT.
THE CONDUCTOR WAS IN THE CORRIDOR THE WHOLE TIME AND DIDN'T SEE ANYONE ENTER OR LEAVE THE CABIN.
ONLY ONE EXPLANATION! MUROBASHI SHOT HIM-SELF!
BUT THERE WERE NO BURN MARKS AROUND THE BULLET WOUND.
AND THERE WAS A GUNSHOT MARK ON THE SEAT ACROSS FROM THE BODY.
EVERY-ONE ON THIS TRAIN IS A MYSTERY BUFF.
HE RIGGED HIS DEATH TO MAKE IT LOOK LIKE A MURDER ...
...TO CHALLENGE THE OTHER PASSENGERS TO CRACK THE CASE!
BRILLIANT DEDUCTION, SLEEPING MOORE!!
TODAY, CALL ME *MOOIROT.*
HE DIDN'T SEEM SUICIDAL WHEN HE SWAPPED ROOMS WITH RACHEL AND SERENA. HE WAS INTO THE MYSTERY GAME.

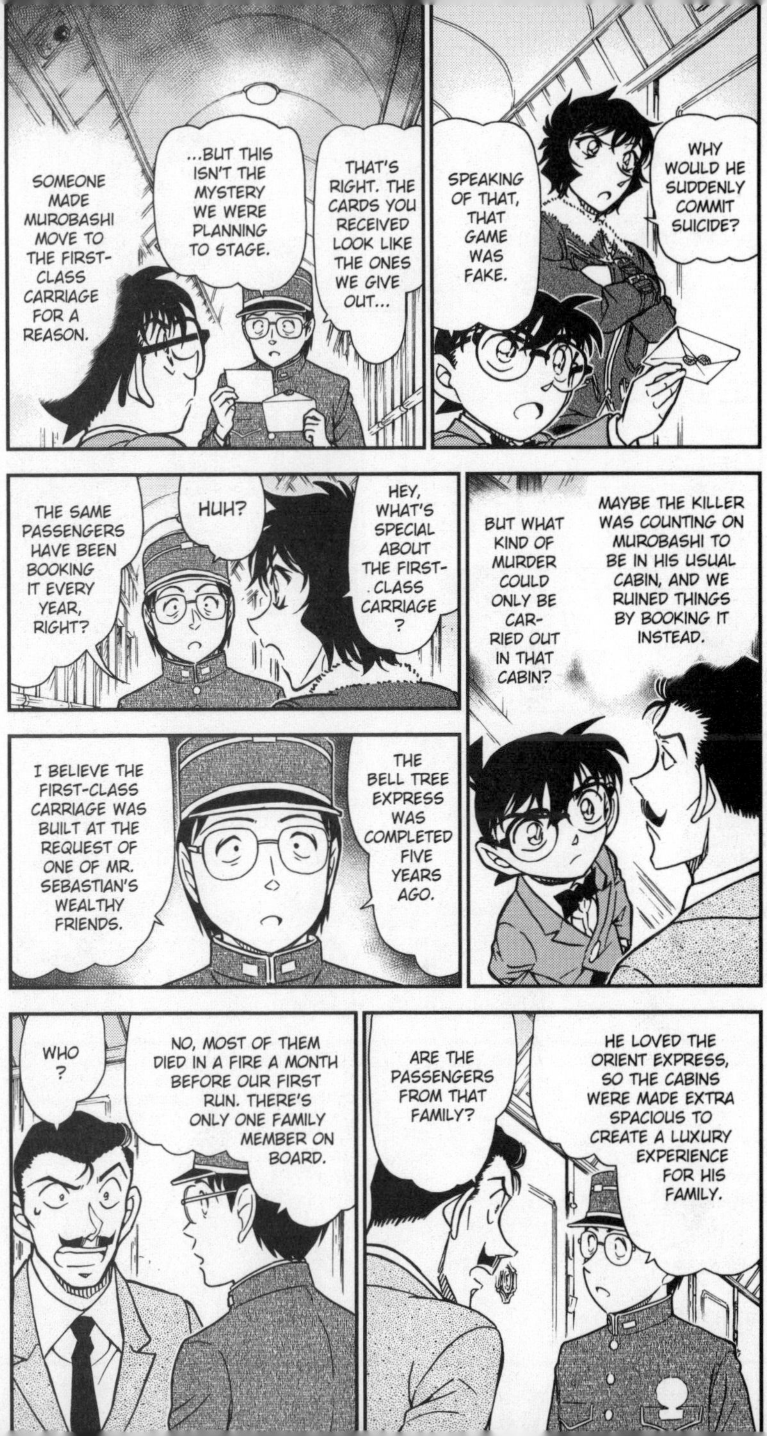
WHY WOULD HE SUDDENLY COMMIT SUICIDE?
SPEAKING OF THAT, THAT GAME WAS FAKE.
THAT'S RIGHT. THE CARDS YOU RECEIVED LOOK LIKE THE ONES WE GIVE OUT...
...BUT THIS ISN'T THE MYSTERY WE WERE PLANNING TO STAGE.
SOMEONE MADE MUROBASHI MOVE TO THE FIRST-CLASS CARRIAGE FOR A REASON.
MAYBE THE KILLER WAS COUNTING ON MUROBASHI TO BE IN HIS USUAL CABIN, AND WE RUINED THINGS BY BOOKING IT INSTEAD.
BUT WHAT KIND OF MURDER COULD ONLY BE CAR-RIED OUT IN THAT CABIN?
HEY, WHAT'S SPECIAL ABOUT THE FIRST-CLASS CARRIAGE?
HUH?
THE SAME PASSENGERS HAVE BEEN BOOKING IT EVERY YEAR, RIGHT?
THE BELL TREE EXPRESS WAS COMPLETED FIVE YEARS AGO.
I BELIEVE THE FIRST-CLASS CARRIAGE WAS BUILT AT THE REQUEST OF ONE OF MR. SEBASTIAN'S WEALTHY FRIENDS.
HE LOVED THE ORIENT EXPRESS, SO THE CABINS WERE MADE EXTRA SPACIOUS TO CREATE A LUXURY EXPERIENCE FOR HIS FAMILY.
ARE THE PASSENGERS FROM THAT FAMILY?
NO, MOST OF THEM DIED IN A FIRE A MONTH BEFORE OUR FIRST RUN. THERE'S ONLY ONE FAMILY MEMBER ON BOARD.
WHO?

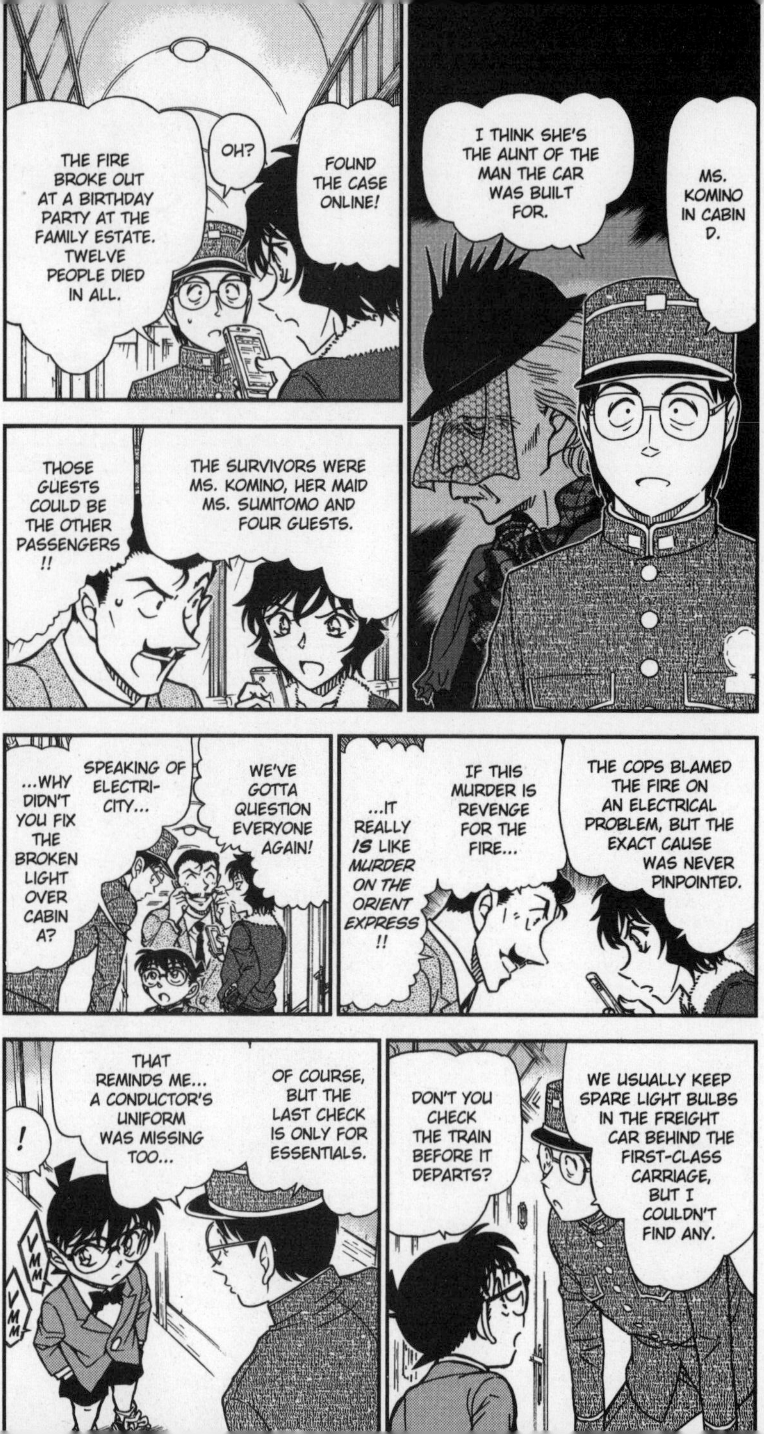
MS. KOMINO IN CABIN D.
I THINK SHE'S THE AUNT OF THE MAN THE CAR WAS BUILT FOR.
FOUND THE CASE ONLINE!
OH?
THE FIRE BROKE OUT AT A BIRTHDAY PARTY AT THE FAMILY ESTATE. TWELVE PEOPLE DIED IN ALL.
THE SURVIVORS WERE MS. KOMINO, HER MAID MS. SUMITOMO AND FOUR GUESTS.
THOSE GUESTS COULD BE THE OTHER PASSENGERS!!
THE COPS BLAMED THE FIRE ON AN ELECTRICAL PROBLEM, BUT THE EXACT CAUSE WAS NEVER PINPOINTED.
IF THIS MURDER IS REVENGE FOR THE FIRE...
...IT REALLY IS LIKE MURDER ON THE ORIENT EXPRESS!!
WE'VE GOTTA QUESTION EVERYONE AGAIN!
SPEAKING OF ELECTRI-CITY...
...WHY DIDN'T YOU FIX THE BROKEN LIGHT OVER CABIN A?
WE USUALLY KEEP SPARE LIGHT BULBS IN THE FREIGHT CAR BEHIND THE FIRST-CLASS CARRIAGE, BUT I COULDN'T FIND ANY.
DON'T YOU CHECK THE TRAIN BEFORE IT DEPARTS?
OF COURSE, BUT THE LAST CHECK IS ONLY FOR ESSENTIALS.
THAT REMINDS ME... A CONDUCTOR'S UNIFORM WAS MISSING TOO...
!
VMM
VMM

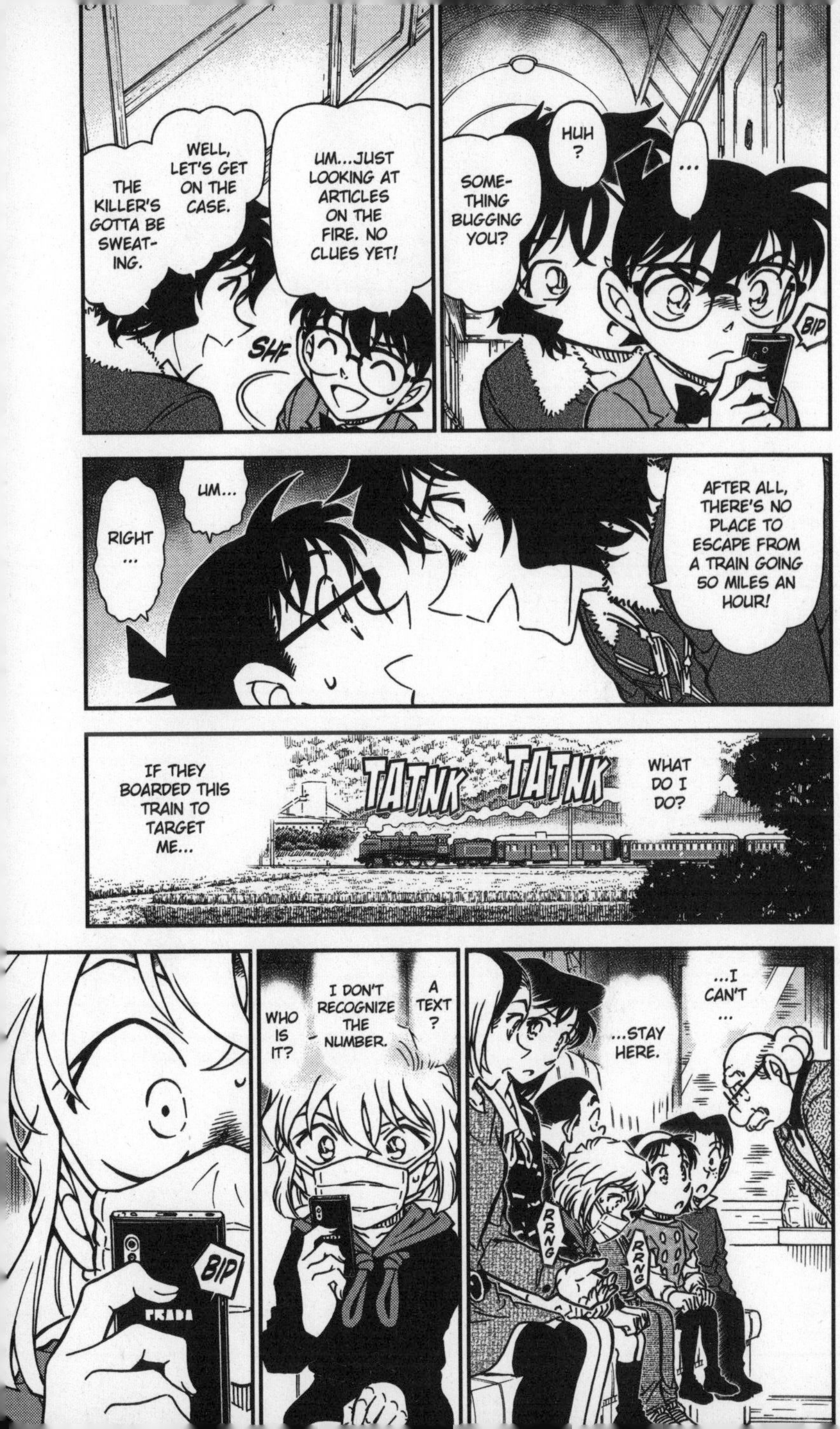
...
HUH ?
SOME-THING BUGGING YOU?
BIP
UM...JUST LOOKING AT ARTICLES ON THE FIRE. NO CLUES YET!
WELL, LET'S GET ON THE CASE.
THE KILLER'S GOTTA BE SWEAT-ING.
SHF
AFTER ALL, THERE'S NO PLACE TO ESCAPE FROM A TRAIN GOING 50 MILES AN HOUR!
UM...
RIGHT ...
WHAT DO I DO?
TATNK
TATNK
IF THEY BOARDED THIS TRAIN TO TARGET ME...
...I CAN'T ...
...STAY HERE.
RRNG
RRNG
A TEXT ?
I DON'T RECOGNIZE THE NUMBER.
WHO IS IT?
BIP
PRADA

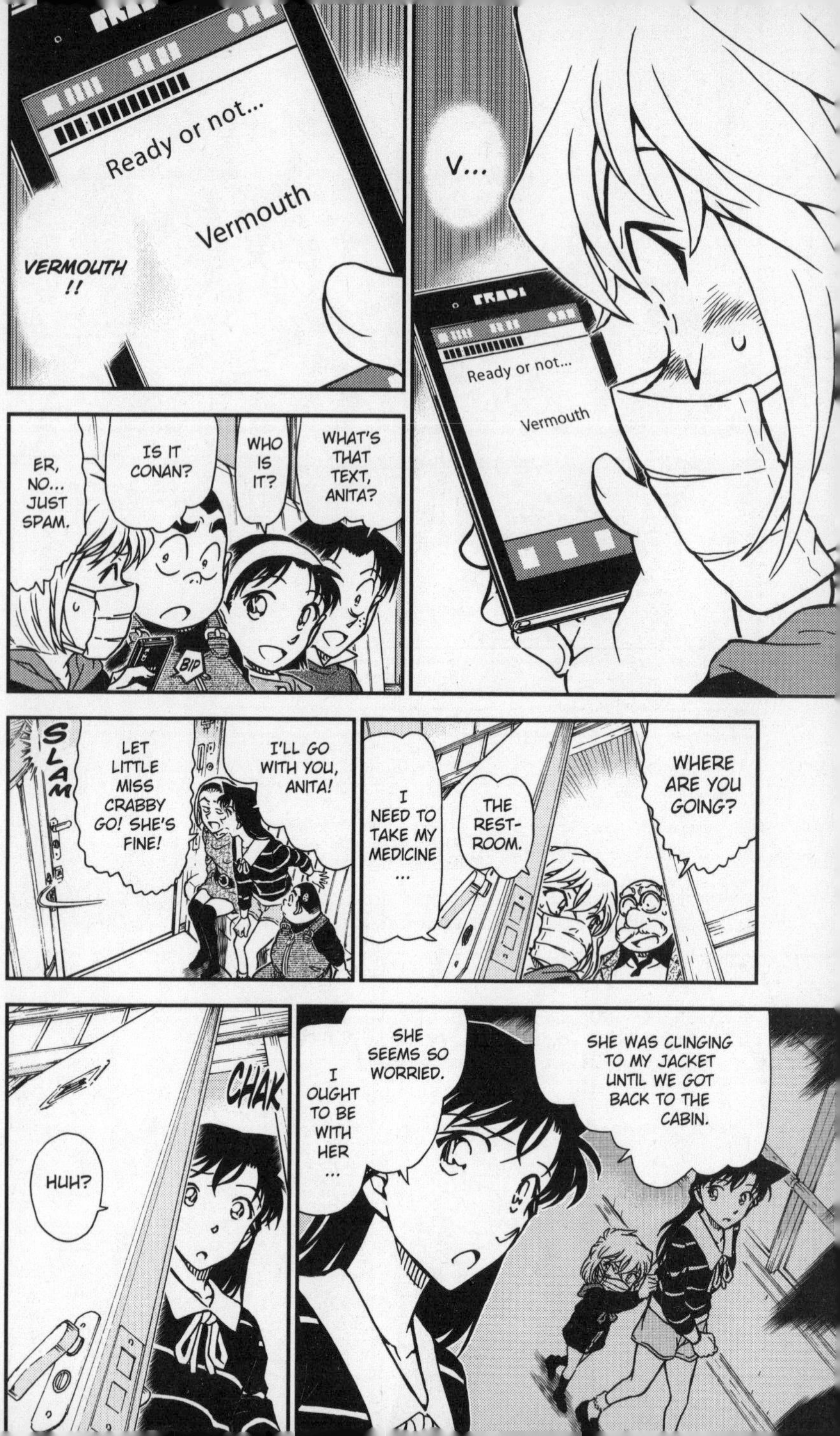
V...
Ready or not...
Vermouth
Ready or not...
Vermouth
VERMOUTH !!
WHAT'S THAT TEXT, ANITA?
WHO IS IT?
IS IT CONAN?
ER, NO... JUST SPAM.
BIP
WHERE ARE YOU GOING?
THE REST-ROOM.
I NEED TO TAKE MY MEDICINE ...
I'LL GO WITH YOU, ANITA!
LET LITTLE MISS CRABBY GO! SHE'S FINE!
SLAM
SHE WAS CLINGING TO MY JACKET UNTIL WE GOT BACK TO THE CABIN.
SHE SEEMS SO WORRIED.
I OUGHT TO BE WITH HER ...
CHAK
HUH?

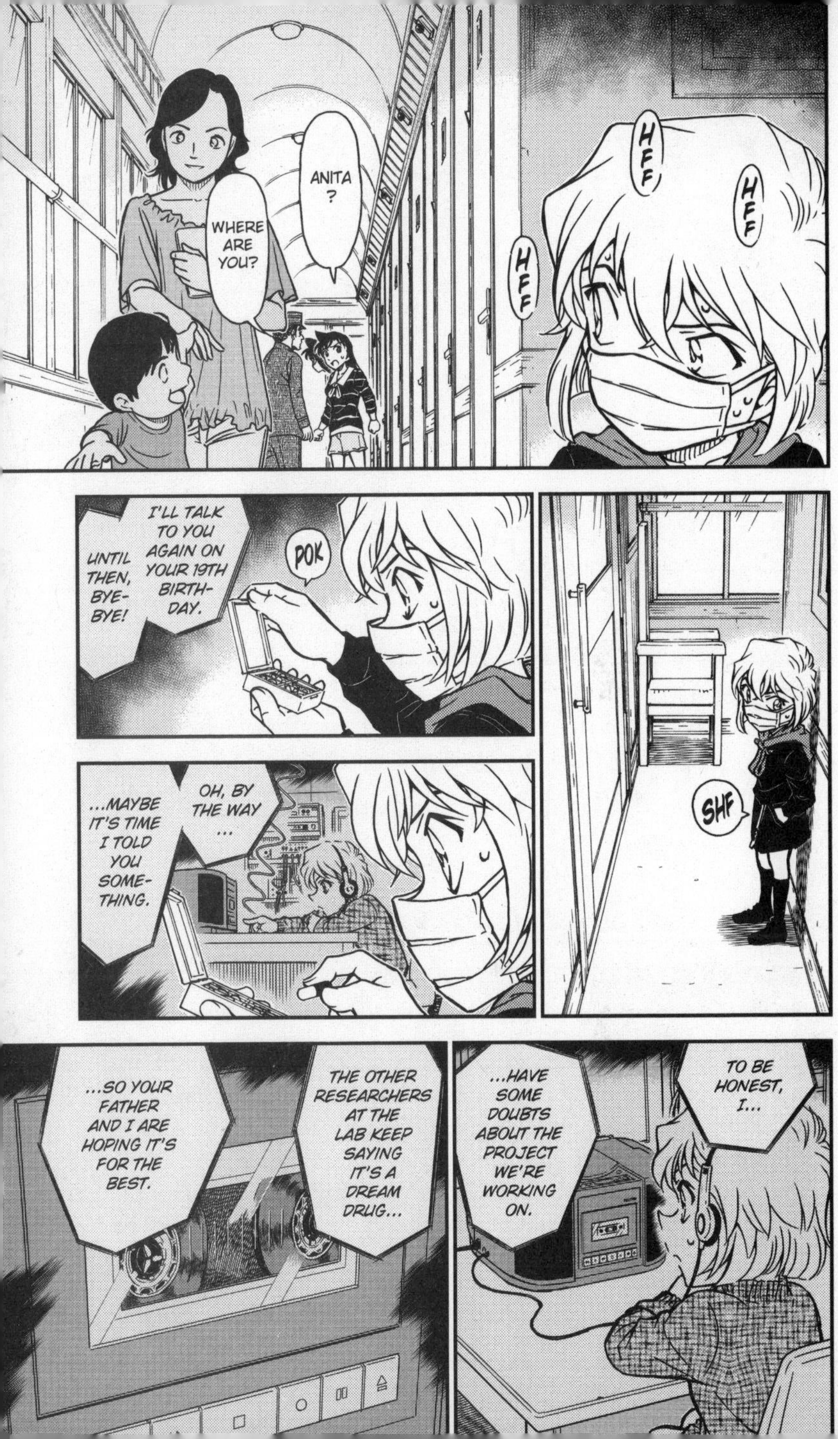
HFF
HFF
HFF
ANITA ?
WHERE ARE YOU?
SHF
POK
I'LL TALK TO YOU AGAIN ON YOUR 19TH BIRTH-DAY.
UNTIL THEN, BYE-BYE!
OH, BY THE WAY ...
...MAYBE IT'S TIME I TOLD YOU SOME-THING.
TO BE HONEST, I...
...HAVE SOME DOUBTS ABOUT THE PROJECT WE'RE WORKING ON.
THE OTHER RESEARCHERS AT THE LAB KEEP SAYING IT'S A DREAM DRUG...
...SO YOUR FATHER AND I ARE HOPING IT'S FOR THE BEST.

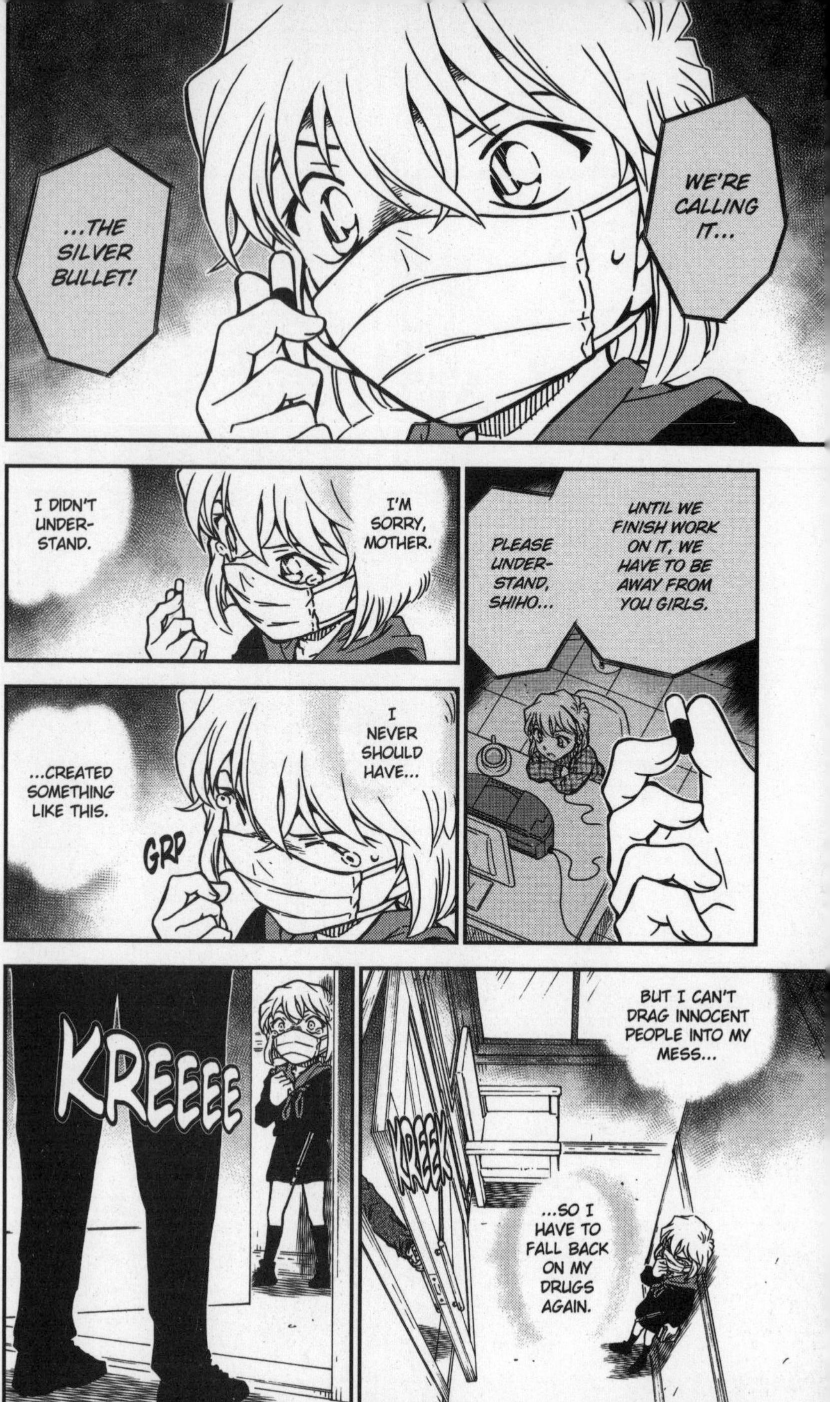
WE'RE CALLING IT...
...THE SILVER BULLET!
UNTIL WE FINISH WORK ON IT, WE HAVE TO BE AWAY FROM YOU GIRLS.
PLEASE UNDER-STAND, SHIHO...
I'M SORRY, MOTHER.
I DIDN'T UNDER-STAND.
I NEVER SHOULD HAVE...
...CREATED SOMETHING LIKE THIS.
GRP
BUT I CAN'T DRAG INNOCENT PEOPLE INTO MY MESS...
...SO I HAVE TO FALL BACK ON MY DRUGS AGAIN.
KREEEE

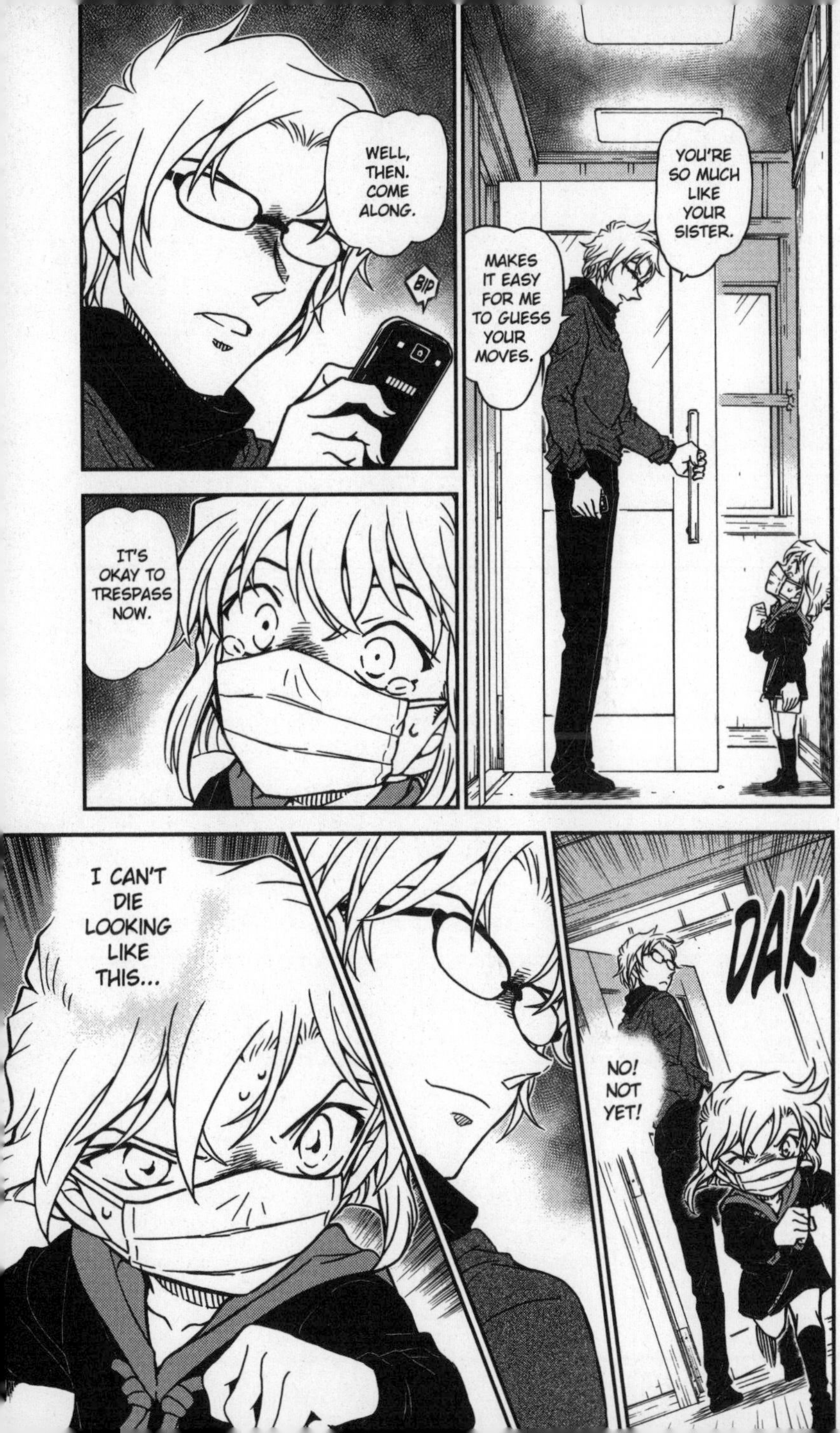
YOU'RE SO MUCH LIKE YOUR SISTER.
MAKES IT EASY FOR ME TO GUESS YOUR MOVES.
WELL, THEN. COME ALONG.
BIP
IT'S OKAY TO TRESPASS NOW.
DAK
NO! NOT YET!
I CAN'T DIE LOOKING LIKE THIS...

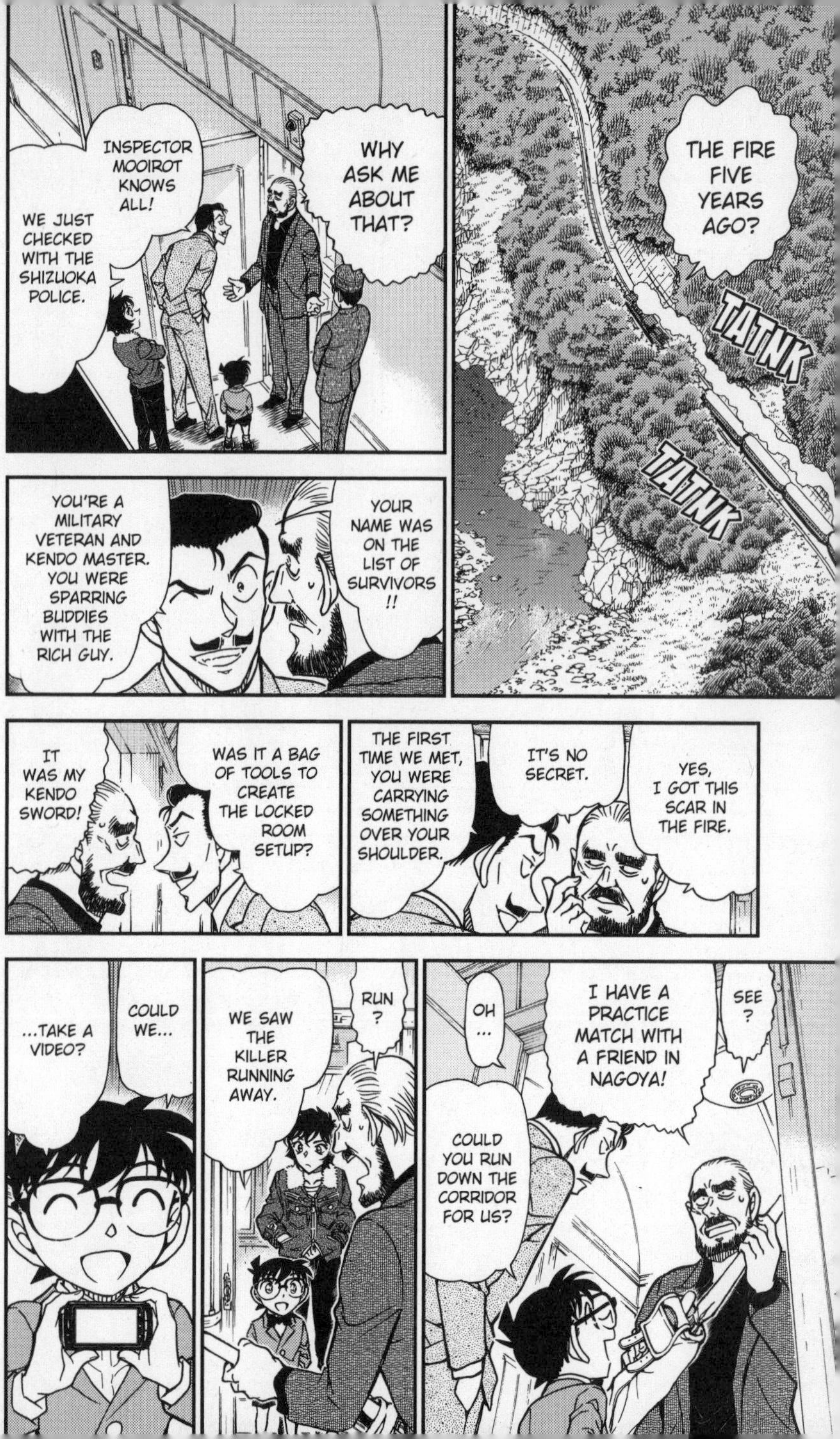
THE FIRE FIVE YEARS AGO?
TATNK
TATNK
WHY ASK ME ABOUT THAT?
INSPECTOR MOOIROT KNOWS ALL!
WE JUST CHECKED WITH THE SHIZUOKA POLICE.
YOUR NAME WAS ON THE LIST OF SURVIVORS!!
YOU'RE A MILITARY VETERAN AND KENDO MASTER. YOU WERE SPARRING BUDDIES WITH THE RICH GUY.
YES, I GOT THIS SCAR IN THE FIRE.
IT'S NO SECRET.
THE FIRST TIME WE MET, YOU WERE CARRYING SOMETHING OVER YOUR SHOULDER.
WAS IT A BAG OF TOOLS TO CREATE THE LOCKED ROOM SETUP?
IT WAS MY KENDO SWORD!
SEE?
I HAVE A PRACTICE MATCH WITH A FRIEND IN NAGOYA!
OH ...
COULD YOU RUN DOWN THE CORRIDOR FOR US?
RUN?
WE SAW THE KILLER RUNNING AWAY.
COULD WE...
...TAKE A VIDEO?

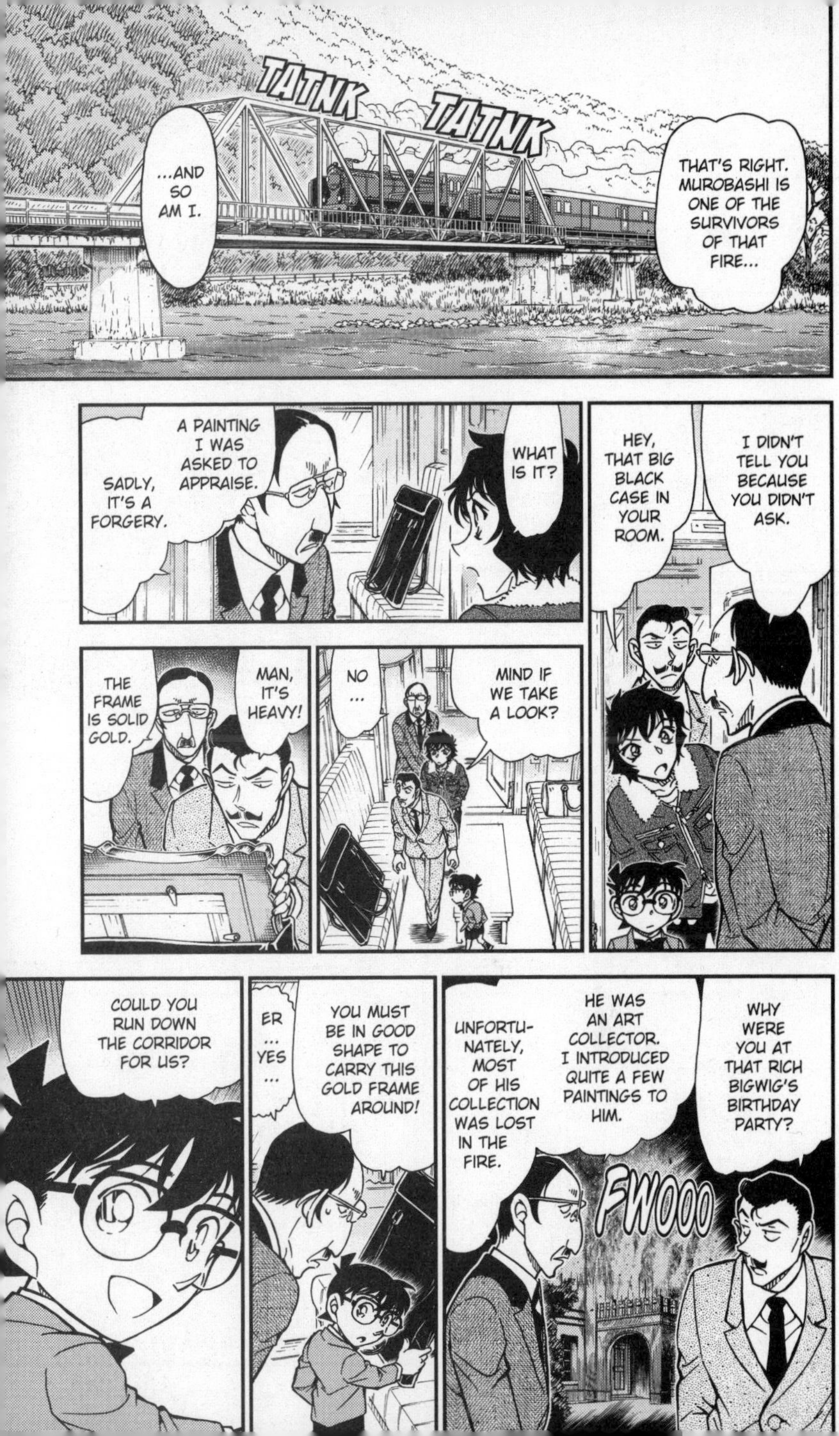
THAT'S RIGHT. MUROBASHI IS ONE OF THE SURVIVORS OF THAT FIRE...
TATNK
TATNK
...AND SO AM I.
I DIDN'T TELL YOU BECAUSE YOU DIDN'T ASK.
HEY, THAT BIG BLACK CASE IN YOUR ROOM.
WHAT IS IT?
A PAINTING I WAS ASKED TO APPRAISE.
SADLY, IT'S A FORGERY.
MIND IF WE TAKE A LOOK?
NO ...
MAN, IT'S HEAVY!
THE FRAME IS SOLID GOLD.
WHY WERE YOU AT THAT RICH BIGWIG'S BIRTHDAY PARTY?
HE WAS AN ART COLLECTOR. I INTRODUCED QUITE A FEW PAINTINGS TO HIM.
UNFORTU-NATELY, MOST OF HIS COLLECTION WAS LOST IN THE FIRE.
FWOOO
YOU MUST BE IN GOOD SHAPE TO CARRY THIS GOLD FRAME AROUND!
ER ... YES ...
COULD YOU RUN DOWN THE CORRIDOR FOR US?

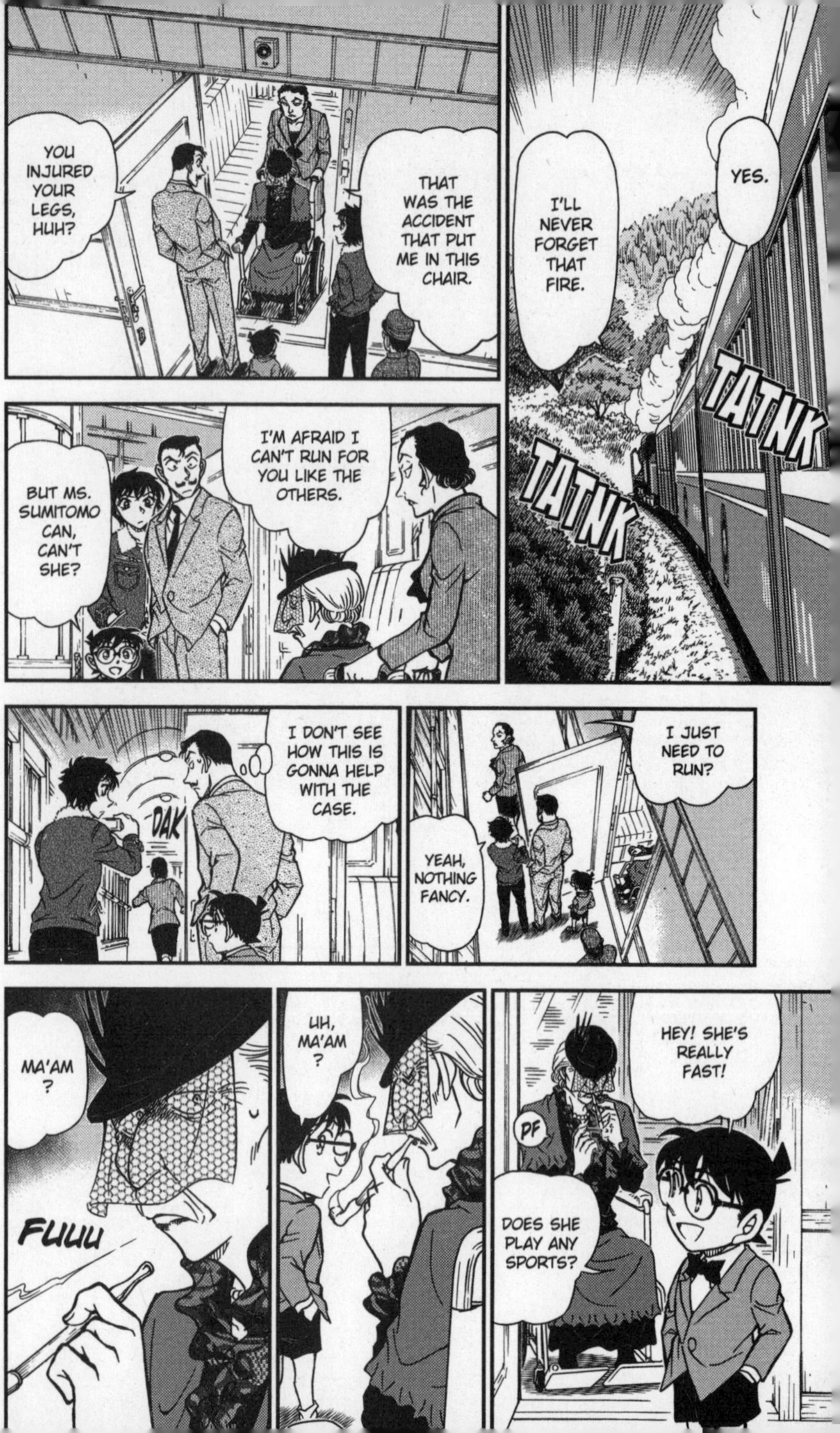
YES.
I'LL NEVER FORGET THAT FIRE.
TATNK
TATNK
THAT WAS THE ACCIDENT THAT PUT ME IN THIS CHAIR.
YOU INJURED YOUR LEGS, HUH?
I'M AFRAID I CAN'T RUN FOR YOU LIKE THE OTHERS.
BUT MS. SUMITOMO CAN, CAN'T SHE?
I JUST NEED TO RUN?
YEAH, NOTHING FANCY.
I DON'T SEE HOW THIS IS GONNA HELP WITH THE CASE.
DAK
HEY! SHE'S REALLY FAST!
PF
DOES SHE PLAY ANY SPORTS?
UH, MA'AM?
MA'AM?
FUUU

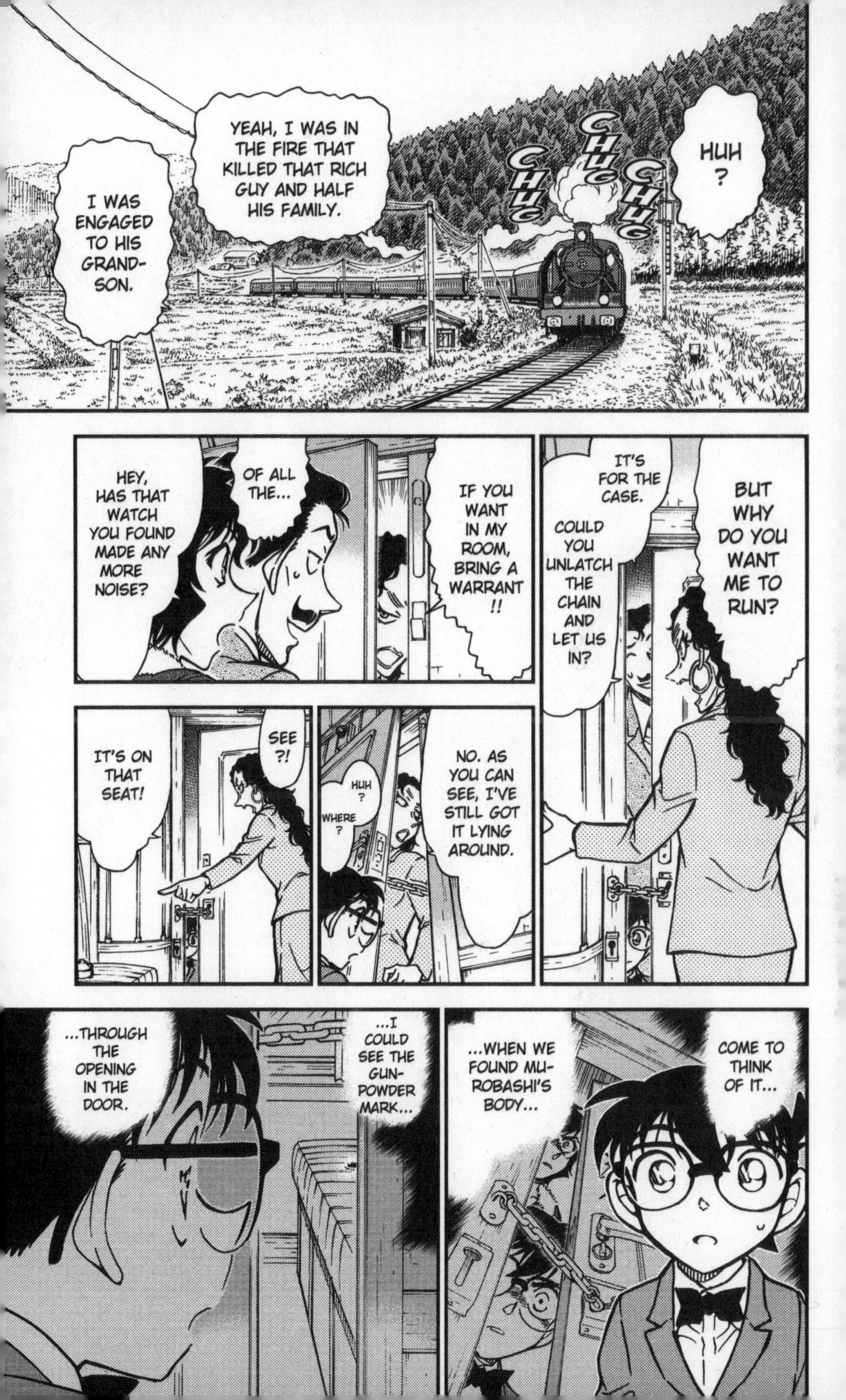
HUH ?
CHUG CHUG CHUG
YEAH, I WAS IN THE FIRE THAT KILLED THAT RICH GUY AND HALF HIS FAMILY.
I WAS ENGAGED TO HIS GRAND-SON.
BUT WHY DO YOU WANT ME TO RUN?
IT'S FOR THE CASE.
COULD YOU UNLATCH THE CHAIN AND LET US IN?
IF YOU WANT IN MY ROOM, BRING A WARRANT !!
OF ALL THE...
HEY, HAS THAT WATCH YOU FOUND MADE ANY MORE NOISE?
NO. AS YOU CAN SEE, I'VE STILL GOT IT LYING AROUND.
HUH ?
WHERE ?
SEE ?!
IT'S ON THAT SEAT!
COME TO THINK OF IT...
...WHEN WE FOUND MU-ROBASHI'S BODY...
...I COULD SEE THE GUN-POWDER MARK...
...THROUGH THE OPENING IN THE DOOR.

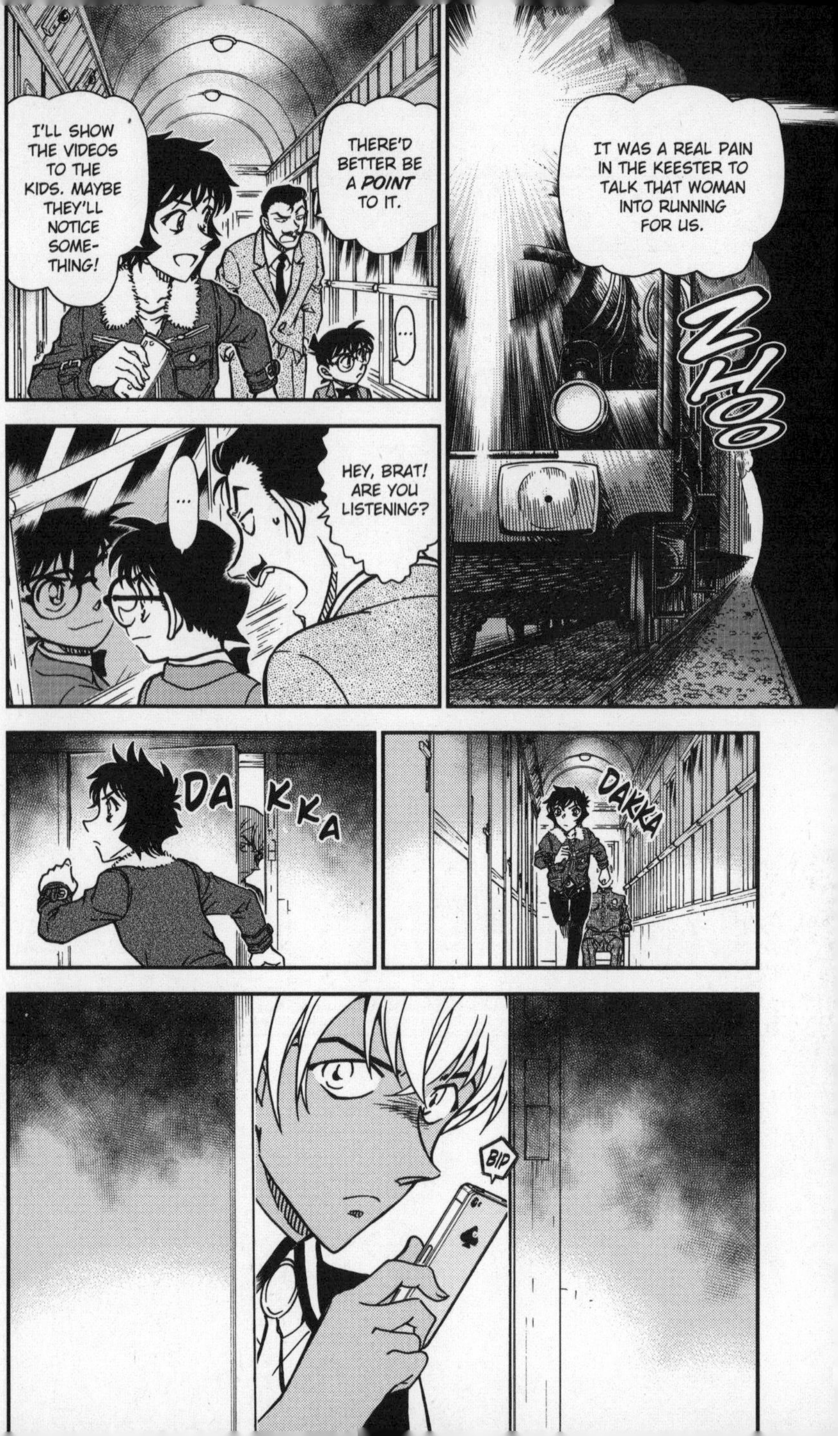
IT WAS A REAL PAIN IN THE KEESTER TO TALK THAT WOMAN INTO RUNNING FOR US.
ZHOO
THERE'D BETTER BE A POINT TO IT.
I'LL SHOW THE VIDEOS TO THE KIDS. MAYBE THEY'LL NOTICE SOME-THING!
...
HEY, BRAT! ARE YOU LISTENING?
...
DAKKA
DA KKA
BIP

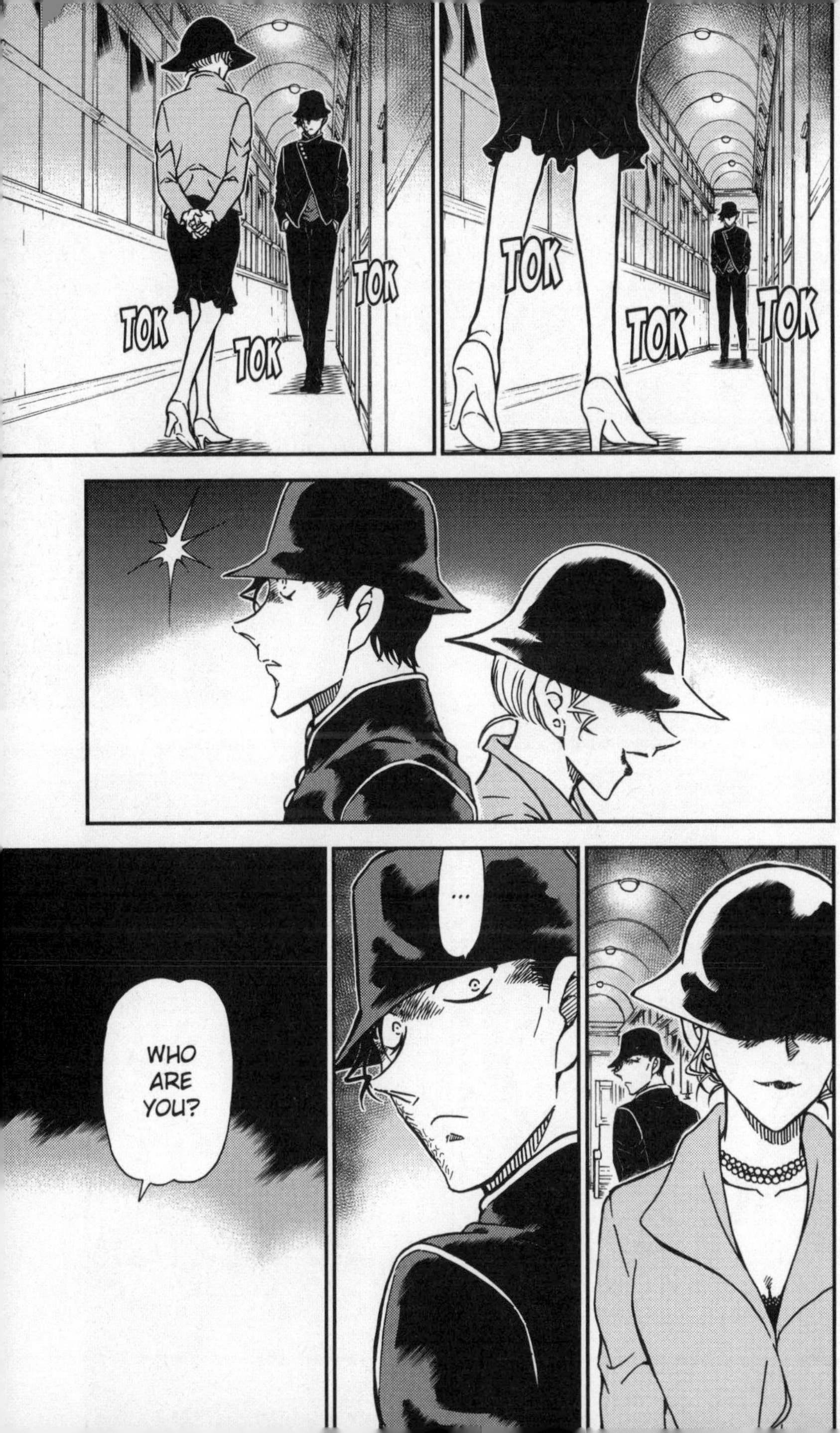

TOK
TOK
TOK
TOK
TOK
TOK
...
WHO ARE YOU?

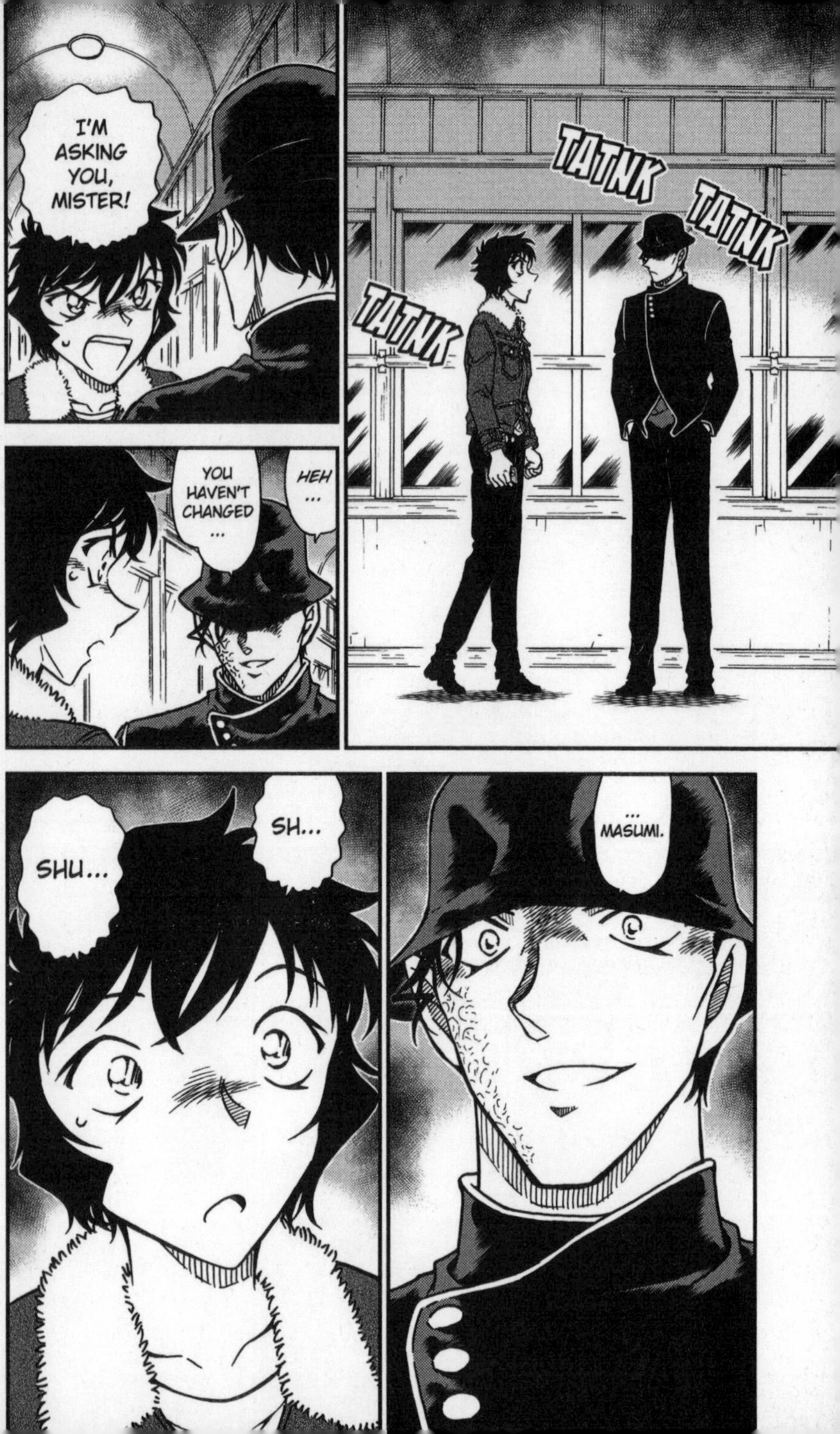
TATNK
TATNK
TATNK
I'M ASKING YOU, MISTER!
HEH...
YOU HAVEN'T CHANGED...
... MASUMI.
SH...
SHU...

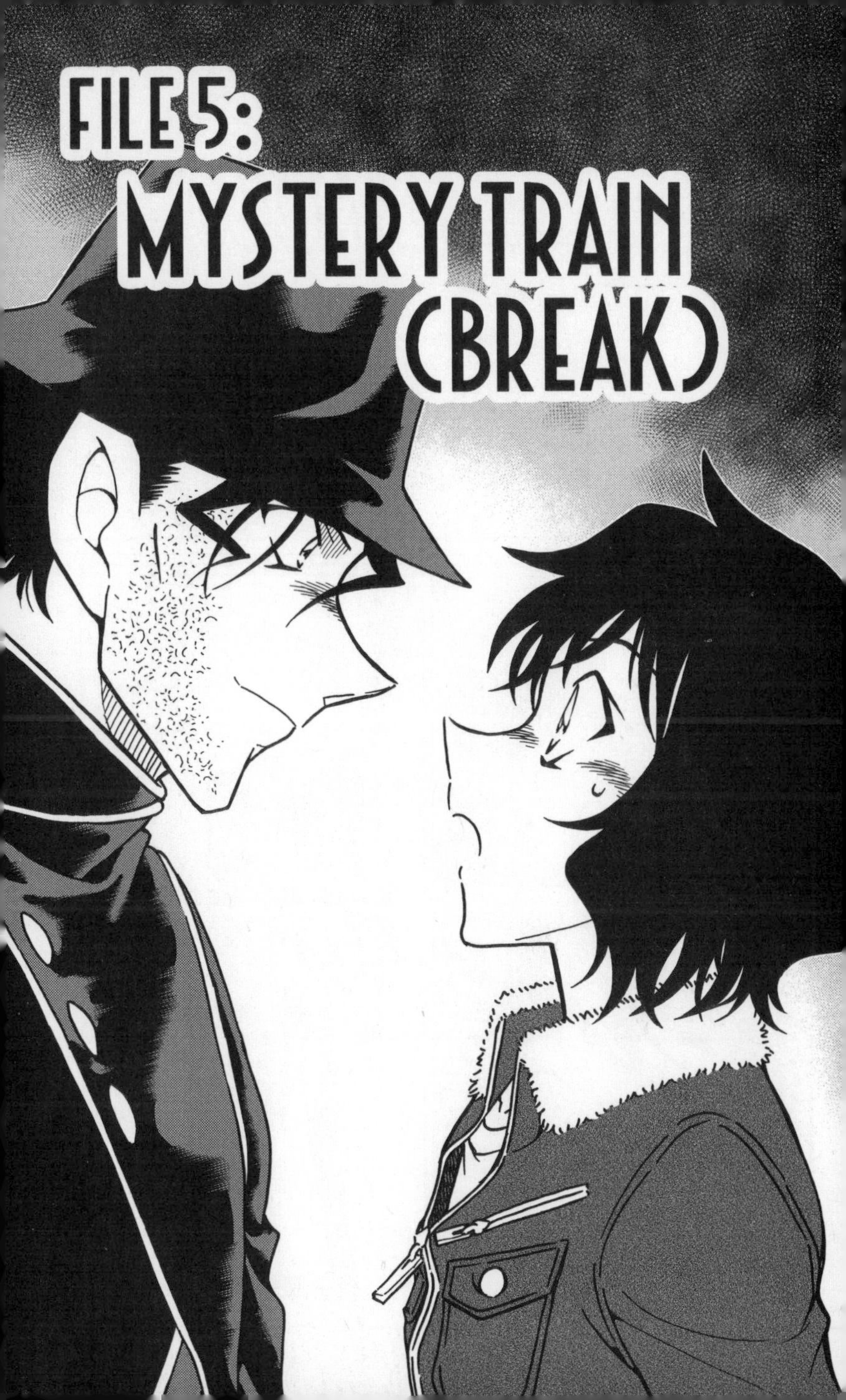
FILE 5:
MYSTERY TRAIN
(BREAK)

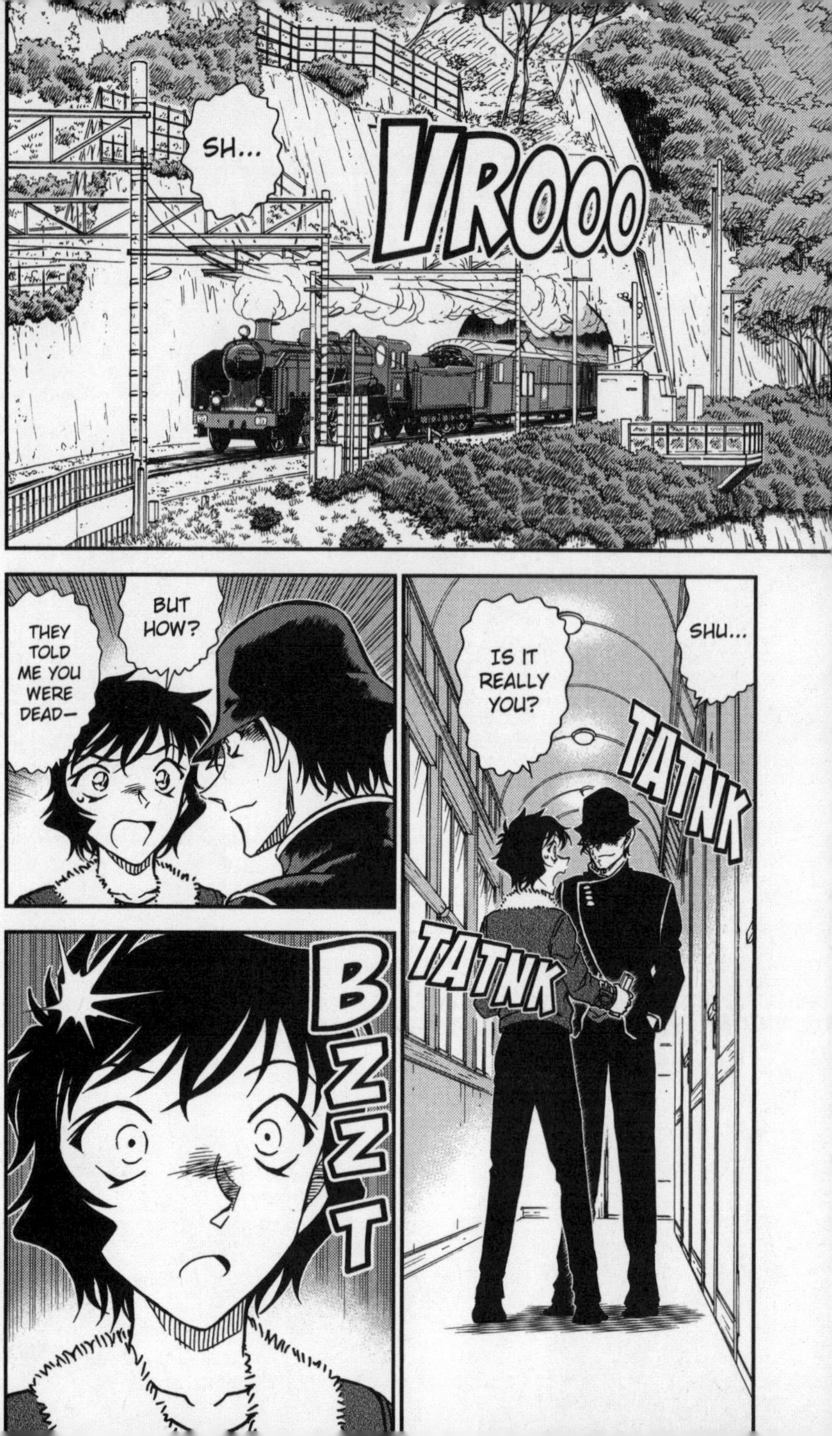
SH...
VROOO
SHU...
IS IT REALLY YOU?
TATNK
TATNK
BUT HOW?
THEY TOLD ME YOU WERE DEAD—
BZZZT

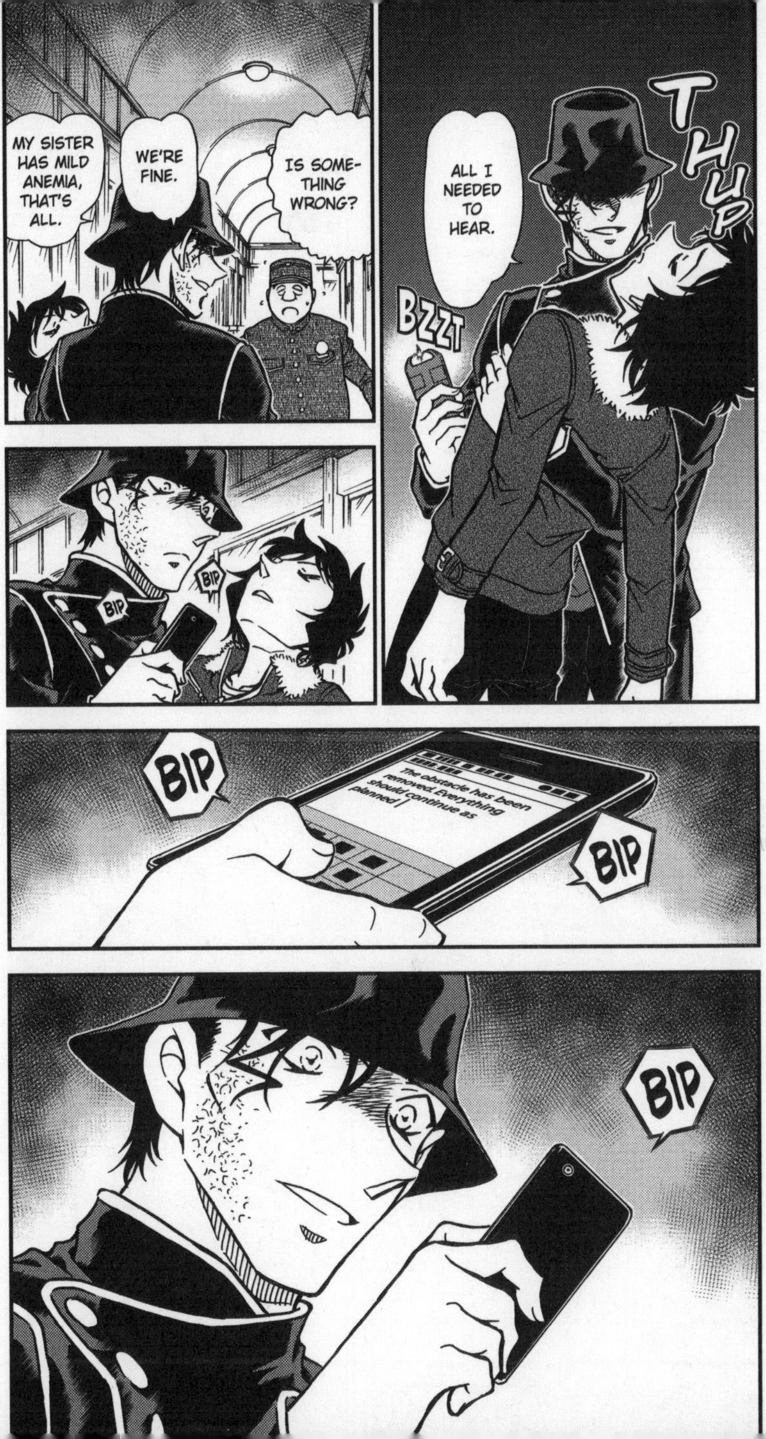
THUP
ALL I NEEDED TO HEAR.
BZZT
IS SOME-THING WRONG?
WE'RE FINE.
MY SISTER HAS MILD ANEMIA, THAT'S ALL.
BIP
BIP
BIP
The obstacle has been removed. Everything should continue as planned |
BIP
BIP

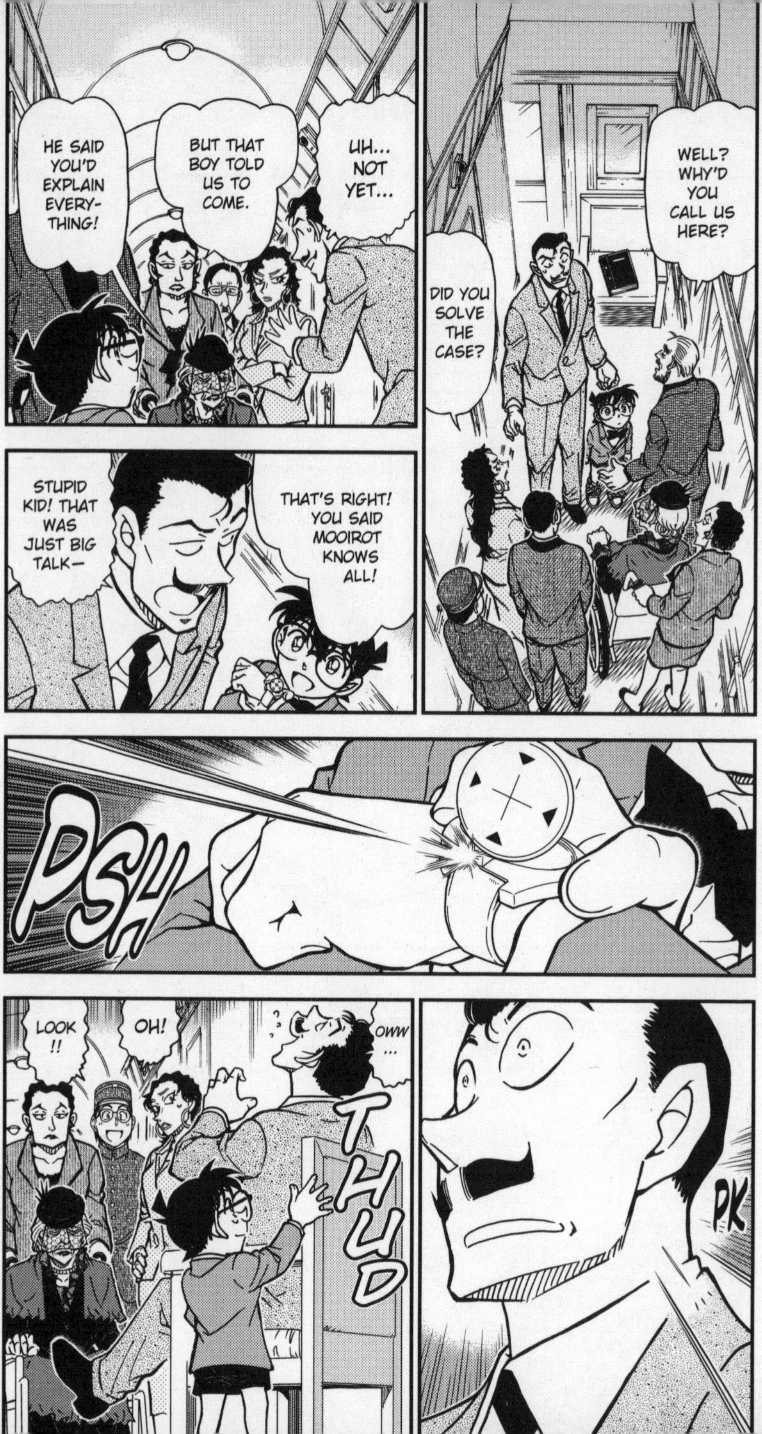
WELL? WHY'D YOU CALL US HERE?
DID YOU SOLVE THE CASE?
UH... NOT YET...
BUT THAT BOY TOLD US TO COME.
HE SAID YOU'D EXPLAIN EVERY-THING!
THAT'S RIGHT! YOU SAID MOOIROT KNOWS ALL!
STUPID KID! THAT WAS JUST BIG TALK—
PSH
DK
OWW ...
THUD
OH!
LOOK !!

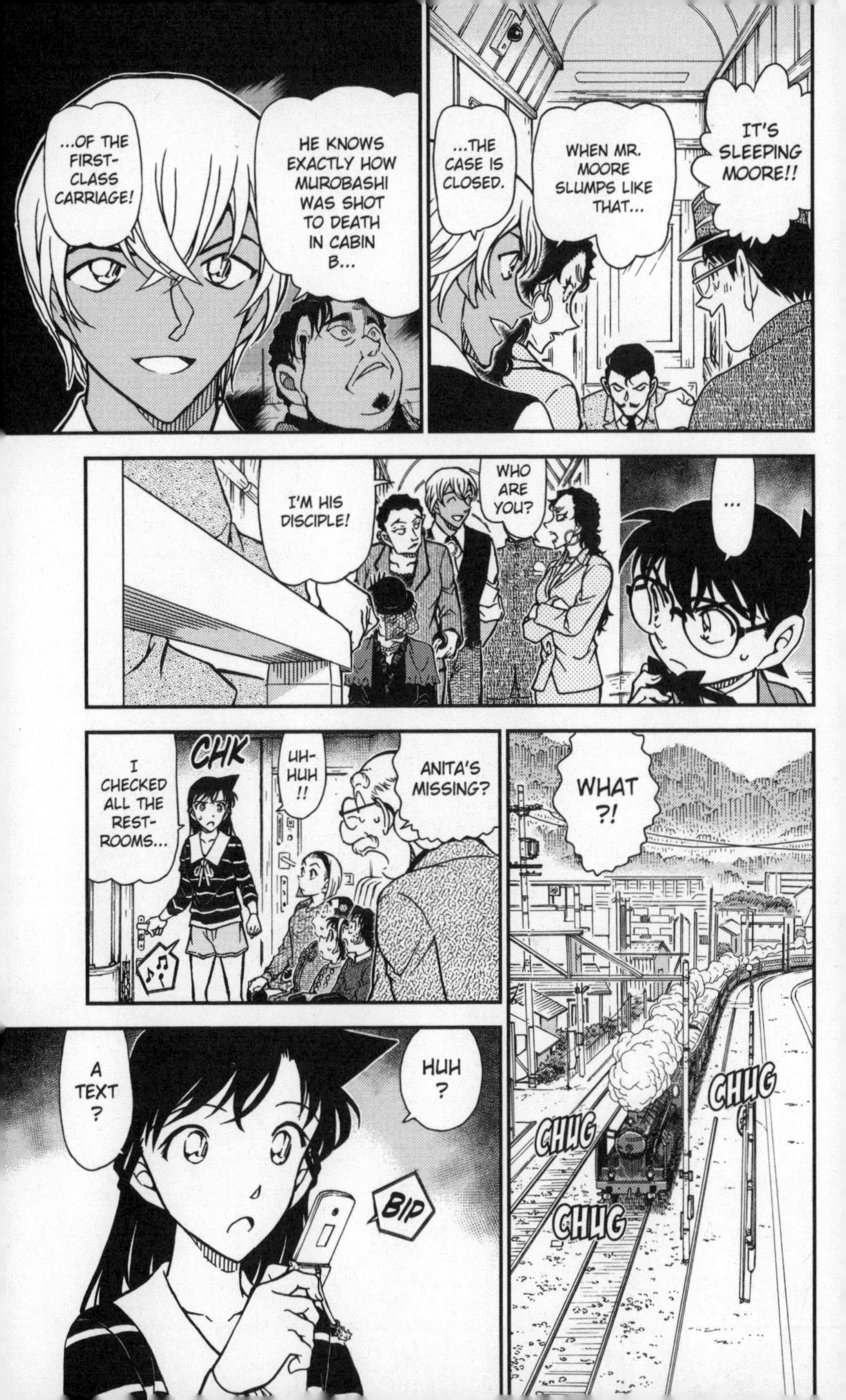
IT'S SLEEPING MOORE!!
WHEN MR. MOORE SLUMPS LIKE THAT...
...THE CASE IS CLOSED.
HE KNOWS EXACTLY HOW MUROBASHI WAS SHOT TO DEATH IN CABIN B...
...OF THE FIRST-CLASS CARRIAGE!
...
WHO ARE YOU?
I'M HIS DISCIPLE!
WHAT?!
CHUG
CHUG
CHUG
ANITA'S MISSING?
UH-HUH!!
CHK
I CHECKED ALL THE REST-ROOMS...
HUH?
BIP
A TEXT?

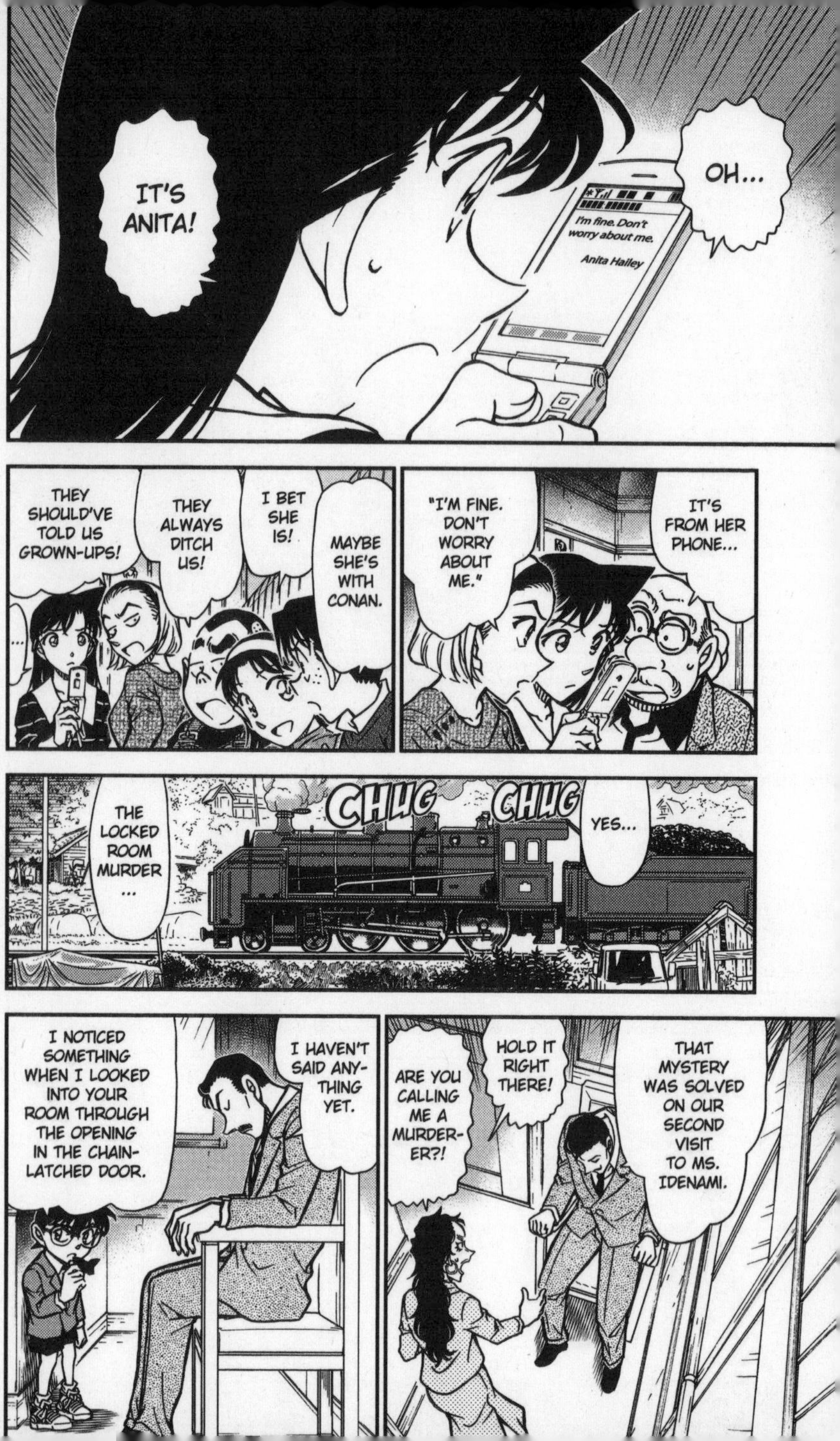
OH...
I'm fine. Don't worry about me.
Anita Hailey
IT'S ANITA!
IT'S FROM HER PHONE...
"I'M FINE. DON'T WORRY ABOUT ME."
MAYBE SHE'S WITH CONAN.
I BET SHE IS!
THEY ALWAYS DITCH US!
THEY SHOULD'VE TOLD US GROWN-UPS!
...
YES...
CHUG CHUG
THE LOCKED ROOM MURDER...
THAT MYSTERY WAS SOLVED ON OUR SECOND VISIT TO MS. IDENAMI.
HOLD IT RIGHT THERE!
ARE YOU CALLING ME A MURDER-ER?!
I HAVEN'T SAID ANY-THING YET.
I NOTICED SOMETHING WHEN I LOOKED INTO YOUR ROOM THROUGH THE OPENING IN THE CHAIN-LATCHED DOOR.

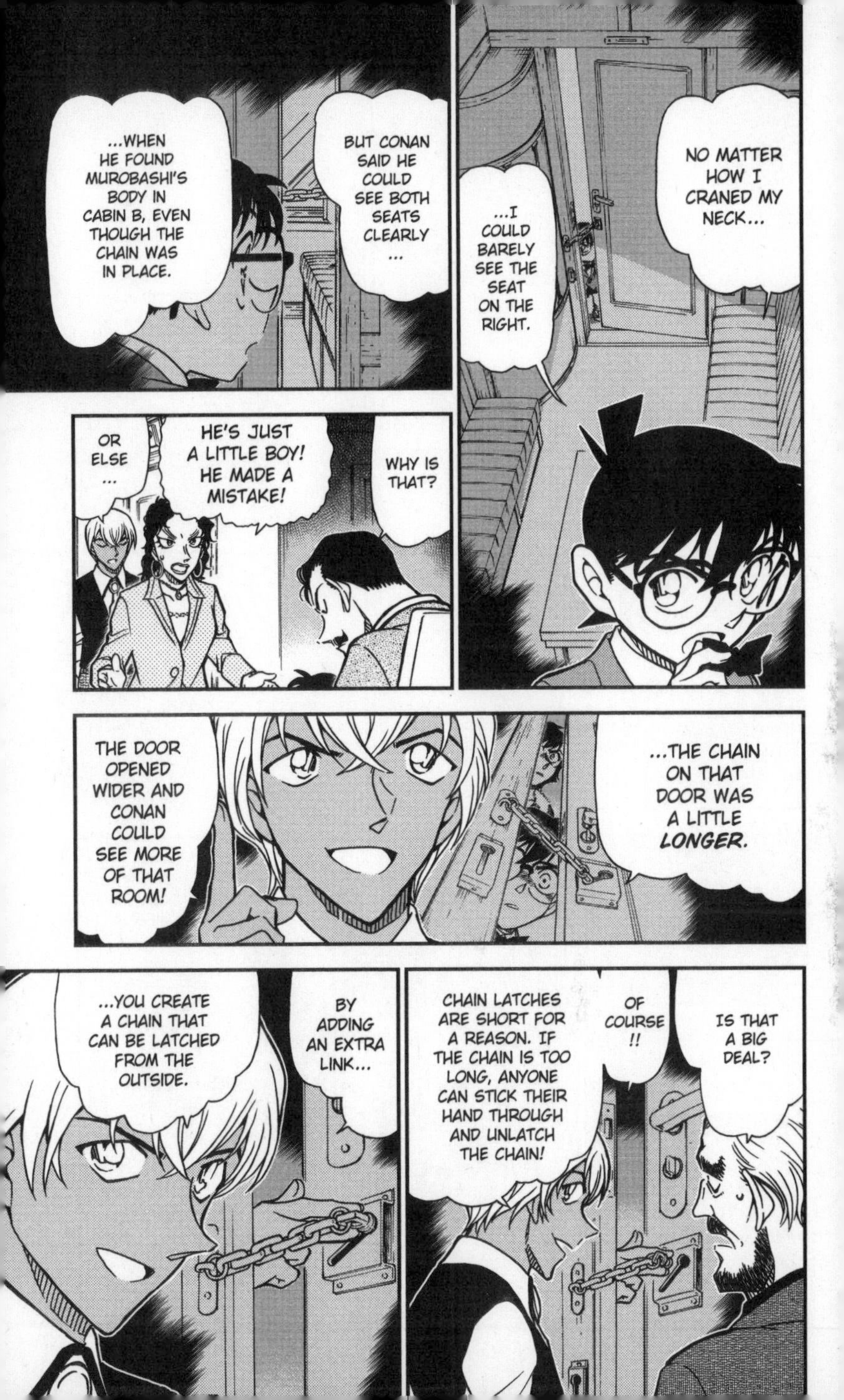
NO MATTER HOW I CRANED MY NECK...
...I COULD BARELY SEE THE SEAT ON THE RIGHT.
BUT CONAN SAID HE COULD SEE BOTH SEATS CLEARLY ...
...WHEN HE FOUND MUROBASHI'S BODY IN CABIN B, EVEN THOUGH THE CHAIN WAS IN PLACE.
WHY IS THAT?
HE'S JUST A LITTLE BOY! HE MADE A MISTAKE!
OR ELSE ...
...THE CHAIN ON THAT DOOR WAS A LITTLE **LONGER.**
THE DOOR OPENED WIDER AND CONAN COULD SEE MORE OF THAT ROOM!
IS THAT A BIG DEAL?
OF COURSE !!
CHAIN LATCHES ARE SHORT FOR A REASON. IF THE CHAIN IS TOO LONG, ANYONE CAN STICK THEIR HAND THROUGH AND UNLATCH THE CHAIN!
BY ADDING AN EXTRA LINK...
...YOU CREATE A CHAIN THAT CAN BE LATCHED FROM THE OUTSIDE.

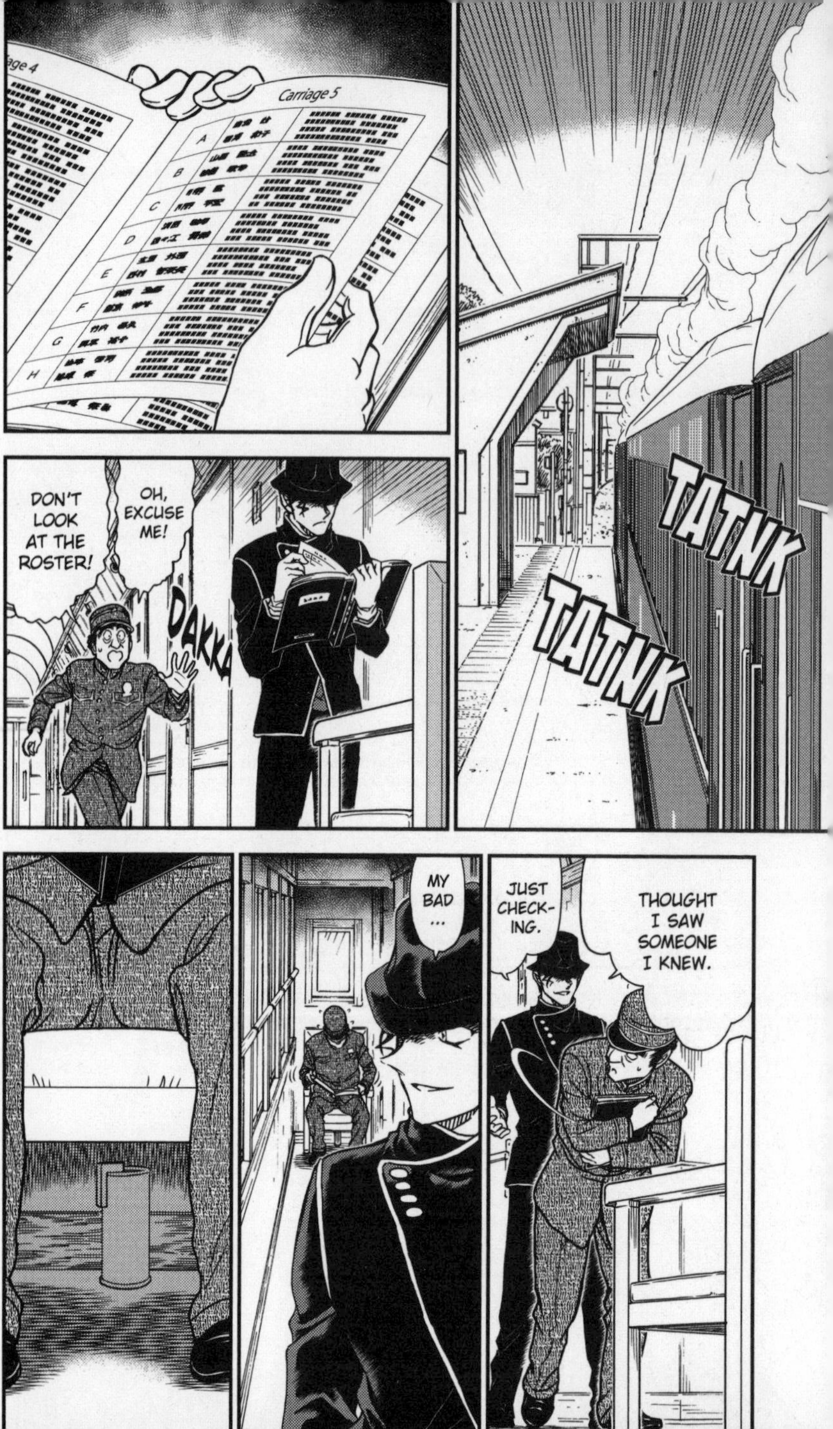
TATNK
TATNK
age 4
Carriage 5
A
B
C
D
E
F
G
H
OH, EXCUSE ME!
DON'T LOOK AT THE ROSTER!
DAKKA
THOUGHT I SAW SOMEONE I KNEW.
JUST CHECKING.
MY BAD ...

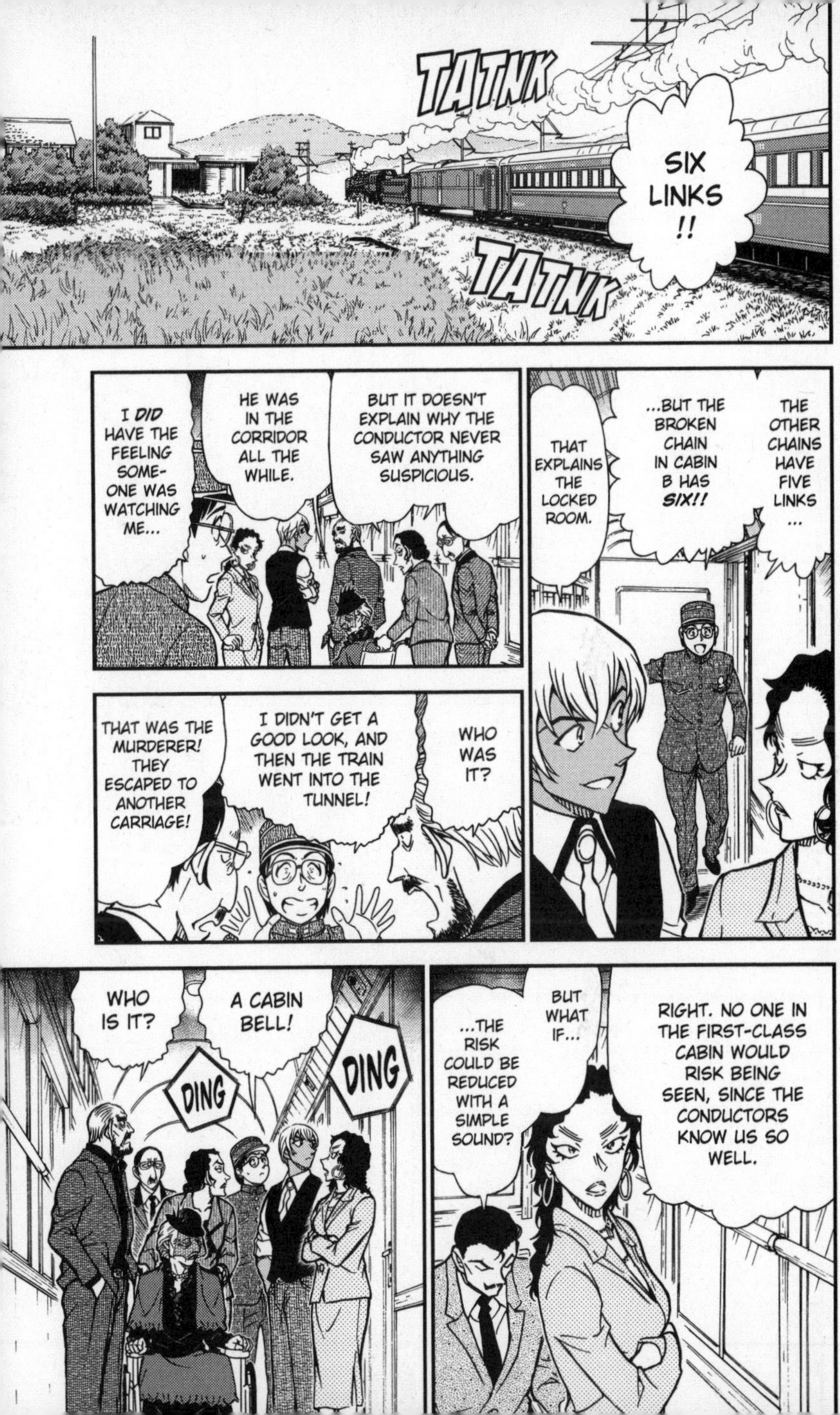
TATNK
SIX LINKS!!
TATNK
THE OTHER CHAINS HAVE FIVE LINKS...
...BUT THE BROKEN CHAIN IN CABIN B HAS *SIX!!*
THAT EXPLAINS THE LOCKED ROOM.
BUT IT DOESN'T EXPLAIN WHY THE CONDUCTOR NEVER SAW ANYTHING SUSPICIOUS.
HE WAS IN THE CORRIDOR ALL THE WHILE.
I *DID* HAVE THE FEELING SOME-ONE WAS WATCHING ME...
WHO WAS IT?
I DIDN'T GET A GOOD LOOK, AND THEN THE TRAIN WENT INTO THE TUNNEL!
THAT WAS THE MURDERER! THEY ESCAPED TO ANOTHER CARRIAGE!
RIGHT. NO ONE IN THE FIRST-CLASS CABIN WOULD RISK BEING SEEN, SINCE THE CONDUCTORS KNOW US SO WELL.
BUT WHAT IF...
...THE RISK COULD BE REDUCED WITH A SIMPLE SOUND?
DING
A CABIN BELL!
WHO IS IT?
DING

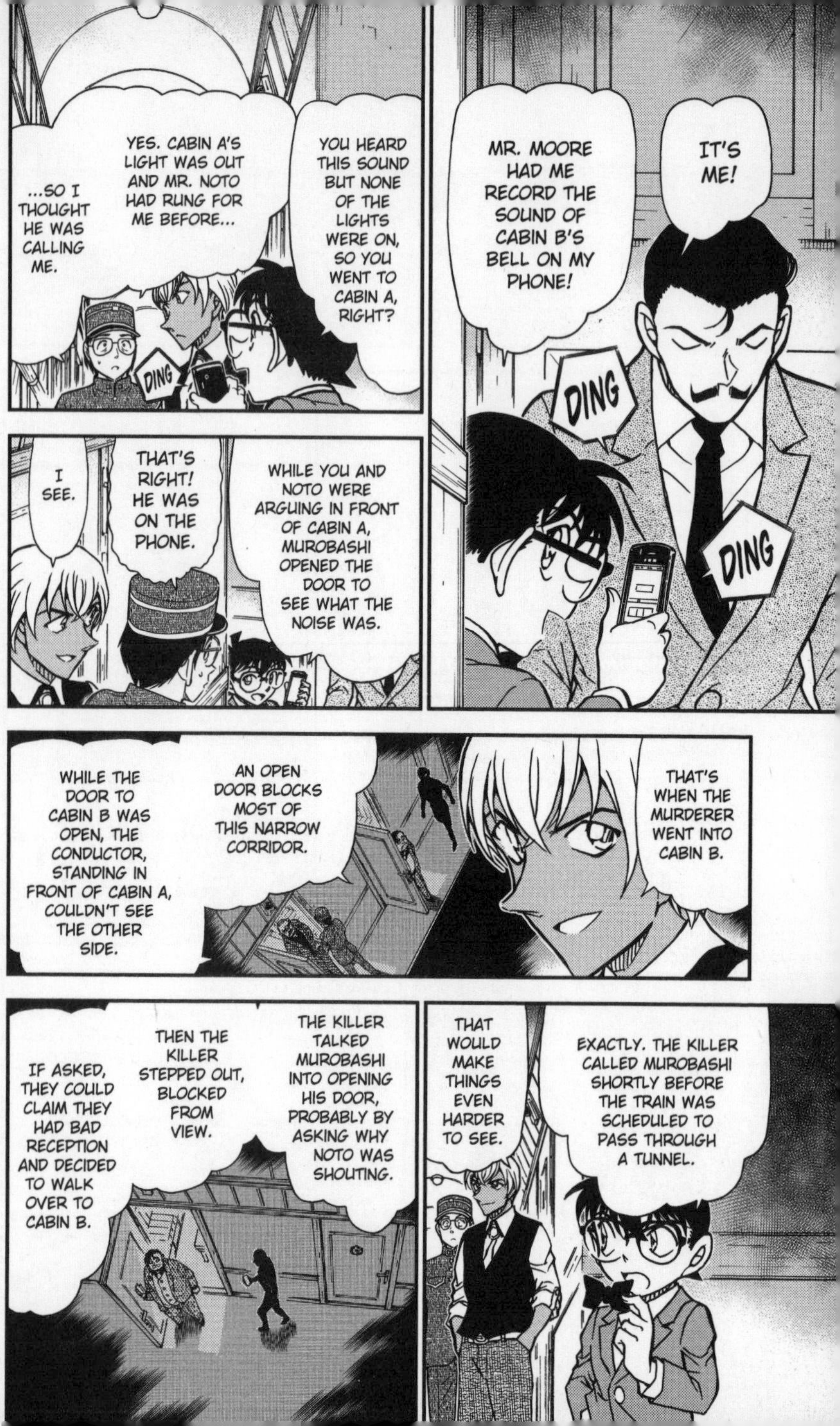
IT'S ME!
MR. MOORE HAD ME RECORD THE SOUND OF CABIN B'S BELL ON MY PHONE!
DING
DING
YOU HEARD THIS SOUND BUT NONE OF THE LIGHTS WERE ON, SO YOU WENT TO CABIN A, RIGHT?
YES. CABIN A'S LIGHT WAS OUT AND MR. NOTO HAD RUNG FOR ME BEFORE...
...SO I THOUGHT HE WAS CALLING ME.
DING
WHILE YOU AND NOTO WERE ARGUING IN FRONT OF CABIN A, MUROBASHI OPENED THE DOOR TO SEE WHAT THE NOISE WAS.
THAT'S RIGHT! HE WAS ON THE PHONE.
I SEE.
THAT'S WHEN THE MURDERER WENT INTO CABIN B.
AN OPEN DOOR BLOCKS MOST OF THIS NARROW CORRIDOR.
WHILE THE DOOR TO CABIN B WAS OPEN, THE CONDUCTOR, STANDING IN FRONT OF CABIN A, COULDN'T SEE THE OTHER SIDE.
EXACTLY. THE KILLER CALLED MUROBASHI SHORTLY BEFORE THE TRAIN WAS SCHEDULED TO PASS THROUGH A TUNNEL.
THAT WOULD MAKE THINGS EVEN HARDER TO SEE.
THE KILLER TALKED MUROBASHI INTO OPENING HIS DOOR, PROBABLY BY ASKING WHY NOTO WAS SHOUTING.
THEN THE KILLER STEPPED OUT, BLOCKED FROM VIEW.
IF ASKED, THEY COULD CLAIM THEY HAD BAD RECEPTION AND DECIDED TO WALK OVER TO CABIN B.

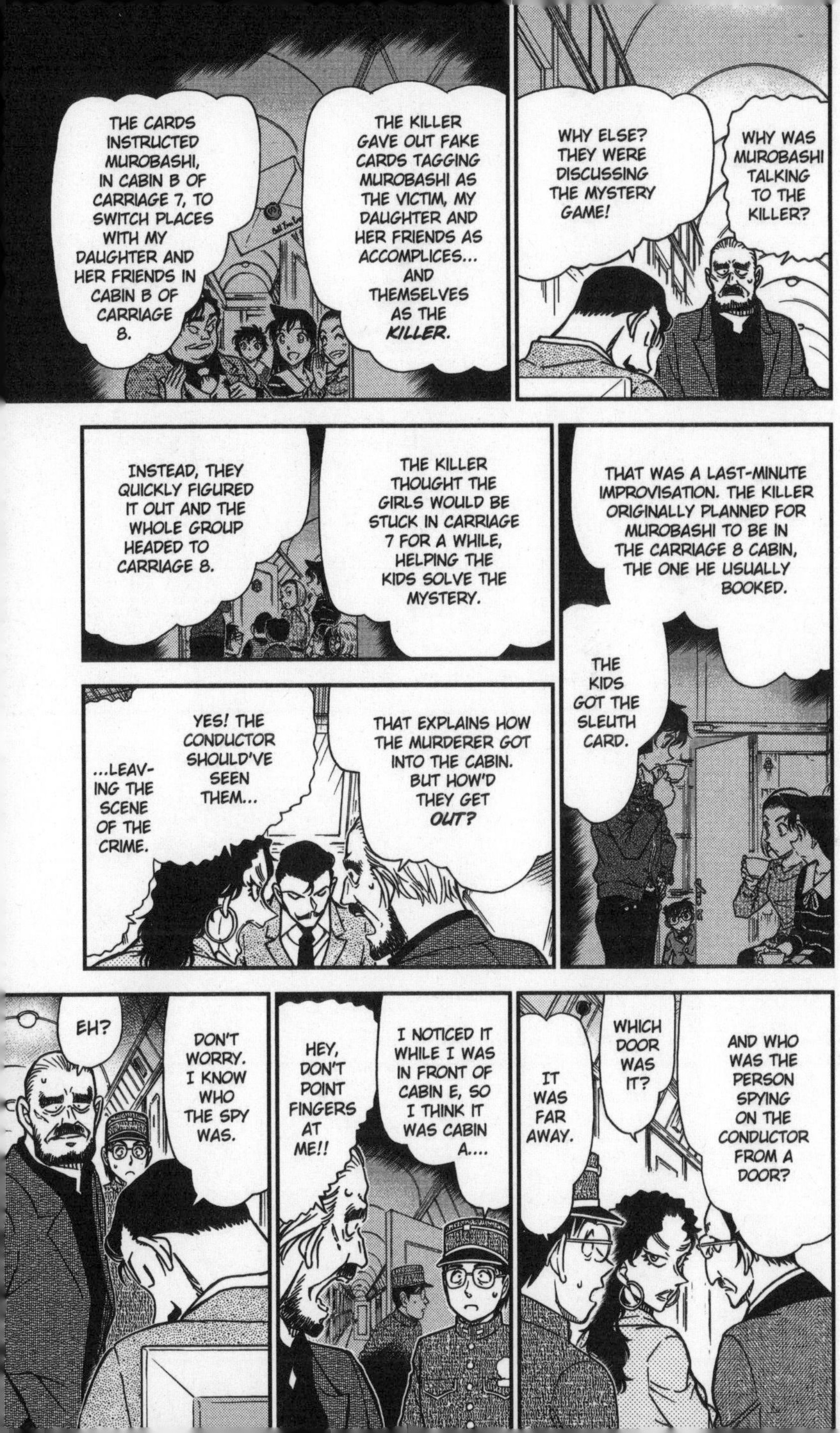
WHY WAS MUROBASHI TALKING TO THE KILLER?
WHY ELSE? THEY WERE DISCUSSING THE MYSTERY GAME!
THE KILLER GAVE OUT FAKE CARDS TAGGING MUROBASHI AS THE VICTIM, MY DAUGHTER AND HER FRIENDS AS ACCOMPLICES... AND THEMSELVES AS THE *KILLER*.
THE CARDS INSTRUCTED MUROBASHI, IN CABIN B OF CARRIAGE 7, TO SWITCH PLACES WITH MY DAUGHTER AND HER FRIENDS IN CABIN B OF CARRIAGE 8.
THAT WAS A LAST-MINUTE IMPROVISATION. THE KILLER ORIGINALLY PLANNED FOR MUROBASHI TO BE IN THE CARRIAGE 8 CABIN, THE ONE HE USUALLY BOOKED.
THE KIDS GOT THE SLEUTH CARD.
THE KILLER THOUGHT THE GIRLS WOULD BE STUCK IN CARRIAGE 7 FOR A WHILE, HELPING THE KIDS SOLVE THE MYSTERY.
INSTEAD, THEY QUICKLY FIGURED IT OUT AND THE WHOLE GROUP HEADED TO CARRIAGE 8.
THAT EXPLAINS HOW THE MURDERER GOT INTO THE CABIN. BUT HOW'D THEY GET *OUT?*
YES! THE CONDUCTOR SHOULD'VE SEEN THEM...
...LEAV-ING THE SCENE OF THE CRIME.
AND WHO WAS THE PERSON SPYING ON THE CONDUCTOR FROM A DOOR?
WHICH DOOR WAS IT?
IT WAS FAR AWAY.
I NOTICED IT WHILE I WAS IN FRONT OF CABIN E, SO I THINK IT WAS CABIN A....
HEY, DON'T POINT FINGERS AT ME!!
DON'T WORRY. I KNOW WHO THE SPY WAS.
EH?

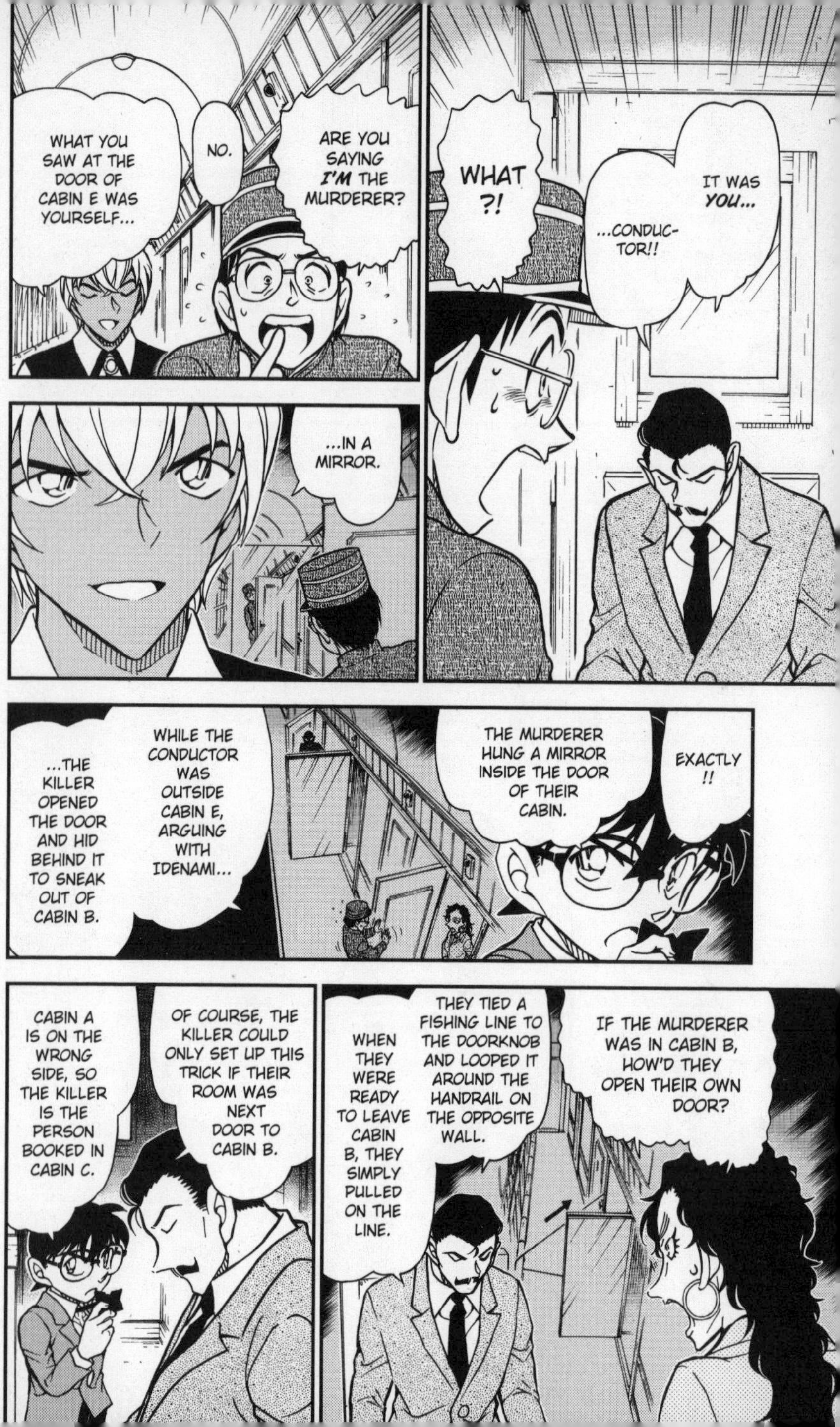
IT WAS YOU...
...CONDUC-TOR!!
WHAT ?!
ARE YOU SAYING I'M THE MURDERER?
NO.
WHAT YOU SAW AT THE DOOR OF CABIN E WAS YOURSELF...
...IN A MIRROR.
EXACTLY !!
THE MURDERER HUNG A MIRROR INSIDE THE DOOR OF THEIR CABIN.
WHILE THE CONDUCTOR WAS OUTSIDE CABIN E, ARGUING WITH IDENAMI...
...THE KILLER OPENED THE DOOR AND HID BEHIND IT TO SNEAK OUT OF CABIN B.
IF THE MURDERER WAS IN CABIN B, HOW'D THEY OPEN THEIR OWN DOOR?
THEY TIED A FISHING LINE TO THE DOORKNOB AND LOOPED IT AROUND THE HANDRAIL ON THE OPPOSITE WALL.
WHEN THEY WERE READY TO LEAVE CABIN B, THEY SIMPLY PULLED ON THE LINE.
OF COURSE, THE KILLER COULD ONLY SET UP THIS TRICK IF THEIR ROOM WAS NEXT DOOR TO CABIN B.
CABIN A IS ON THE WRONG SIDE, SO THE KILLER IS THE PERSON BOOKED IN CABIN C.

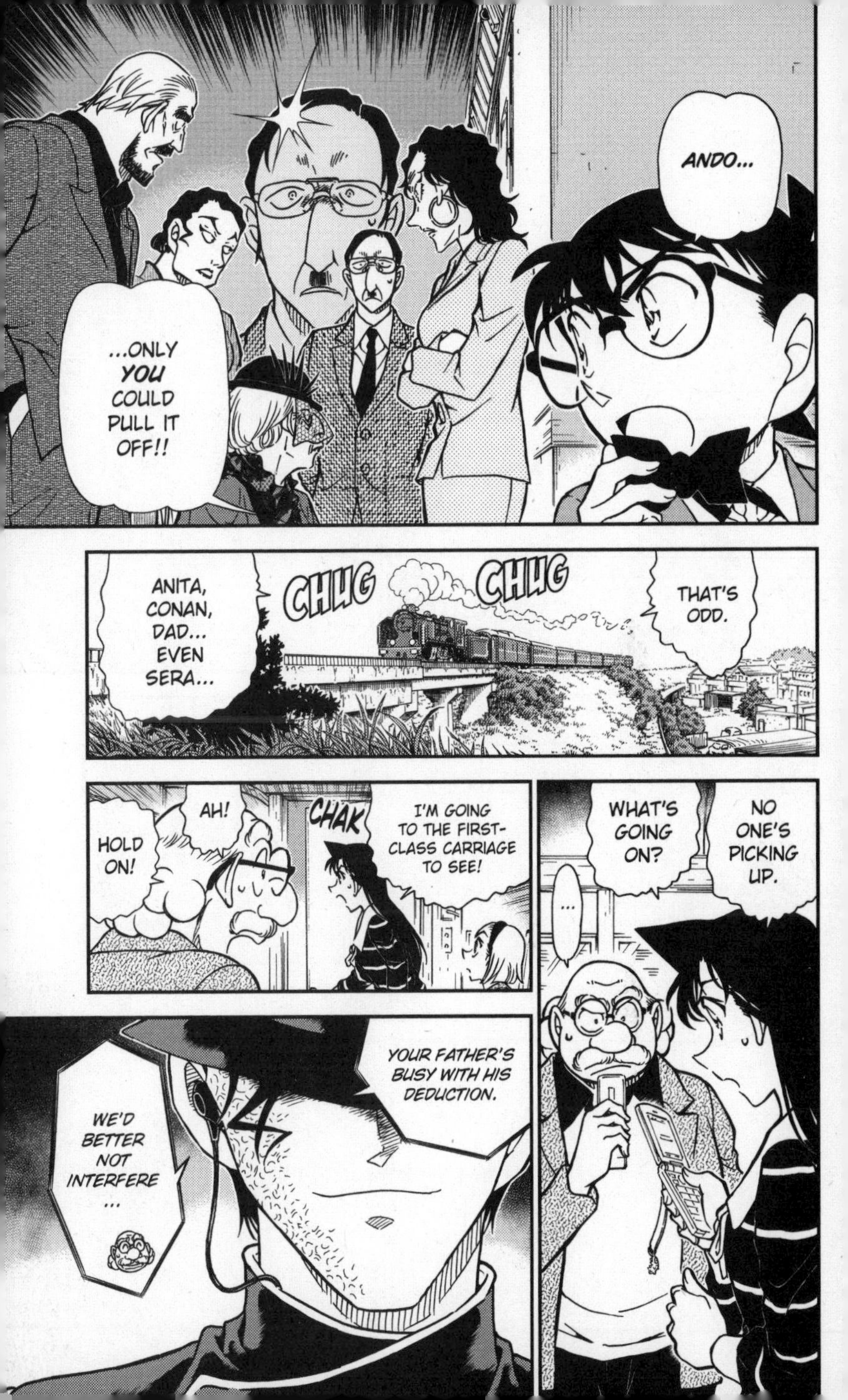
ANDO...
...ONLY YOU COULD PULL IT OFF!!
THAT'S ODD.
CHUG CHUG
ANITA, CONAN, DAD... EVEN SERA...
NO ONE'S PICKING UP.
WHAT'S GOING ON?
...
I'M GOING TO THE FIRST-CLASS CARRIAGE TO SEE!
CHAK
AH!
HOLD ON!
YOUR FATHER'S BUSY WITH HIS DEDUCTION.
WE'D BETTER NOT INTERFERE...

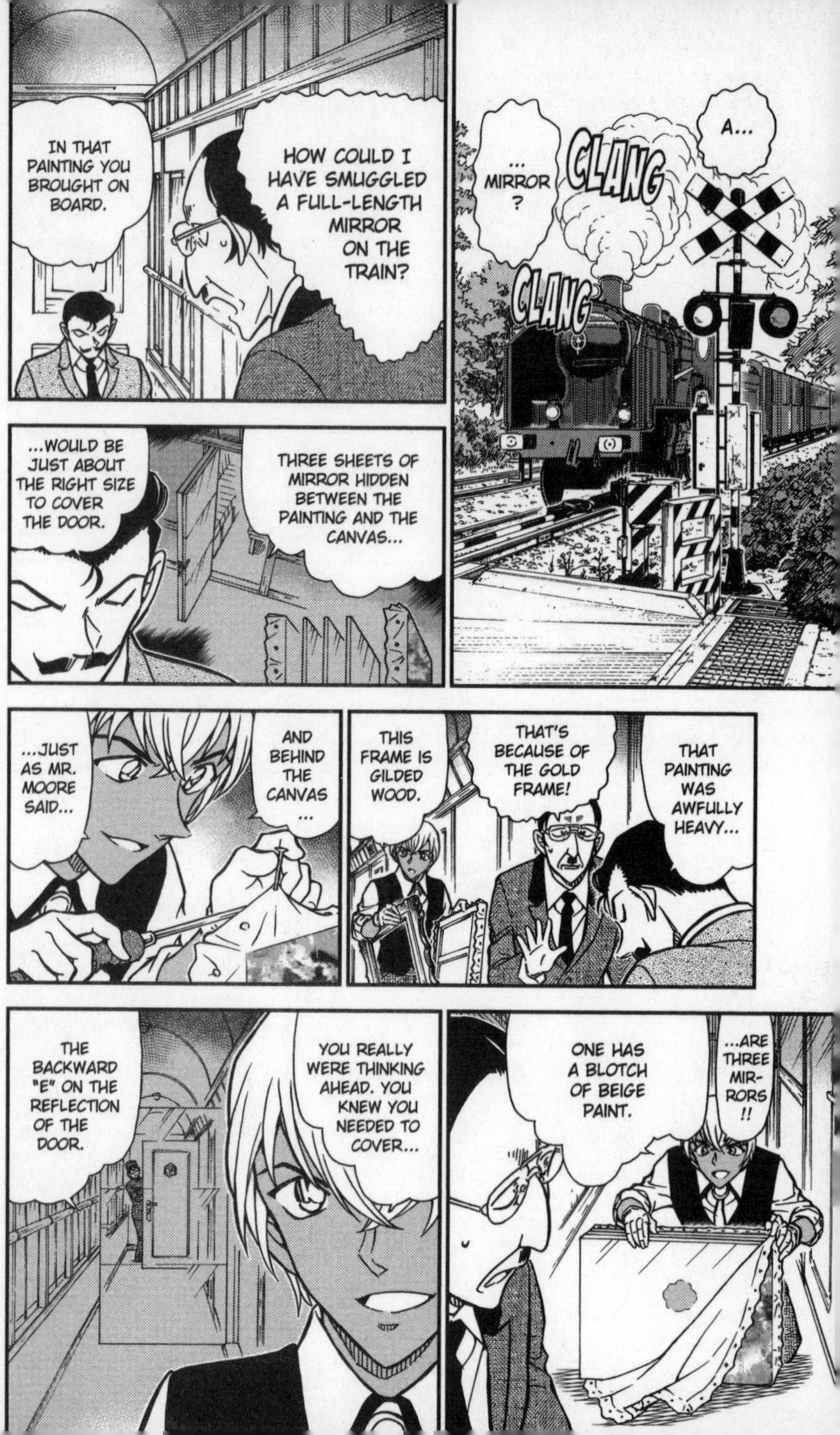
A...
... MIRROR ?
CLANG
CLANG
HOW COULD I HAVE SMUGGLED A FULL-LENGTH MIRROR ON THE TRAIN?
IN THAT PAINTING YOU BROUGHT ON BOARD.
THREE SHEETS OF MIRROR HIDDEN BETWEEN THE PAINTING AND THE CANVAS...
...WOULD BE JUST ABOUT THE RIGHT SIZE TO COVER THE DOOR.
THAT PAINTING WAS AWFULLY HEAVY...
THAT'S BECAUSE OF THE GOLD FRAME!
THIS FRAME IS GILDED WOOD.
AND BEHIND THE CANVAS ...
...JUST AS MR. MOORE SAID...
...ARE THREE MIR-RORS !!
ONE HAS A BLOTCH OF BEIGE PAINT.
YOU REALLY WERE THINKING AHEAD. YOU KNEW YOU NEEDED TO COVER...
THE BACKWARD "E" ON THE REFLECTION OF THE DOOR.

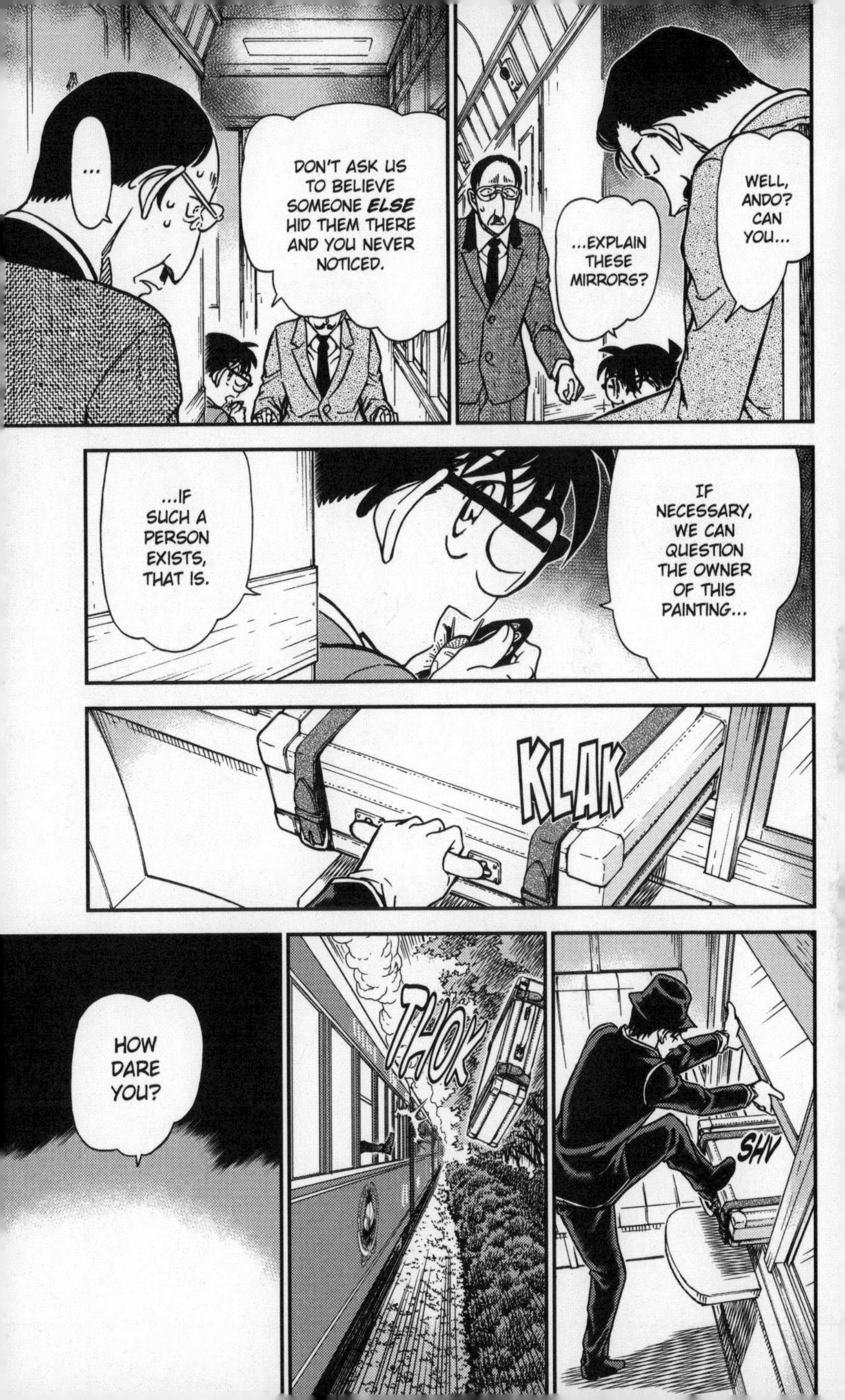
WELL, ANDO? CAN YOU...
...EXPLAIN THESE MIRRORS?
DON'T ASK US TO BELIEVE SOMEONE ELSE HID THEM THERE AND YOU NEVER NOTICED.
...
IF NECESSARY, WE CAN QUESTION THE OWNER OF THIS PAINTING...
...IF SUCH A PERSON EXISTS, THAT IS.
KLAK
SHV
THOK
HOW DARE YOU?

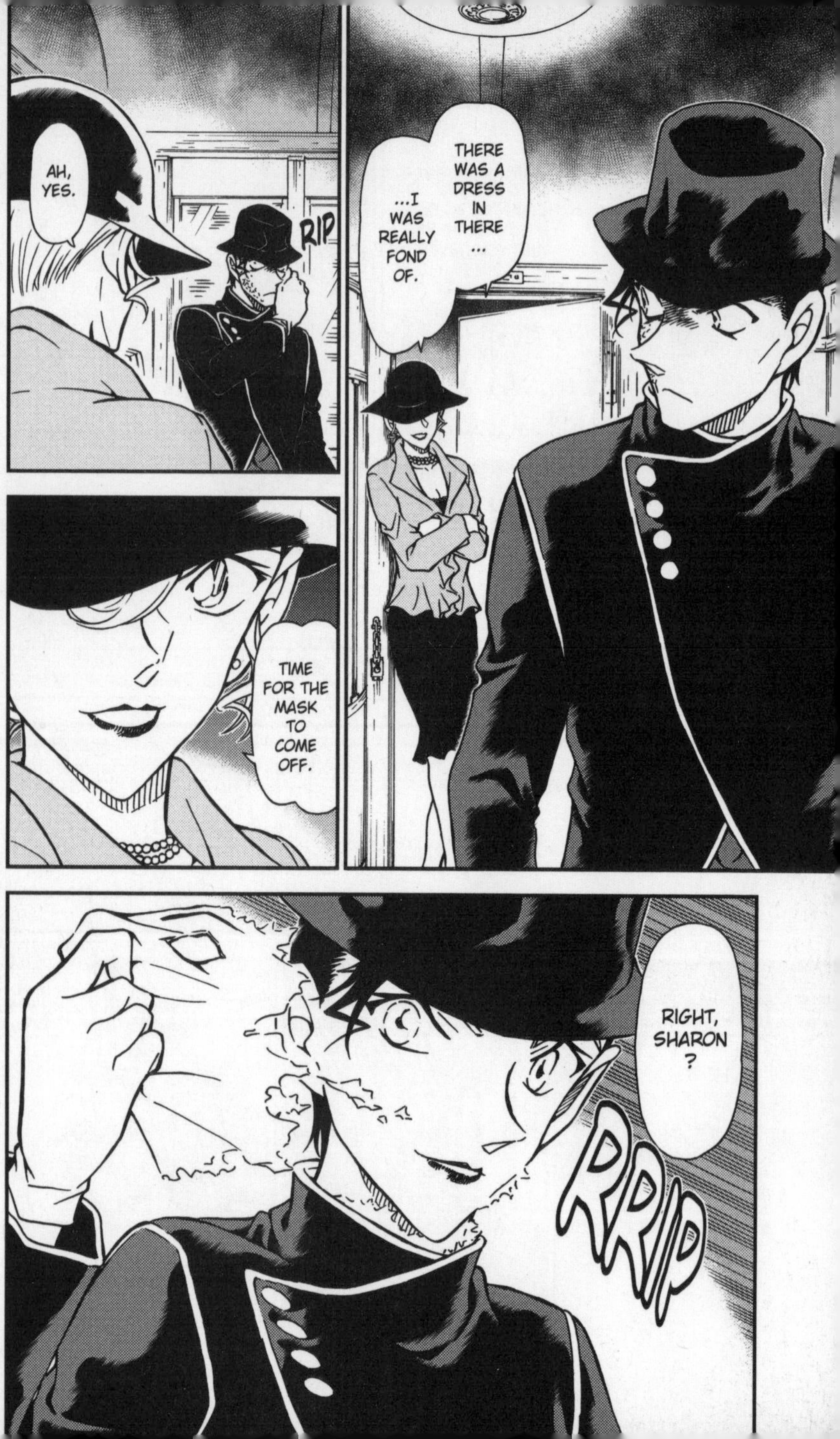
THERE WAS A DRESS IN THERE ...
...I WAS REALLY FOND OF.
AH, YES.
RIP
TIME FOR THE MASK TO COME OFF.
RIGHT, SHARON?
RRIP

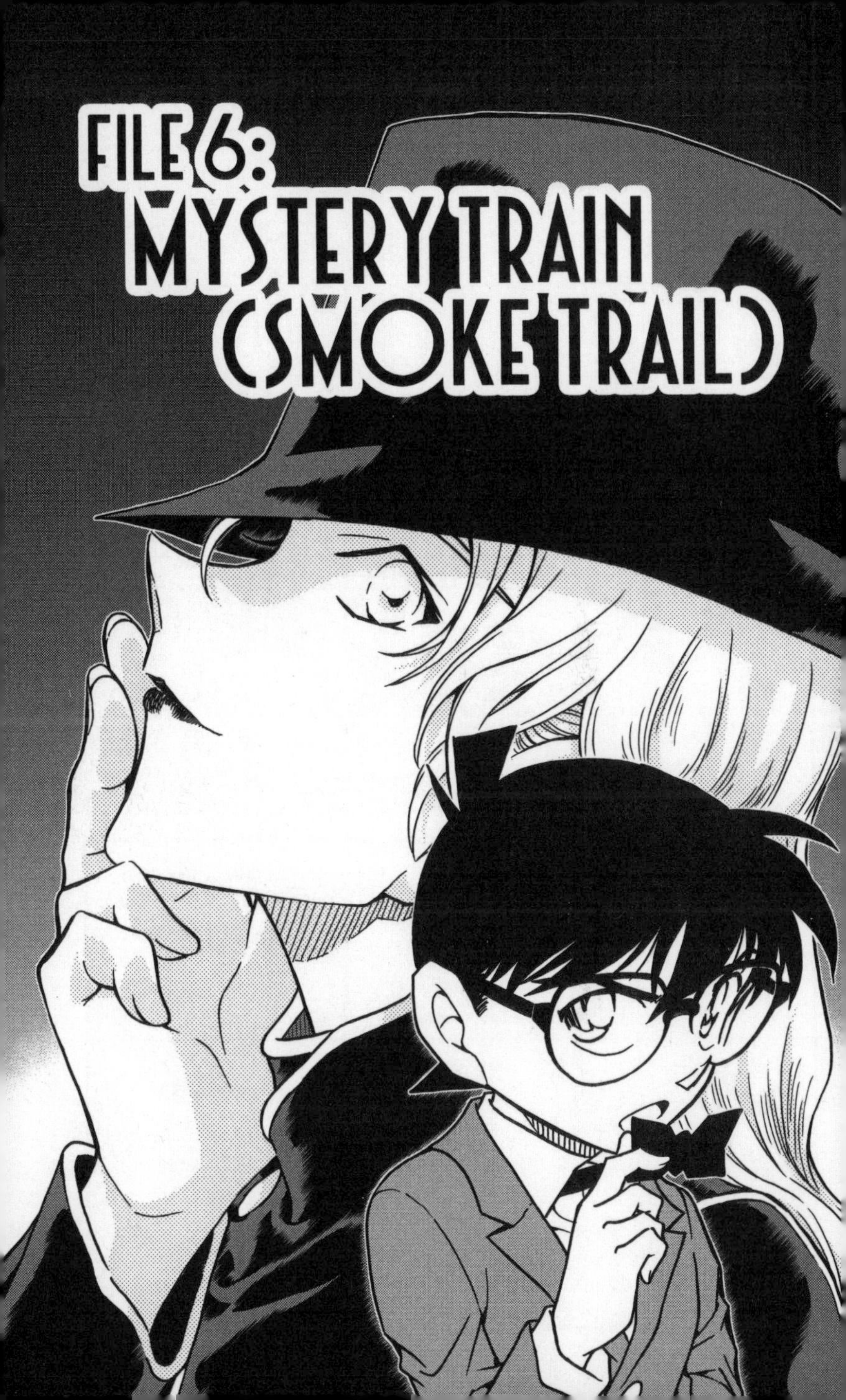
FILE 6:
MYSTERY TRAIN
(SMOKE TRAIL)

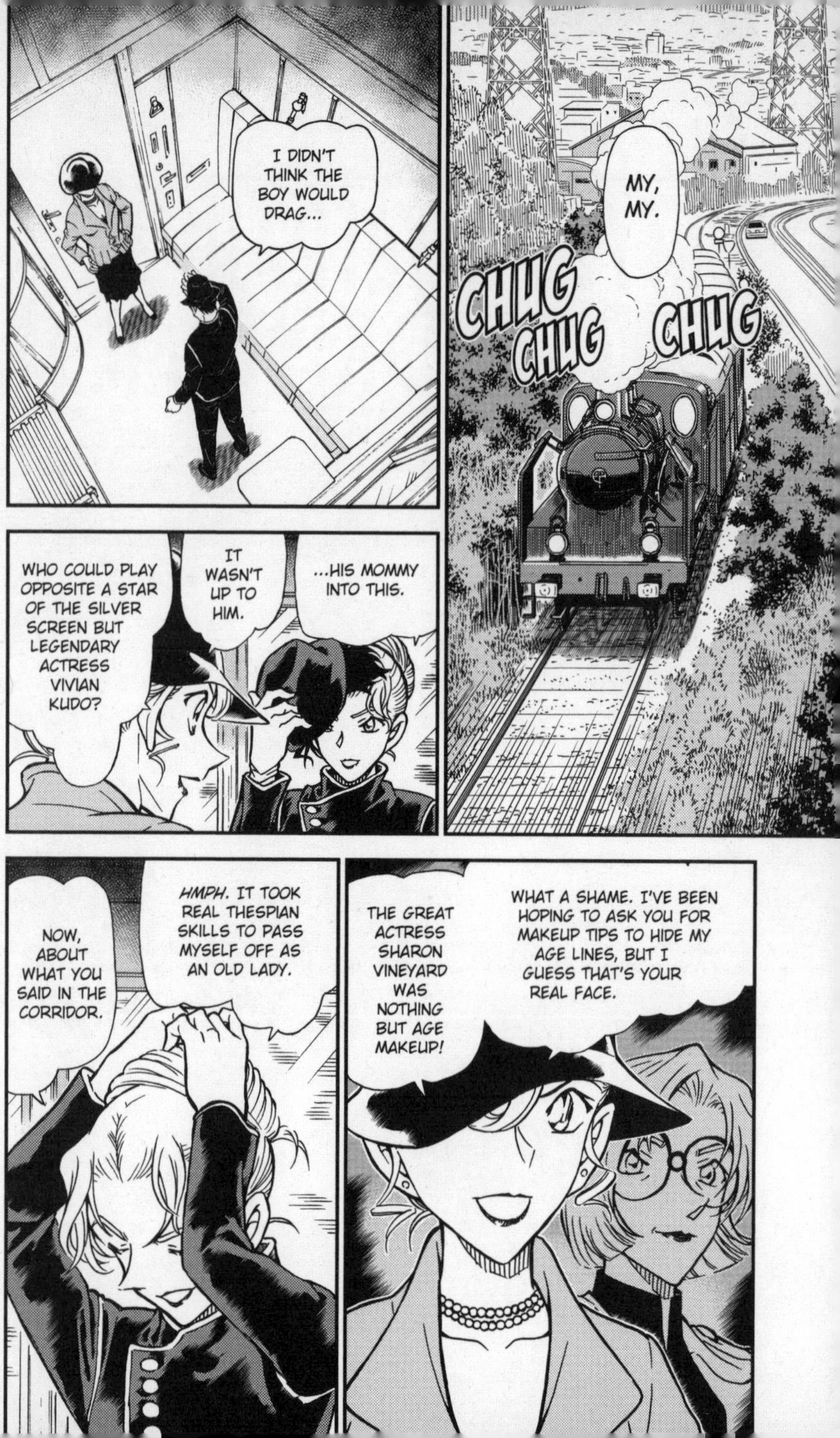
MY, MY.
CHUG
CHUG
CHUG
I DIDN'T THINK THE BOY WOULD DRAG...
...HIS MOMMY INTO THIS.
IT WASN'T UP TO HIM.
WHO COULD PLAY OPPOSITE A STAR OF THE SILVER SCREEN BUT LEGENDARY ACTRESS VIVIAN KUDO?
WHAT A SHAME. I'VE BEEN HOPING TO ASK YOU FOR MAKEUP TIPS TO HIDE MY AGE LINES, BUT I GUESS THAT'S YOUR REAL FACE.
THE GREAT ACTRESS SHARON VINEYARD WAS NOTHING BUT AGE MAKEUP!
HMPH. IT TOOK REAL THESPIAN SKILLS TO PASS MYSELF OFF AS AN OLD LADY.
NOW, ABOUT WHAT YOU SAID IN THE CORRIDOR.

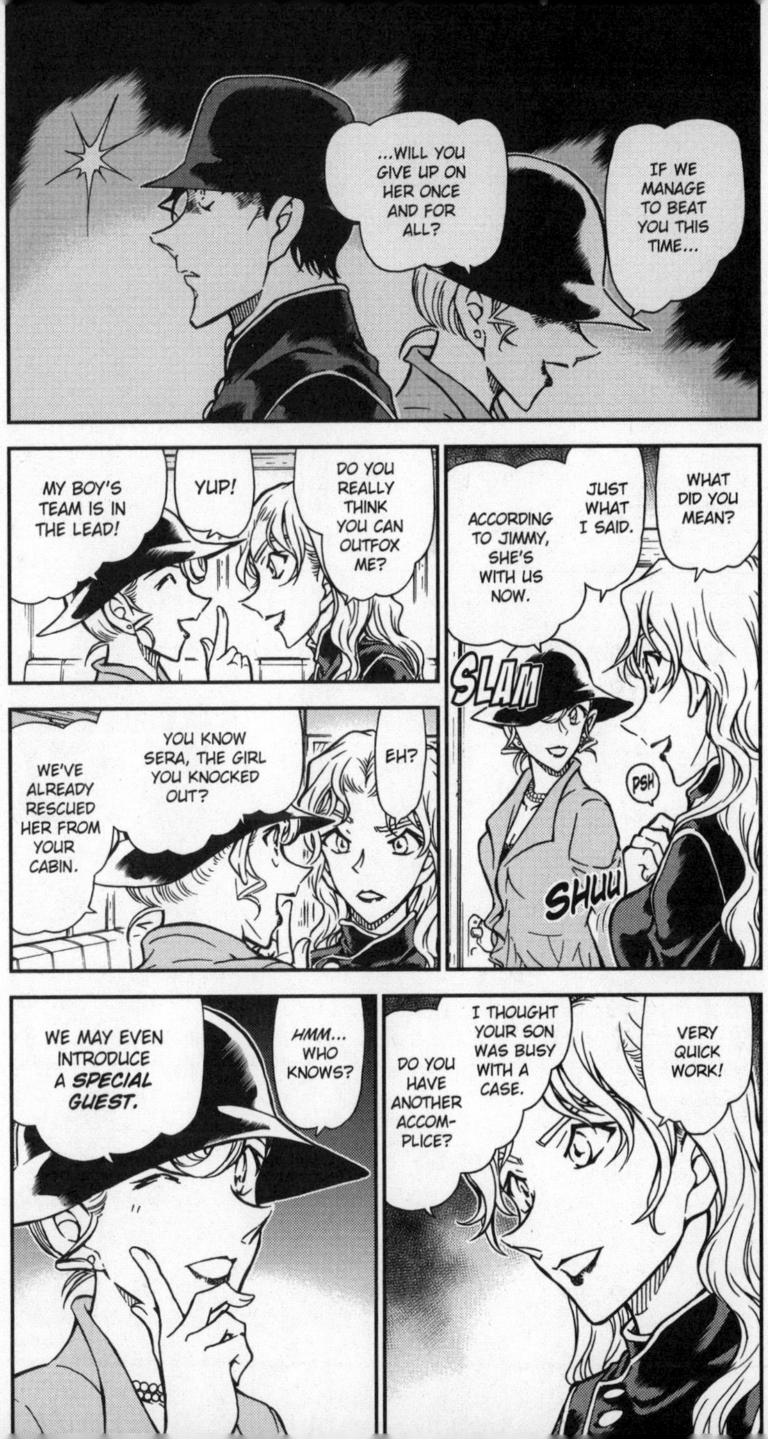
IF WE MANAGE TO BEAT YOU THIS TIME...
...WILL YOU GIVE UP ON HER ONCE AND FOR ALL?
WHAT DID YOU MEAN?
JUST WHAT I SAID.
ACCORDING TO JIMMY, SHE'S WITH US NOW.
SLAM
PSH
SHUU
DO YOU REALLY THINK YOU CAN OUTFOX ME?
YUP!
MY BOY'S TEAM IS IN THE LEAD!
EH?
YOU KNOW SERA, THE GIRL YOU KNOCKED OUT?
WE'VE ALREADY RESCUED HER FROM YOUR CABIN.
VERY QUICK WORK!
I THOUGHT YOUR SON WAS BUSY WITH A CASE.
DO YOU HAVE ANOTHER ACCOMPLICE?
HMM... WHO KNOWS?
WE MAY EVEN INTRODUCE A ***SPECIAL GUEST.***

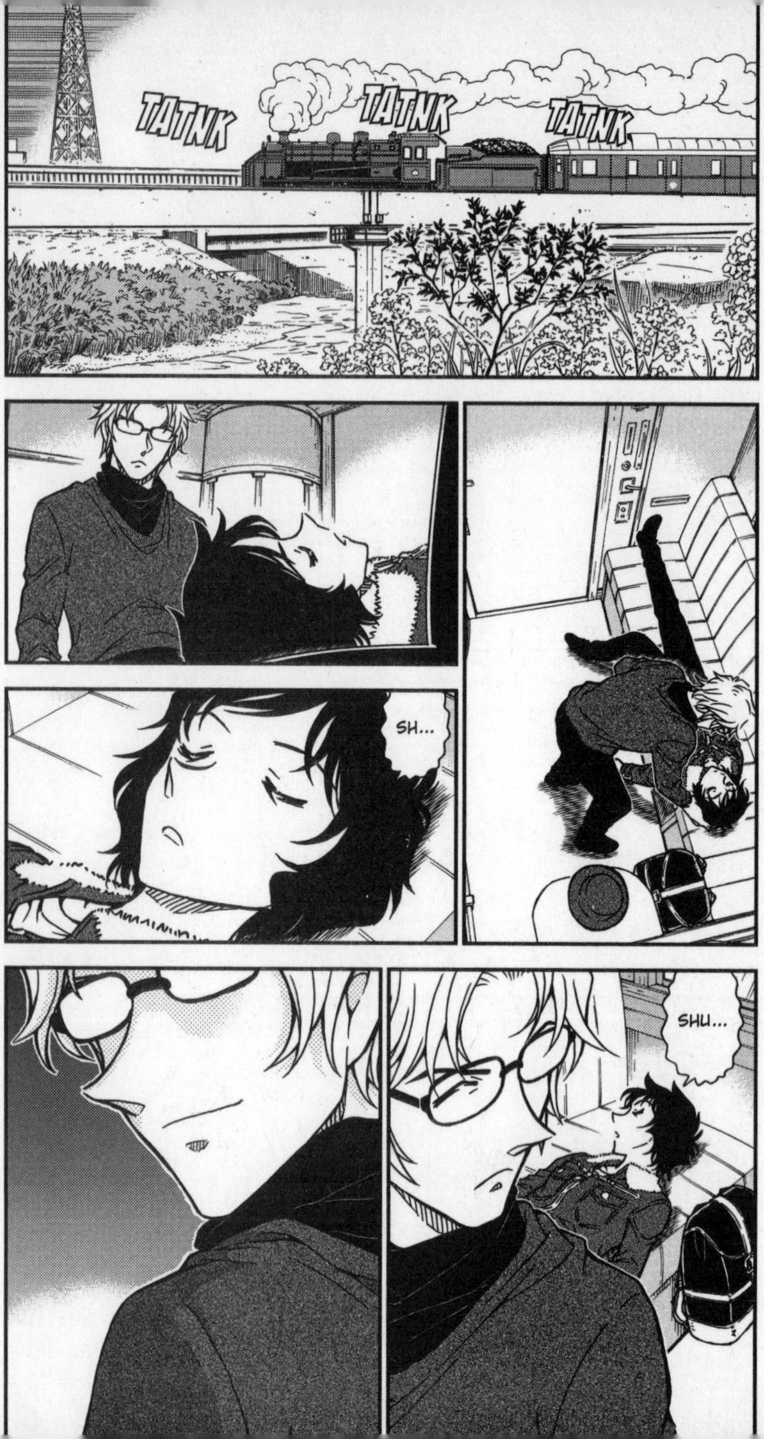
TATNK
TATNK
TATNK
SH...
SHU...

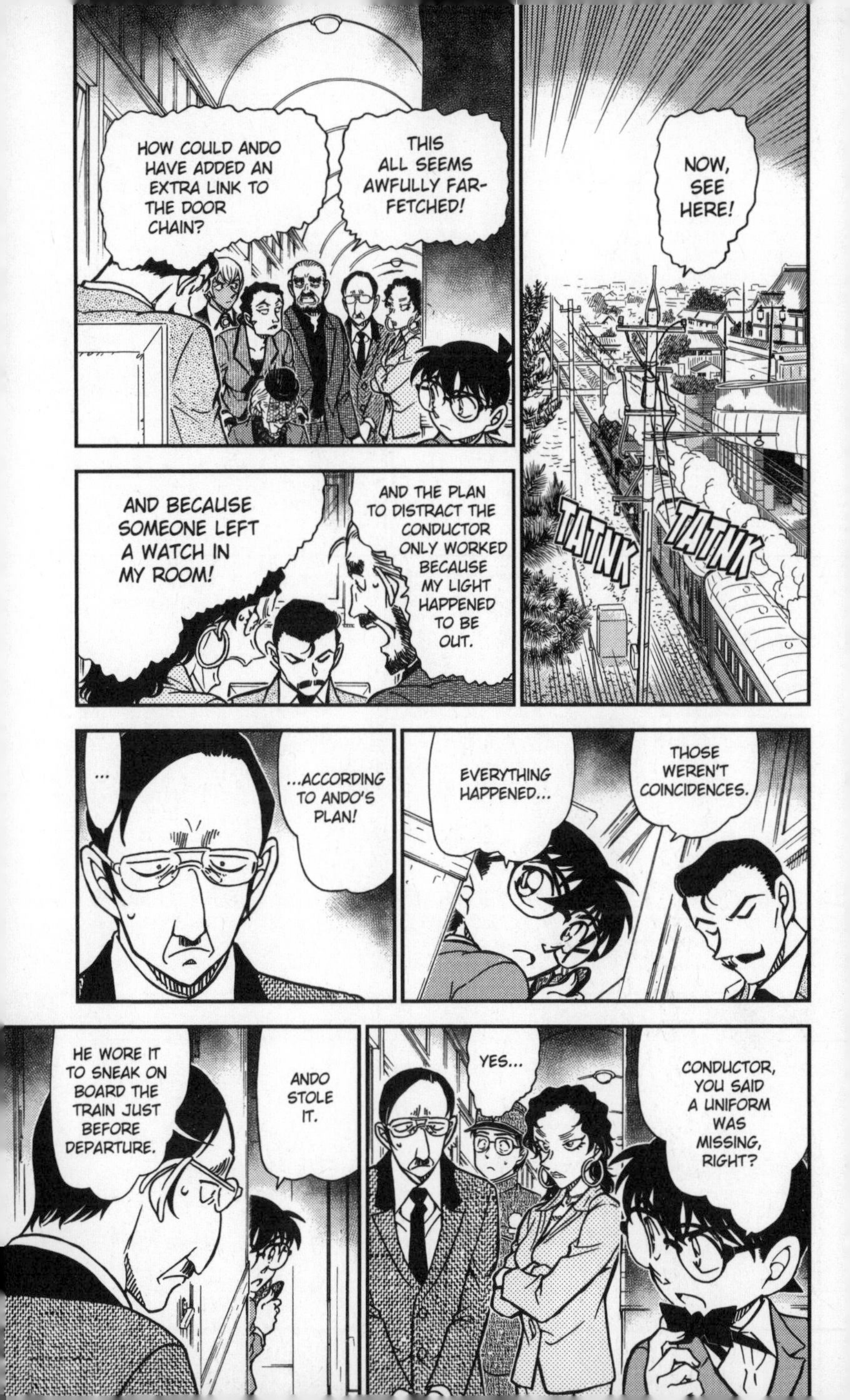
NOW, SEE HERE!
TATNK
TATNK
THIS ALL SEEMS AWFULLY FAR-FETCHED!
HOW COULD ANDO HAVE ADDED AN EXTRA LINK TO THE DOOR CHAIN?
AND THE PLAN TO DISTRACT THE CONDUCTOR ONLY WORKED BECAUSE MY LIGHT HAPPENED TO BE OUT.
AND BECAUSE SOMEONE LEFT A WATCH IN MY ROOM!
THOSE WEREN'T COINCIDENCES.
EVERYTHING HAPPENED...
...ACCORDING TO ANDO'S PLAN!
...
CONDUCTOR, YOU SAID A UNIFORM WAS MISSING, RIGHT?
YES...
ANDO STOLE IT.
HE WORE IT TO SNEAK ON BOARD THE TRAIN JUST BEFORE DEPARTURE.

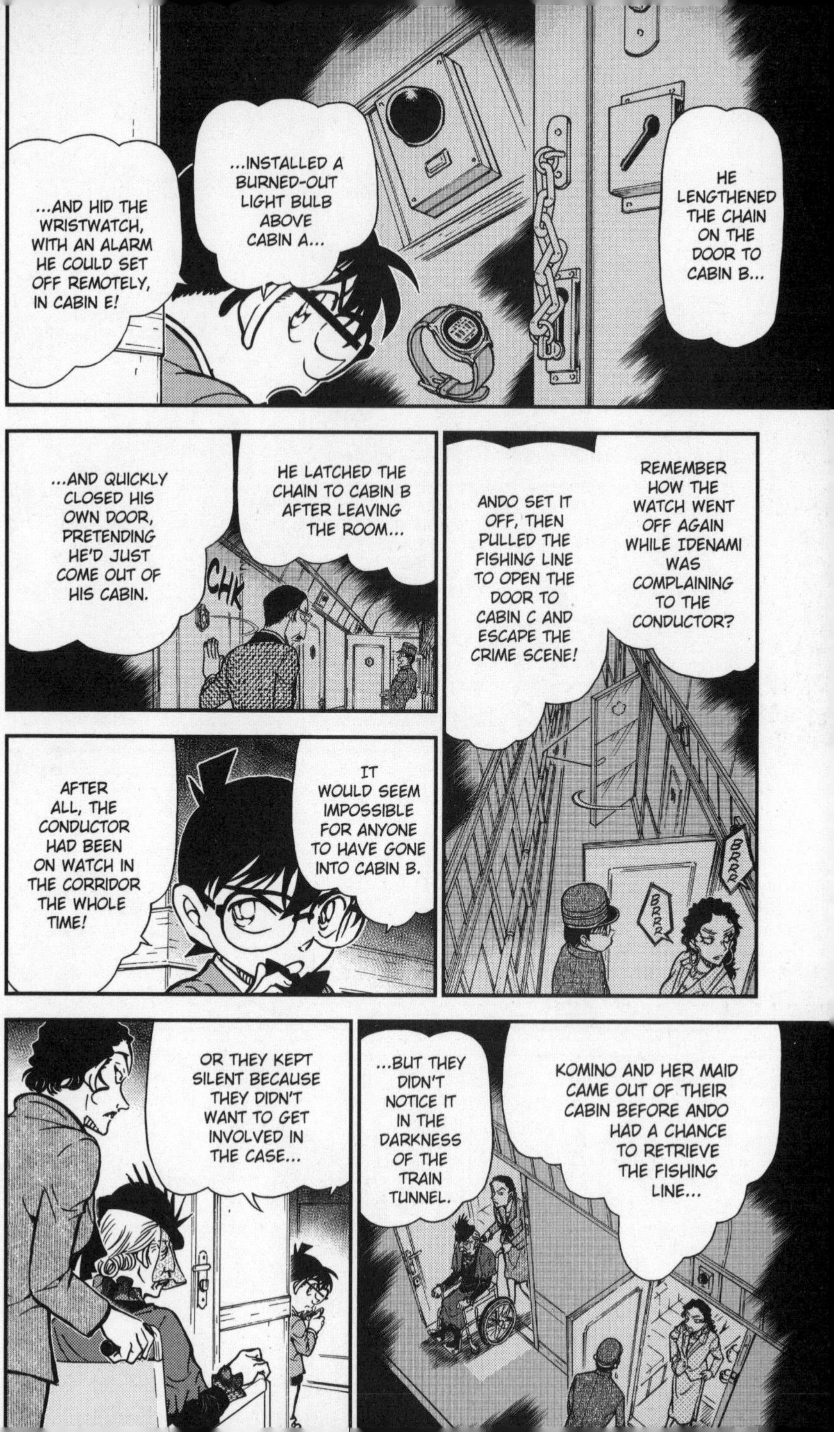
HE LENGTHENED THE CHAIN ON THE DOOR TO CABIN B...
...INSTALLED A BURNED-OUT LIGHT BULB ABOVE CABIN A...
...AND HID THE WRISTWATCH, WITH AN ALARM HE COULD SET OFF REMOTELY, IN CABIN E!
REMEMBER HOW THE WATCH WENT OFF AGAIN WHILE IDENAMI WAS COMPLAINING TO THE CONDUCTOR?
ANDO SET IT OFF, THEN PULLED THE FISHING LINE TO OPEN THE DOOR TO CABIN C AND ESCAPE THE CRIME SCENE!
BRRR
BRRR
HE LATCHED THE CHAIN TO CABIN B AFTER LEAVING THE ROOM...
...AND QUICKLY CLOSED HIS OWN DOOR, PRETENDING HE'D JUST COME OUT OF HIS CABIN.
CHK
IT WOULD SEEM IMPOSSIBLE FOR ANYONE TO HAVE GONE INTO CABIN B.
AFTER ALL, THE CONDUCTOR HAD BEEN ON WATCH IN THE CORRIDOR THE WHOLE TIME!
KOMINO AND HER MAID CAME OUT OF THEIR CABIN BEFORE ANDO HAD A CHANCE TO RETRIEVE THE FISHING LINE...
...BUT THEY DIDN'T NOTICE IT IN THE DARKNESS OF THE TRAIN TUNNEL.
OR THEY KEPT SILENT BECAUSE THEY DIDN'T WANT TO GET INVOLVED IN THE CASE...

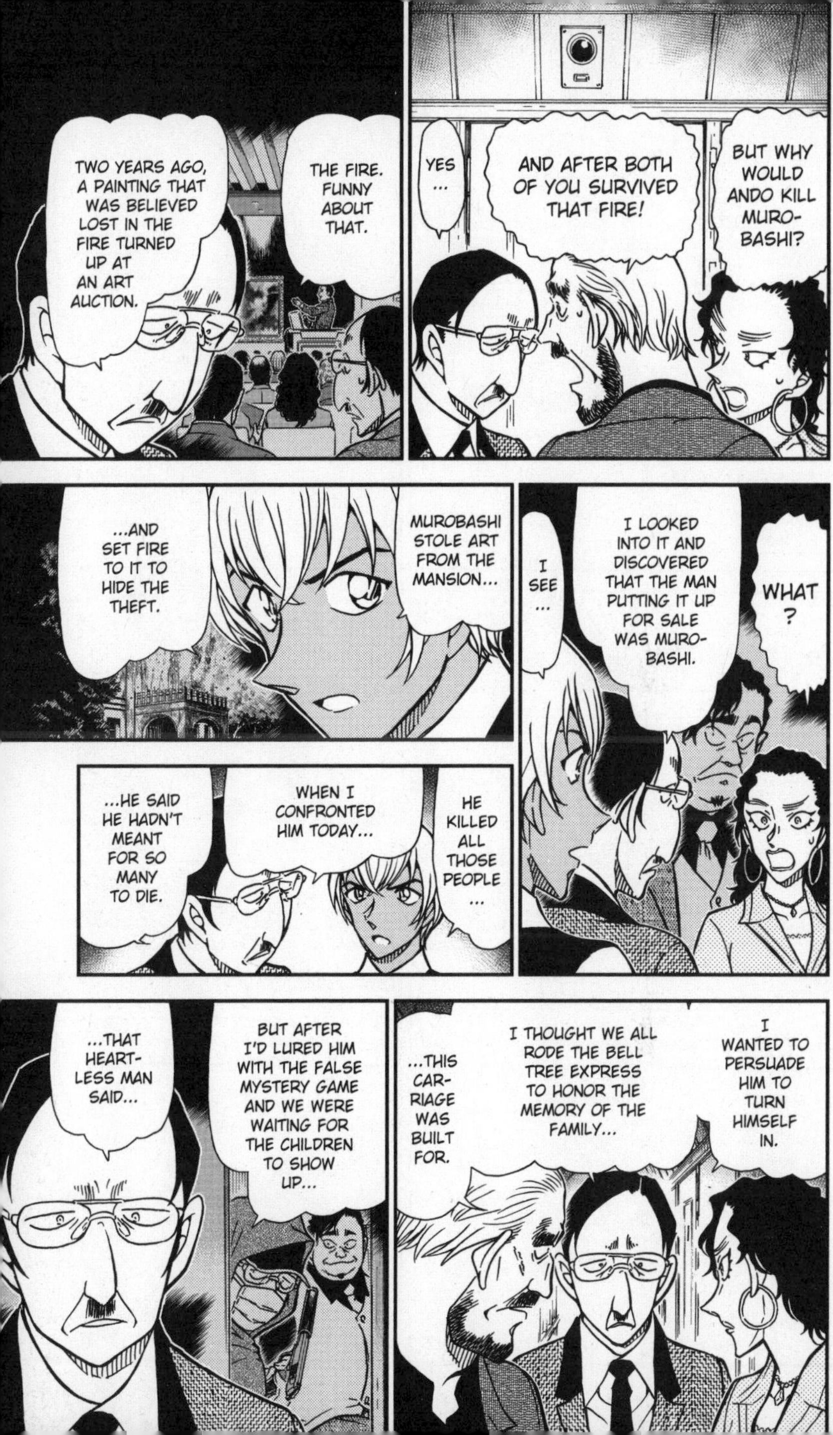
BUT WHY WOULD ANDO KILL MURO-BASHI?
AND AFTER BOTH OF YOU SURVIVED THAT FIRE!
YES ...
THE FIRE. FUNNY ABOUT THAT.
TWO YEARS AGO, A PAINTING THAT WAS BELIEVED LOST IN THE FIRE TURNED UP AT AN ART AUCTION.
WHAT ?
I LOOKED INTO IT AND DISCOVERED THAT THE MAN PUTTING IT UP FOR SALE WAS MURO-BASHI.
I SEE ...
MUROBASHI STOLE ART FROM THE MANSION...
...AND SET FIRE TO IT TO HIDE THE THEFT.
HE KILLED ALL THOSE PEOPLE ...
WHEN I CONFRONTED HIM TODAY...
...HE SAID HE HADN'T MEANT FOR SO MANY TO DIE.
I WANTED TO PERSUADE HIM TO TURN HIMSELF IN.
I THOUGHT WE ALL RODE THE BELL TREE EXPRESS TO HONOR THE MEMORY OF THE FAMILY...
...THIS CAR-RIAGE WAS BUILT FOR.
BUT AFTER I'D LURED HIM WITH THE FALSE MYSTERY GAME AND WE WERE WAITING FOR THE CHILDREN TO SHOW UP...
...THAT HEART-LESS MAN SAID...

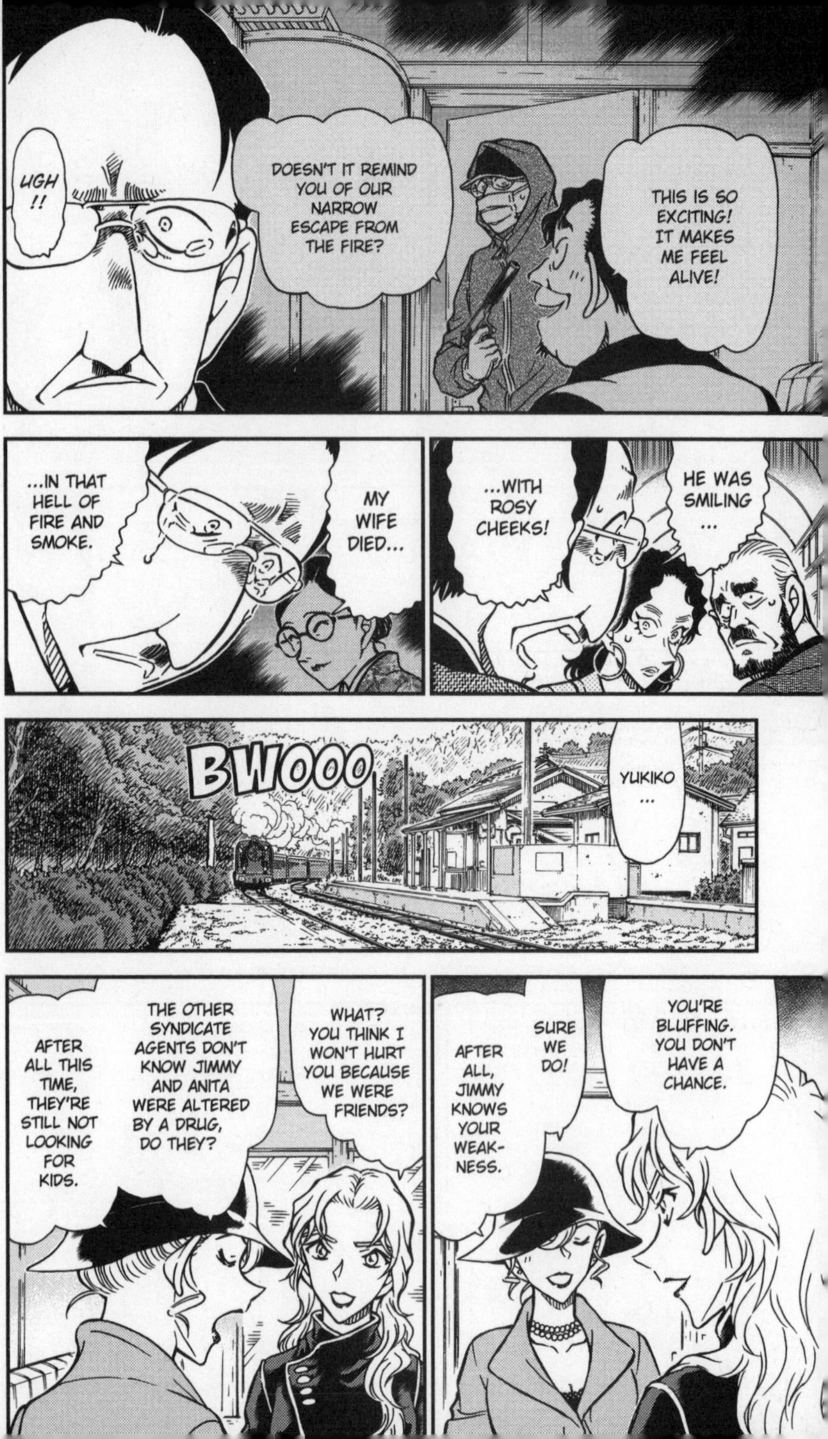
THIS IS SO EXCITING! IT MAKES ME FEEL ALIVE!
DOESN'T IT REMIND YOU OF OUR NARROW ESCAPE FROM THE FIRE?
UGH!!
HE WAS SMILING...
...WITH ROSY CHEEKS!
MY WIFE DIED...
...IN THAT HELL OF FIRE AND SMOKE.
YUKIKO...
BWOOO
YOU'RE BLUFFING. YOU DON'T HAVE A CHANCE.
SURE WE DO!
AFTER ALL, JIMMY KNOWS YOUR WEAK-NESS.
WHAT? YOU THINK I WON'T HURT YOU BECAUSE WE WERE FRIENDS?
THE OTHER SYNDICATE AGENTS DON'T KNOW JIMMY AND ANITA WERE ALTERED BY A DRUG, DO THEY?
AFTER ALL THIS TIME, THEY'RE STILL NOT LOOKING FOR KIDS.

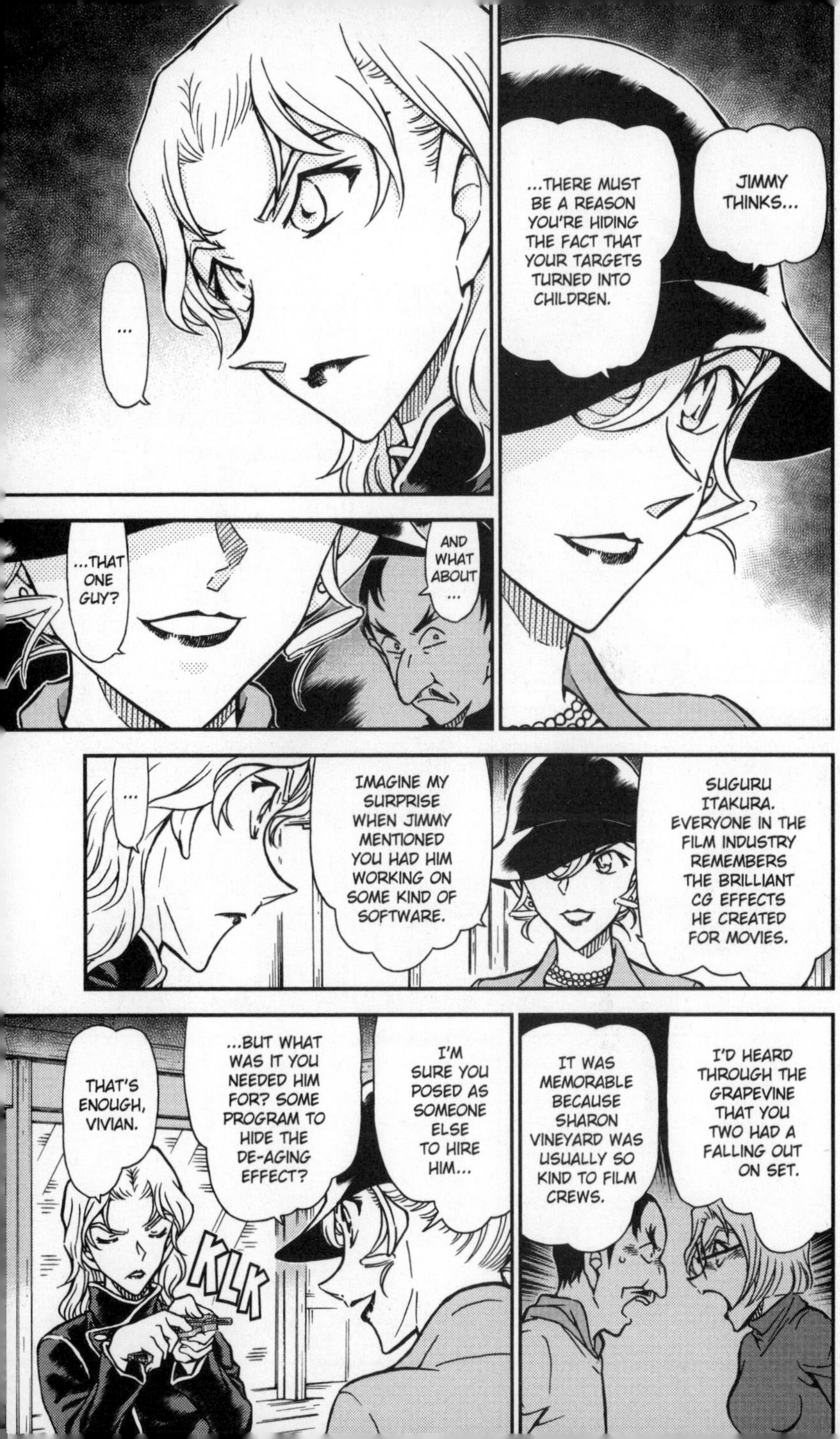
JIMMY THINKS...
...THERE MUST BE A REASON YOU'RE HIDING THE FACT THAT YOUR TARGETS TURNED INTO CHILDREN.
...
AND WHAT ABOUT...
...THAT ONE GUY?
SUGURU ITAKURA. EVERYONE IN THE FILM INDUSTRY REMEMBERS THE BRILLIANT CG EFFECTS HE CREATED FOR MOVIES.
IMAGINE MY SURPRISE WHEN JIMMY MENTIONED YOU HAD HIM WORKING ON SOME KIND OF SOFTWARE.
...
I'D HEARD THROUGH THE GRAPEVINE THAT YOU TWO HAD A FALLING OUT ON SET.
IT WAS MEMORABLE BECAUSE SHARON VINEYARD WAS USUALLY SO KIND TO FILM CREWS.
I'M SURE YOU POSED AS SOMEONE ELSE TO HIRE HIM...
...BUT WHAT WAS IT YOU NEEDED HIM FOR? SOME PROGRAM TO HIDE THE DE-AGING EFFECT?
KLK
THAT'S ENOUGH, VIVIAN.

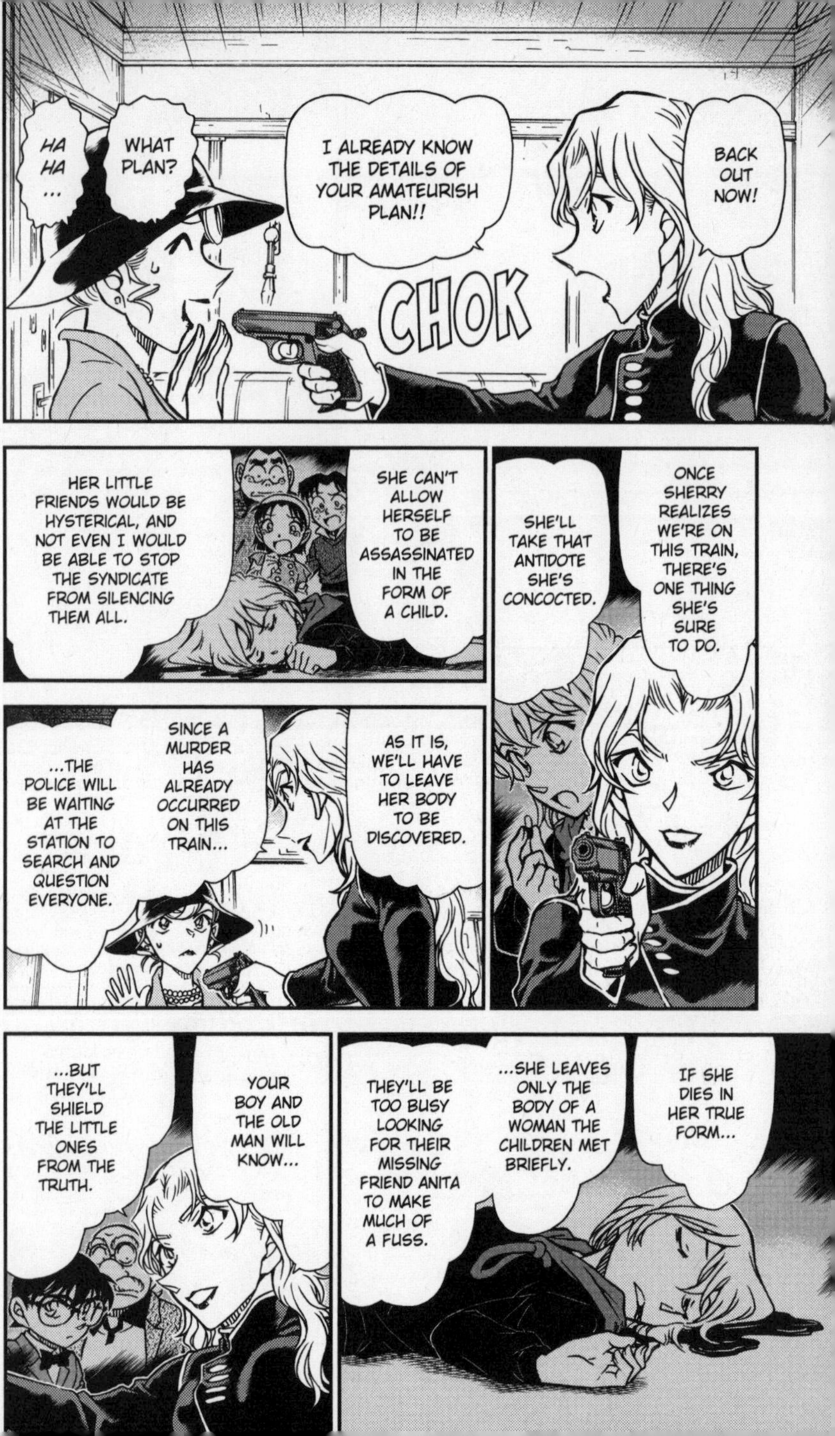
BACK OUT NOW!
I ALREADY KNOW THE DETAILS OF YOUR AMATEURISH PLAN!!
CHOK
WHAT PLAN?
HA HA ...
ONCE SHERRY REALIZES WE'RE ON THIS TRAIN, THERE'S ONE THING SHE'S SURE TO DO.
SHE'LL TAKE THAT ANTIDOTE SHE'S CONCOCTED.
SHE CAN'T ALLOW HERSELF TO BE ASSASSINATED IN THE FORM OF A CHILD.
HER LITTLE FRIENDS WOULD BE HYSTERICAL, AND NOT EVEN I WOULD BE ABLE TO STOP THE SYNDICATE FROM SILENCING THEM ALL.
AS IT IS, WE'LL HAVE TO LEAVE HER BODY TO BE DISCOVERED.
SINCE A MURDER HAS ALREADY OCCURRED ON THIS TRAIN...
...THE POLICE WILL BE WAITING AT THE STATION TO SEARCH AND QUESTION EVERYONE.
IF SHE DIES IN HER TRUE FORM...
...SHE LEAVES ONLY THE BODY OF A WOMAN THE CHILDREN MET BRIEFLY.
THEY'LL BE TOO BUSY LOOKING FOR THEIR MISSING FRIEND ANITA TO MAKE MUCH OF A FUSS.
YOUR BOY AND THE OLD MAN WILL KNOW...
...BUT THEY'LL SHIELD THE LITTLE ONES FROM THE TRUTH.

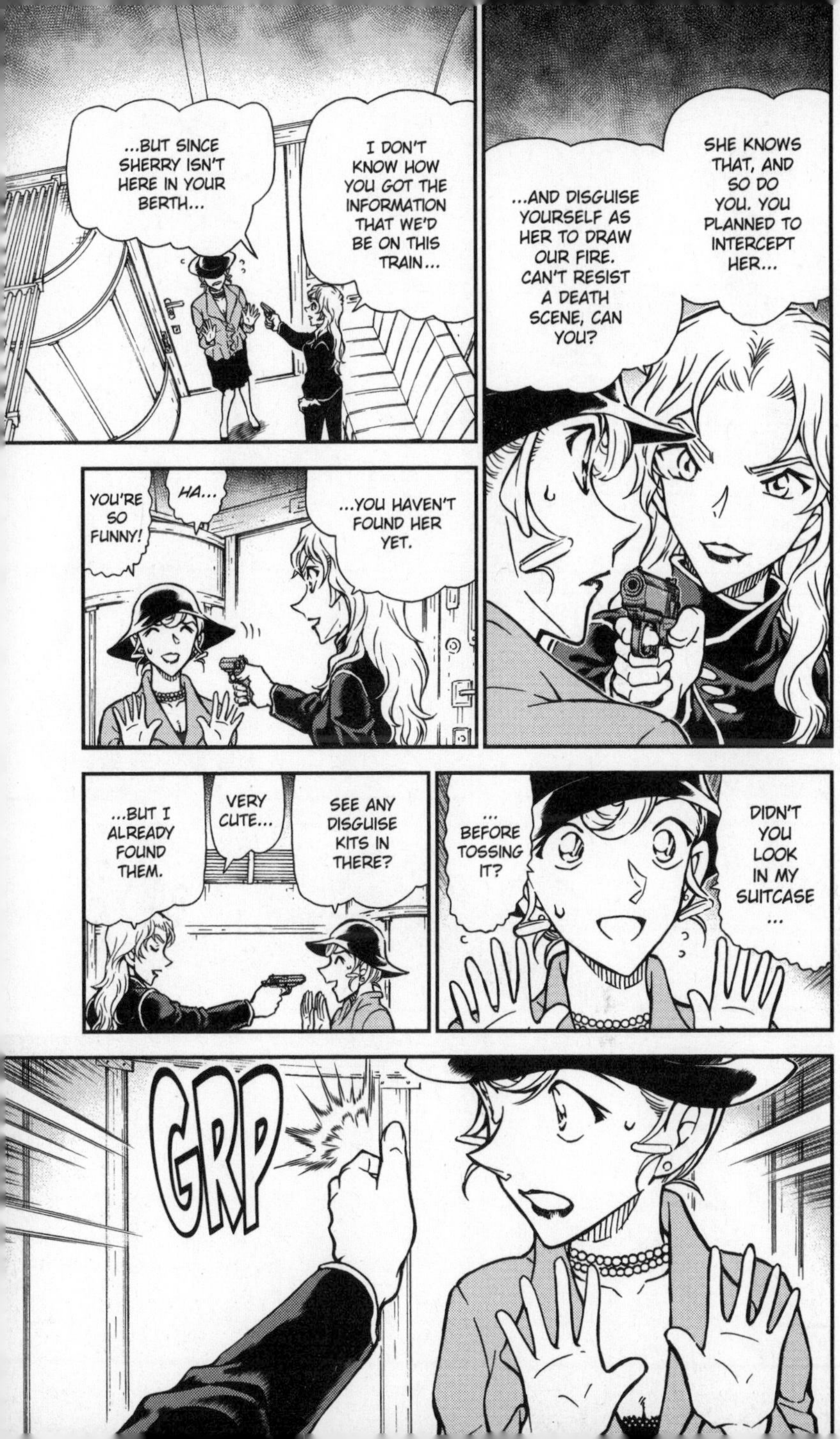
SHE KNOWS THAT, AND SO DO YOU. YOU PLANNED TO INTERCEPT HER...
...AND DISGUISE YOURSELF AS HER TO DRAW OUR FIRE. CAN'T RESIST A DEATH SCENE, CAN YOU?
I DON'T KNOW HOW YOU GOT THE INFORMATION THAT WE'D BE ON THIS TRAIN...
...BUT SINCE SHERRY ISN'T HERE IN YOUR BERTH...
...YOU HAVEN'T FOUND HER YET.
HA...
YOU'RE SO FUNNY!
DIDN'T YOU LOOK IN MY SUITCASE...
...BEFORE TOSSING IT?
SEE ANY DISGUISE KITS IN THERE?
VERY CUTE...
...BUT I ALREADY FOUND THEM.
GRP

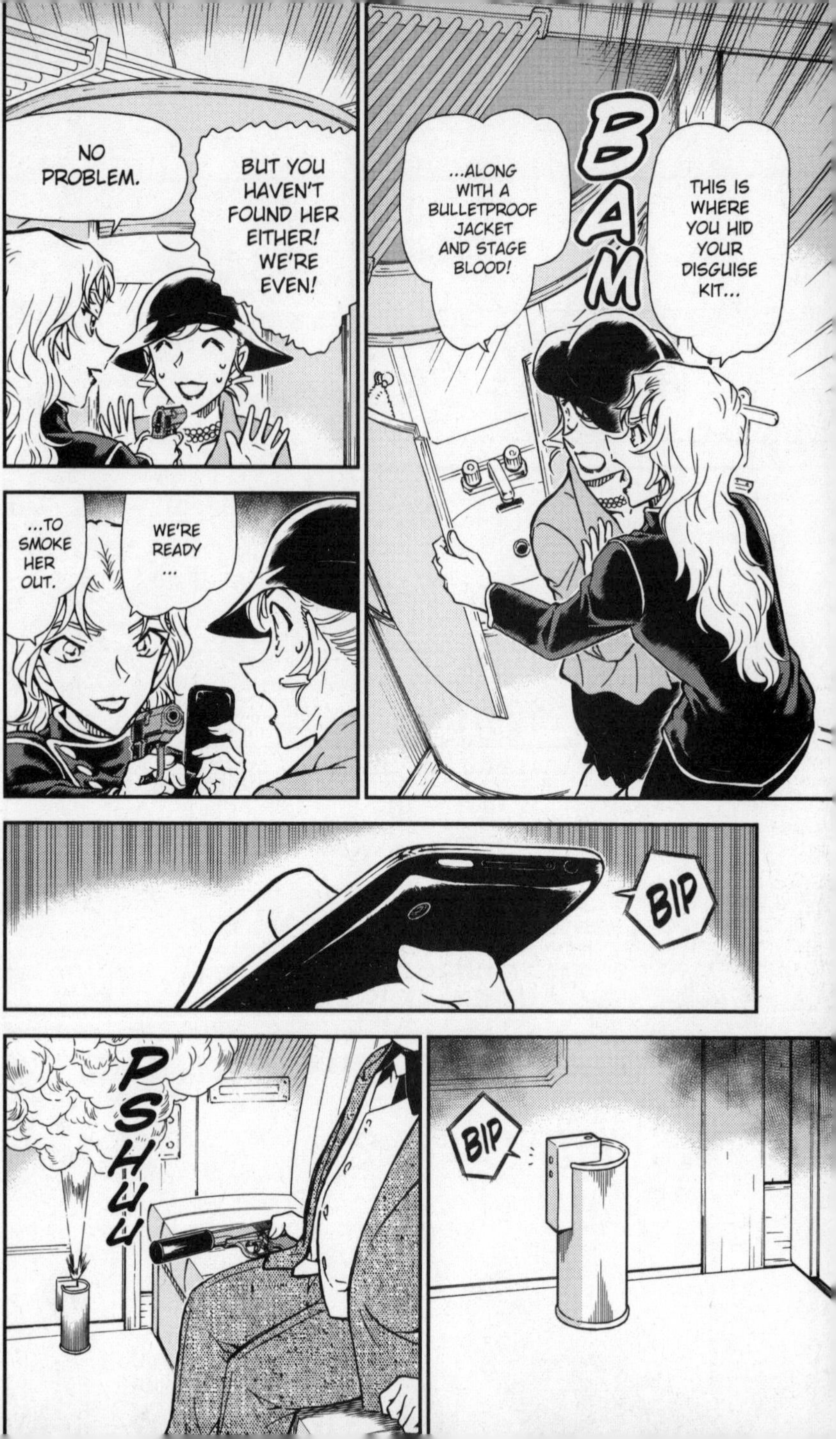

THIS IS WHERE YOU HID YOUR DISGUISE KIT...
BAM
...ALONG WITH A BULLETPROOF JACKET AND STAGE BLOOD!
BUT YOU HAVEN'T FOUND HER EITHER! WE'RE EVEN!
NO PROBLEM.
WE'RE READY...
...TO SMOKE HER OUT.
BIP
BIP
PSHUU

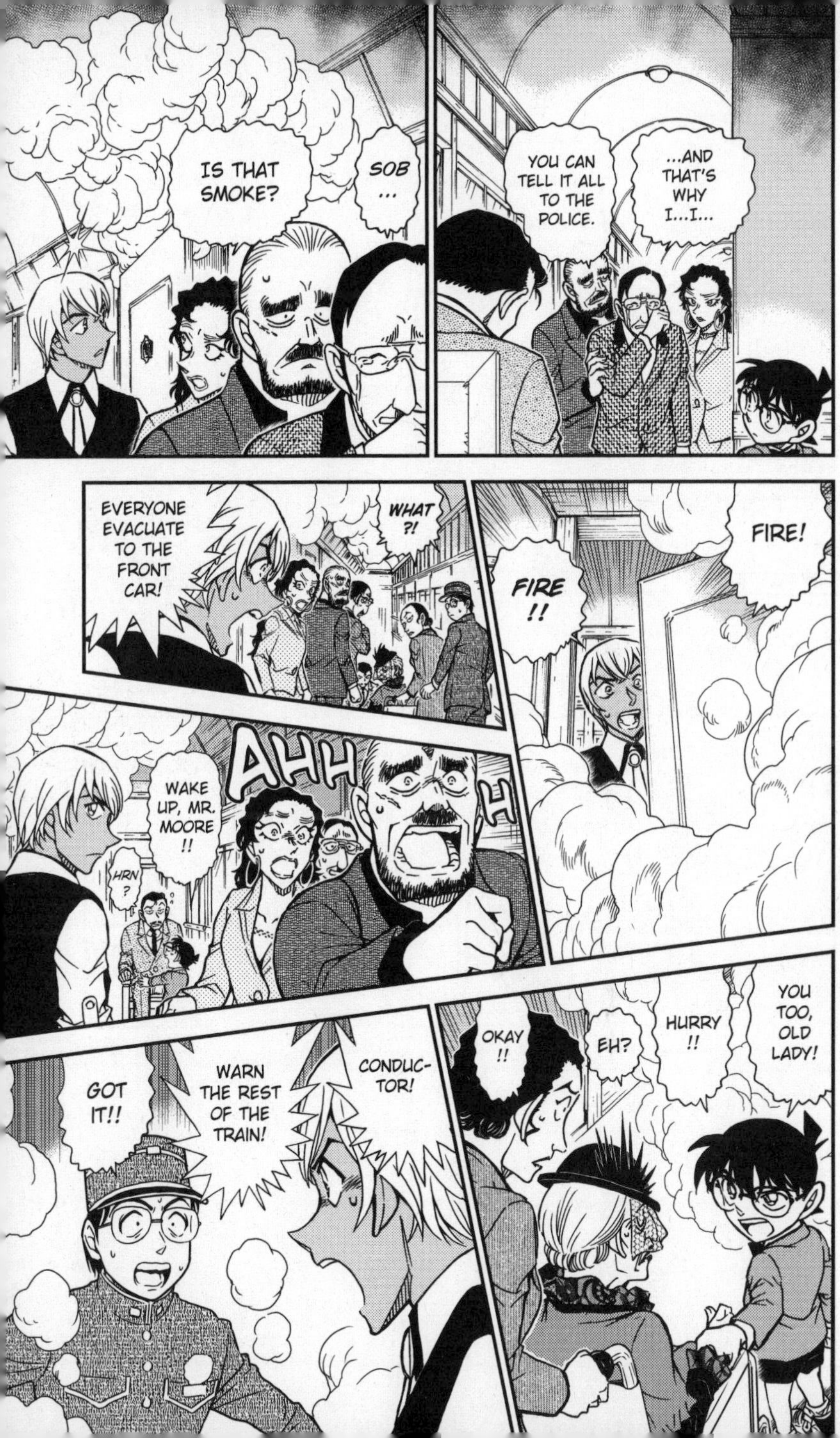
...AND THAT'S WHY I...I...
YOU CAN TELL IT ALL TO THE POLICE.
SOB ...
IS THAT SMOKE?
FIRE!
FIRE !!
WHAT ?!
EVERYONE EVACUATE TO THE FRONT CAR!
AHHH
WAKE UP, MR. MOORE !!
HRN ?
YOU TOO, OLD LADY!
HURRY !!
EH?
OKAY !!
CONDUC-TOR!
WARN THE REST OF THE TRAIN!
GOT IT!!

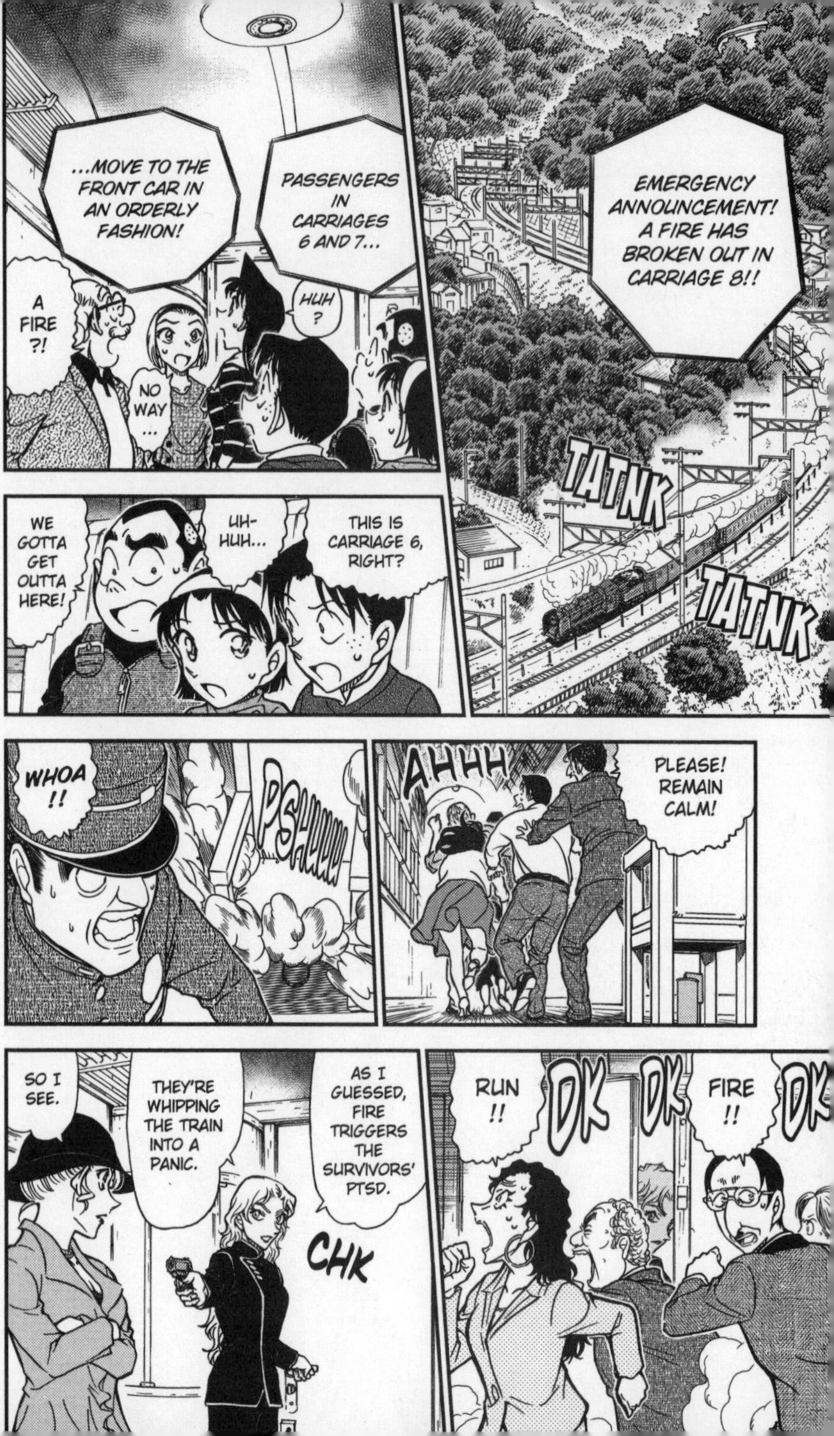
EMERGENCY ANNOUNCEMENT! A FIRE HAS BROKEN OUT IN CARRIAGE 8!!
TATNK
TATNK
PASSENGERS IN CARRIAGES 6 AND 7...
...MOVE TO THE FRONT CAR IN AN ORDERLY FASHION!
HUH?
A FIRE?!
NO WAY...
THIS IS CARRIAGE 6, RIGHT?
UH-HUH...
WE GOTTA GET OUTTA HERE!
PLEASE! REMAIN CALM!
AHHH
WHOA!!
DK
FIRE!!
DK
DK
RUN!!
AS I GUESSED, FIRE TRIGGERS THE SURVIVORS' PTSD.
CHK
THEY'RE WHIPPING THE TRAIN INTO A PANIC.
SO I SEE.

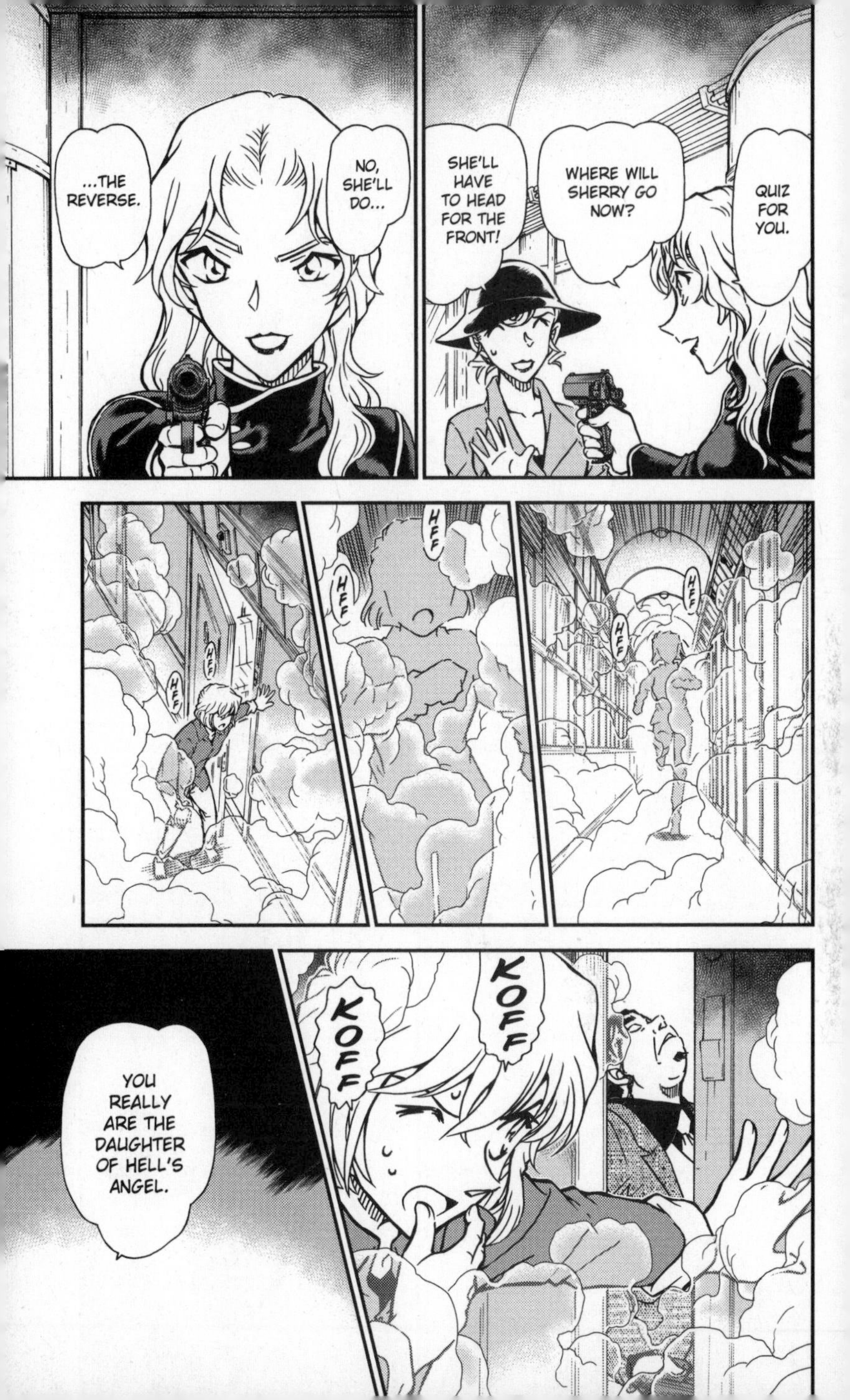
QUIZ FOR YOU.
WHERE WILL SHERRY GO NOW?
SHE'LL HAVE TO HEAD FOR THE FRONT!
NO, SHE'LL DO...
...THE REVERSE.
HFF
HFF
HFF
HFF
HFF
HFF
KOFF
KOFF
YOU REALLY ARE THE DAUGHTER OF HELL'S ANGEL.

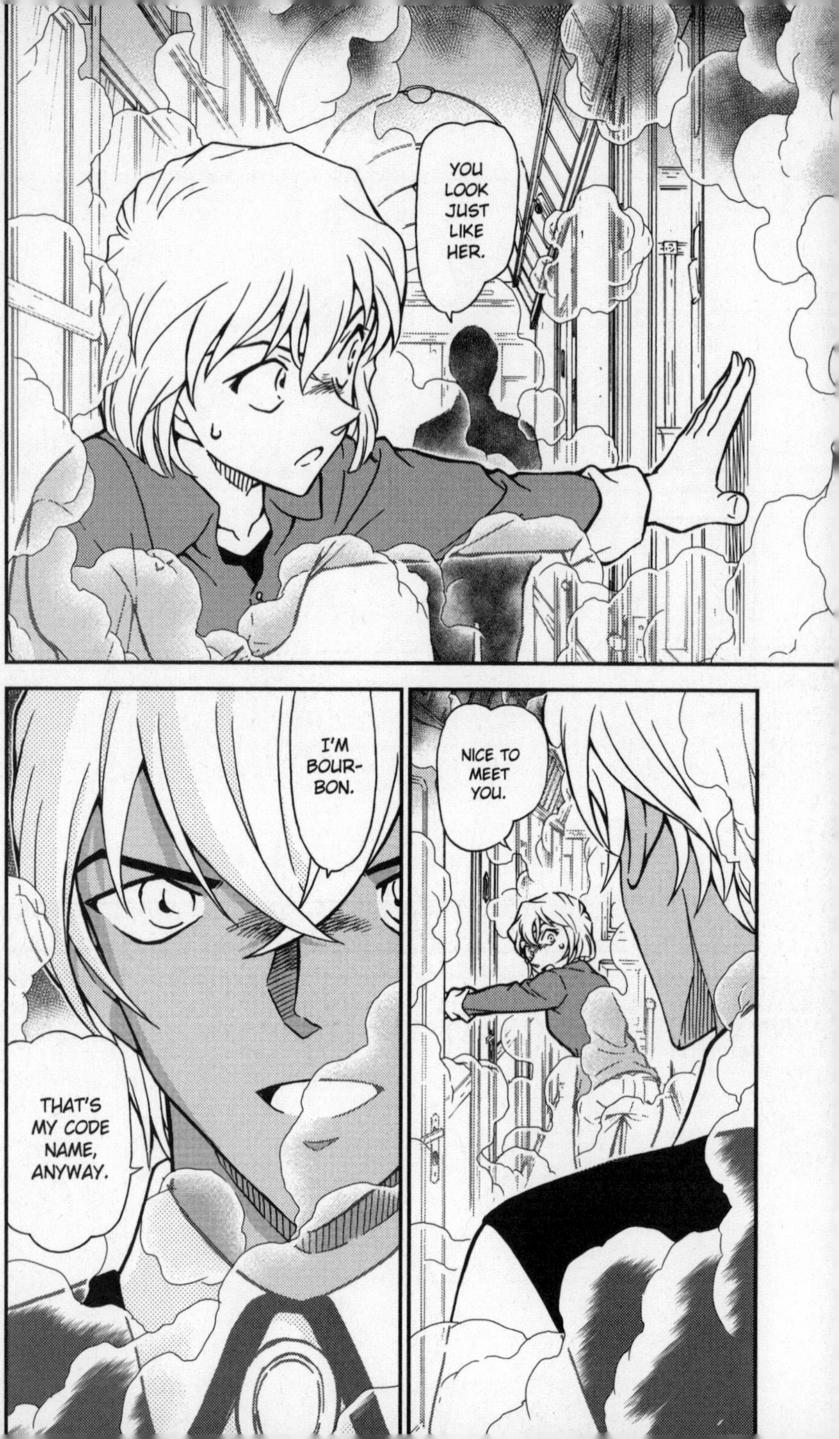
YOU LOOK JUST LIKE HER.
NICE TO MEET YOU.
I'M BOUR-BON.
THAT'S MY CODE NAME, ANYWAY.

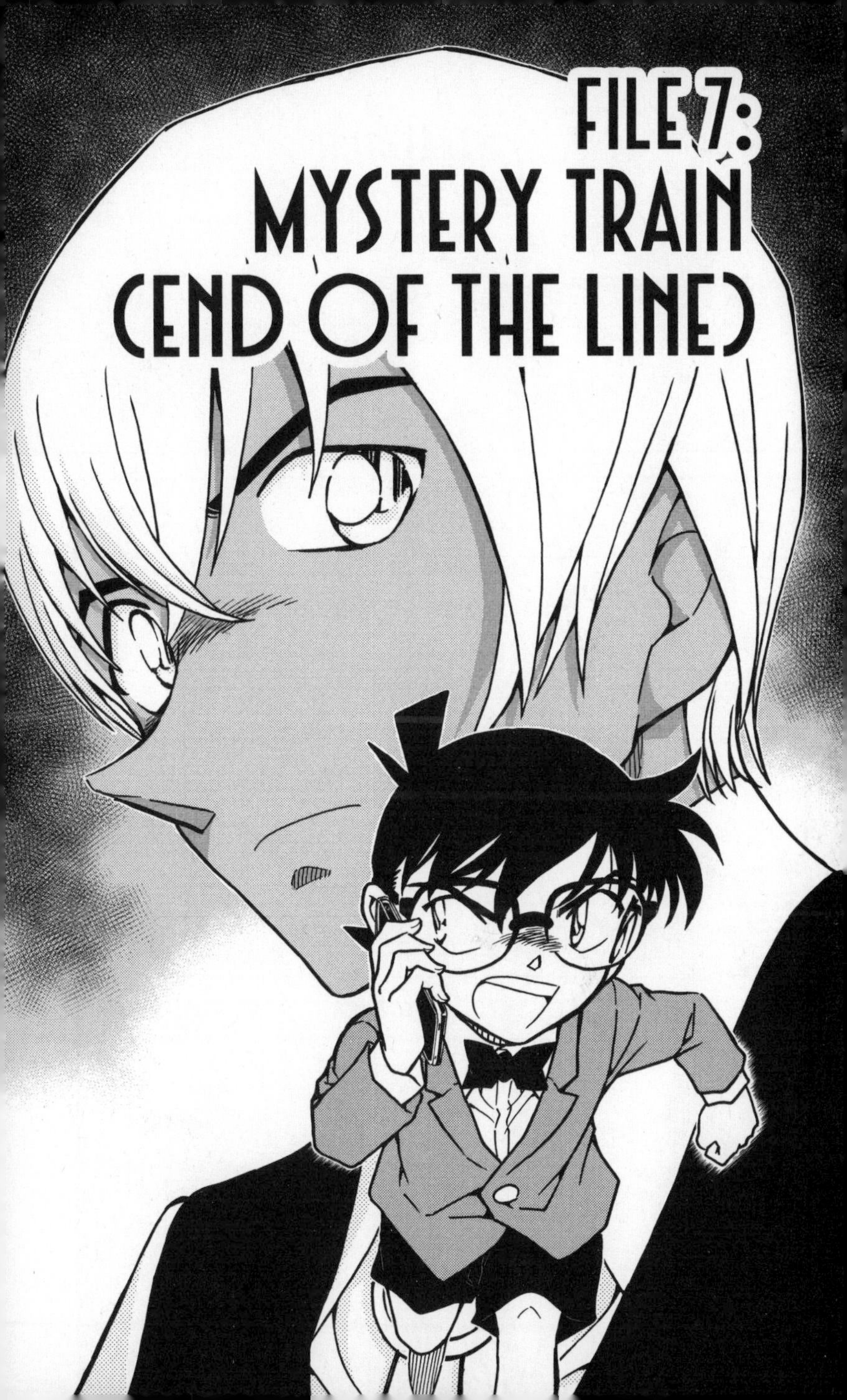
FILE 7:
MYSTERY TRAIN
(END OF THE LINE)

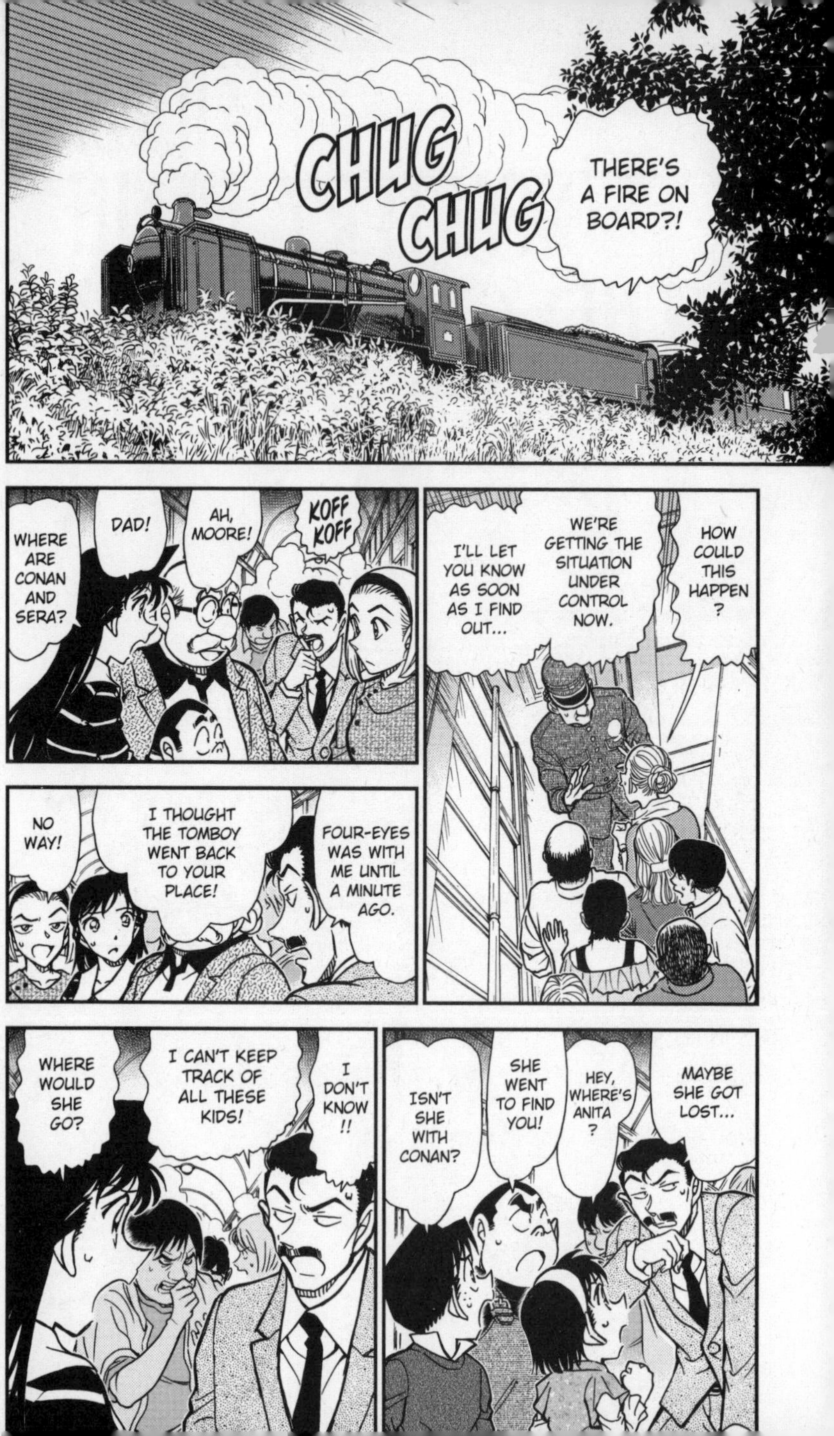
THERE'S A FIRE ON BOARD?!
CHUG CHUG
HOW COULD THIS HAPPEN?
WE'RE GETTING THE SITUATION UNDER CONTROL NOW.
I'LL LET YOU KNOW AS SOON AS I FIND OUT...
KOFF KOFF
AH, MOORE!
DAD!
WHERE ARE CONAN AND SERA?
FOUR-EYES WAS WITH ME UNTIL A MINUTE AGO.
I THOUGHT THE TOMBOY WENT BACK TO YOUR PLACE!
NO WAY!
MAYBE SHE GOT LOST...
HEY, WHERE'S ANITA?
SHE WENT TO FIND YOU!
ISN'T SHE WITH CONAN?
I DON'T KNOW!!
I CAN'T KEEP TRACK OF ALL THESE KIDS!
WHERE WOULD SHE GO?

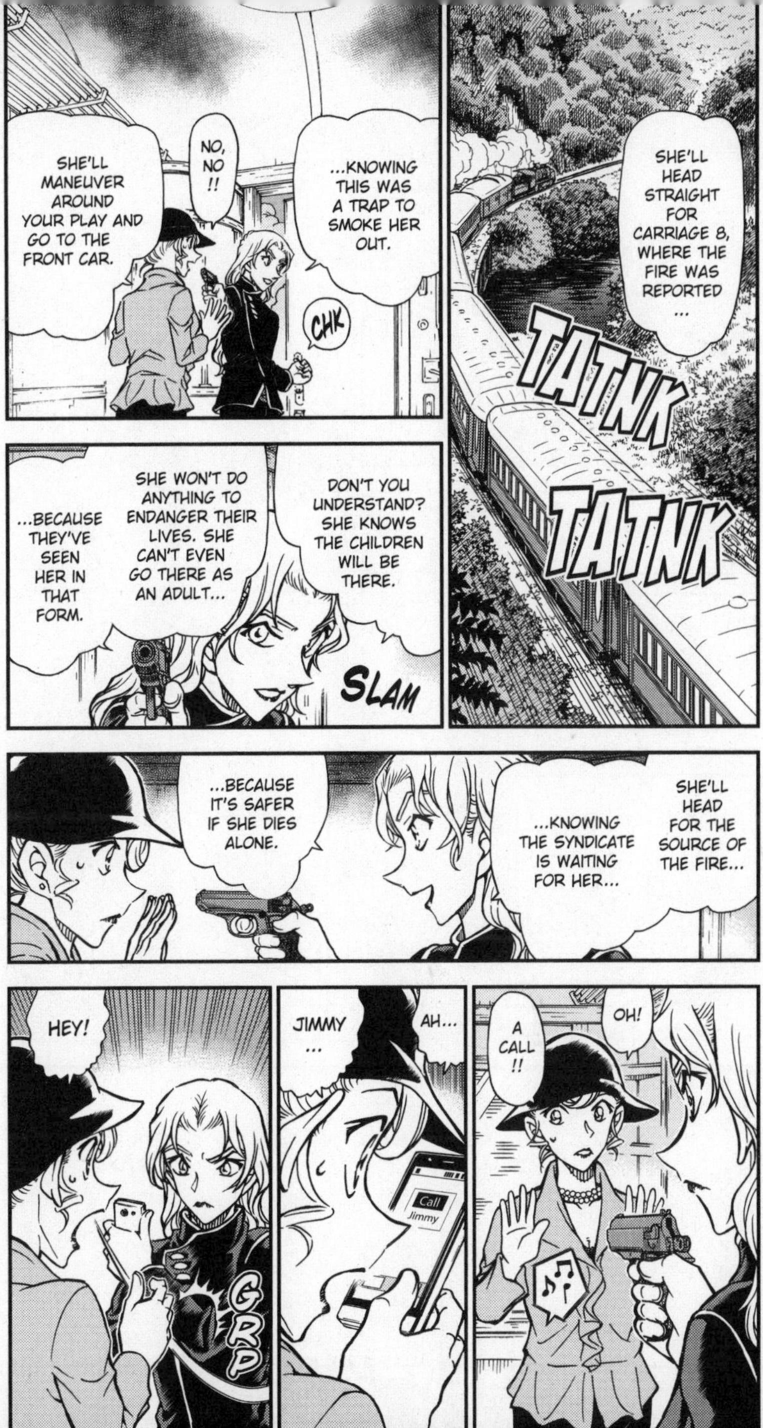
SHE'LL HEAD STRAIGHT FOR CARRIAGE 8, WHERE THE FIRE WAS REPORTED ...
TATNK
TATNK
...KNOWING THIS WAS A TRAP TO SMOKE HER OUT.
NO, NO !!
SHE'LL MANEUVER AROUND YOUR PLAY AND GO TO THE FRONT CAR.
CHK
DON'T YOU UNDERSTAND? SHE KNOWS THE CHILDREN WILL BE THERE.
SHE WON'T DO ANYTHING TO ENDANGER THEIR LIVES. SHE CAN'T EVEN GO THERE AS AN ADULT...
...BECAUSE THEY'VE SEEN HER IN THAT FORM.
SLAM
SHE'LL HEAD FOR THE SOURCE OF THE FIRE...
...KNOWING THE SYNDICATE IS WAITING FOR HER...
...BECAUSE IT'S SAFER IF SHE DIES ALONE.
OH!
A CALL !!
AH...
JIMMY ...
Call
Jimmy
HEY!
GRP

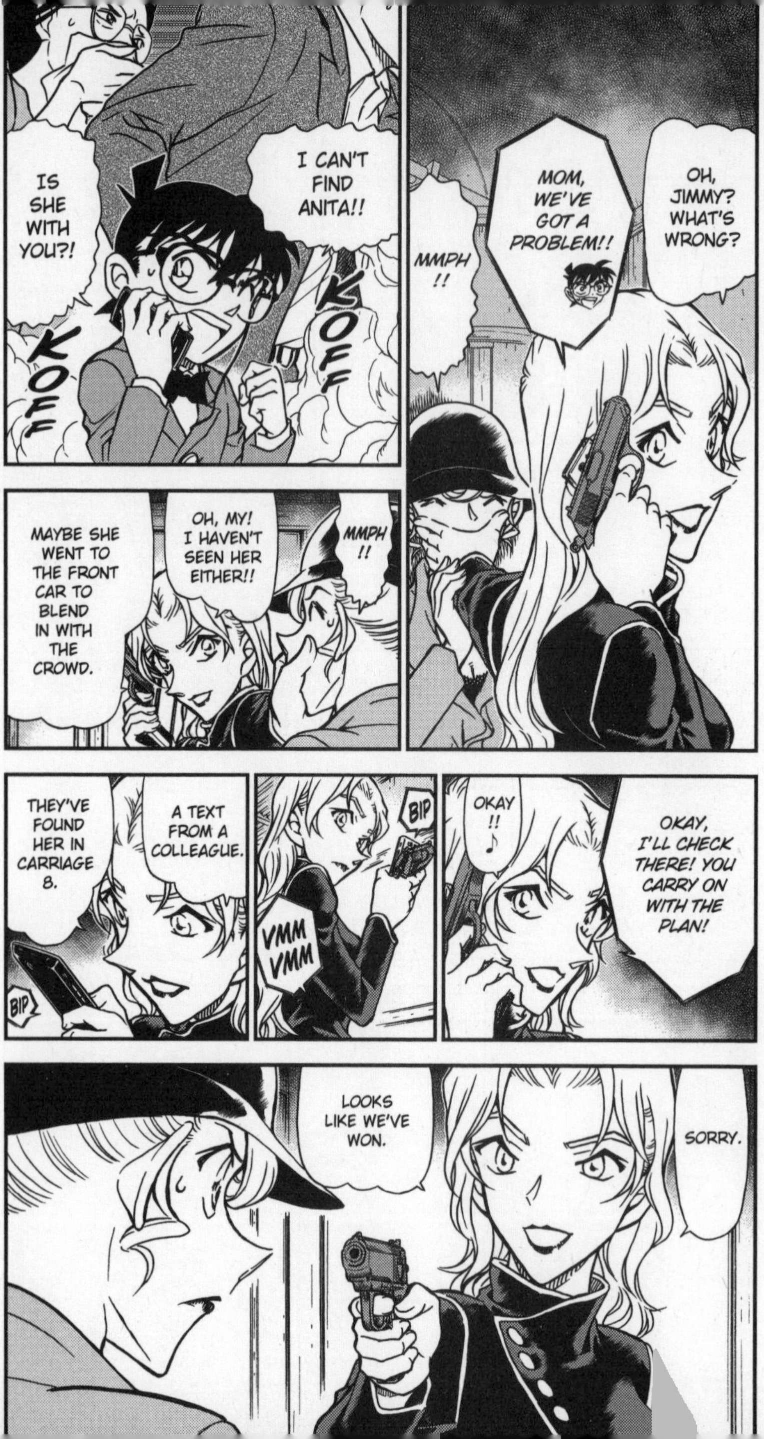
OH, JIMMY? WHAT'S WRONG?
MOM, WE'VE GOT A PROBLEM!!
MMPH !!
I CAN'T FIND ANITA!!
IS SHE WITH YOU?!
KOFF
KOFF
MMPH !!
OH, MY! I HAVEN'T SEEN HER EITHER!!
MAYBE SHE WENT TO THE FRONT CAR TO BLEND IN WITH THE CROWD.
OKAY, I'LL CHECK THERE! YOU CARRY ON WITH THE PLAN!
OKAY !! ♪
BIP
VMM VMM
A TEXT FROM A COLLEAGUE.
THEY'VE FOUND HER IN CARRIAGE 8.
BIP
SORRY.
LOOKS LIKE WE'VE WON.

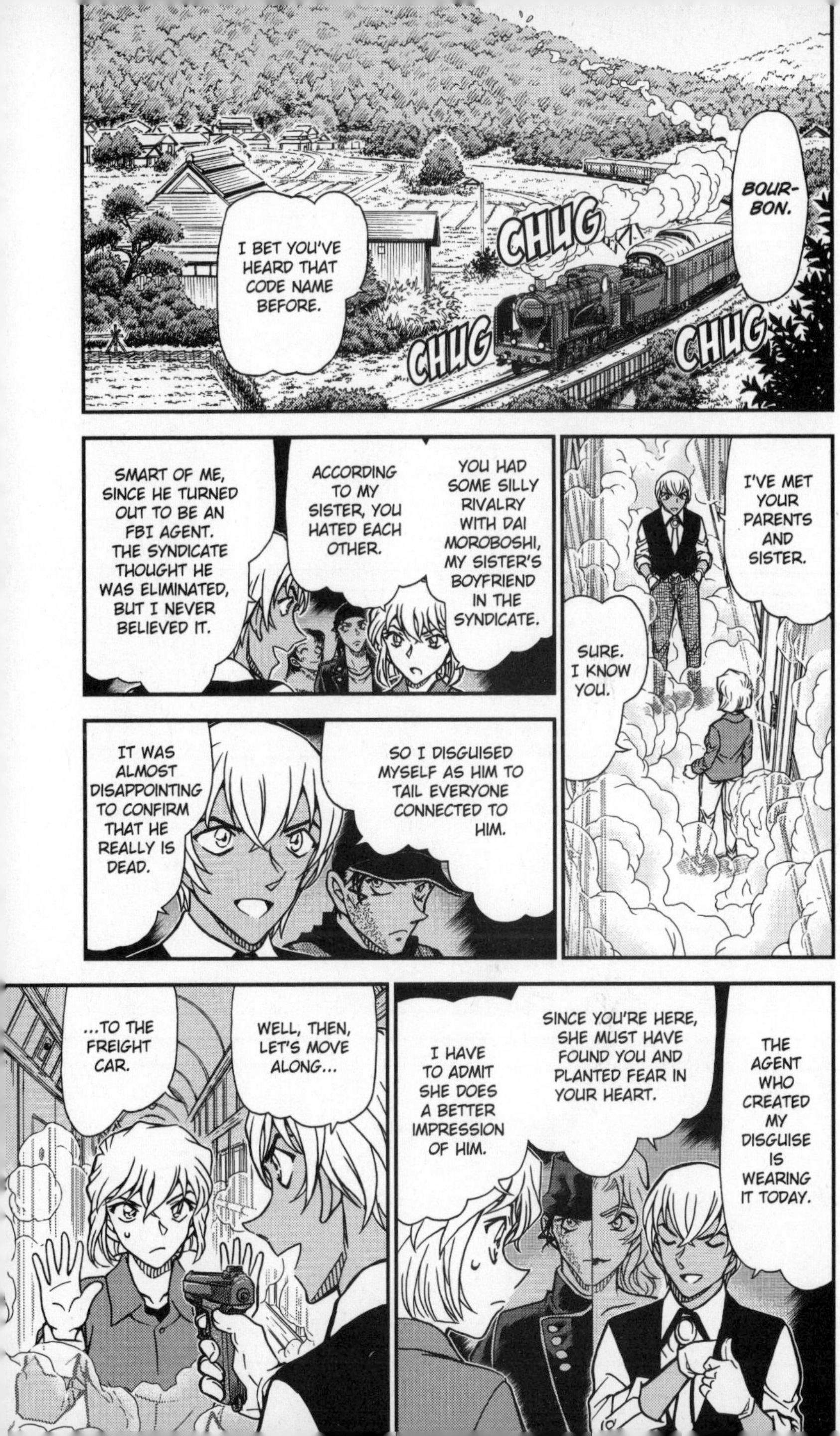
BOUR-BON.
CHUG
I BET YOU'VE HEARD THAT CODE NAME BEFORE.
CHUG
CHUG
I'VE MET YOUR PARENTS AND SISTER.
SURE. I KNOW YOU.
YOU HAD SOME SILLY RIVALRY WITH DAI MOROBOSHI, MY SISTER'S BOYFRIEND IN THE SYNDICATE.
ACCORDING TO MY SISTER, YOU HATED EACH OTHER.
SMART OF ME, SINCE HE TURNED OUT TO BE AN FBI AGENT. THE SYNDICATE THOUGHT HE WAS ELIMINATED, BUT I NEVER BELIEVED IT.
SO I DISGUISED MYSELF AS HIM TO TAIL EVERYONE CONNECTED TO HIM.
IT WAS ALMOST DISAPPOINTING TO CONFIRM THAT HE REALLY IS DEAD.
THE AGENT WHO CREATED MY DISGUISE IS WEARING IT TODAY.
SINCE YOU'RE HERE, SHE MUST HAVE FOUND YOU AND PLANTED FEAR IN YOUR HEART.
I HAVE TO ADMIT SHE DOES A BETTER IMPRESSION OF HIM.
WELL, THEN, LET'S MOVE ALONG...
...TO THE FREIGHT CAR.

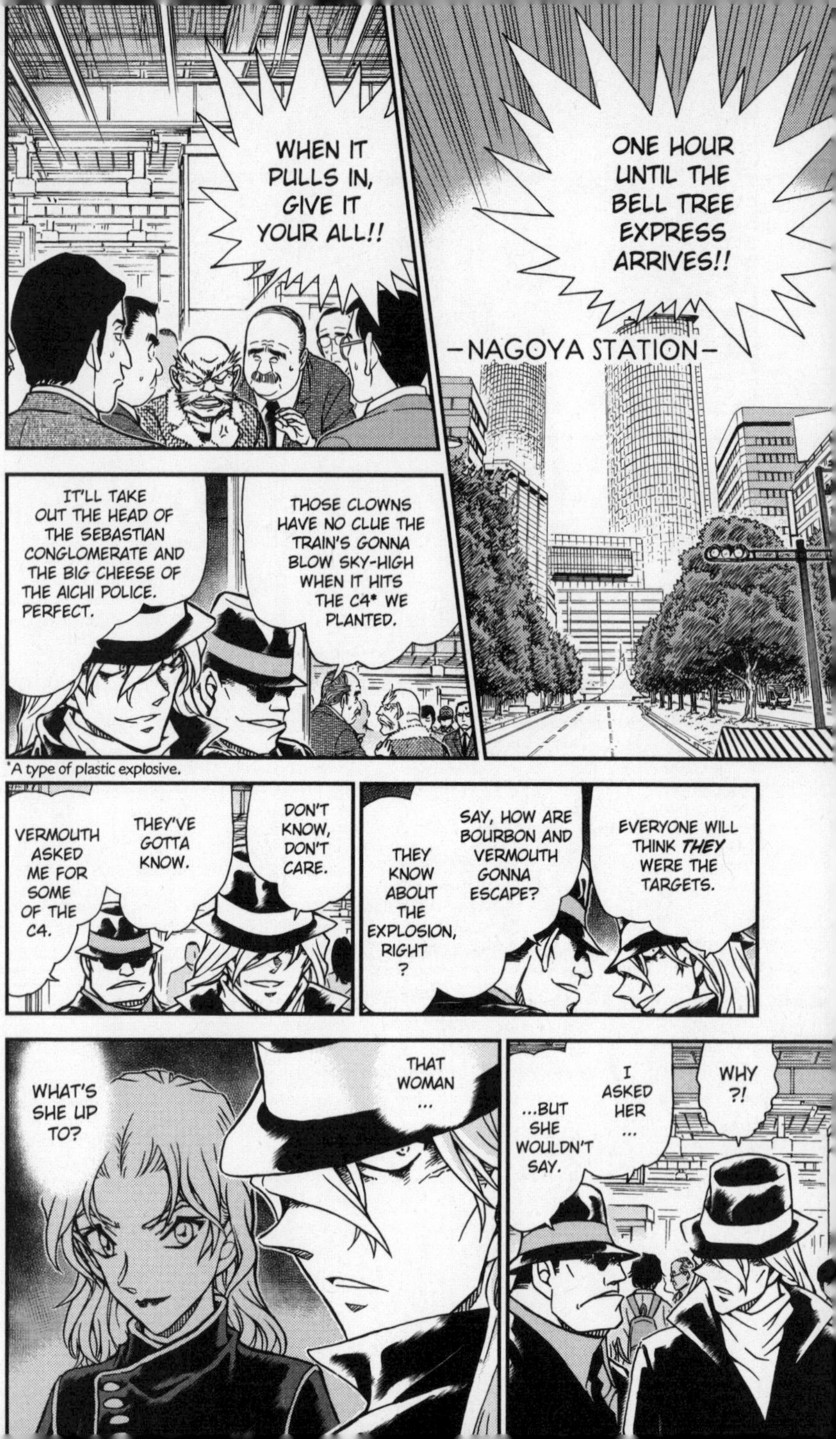
ONE HOUR UNTIL THE BELL TREE EXPRESS ARRIVES!!
—NAGOYA STATION—
WHEN IT PULLS IN, GIVE IT YOUR ALL!!
THOSE CLOWNS HAVE NO CLUE THE TRAIN'S GONNA BLOW SKY-HIGH WHEN IT HITS THE C4* WE PLANTED.
IT'LL TAKE OUT THE HEAD OF THE SEBASTIAN CONGLOMERATE AND THE BIG CHEESE OF THE AICHI POLICE. PERFECT.
EVERYONE WILL THINK *THEY* WERE THE TARGETS.
SAY, HOW ARE BOURBON AND VERMOUTH GONNA ESCAPE?
THEY KNOW ABOUT THE EXPLOSION, RIGHT?
DON'T KNOW, DON'T CARE.
THEY'VE GOTTA KNOW.
VERMOUTH ASKED ME FOR SOME OF THE C4.
WHY?!
I ASKED HER...
...BUT SHE WOULDN'T SAY.
THAT WOMAN...
WHAT'S SHE UP TO?

*A type of plastic explosive.

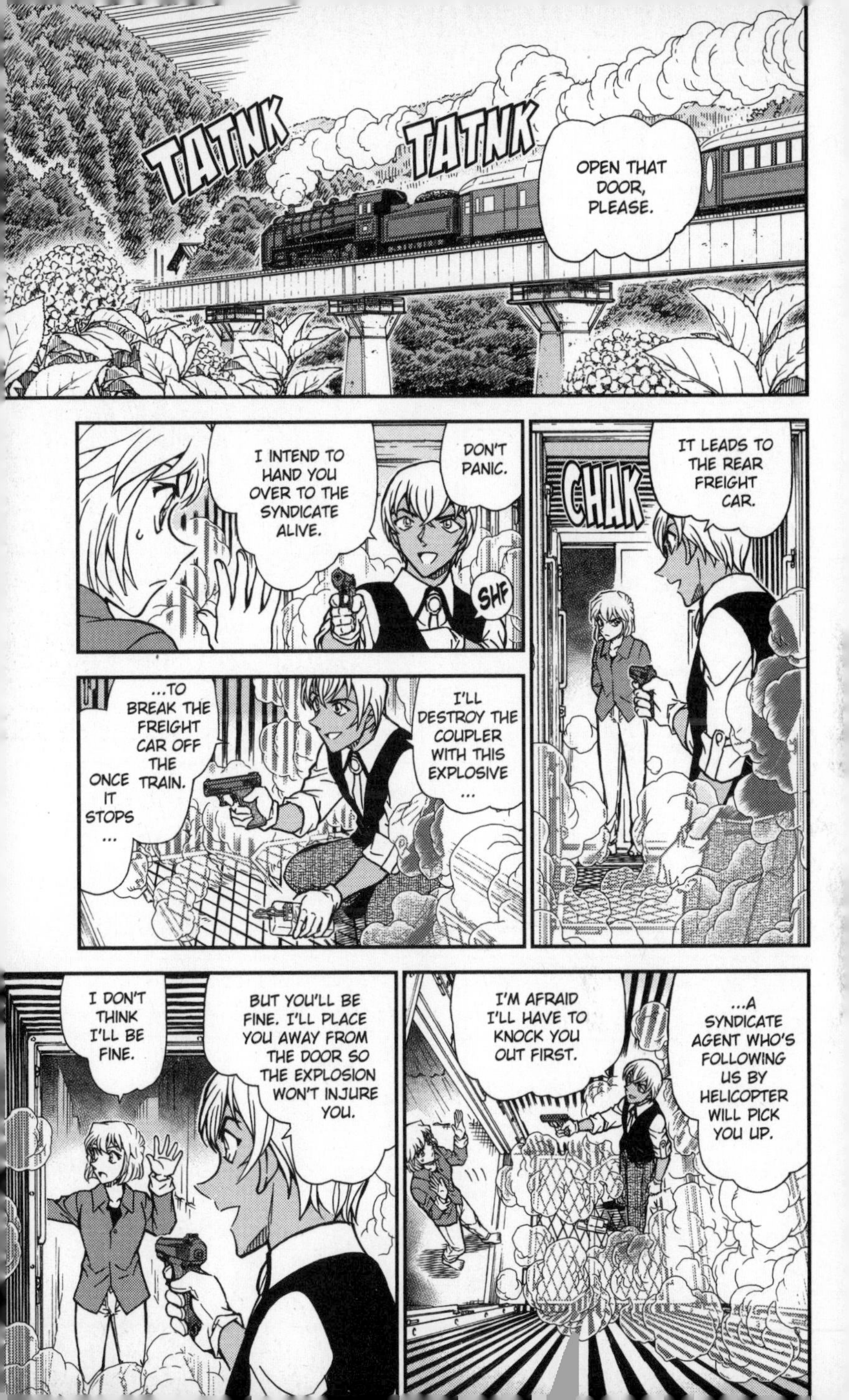
OPEN THAT DOOR, PLEASE.
TATNK
TATNK
IT LEADS TO THE REAR FREIGHT CAR.
CHAK
DON'T PANIC.
I INTEND TO HAND YOU OVER TO THE SYNDICATE ALIVE.
SHF
I'LL DESTROY THE COUPLER WITH THIS EXPLOSIVE ...
...TO BREAK THE FREIGHT CAR OFF THE TRAIN.
ONCE IT STOPS ...
...A SYNDICATE AGENT WHO'S FOLLOWING US BY HELICOPTER WILL PICK YOU UP.
I'M AFRAID I'LL HAVE TO KNOCK YOU OUT FIRST.
BUT YOU'LL BE FINE. I'LL PLACE YOU AWAY FROM THE DOOR SO THE EXPLOSION WON'T INJURE YOU.
I DON'T THINK I'LL BE FINE.

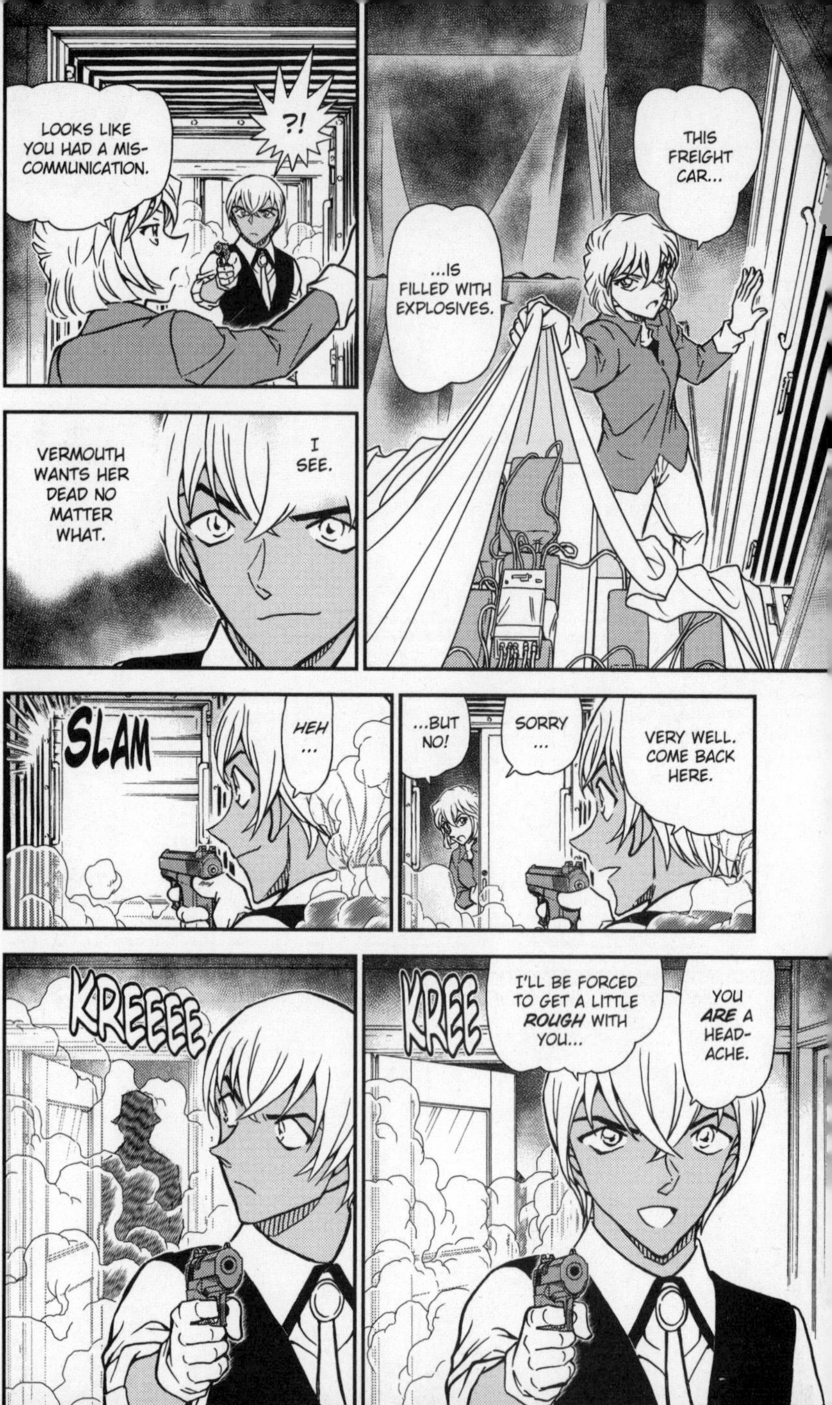
THIS FREIGHT CAR...
...IS FILLED WITH EXPLOSIVES.
?!
LOOKS LIKE YOU HAD A MIS-COMMUNICATION.
I SEE.
VERMOUTH WANTS HER DEAD NO MATTER WHAT.
VERY WELL. COME BACK HERE.
SORRY...
...BUT NO!
HEH...
SLAM
YOU *ARE* A HEAD-ACHE.
I'LL BE FORCED TO GET A LITTLE *ROUGH* WITH YOU...
KREE
KREEEEE

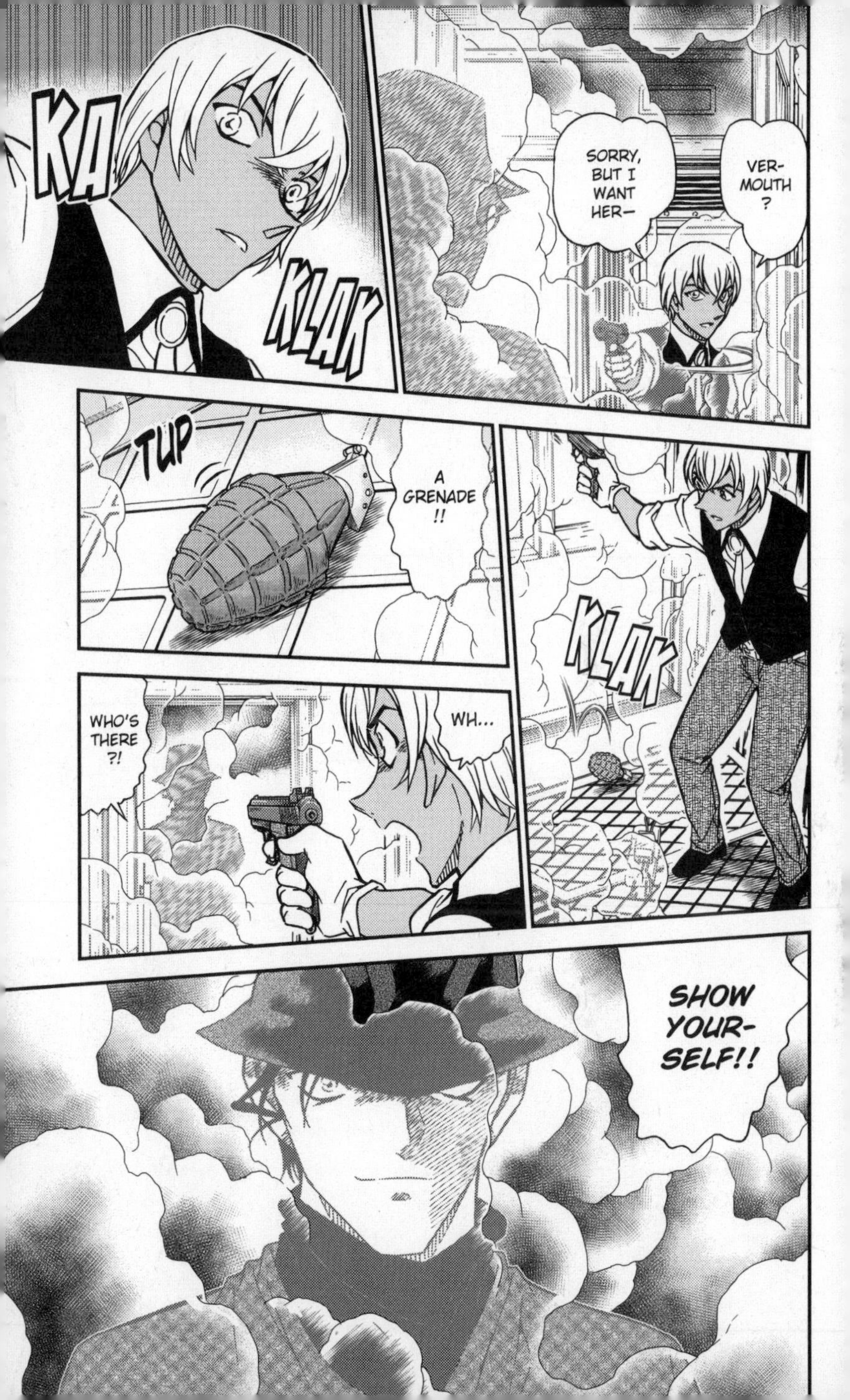
VER-MOUTH?
SORRY, BUT I WANT HER—
KA
KLAK
KLAK
A GRENADE!!
TUP
WH...
WHO'S THERE?!
SHOW YOUR-SELF!!

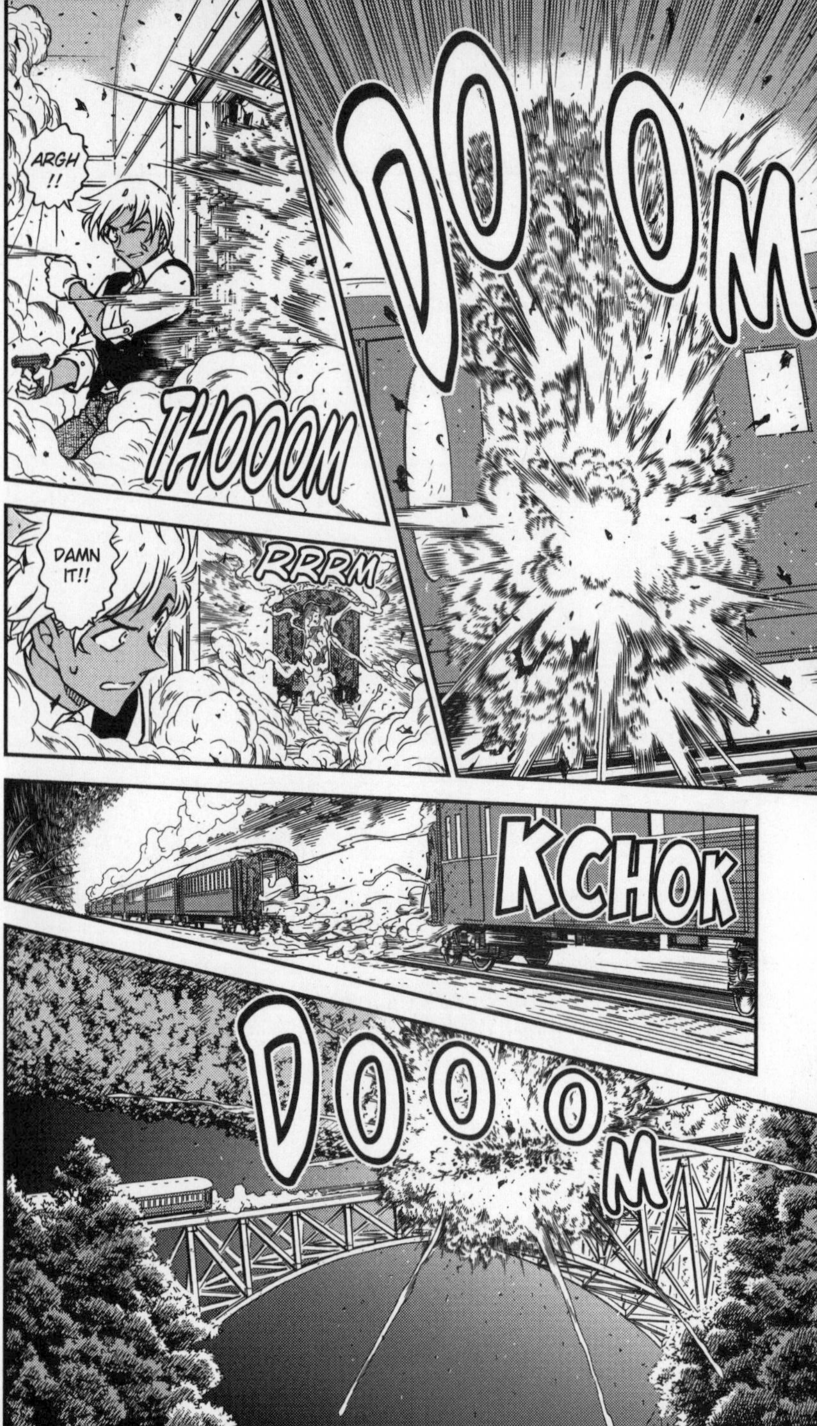
DOOM
ARGH!!
THOOOM
DAMN IT!!
RRRM
KCHOK
DOOOM

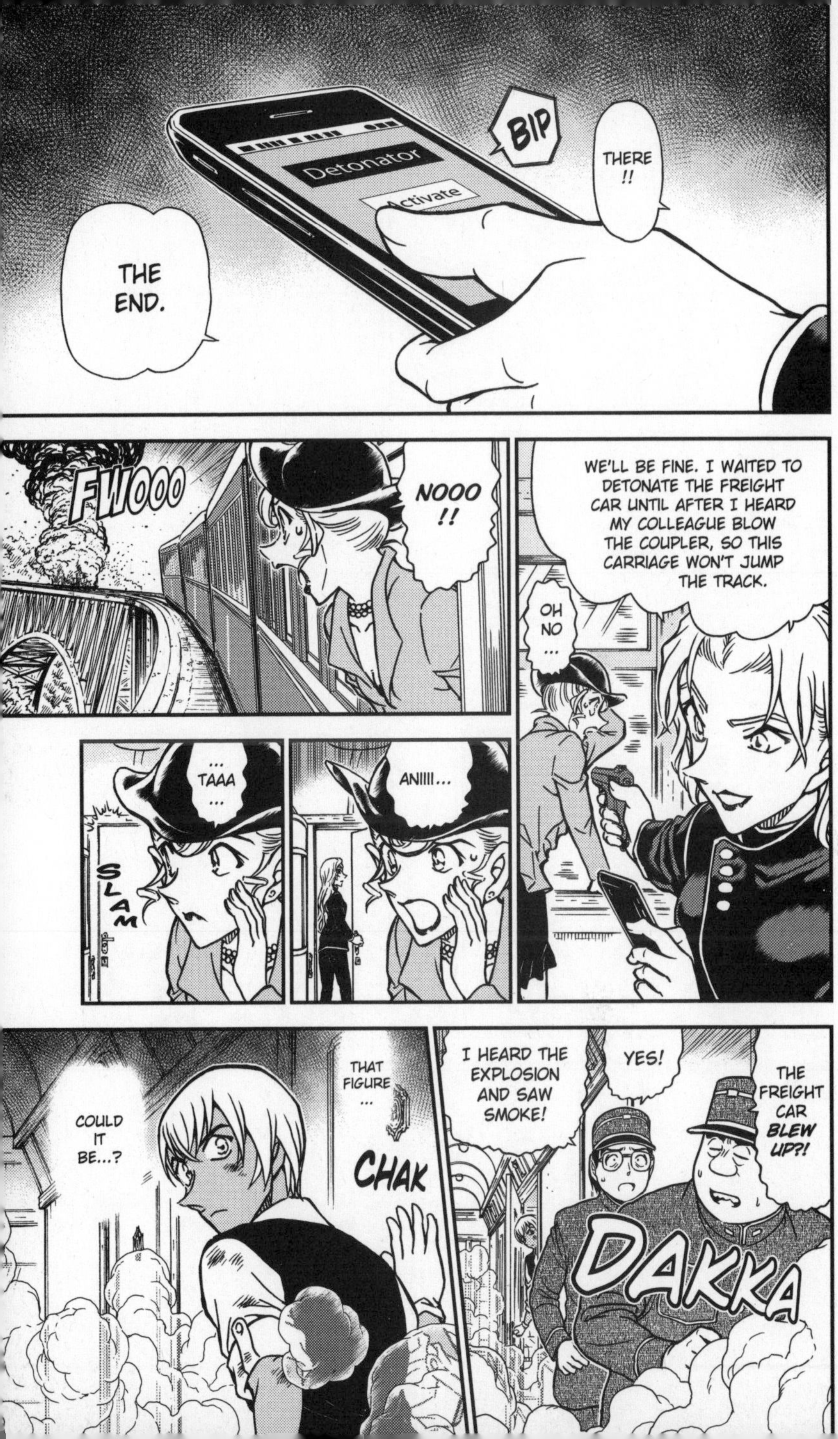
BIP
THERE!!
Detonator
Activate
THE END.
WE'LL BE FINE. I WAITED TO DETONATE THE FREIGHT CAR UNTIL AFTER I HEARD MY COLLEAGUE BLOW THE COUPLER, SO THIS CARRIAGE WON'T JUMP THE TRACK.
OH NO...
NOOO!!
FWOOO
ANIIII...
...TAAA...
SLAM
THE FREIGHT CAR BLEW UP?!
YES!
I HEARD THE EXPLOSION AND SAW SMOKE!
DAKKA
THAT FIGURE...
CHAK
COULD IT BE...?

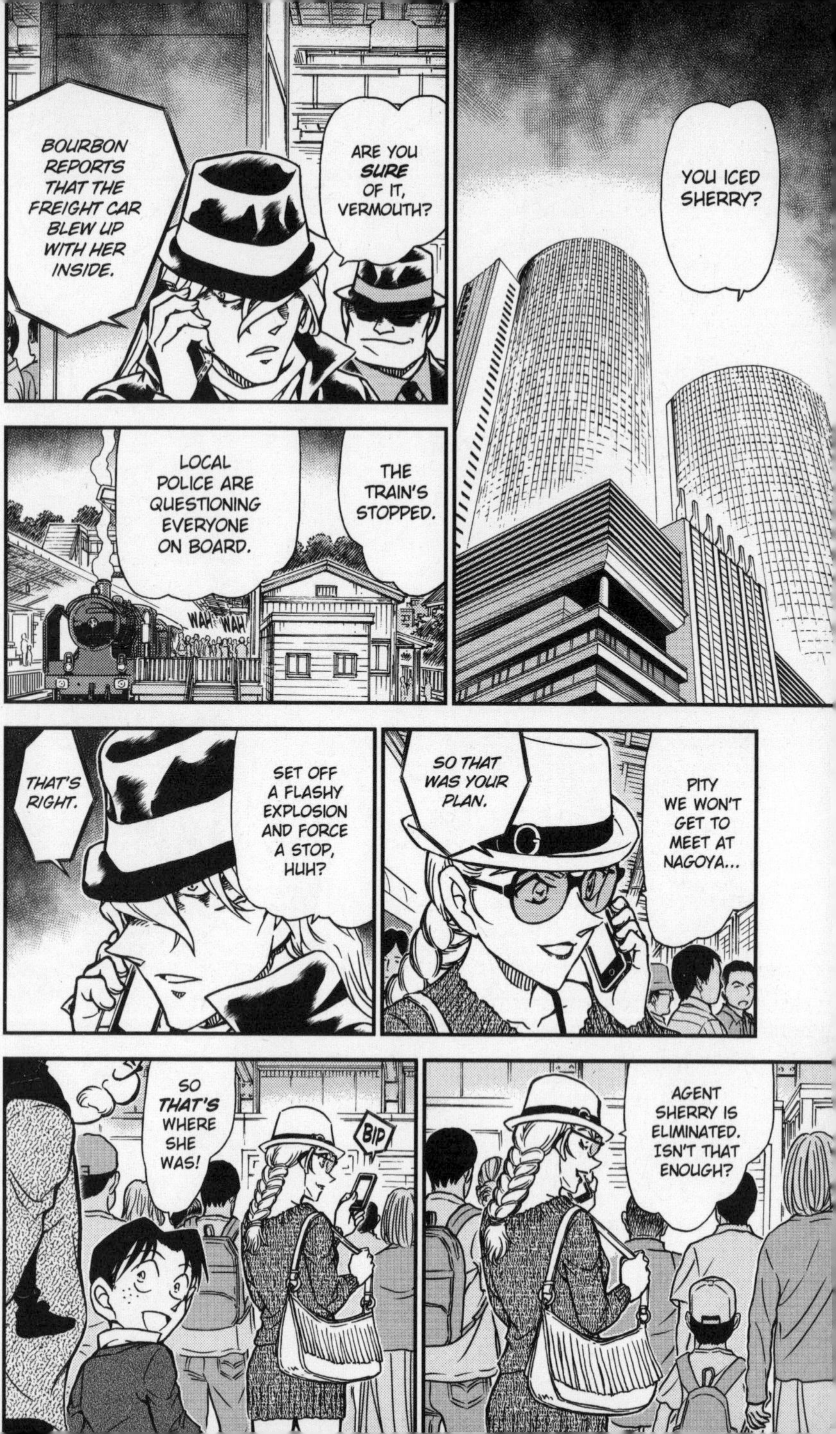
YOU ICED SHERRY?
ARE YOU *SURE* OF IT, VERMOUTH?
BOURBON REPORTS THAT THE FREIGHT CAR BLEW UP WITH HER INSIDE.
THE TRAIN'S STOPPED.
LOCAL POLICE ARE QUESTIONING EVERYONE ON BOARD.
WAH WAH
PITY WE WON'T GET TO MEET AT NAGOYA...
SO THAT WAS YOUR PLAN.
SET OFF A FLASHY EXPLOSION AND FORCE A STOP, HUH?
THAT'S RIGHT.
AGENT SHERRY IS ELIMINATED. ISN'T THAT ENOUGH?
BIP
SO *THAT'S* WHERE SHE WAS!

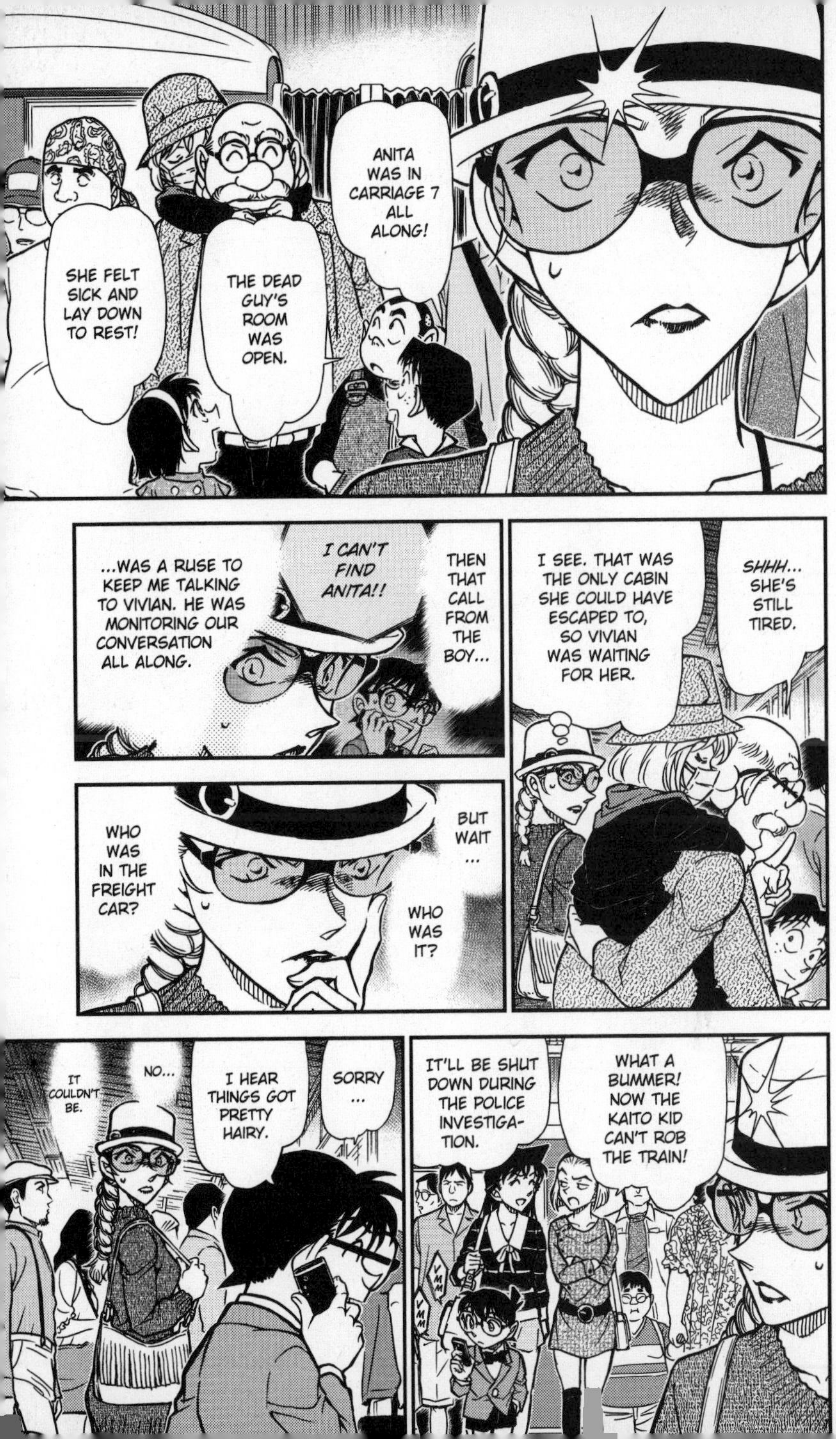
ANITA WAS IN CARRIAGE 7 ALL ALONG!
THE DEAD GUY'S ROOM WAS OPEN.
SHE FELT SICK AND LAY DOWN TO REST!
SHHH... SHE'S STILL TIRED.
I SEE. THAT WAS THE ONLY CABIN SHE COULD HAVE ESCAPED TO, SO VIVIAN WAS WAITING FOR HER.
THEN THAT CALL FROM THE BOY...
I CAN'T FIND ANITA!!
...WAS A RUSE TO KEEP ME TALKING TO VIVIAN. HE WAS MONITORING OUR CONVERSATION ALL ALONG.
BUT WAIT...
WHO WAS IN THE FREIGHT CAR?
WHO WAS IT?
WHAT A BUMMER! NOW THE KAITO KID CAN'T ROB THE TRAIN!
IT'LL BE SHUT DOWN DURING THE POLICE INVESTIGATION.
VMM
VMM
SORRY...
I HEAR THINGS GOT PRETTY HAIRY.
NO...
IT COULDN'T BE.

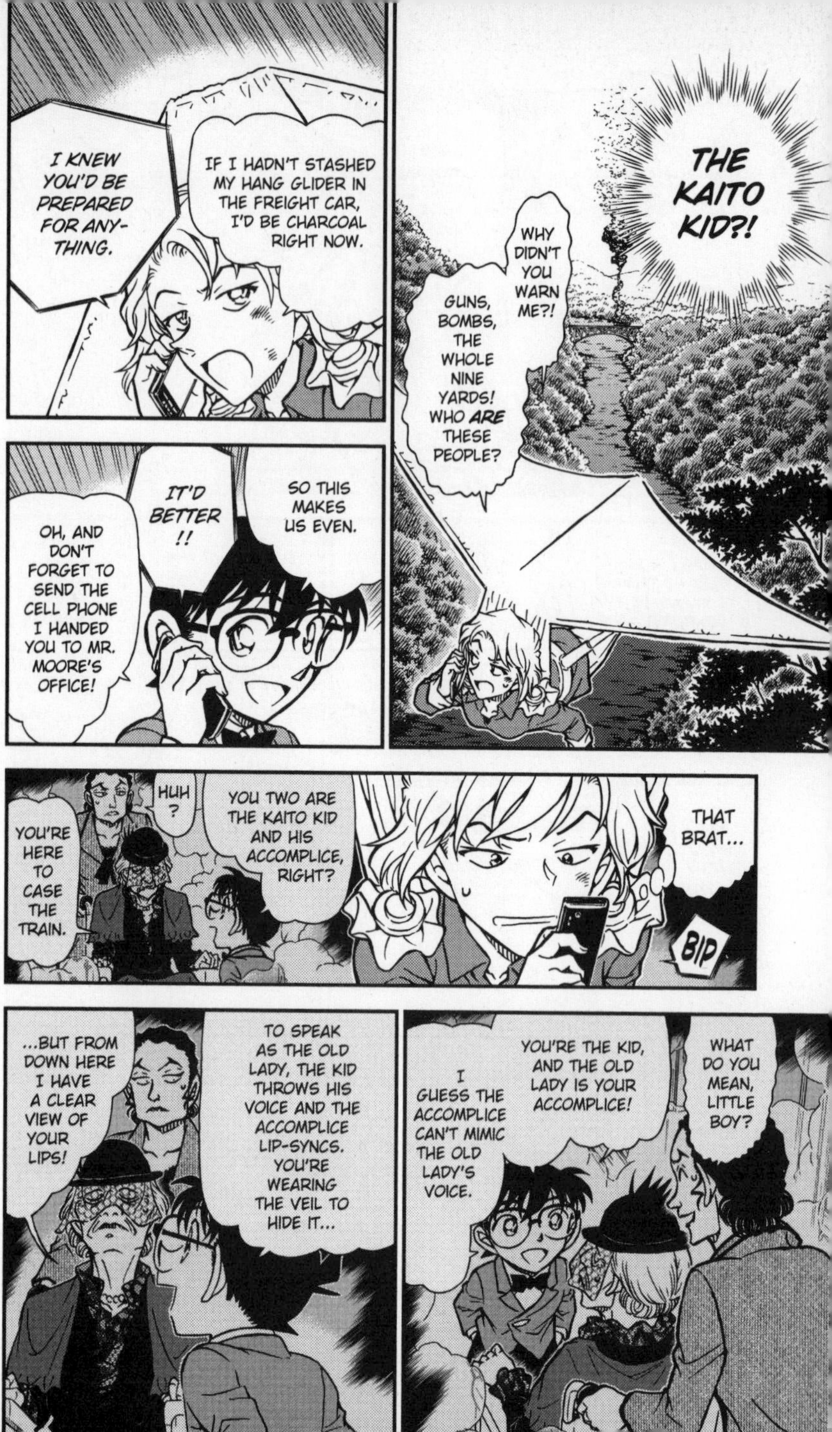
THE KAITO KID?!
WHY DIDN'T YOU WARN ME?!
GUNS, BOMBS, THE WHOLE NINE YARDS! WHO *ARE* THESE PEOPLE?
IF I HADN'T STASHED MY HANG GLIDER IN THE FREIGHT CAR, I'D BE CHARCOAL RIGHT NOW.
I KNEW YOU'D BE PREPARED FOR ANYTHING.
SO THIS MAKES US EVEN.
IT'D BETTER!!
OH, AND DON'T FORGET TO SEND THE CELL PHONE I HANDED YOU TO MR. MOORE'S OFFICE!
THAT BRAT...
BIP
YOU TWO ARE THE KAITO KID AND HIS ACCOMPLICE, RIGHT?
HUH?
YOU'RE HERE TO CASE THE TRAIN.
WHAT DO YOU MEAN, LITTLE BOY?
YOU'RE THE KID, AND THE OLD LADY IS YOUR ACCOMPLICE!
I GUESS THE ACCOMPLICE CAN'T MIMIC THE OLD LADY'S VOICE.
TO SPEAK AS THE OLD LADY, THE KID THROWS HIS VOICE AND THE ACCOMPLICE LIP-SYNCS. YOU'RE WEARING THE VEIL TO HIDE IT...
...BUT FROM DOWN HERE I HAVE A CLEAR VIEW OF YOUR LIPS!

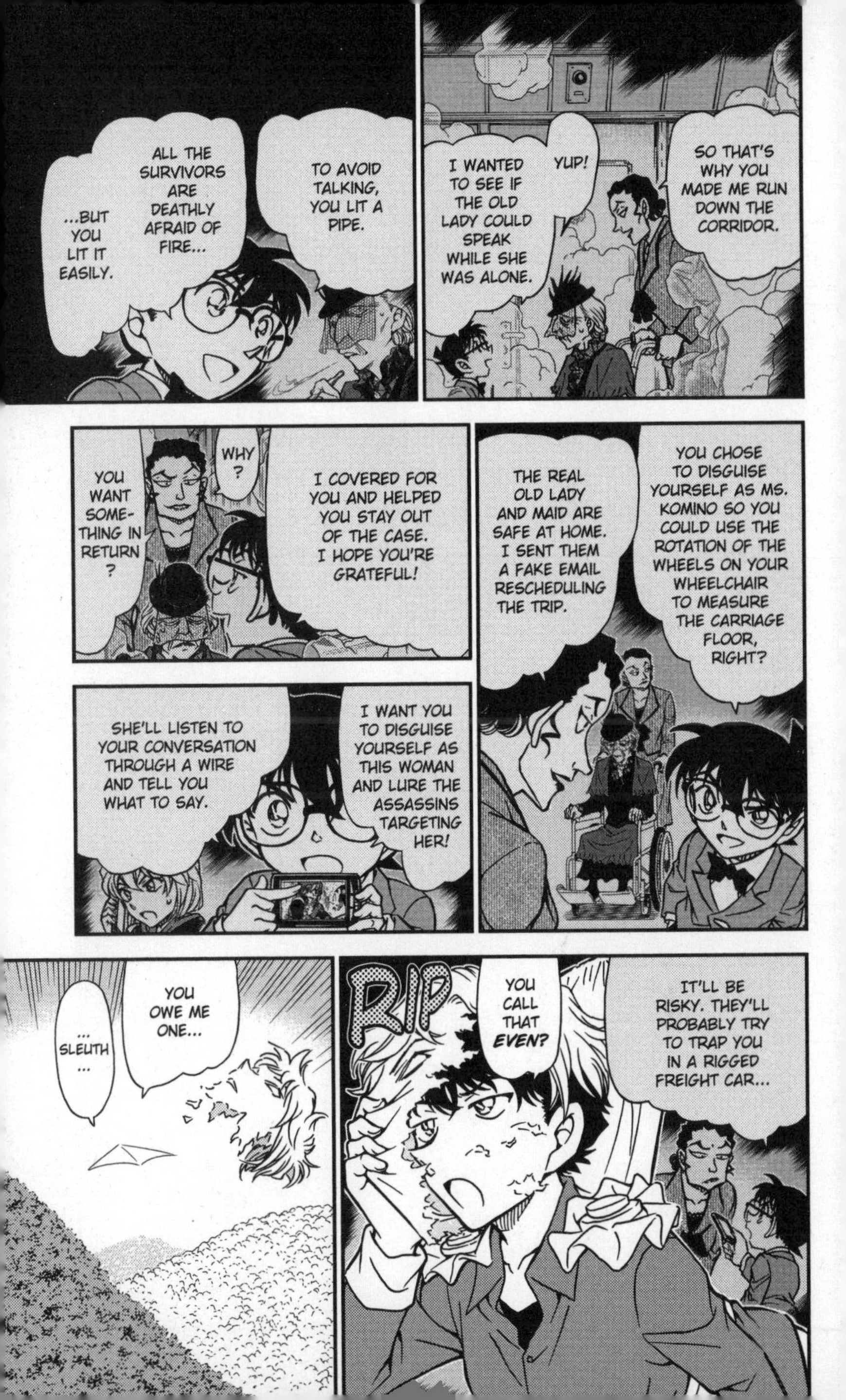

SO THAT'S WHY YOU MADE ME RUN DOWN THE CORRIDOR.
YUP!
I WANTED TO SEE IF THE OLD LADY COULD SPEAK WHILE SHE WAS ALONE.
TO AVOID TALKING, YOU LIT A PIPE.
ALL THE SURVIVORS ARE DEATHLY AFRAID OF FIRE...
...BUT YOU LIT IT EASILY.
YOU CHOSE TO DISGUISE YOURSELF AS MS. KOMINO SO YOU COULD USE THE ROTATION OF THE WHEELS ON YOUR WHEELCHAIR TO MEASURE THE CARRIAGE FLOOR, RIGHT?
THE REAL OLD LADY AND MAID ARE SAFE AT HOME. I SENT THEM A FAKE EMAIL RESCHEDULING THE TRIP.
I COVERED FOR YOU AND HELPED YOU STAY OUT OF THE CASE. I HOPE YOU'RE GRATEFUL!
WHY?
YOU WANT SOMETHING IN RETURN?
I WANT YOU TO DISGUISE YOURSELF AS THIS WOMAN AND LURE THE ASSASSINS TARGETING HER!
SHE'LL LISTEN TO YOUR CONVERSATION THROUGH A WIRE AND TELL YOU WHAT TO SAY.
IT'LL BE RISKY. THEY'LL PROBABLY TRY TO TRAP YOU IN A RIGGED FREIGHT CAR...
RIP
YOU CALL THAT *EVEN?*
YOU OWE ME ONE...
... SLEUTH ...

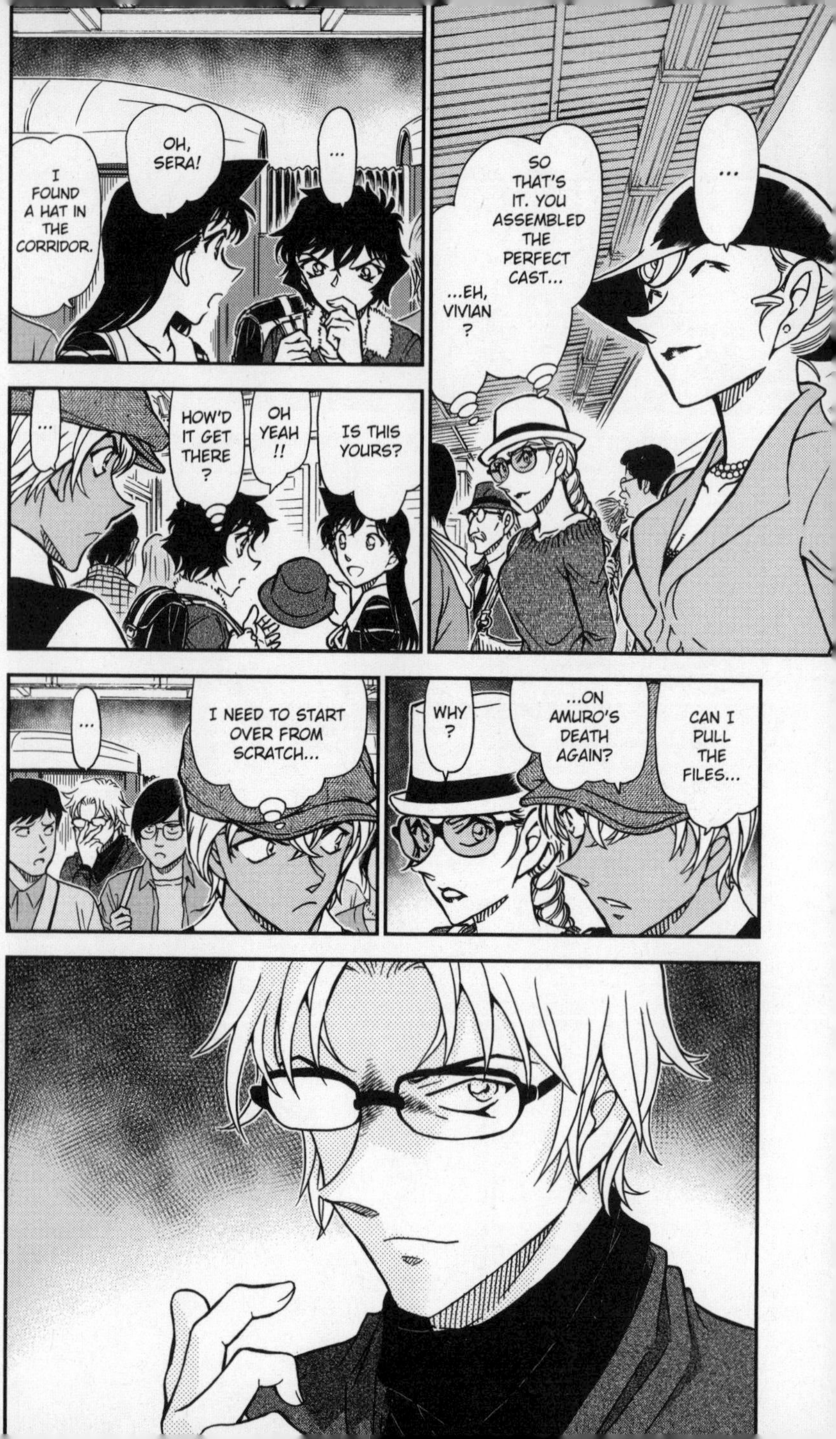
...
SO THAT'S IT. YOU ASSEMBLED THE PERFECT CAST... ...EH, VIVIAN?
...
OH, SERA!
I FOUND A HAT IN THE CORRIDOR.
IS THIS YOURS?
OH YEAH!!
HOW'D IT GET THERE?
...
CAN I PULL THE FILES...
...ON AMURO'S DEATH AGAIN?
WHY?
I NEED TO START OVER FROM SCRATCH...
...

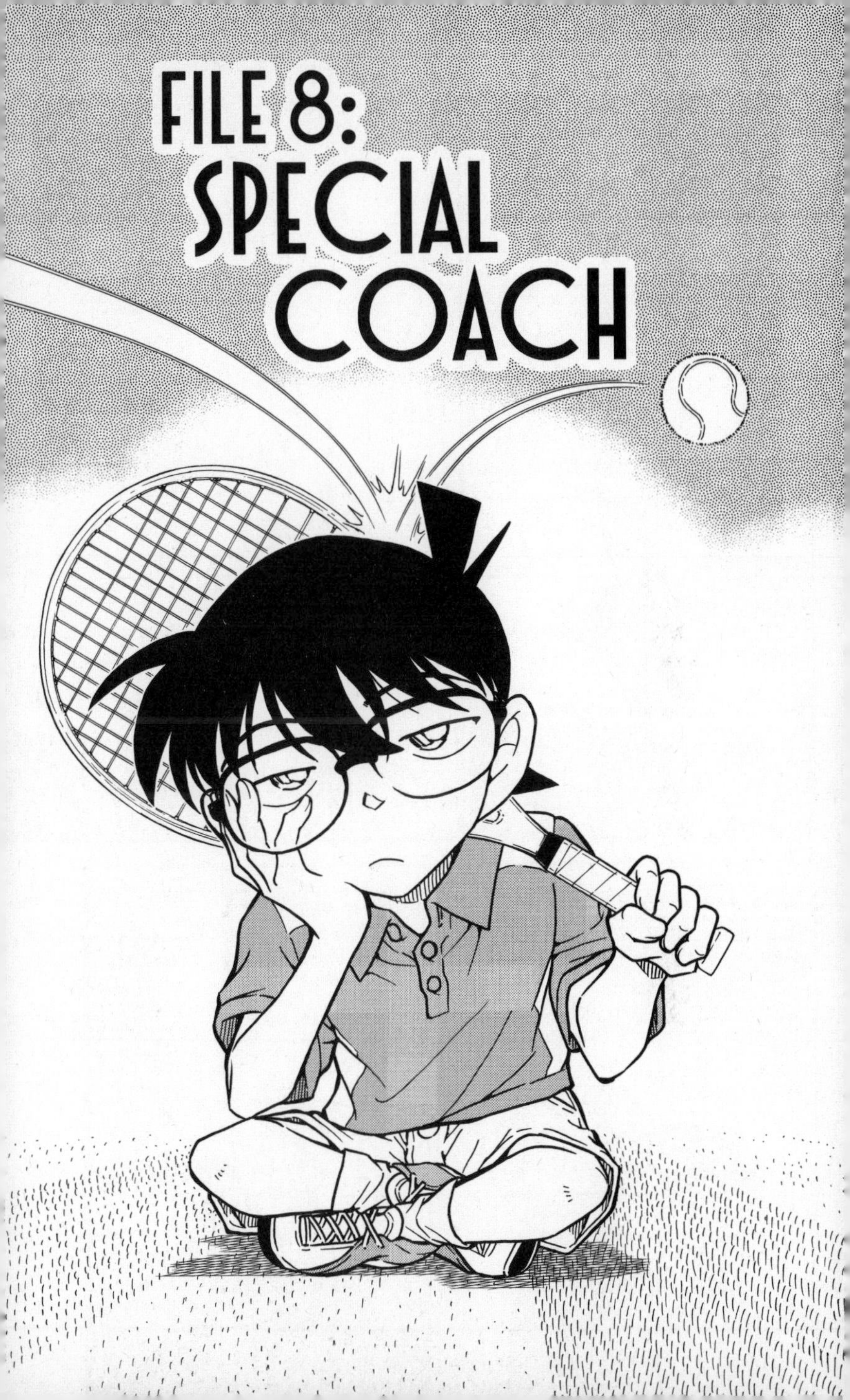
FILE 8:
SPECIAL
COACH

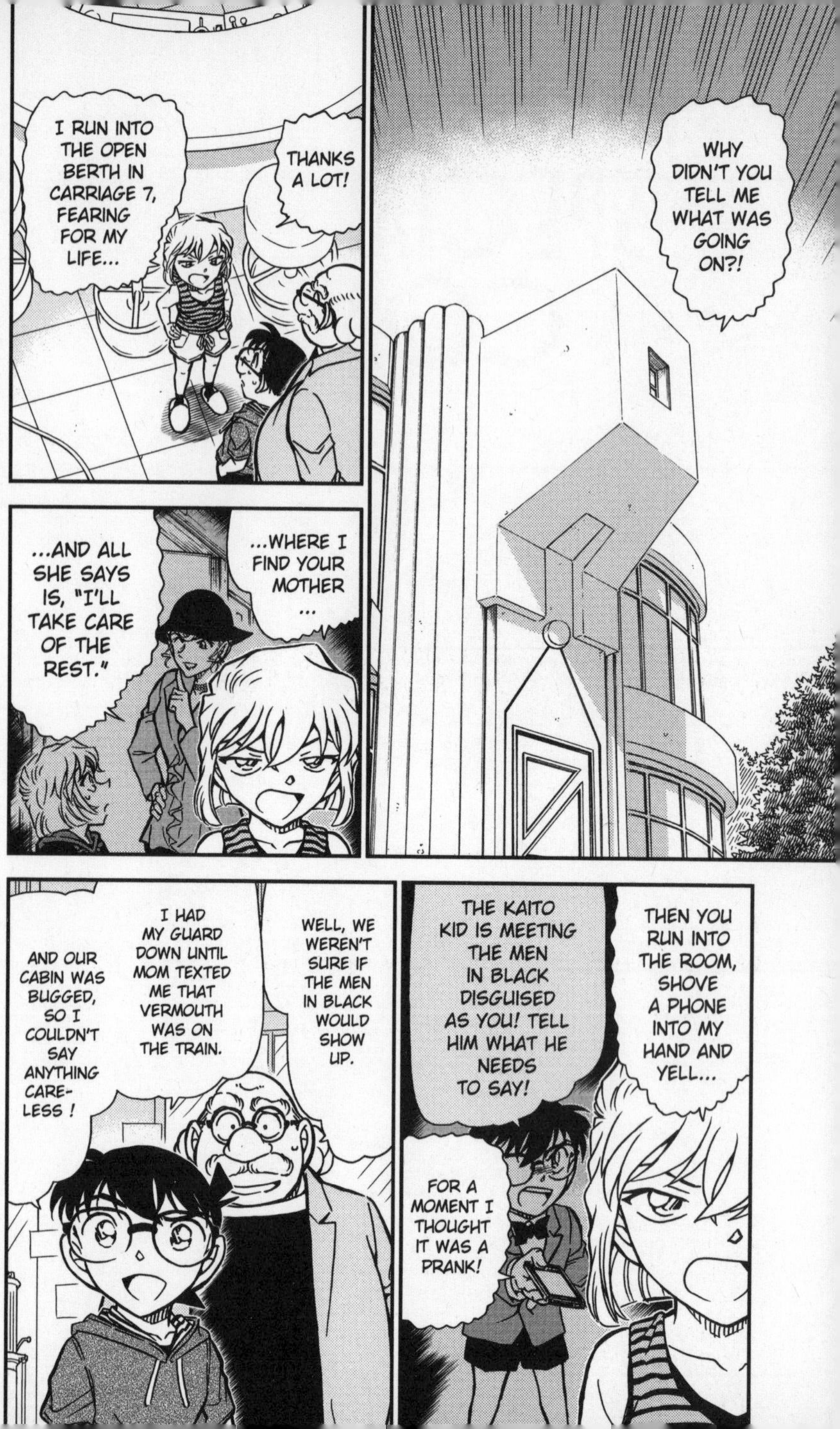
WHY DIDN'T YOU TELL ME WHAT WAS GOING ON?!
THANKS A LOT!
I RUN INTO THE OPEN BERTH IN CARRIAGE 7, FEARING FOR MY LIFE...
...WHERE I FIND YOUR MOTHER ...
...AND ALL SHE SAYS IS, "I'LL TAKE CARE OF THE REST."
THEN YOU RUN INTO THE ROOM, SHOVE A PHONE INTO MY HAND AND YELL...
THE KAITO KID IS MEETING THE MEN IN BLACK DISGUISED AS YOU! TELL HIM WHAT HE NEEDS TO SAY!
FOR A MOMENT I THOUGHT IT WAS A PRANK!
WELL, WE WEREN'T SURE IF THE MEN IN BLACK WOULD SHOW UP.
I HAD MY GUARD DOWN UNTIL MOM TEXTED ME THAT VERMOUTH WAS ON THE TRAIN.
AND OUR CABIN WAS BUGGED, SO I COULDN'T SAY ANYTHING CARE-LESS !

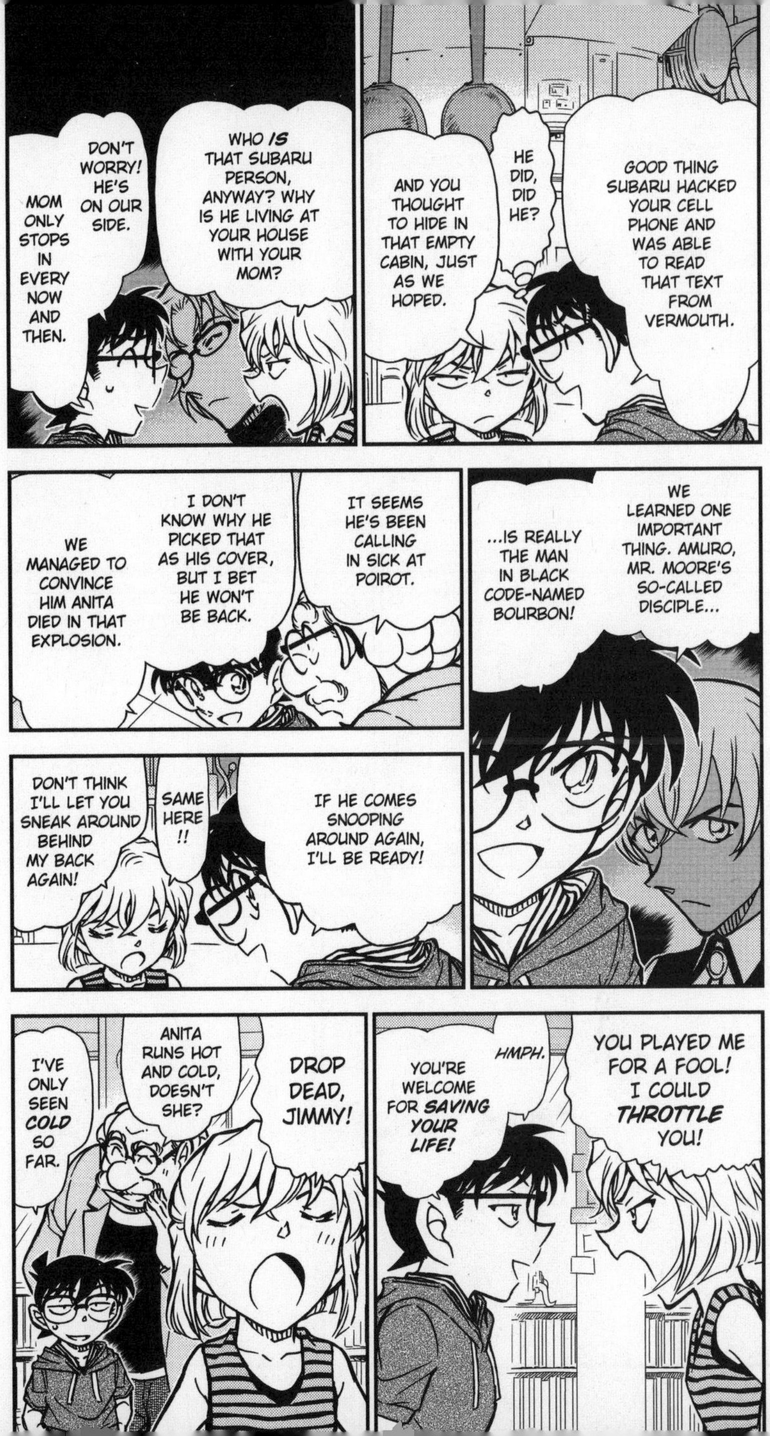
GOOD THING SUBARU HACKED YOUR CELL PHONE AND WAS ABLE TO READ THAT TEXT FROM VERMOUTH.
HE DID, DID HE?
AND YOU THOUGHT TO HIDE IN THAT EMPTY CABIN, JUST AS WE HOPED.
WHO *IS* THAT SUBARU PERSON, ANYWAY? WHY IS HE LIVING AT YOUR HOUSE WITH YOUR MOM?
DON'T WORRY! HE'S ON OUR SIDE.
MOM ONLY STOPS IN EVERY NOW AND THEN.
WE LEARNED ONE IMPORTANT THING. AMURO, MR. MOORE'S SO-CALLED DISCIPLE...
...IS REALLY THE MAN IN BLACK CODE-NAMED BOURBON!
IT SEEMS HE'S BEEN CALLING IN SICK AT POIROT.
I DON'T KNOW WHY HE PICKED THAT AS HIS COVER, BUT I BET HE WON'T BE BACK.
WE MANAGED TO CONVINCE HIM ANITA DIED IN THAT EXPLOSION.
IF HE COMES SNOOPING AROUND AGAIN, I'LL BE READY!
SAME HERE!!
DON'T THINK I'LL LET YOU SNEAK AROUND BEHIND MY BACK AGAIN!
YOU PLAYED ME FOR A FOOL! I COULD **THROTTLE** YOU!
HMPH.
YOU'RE WELCOME FOR ***SAVING YOUR LIFE!***
DROP DEAD, JIMMY!
ANITA RUNS HOT AND COLD, DOESN'T SHE?
I'VE ONLY SEEN ***COLD*** SO FAR.

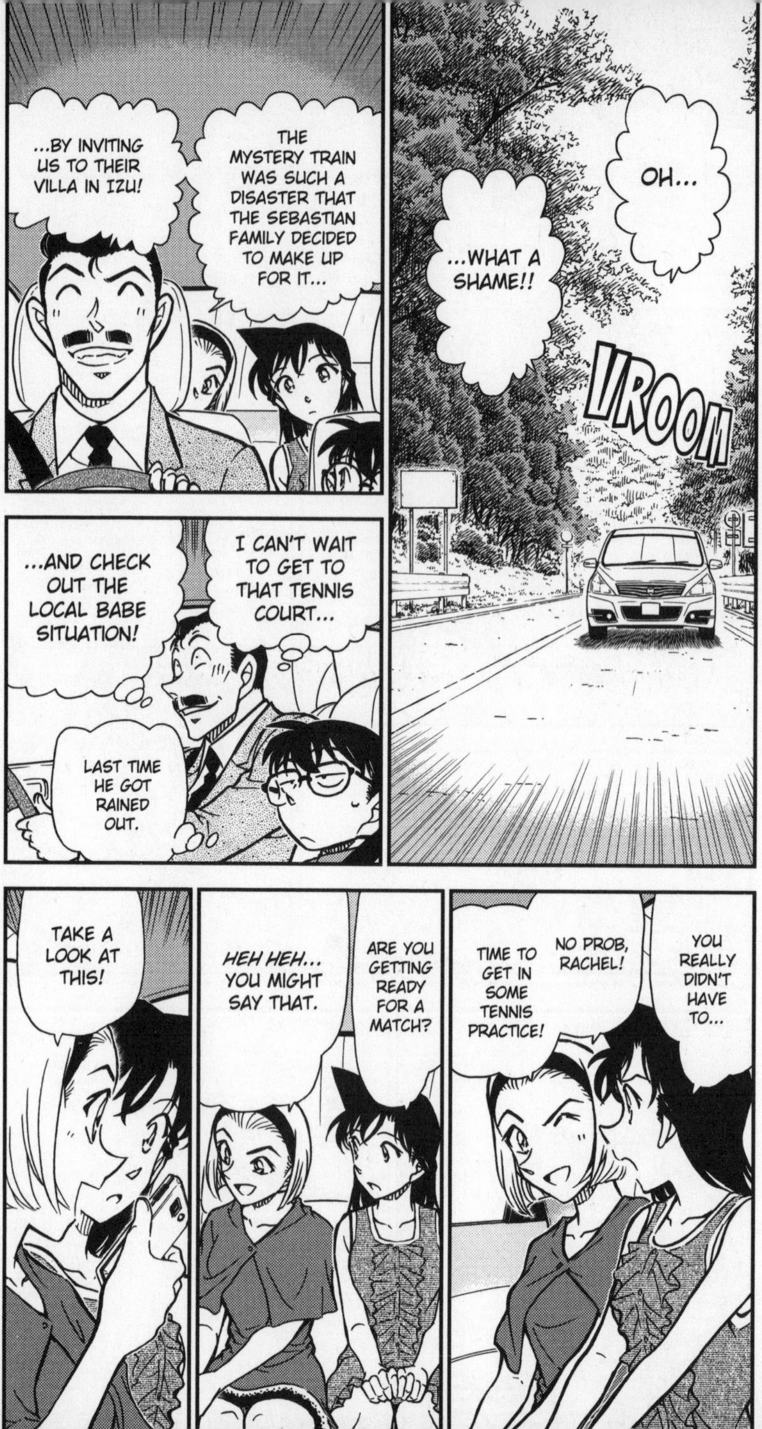
OH...
...WHAT A SHAME!!
VROOM
THE MYSTERY TRAIN WAS SUCH A DISASTER THAT THE SEBASTIAN FAMILY DECIDED TO MAKE UP FOR IT...
...BY INVITING US TO THEIR VILLA IN IZU!
I CAN'T WAIT TO GET TO THAT TENNIS COURT...
...AND CHECK OUT THE LOCAL BABE SITUATION!
LAST TIME HE GOT RAINED OUT.
YOU REALLY DIDN'T HAVE TO...
NO PROB, RACHEL!
TIME TO GET IN SOME TENNIS PRACTICE!
ARE YOU GETTING READY FOR A MATCH?
HEH HEH... YOU MIGHT SAY THAT.
TAKE A LOOK AT THIS!

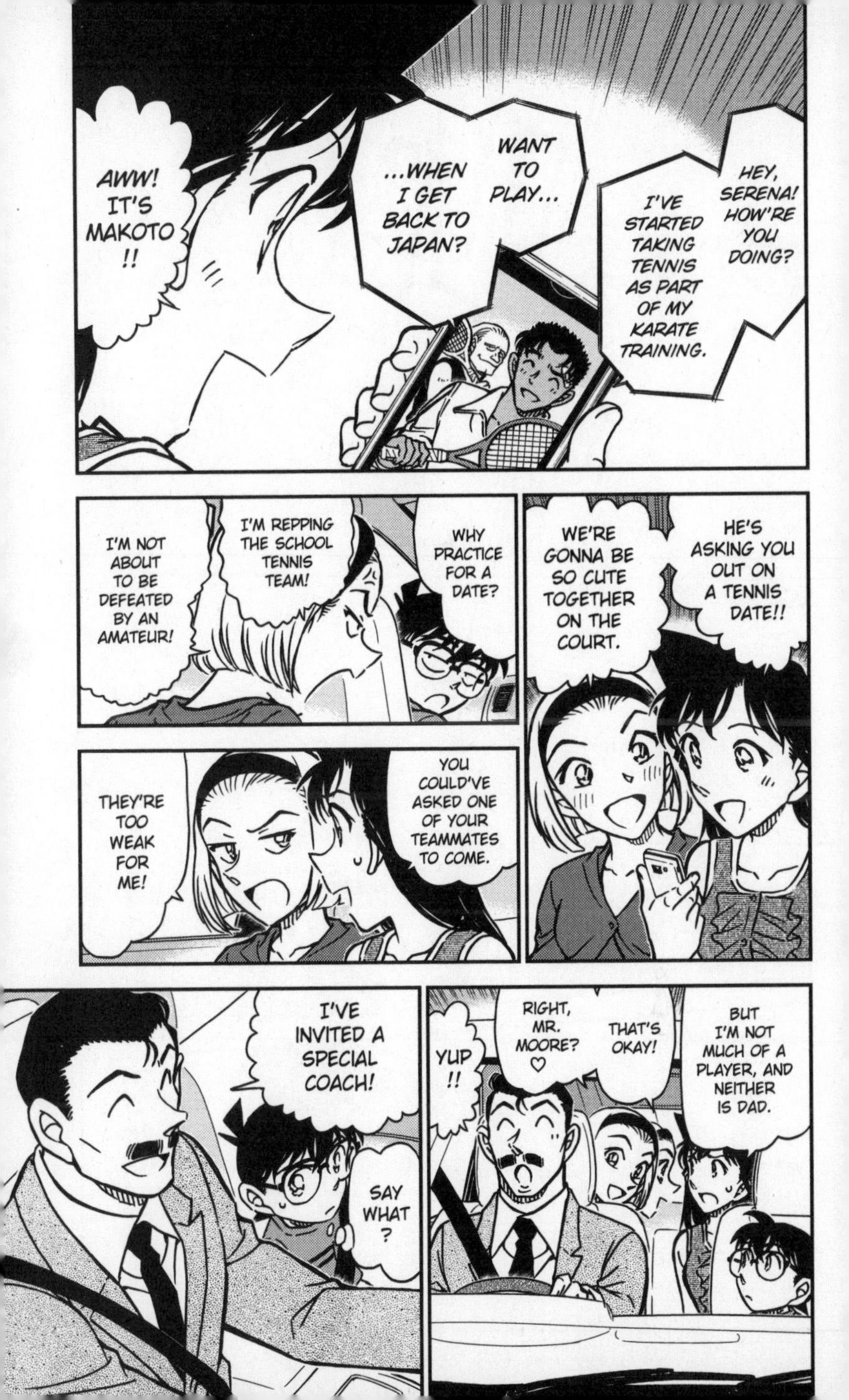
HEY, SERENA! HOW'RE YOU DOING?
I'VE STARTED TAKING TENNIS AS PART OF MY KARATE TRAINING.
WANT TO PLAY...
...WHEN I GET BACK TO JAPAN?
AWW! IT'S MAKOTO !!
HE'S ASKING YOU OUT ON A TENNIS DATE!!
WE'RE GONNA BE SO CUTE TOGETHER ON THE COURT.
WHY PRACTICE FOR A DATE?
I'M REPPING THE SCHOOL TENNIS TEAM!
I'M NOT ABOUT TO BE DEFEATED BY AN AMATEUR!
YOU COULD'VE ASKED ONE OF YOUR TEAMMATES TO COME.
THEY'RE TOO WEAK FOR ME!
BUT I'M NOT MUCH OF A PLAYER, AND NEITHER IS DAD.
THAT'S OKAY!
RIGHT, MR. MOORE? ♡
YUP !!
I'VE INVITED A SPECIAL COACH!
SAY WHAT ?

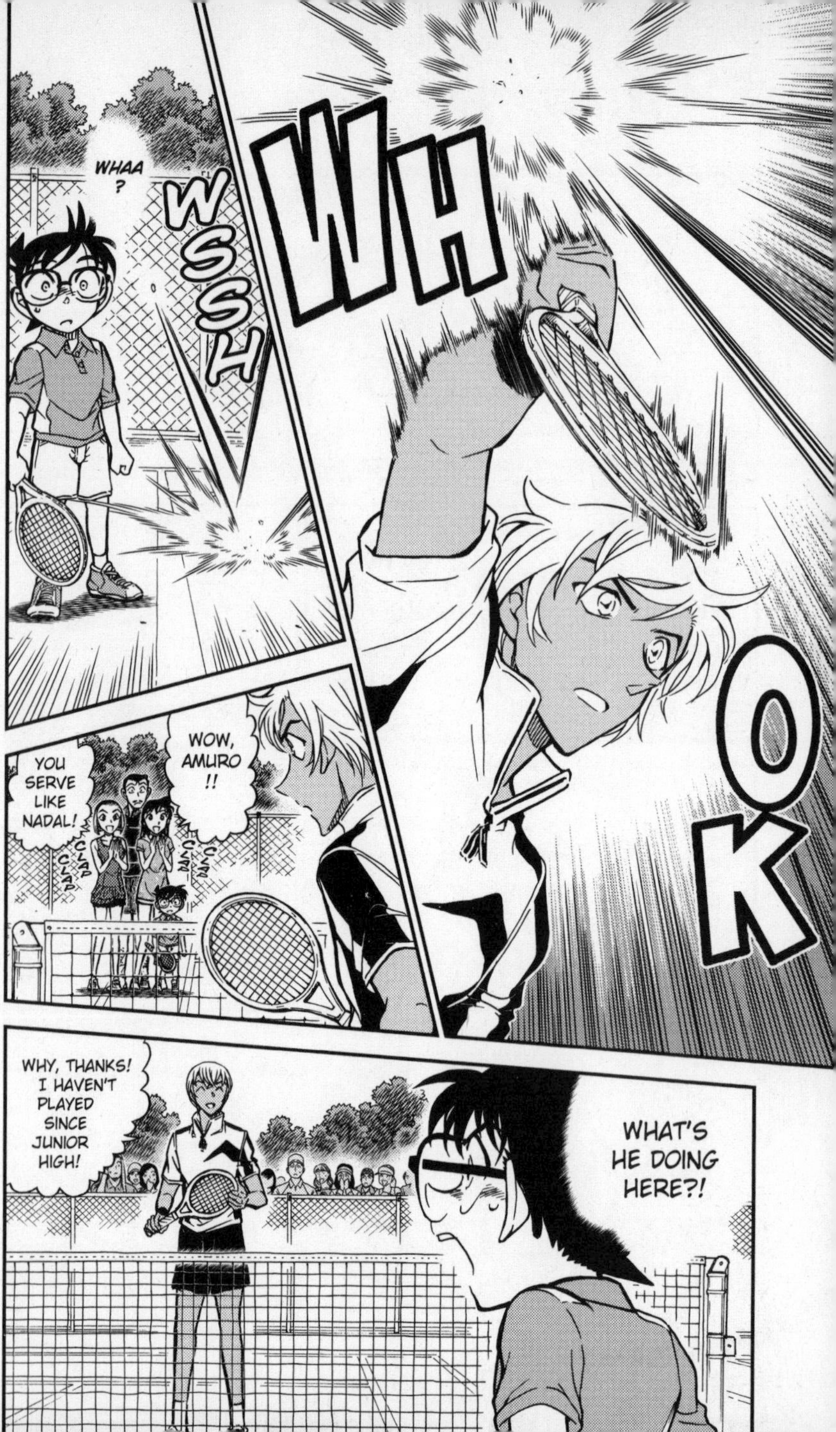
WHOK
WHAA ?
WSSH
WOW, AMURO!!
YOU SERVE LIKE NADAL!
CLAP CLAP
CLAP CLAP
WHAT'S HE DOING HERE?!
WHY, THANKS! I HAVEN'T PLAYED SINCE JUNIOR HIGH!

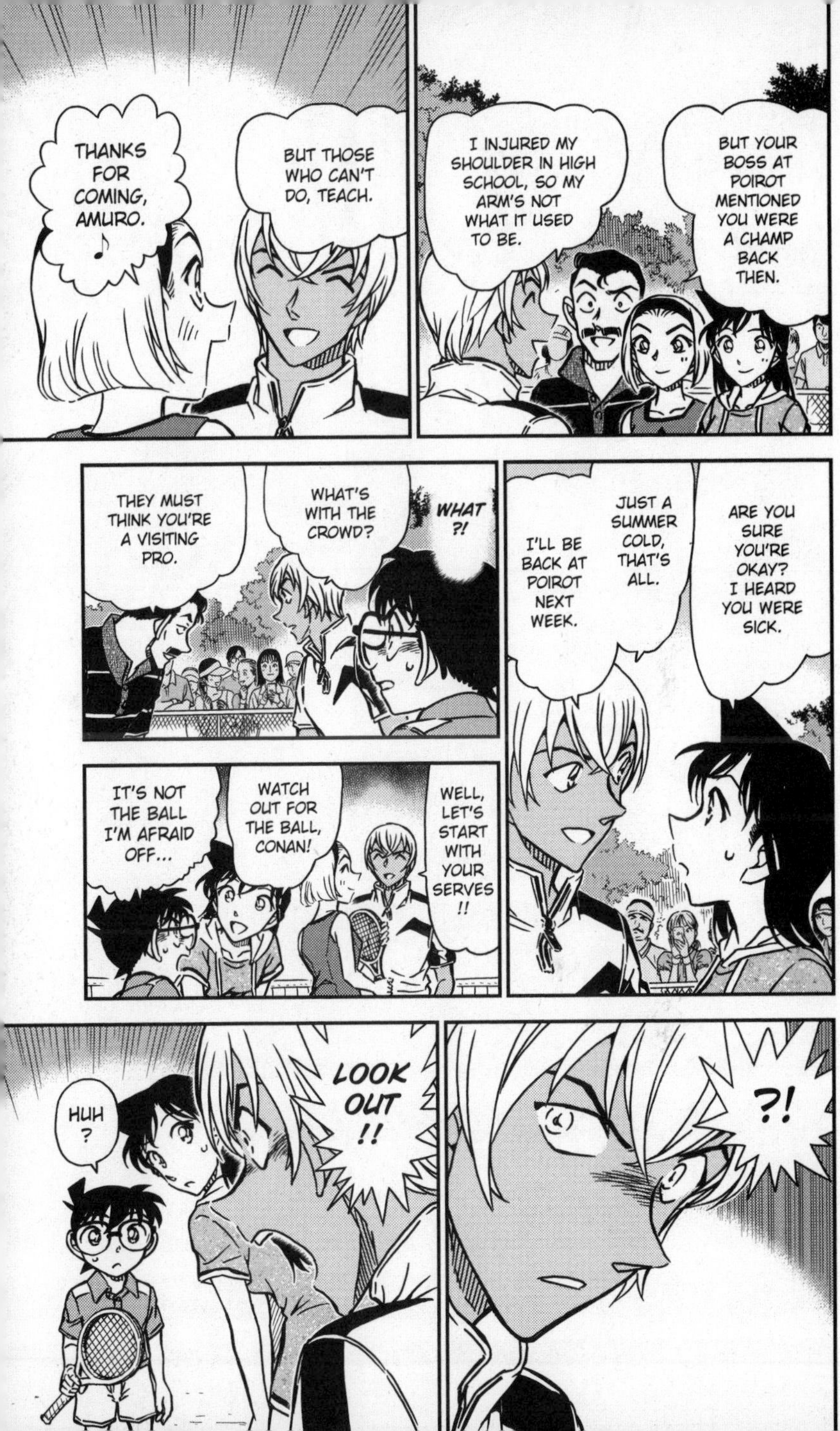
BUT YOUR BOSS AT POIROT MENTIONED YOU WERE A CHAMP BACK THEN.
I INJURED MY SHOULDER IN HIGH SCHOOL, SO MY ARM'S NOT WHAT IT USED TO BE.
BUT THOSE WHO CAN'T DO, TEACH.
THANKS FOR COMING, AMURO. ♪
ARE YOU SURE YOU'RE OKAY? I HEARD YOU WERE SICK.
JUST A SUMMER COLD, THAT'S ALL.
I'LL BE BACK AT POIROT NEXT WEEK.
WHAT ?!
WHAT'S WITH THE CROWD?
THEY MUST THINK YOU'RE A VISITING PRO.
WELL, LET'S START WITH YOUR SERVES !!
WATCH OUT FOR THE BALL, CONAN!
IT'S NOT THE BALL I'M AFRAID OFF...
?!
LOOK OUT !!
HUH ?

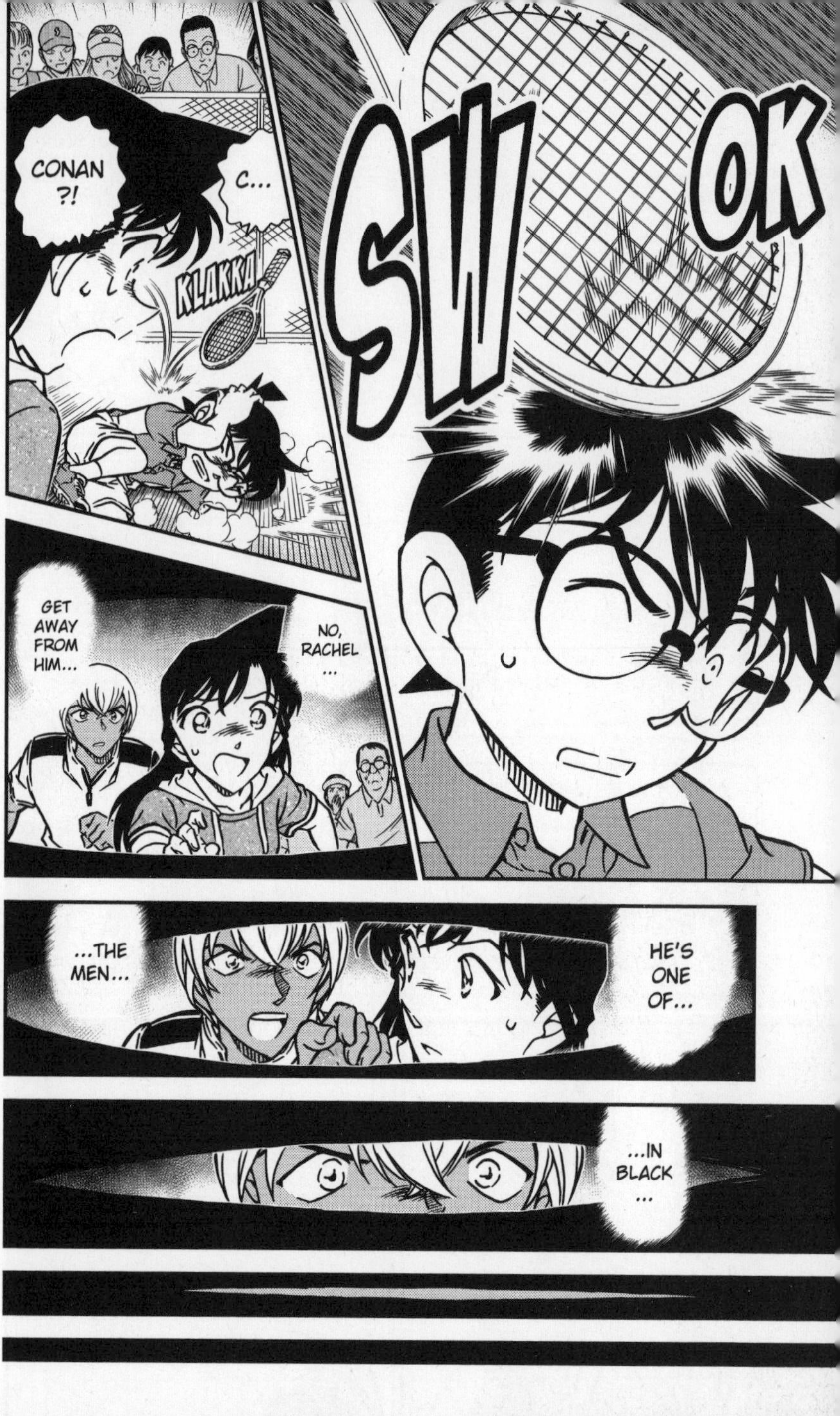
SWOOK
C...
CONAN ?!
KLAKKA
NO, RACHEL ...
GET AWAY FROM HIM...
HE'S ONE OF...
...THE MEN...
...IN BLACK ...

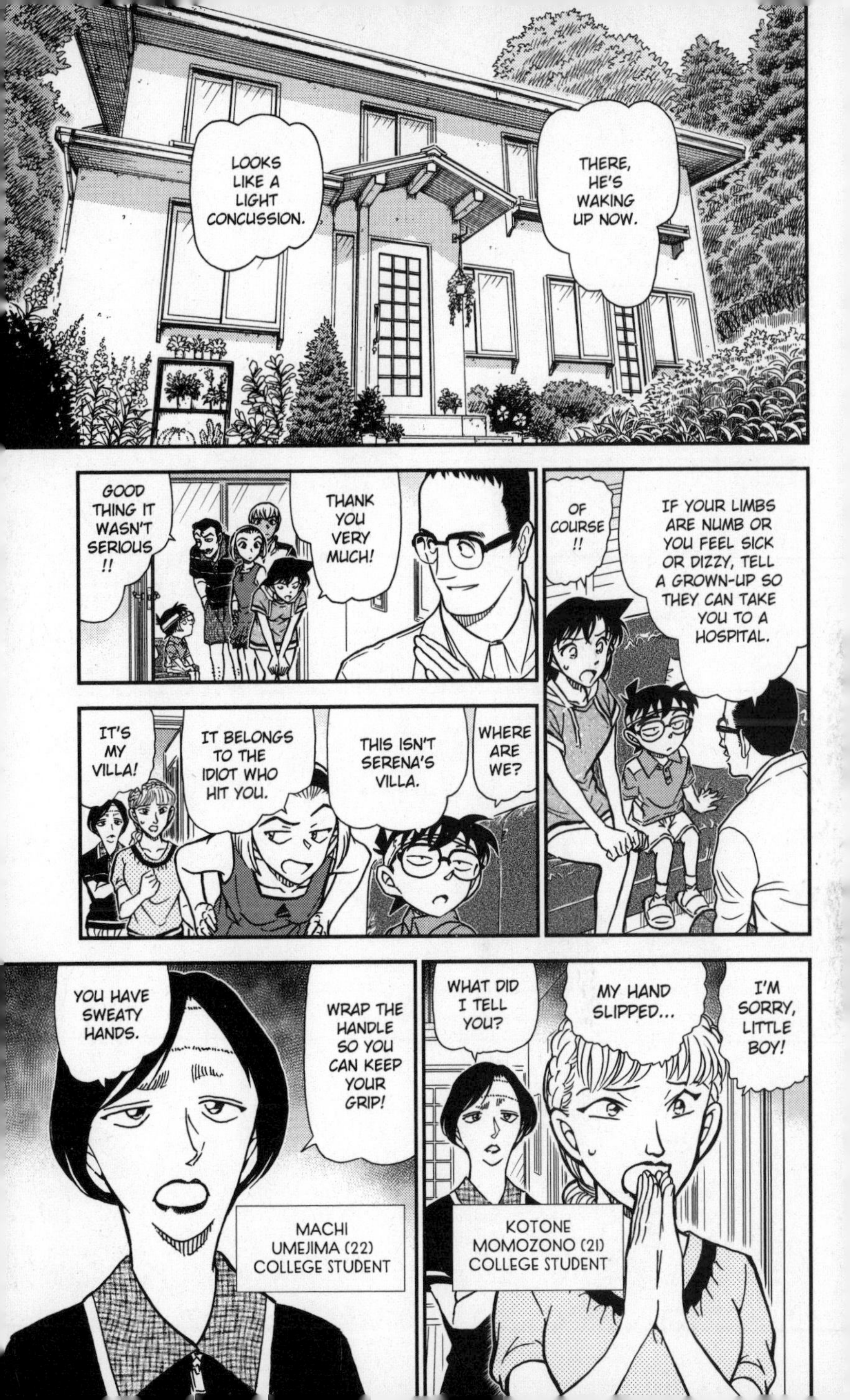
THERE, HE'S WAKING UP NOW.
LOOKS LIKE A LIGHT CONCUSSION.
IF YOUR LIMBS ARE NUMB OR YOU FEEL SICK OR DIZZY, TELL A GROWN-UP SO THEY CAN TAKE YOU TO A HOSPITAL.
OF COURSE!!
THANK YOU VERY MUCH!
GOOD THING IT WASN'T SERIOUS!!
WHERE ARE WE?
THIS ISN'T SERENA'S VILLA.
IT BELONGS TO THE IDIOT WHO HIT YOU.
IT'S MY VILLA!
I'M SORRY, LITTLE BOY!
MY HAND SLIPPED...
WHAT DID I TELL YOU?
KOTONE MOMOZONO (21) COLLEGE STUDENT
WRAP THE HANDLE SO YOU CAN KEEP YOUR GRIP!
YOU HAVE SWEATY HANDS.
MACHI UMEJIMA (22) COLLEGE STUDENT

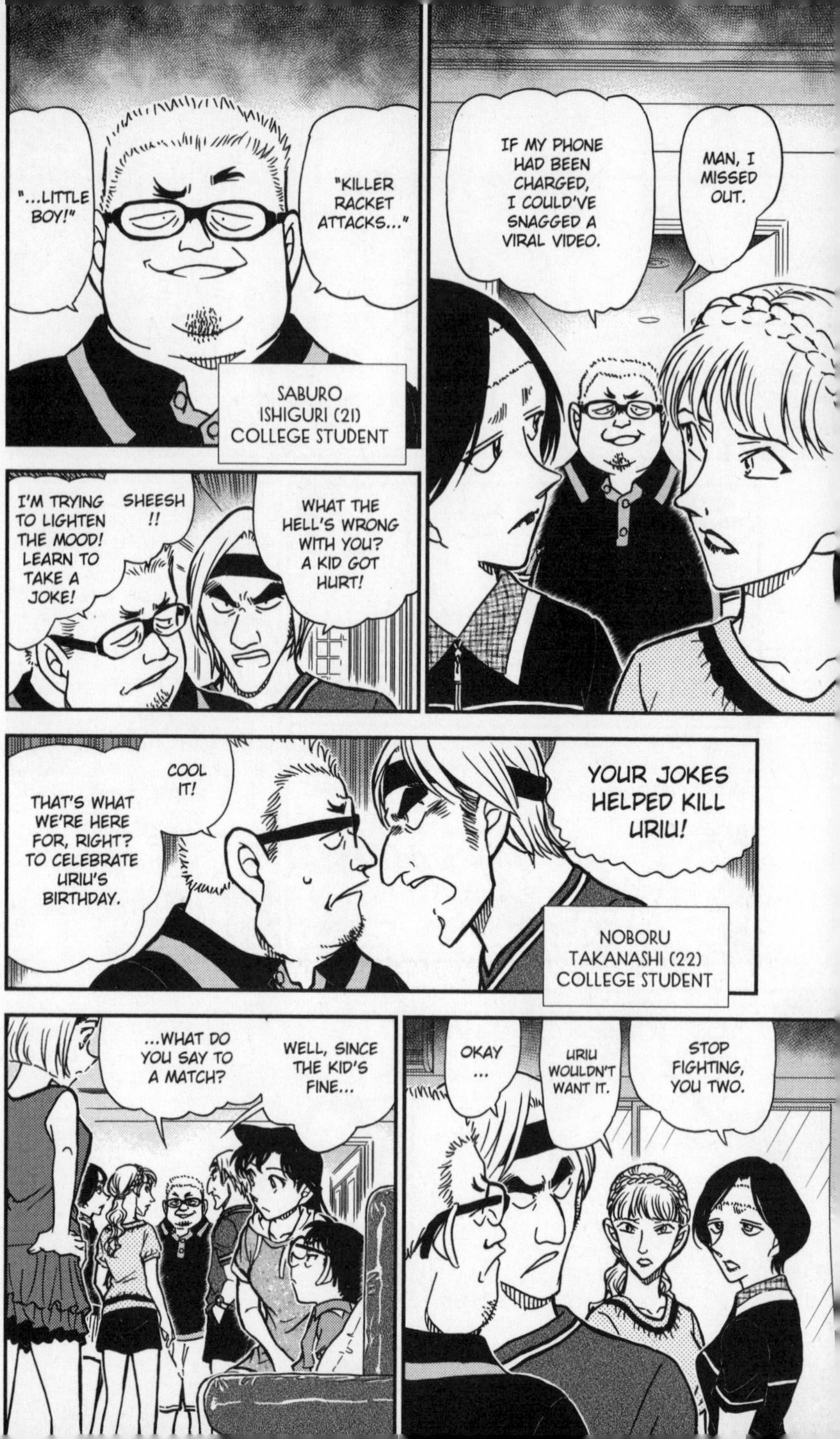
MAN, I MISSED OUT.
IF MY PHONE HAD BEEN CHARGED, I COULD'VE SNAGGED A VIRAL VIDEO.
"KILLER RACKET ATTACKS..."
"...LITTLE BOY!"
SABURO ISHIGURI (21) COLLEGE STUDENT
WHAT THE HELL'S WRONG WITH YOU? A KID GOT HURT!
SHEESH !!
I'M TRYING TO LIGHTEN THE MOOD! LEARN TO TAKE A JOKE!
YOUR JOKES HELPED KILL URIU!
NOBORU TAKANASHI (22) COLLEGE STUDENT
COOL IT!
THAT'S WHAT WE'RE HERE FOR, RIGHT? TO CELEBRATE URIU'S BIRTHDAY.
STOP FIGHTING, YOU TWO.
URIU WOULDN'T WANT IT.
OKAY ...
WELL, SINCE THE KID'S FINE...
...WHAT DO YOU SAY TO A MATCH?

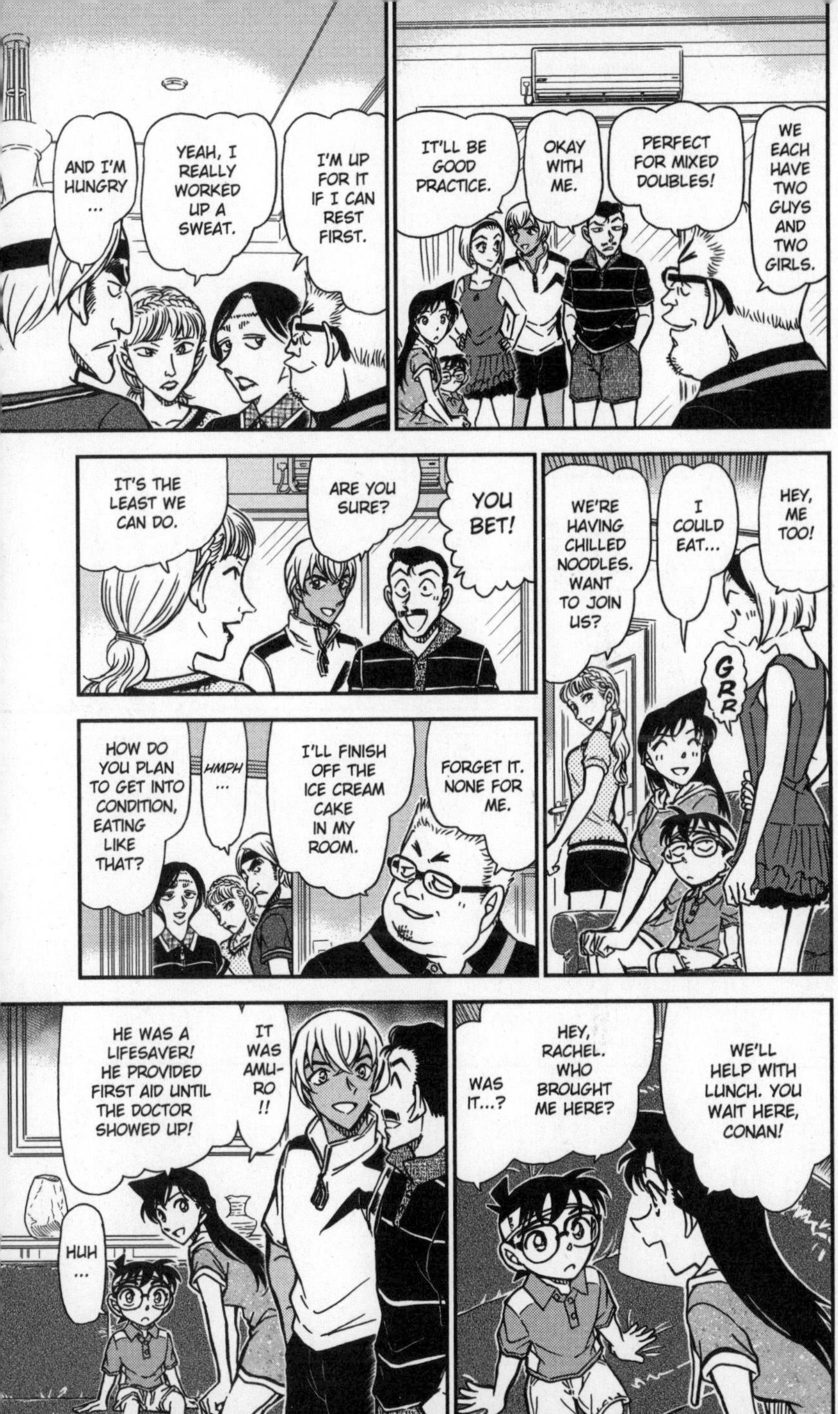
WE EACH HAVE TWO GUYS AND TWO GIRLS.
PERFECT FOR MIXED DOUBLES!
OKAY WITH ME.
IT'LL BE GOOD PRACTICE.
I'M UP FOR IT IF I CAN REST FIRST.
YEAH, I REALLY WORKED UP A SWEAT.
AND I'M HUNGRY ...
HEY, ME TOO!
I COULD EAT...
GRR
WE'RE HAVING CHILLED NOODLES. WANT TO JOIN US?
YOU BET!
ARE YOU SURE?
IT'S THE LEAST WE CAN DO.
FORGET IT. NONE FOR ME.
I'LL FINISH OFF THE ICE CREAM CAKE IN MY ROOM.
HMPH ...
HOW DO YOU PLAN TO GET INTO CONDITION, EATING LIKE THAT?
WE'LL HELP WITH LUNCH. YOU WAIT HERE, CONAN!
HEY, RACHEL. WHO BROUGHT ME HERE?
WAS IT...?
IT WAS AMU-RO !!
HE WAS A LIFESAVER! HE PROVIDED FIRST AID UNTIL THE DOCTOR SHOWED UP!
HUH ...

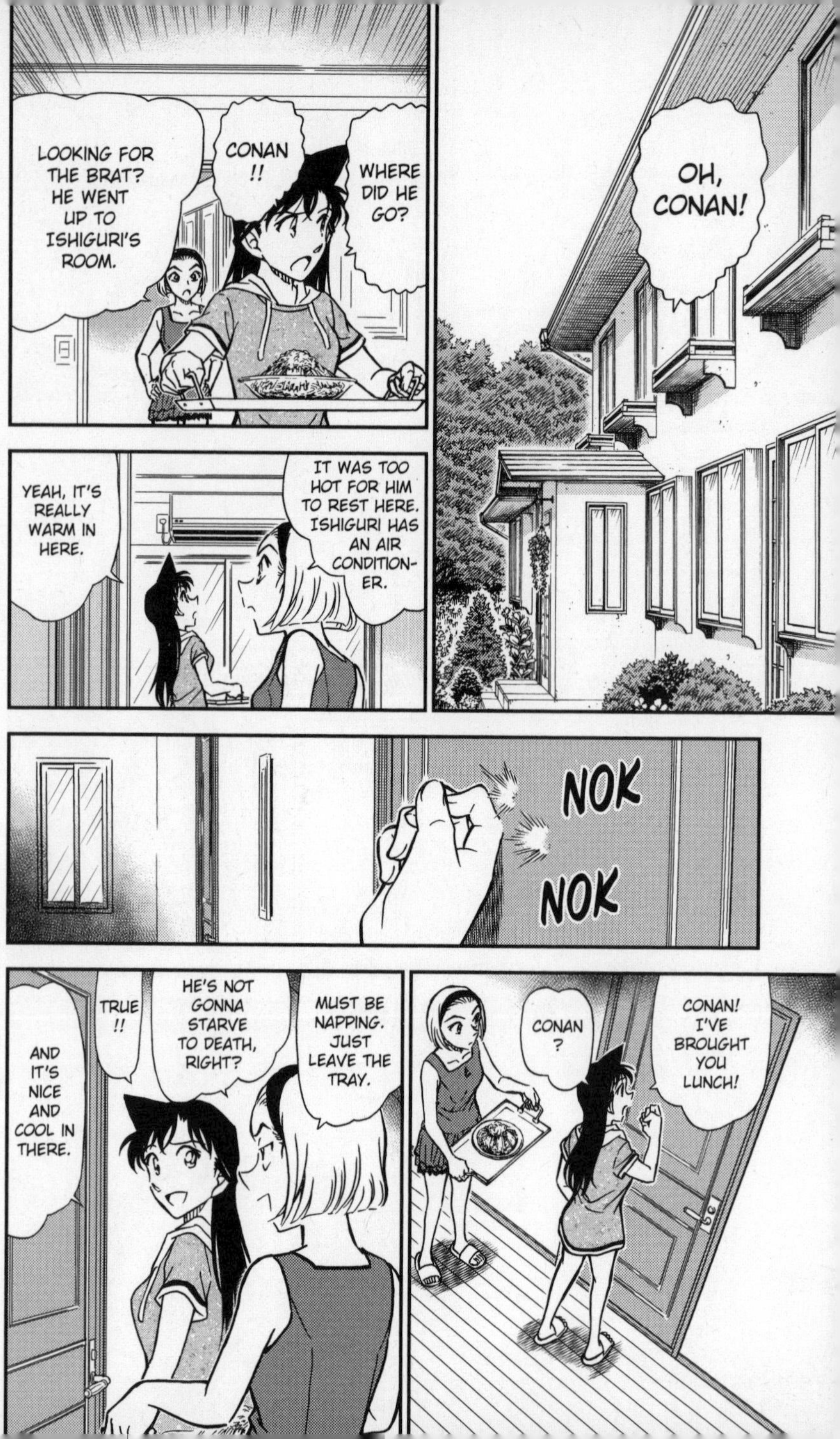
OH, CONAN!
WHERE DID HE GO?
CONAN !!
LOOKING FOR THE BRAT? HE WENT UP TO ISHIGURI'S ROOM.
IT WAS TOO HOT FOR HIM TO REST HERE. ISHIGURI HAS AN AIR CONDITIONER.
YEAH, IT'S REALLY WARM IN HERE.
NOK
NOK
CONAN! I'VE BROUGHT YOU LUNCH!
CONAN ?
MUST BE NAPPING. JUST LEAVE THE TRAY.
HE'S NOT GONNA STARVE TO DEATH, RIGHT?
TRUE !!
AND IT'S NICE AND COOL IN THERE.

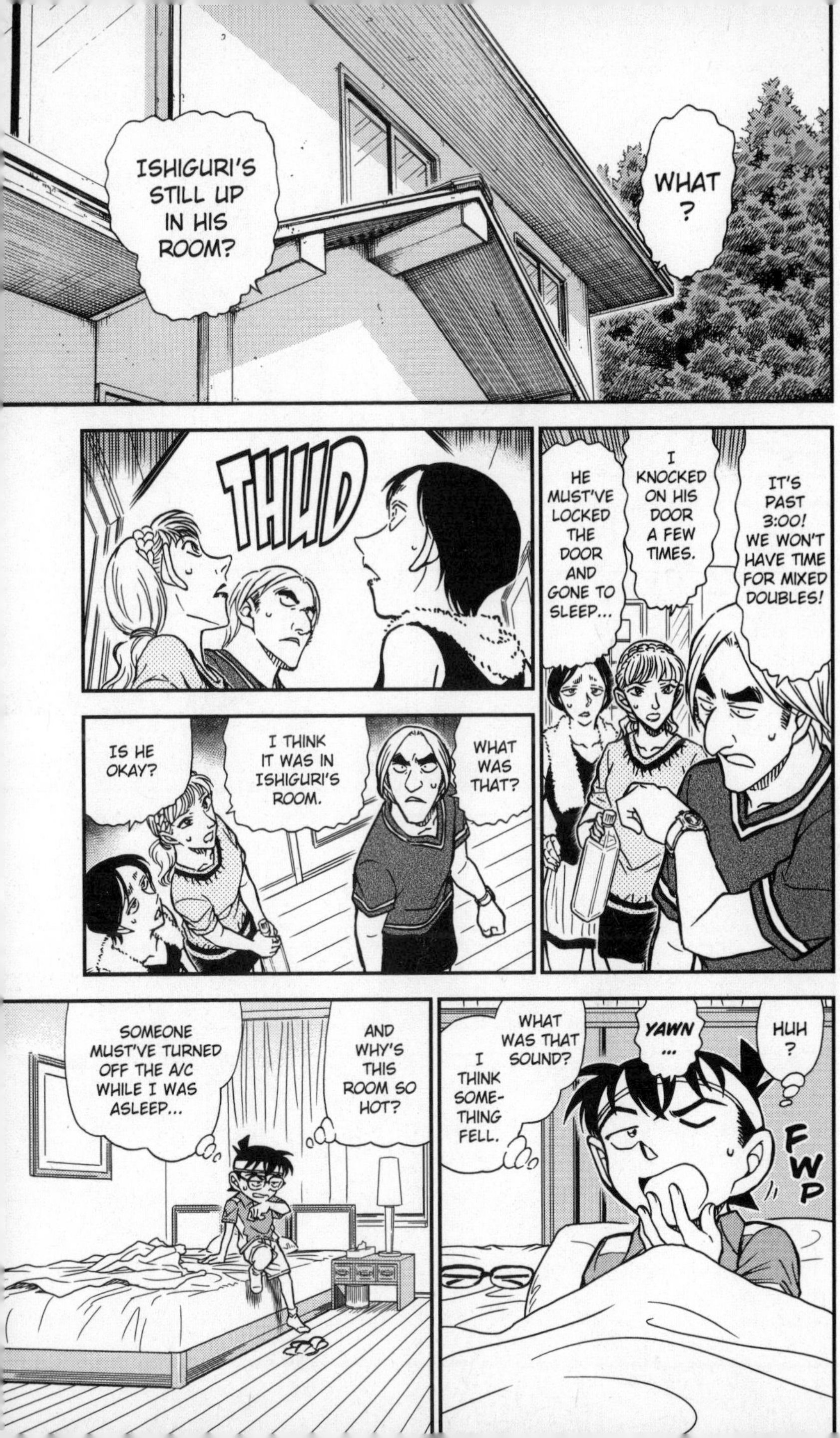
WHAT ?
ISHIGURI'S STILL UP IN HIS ROOM?
IT'S PAST 3:00! WE WON'T HAVE TIME FOR MIXED DOUBLES!
I KNOCKED ON HIS DOOR A FEW TIMES.
HE MUST'VE LOCKED THE DOOR AND GONE TO SLEEP...
THUD
WHAT WAS THAT?
I THINK IT WAS IN ISHIGURI'S ROOM.
IS HE OKAY?
HUH ?
YAWN ...
WHAT WAS THAT SOUND?
I THINK SOME-THING FELL.
FWP
AND WHY'S THIS ROOM SO HOT?
SOMEONE MUST'VE TURNED OFF THE A/C WHILE I WAS ASLEEP...

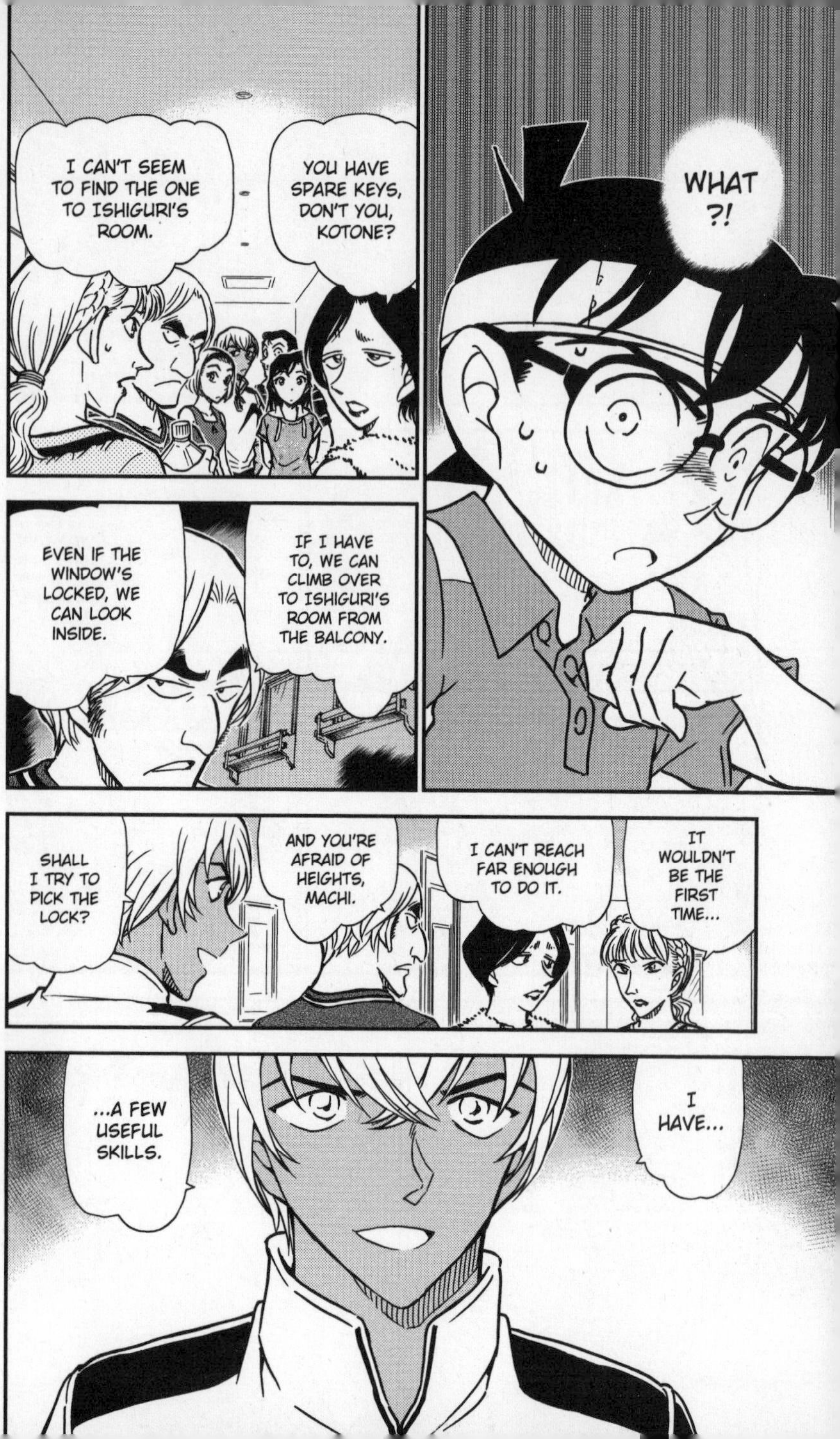
WHAT?!
YOU HAVE SPARE KEYS, DON'T YOU, KOTONE?
I CAN'T SEEM TO FIND THE ONE TO ISHIGURI'S ROOM.
IF I HAVE TO, WE CAN CLIMB OVER TO ISHIGURI'S ROOM FROM THE BALCONY.
EVEN IF THE WINDOW'S LOCKED, WE CAN LOOK INSIDE.
IT WOULDN'T BE THE FIRST TIME...
I CAN'T REACH FAR ENOUGH TO DO IT.
AND YOU'RE AFRAID OF HEIGHTS, MACHI.
SHALL I TRY TO PICK THE LOCK?
I HAVE...
...A FEW USEFUL SKILLS.

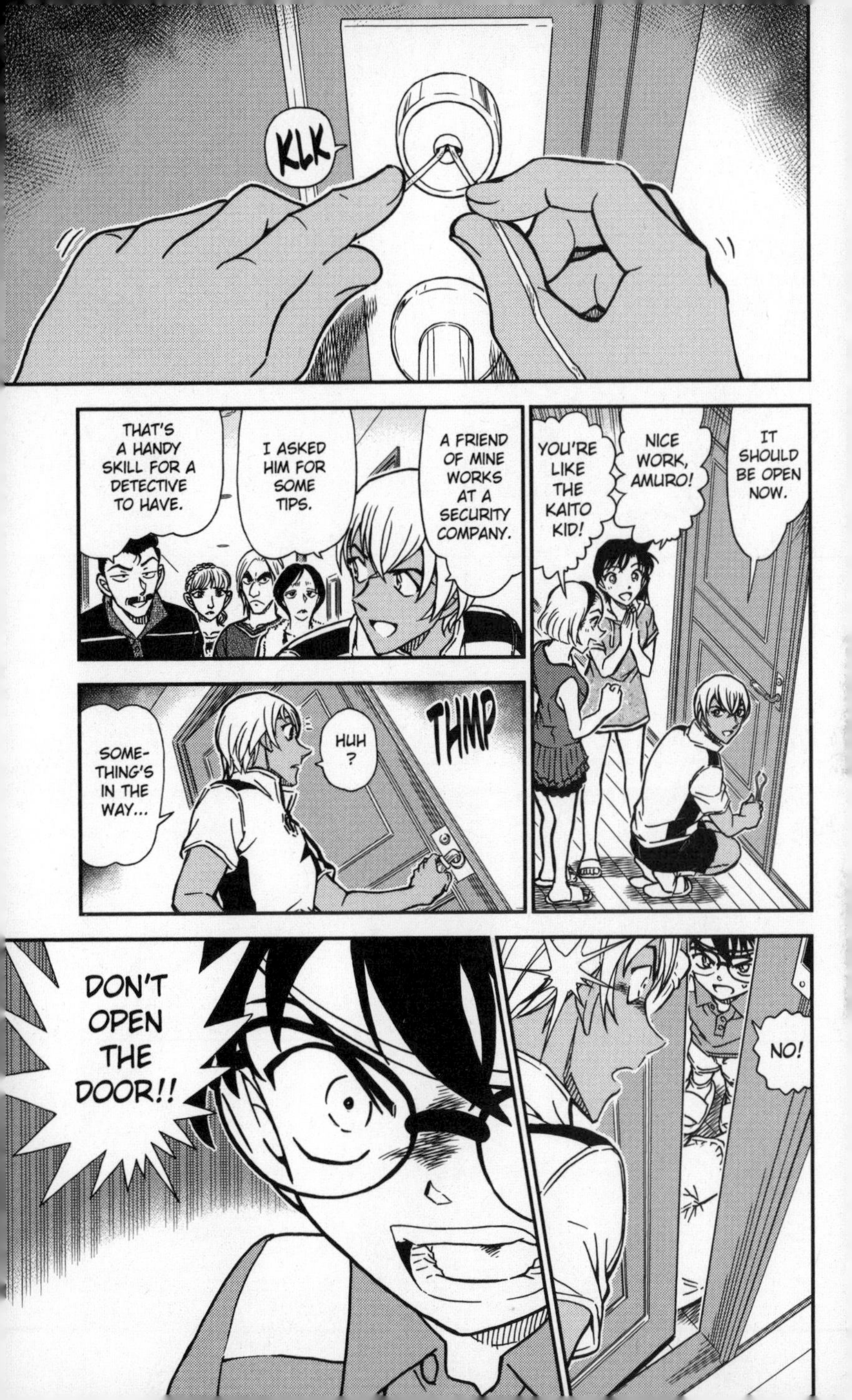
KLK
IT SHOULD BE OPEN NOW.
NICE WORK, AMURO!
YOU'RE LIKE THE KAITO KID!
A FRIEND OF MINE WORKS AT A SECURITY COMPANY.
I ASKED HIM FOR SOME TIPS.
THAT'S A HANDY SKILL FOR A DETECTIVE TO HAVE.
THMP
HUH?
SOME-THING'S IN THE WAY...
NO!
DON'T OPEN THE DOOR!!

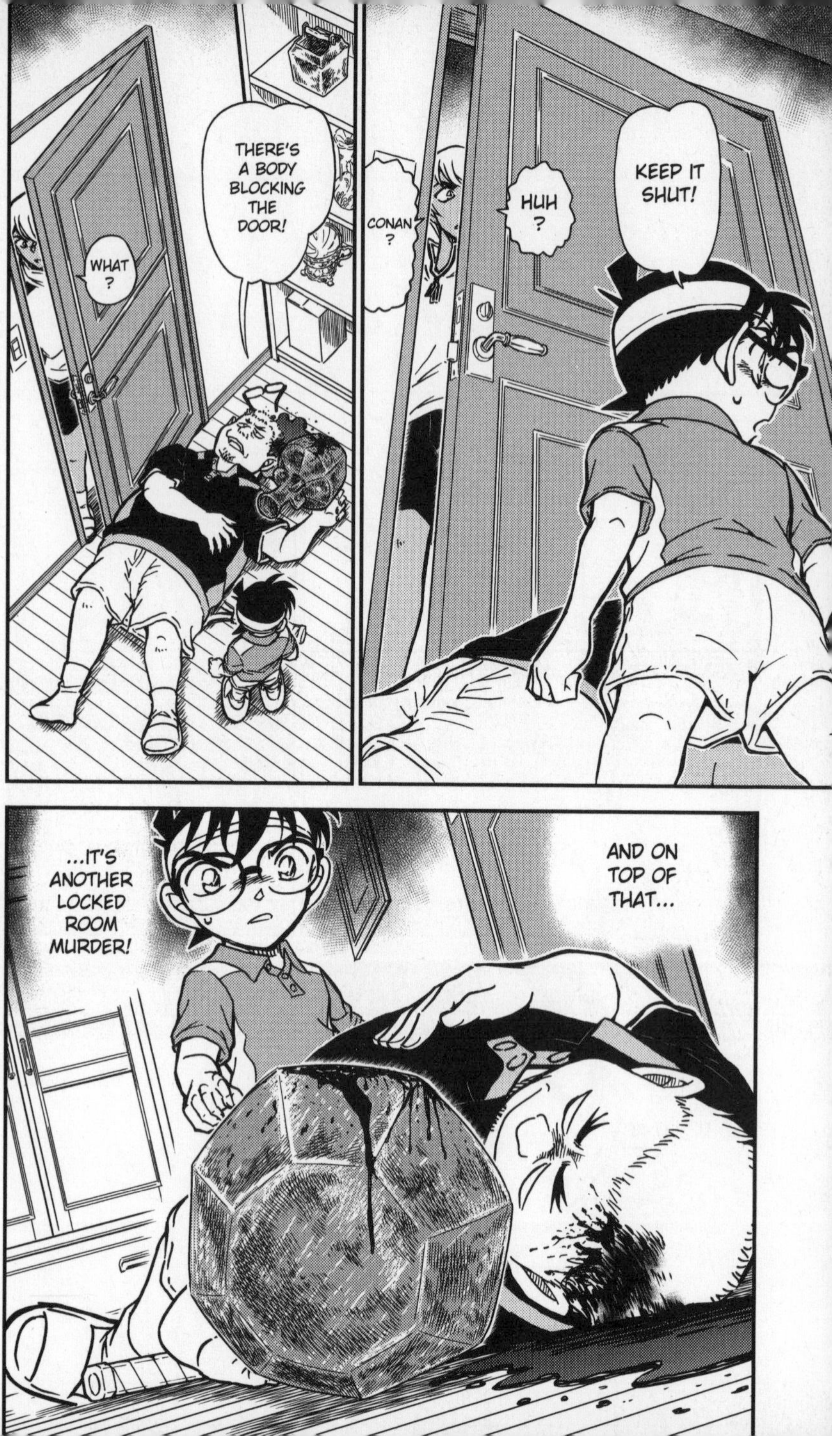
KEEP IT SHUT!
HUH?
CONAN?
THERE'S A BODY BLOCKING THE DOOR!
WHAT?
AND ON TOP OF THAT...
...IT'S ANOTHER LOCKED ROOM MURDER!

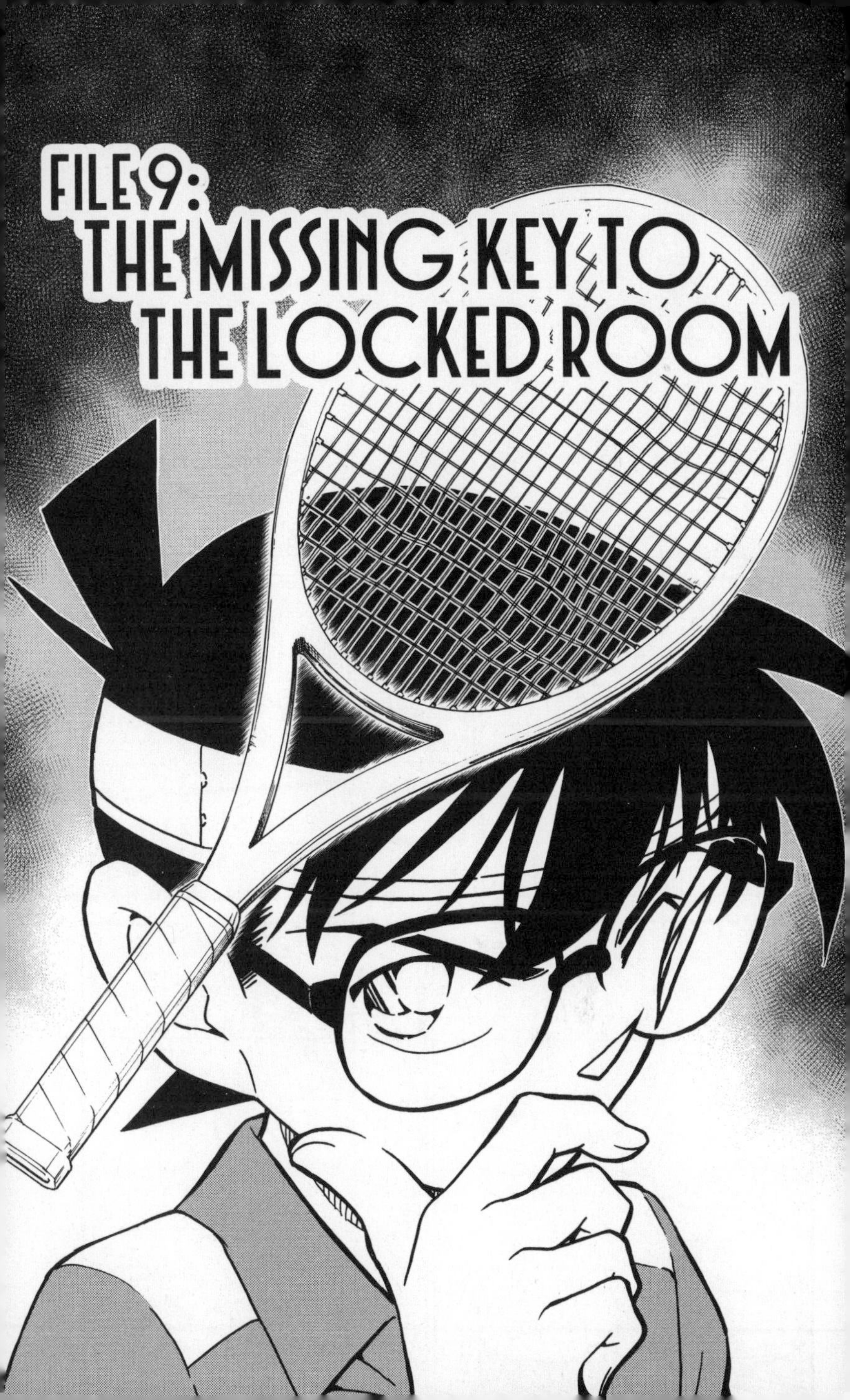
FILE 9:
THE MISSING KEY TO
THE LOCKED ROOM

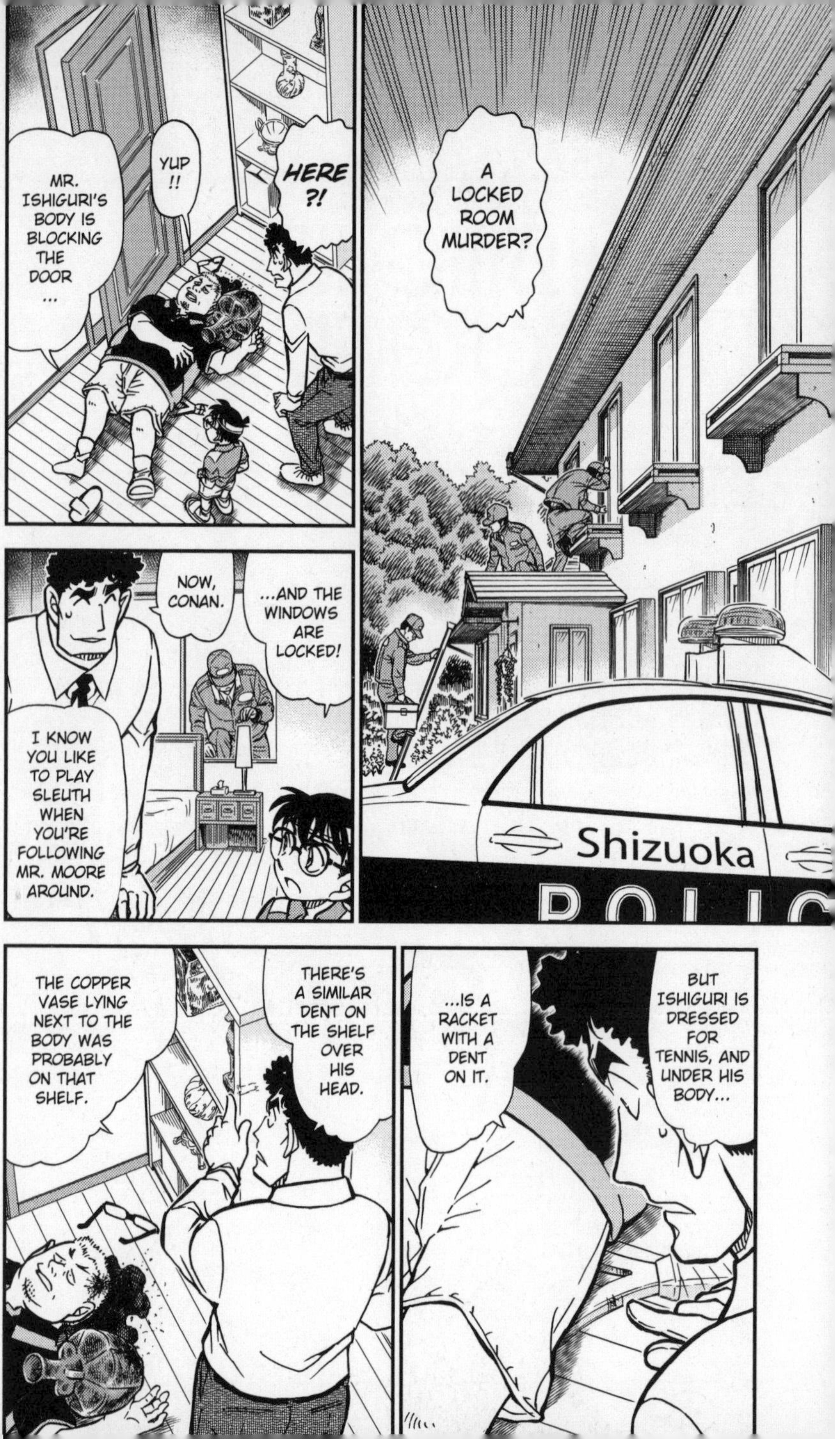
A LOCKED ROOM MURDER?
Shizuoka
POLIC
HERE ?!
YUP !!
MR. ISHIGURI'S BODY IS BLOCKING THE DOOR ...
...AND THE WINDOWS ARE LOCKED!
NOW, CONAN.
I KNOW YOU LIKE TO PLAY SLEUTH WHEN YOU'RE FOLLOWING MR. MOORE AROUND.
BUT ISHIGURI IS DRESSED FOR TENNIS, AND UNDER HIS BODY...
...IS A RACKET WITH A DENT ON IT.
THERE'S A SIMILAR DENT ON THE SHELF OVER HIS HEAD.
THE COPPER VASE LYING NEXT TO THE BODY WAS PROBABLY ON THAT SHELF.

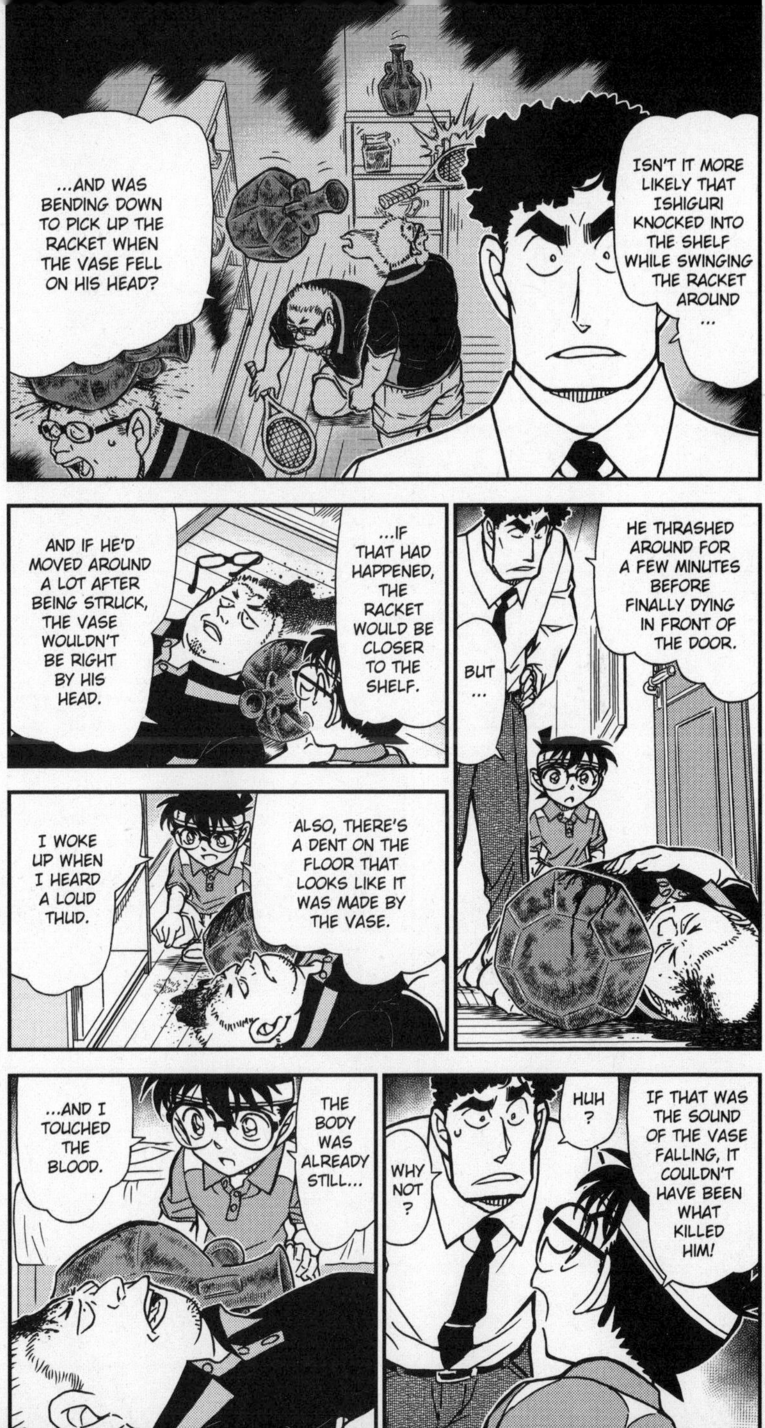
ISN'T IT MORE LIKELY THAT ISHIGURI KNOCKED INTO THE SHELF WHILE SWINGING THE RACKET AROUND ...
...AND WAS BENDING DOWN TO PICK UP THE RACKET WHEN THE VASE FELL ON HIS HEAD?
HE THRASHED AROUND FOR A FEW MINUTES BEFORE FINALLY DYING IN FRONT OF THE DOOR.
BUT ...
...IF THAT HAD HAPPENED, THE RACKET WOULD BE CLOSER TO THE SHELF.
AND IF HE'D MOVED AROUND A LOT AFTER BEING STRUCK, THE VASE WOULDN'T BE RIGHT BY HIS HEAD.
ALSO, THERE'S A DENT ON THE FLOOR THAT LOOKS LIKE IT WAS MADE BY THE VASE.
I WOKE UP WHEN I HEARD A LOUD THUD.
IF THAT WAS THE SOUND OF THE VASE FALLING, IT COULDN'T HAVE BEEN WHAT KILLED HIM!
HUH ?
WHY NOT ?
THE BODY WAS ALREADY STILL...
...AND I TOUCHED THE BLOOD.

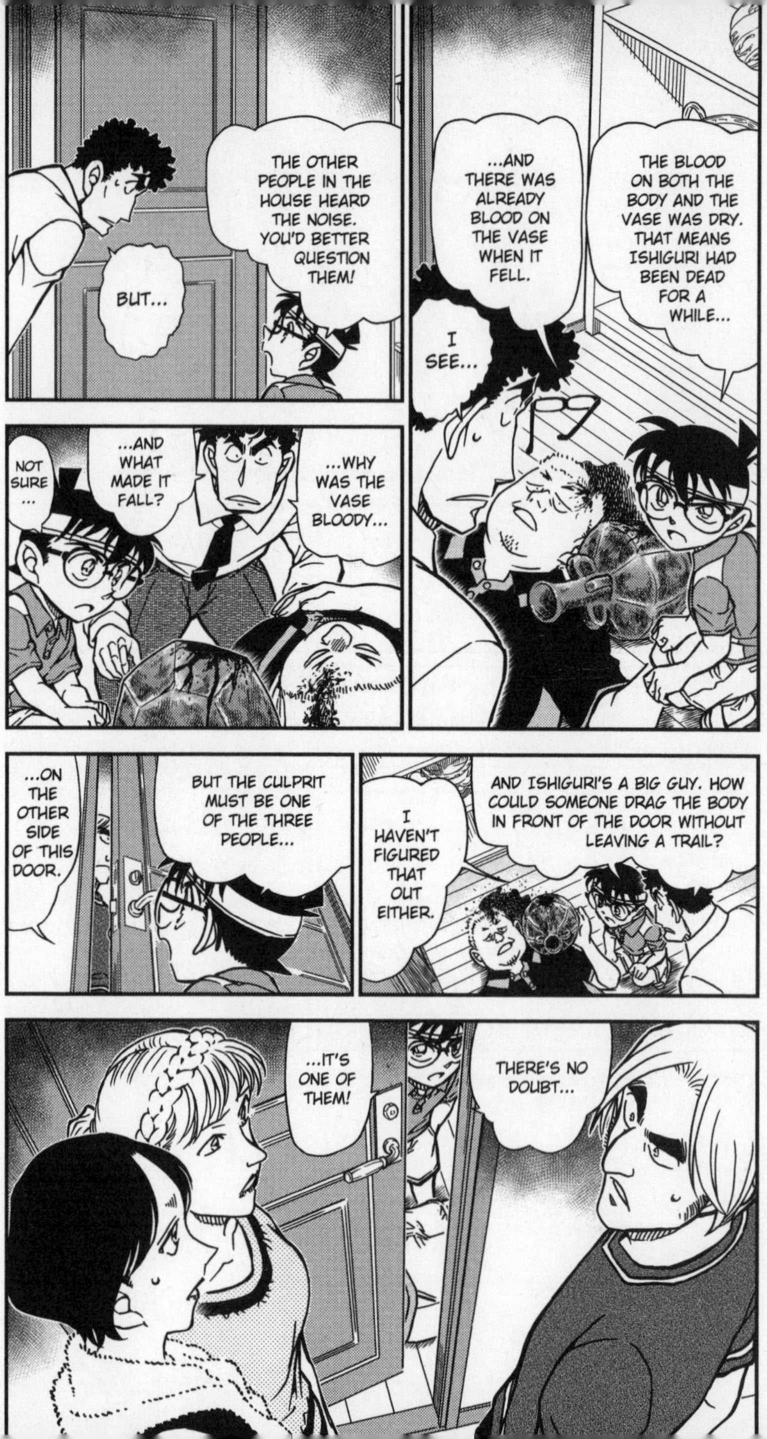
THE BLOOD ON BOTH THE BODY AND THE VASE WAS DRY. THAT MEANS ISHIGURI HAD BEEN DEAD FOR A WHILE...
...AND THERE WAS ALREADY BLOOD ON THE VASE WHEN IT FELL.
I SEE...
THE OTHER PEOPLE IN THE HOUSE HEARD THE NOISE. YOU'D BETTER QUESTION THEM!
BUT...
...WHY WAS THE VASE BLOODY...
...AND WHAT MADE IT FALL?
NOT SURE ...
AND ISHIGURI'S A BIG GUY. HOW COULD SOMEONE DRAG THE BODY IN FRONT OF THE DOOR WITHOUT LEAVING A TRAIL?
I HAVEN'T FIGURED THAT OUT EITHER.
BUT THE CULPRIT MUST BE ONE OF THE THREE PEOPLE...
...ON THE OTHER SIDE OF THIS DOOR.
THERE'S NO DOUBT...
...IT'S ONE OF THEM!

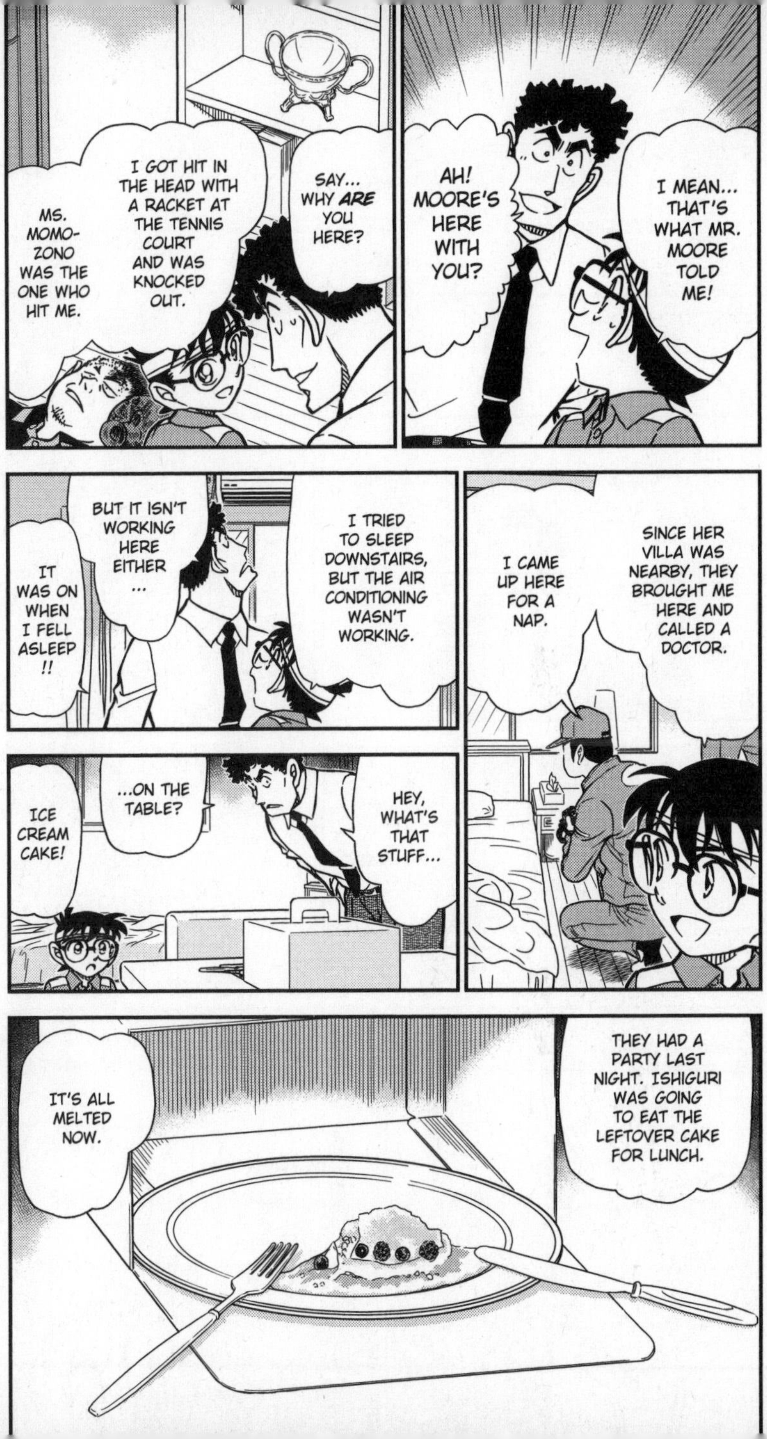
I MEAN... THAT'S WHAT MR. MOORE TOLD ME!
AH! MOORE'S HERE WITH YOU?
SAY... WHY ARE YOU HERE?
I GOT HIT IN THE HEAD WITH A RACKET AT THE TENNIS COURT AND WAS KNOCKED OUT.
MS. MOMO-ZONO WAS THE ONE WHO HIT ME.
SINCE HER VILLA WAS NEARBY, THEY BROUGHT ME HERE AND CALLED A DOCTOR.
I CAME UP HERE FOR A NAP.
I TRIED TO SLEEP DOWNSTAIRS, BUT THE AIR CONDITIONING WASN'T WORKING.
BUT IT ISN'T WORKING HERE EITHER ...
IT WAS ON WHEN I FELL ASLEEP !!
HEY, WHAT'S THAT STUFF...
...ON THE TABLE?
ICE CREAM CAKE!
THEY HAD A PARTY LAST NIGHT. ISHIGURI WAS GOING TO EAT THE LEFTOVER CAKE FOR LUNCH.
IT'S ALL MELTED NOW.

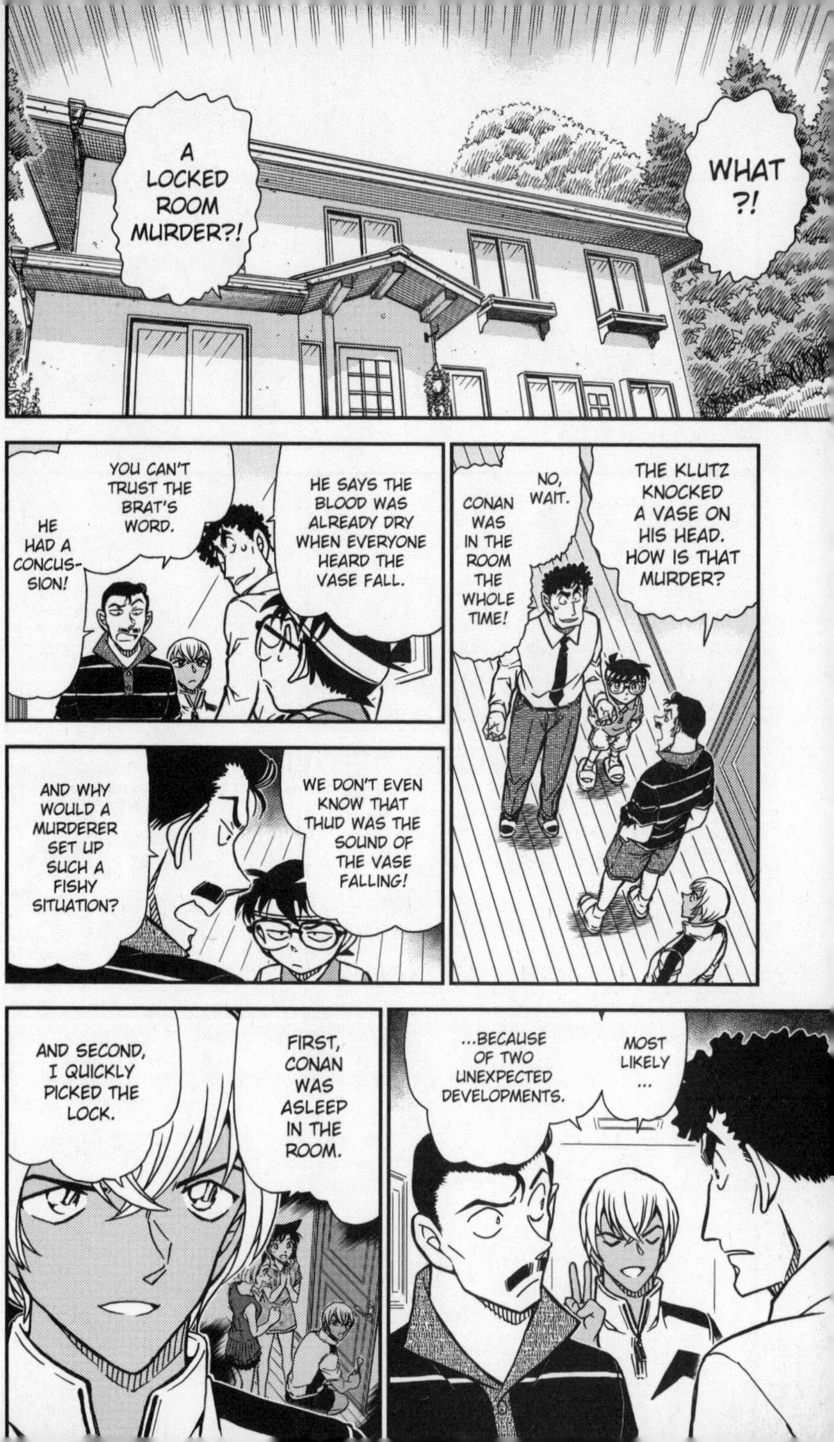
WHAT ?!
A LOCKED ROOM MURDER?!
THE KLUTZ KNOCKED A VASE ON HIS HEAD. HOW IS THAT MURDER?
NO, WAIT.
CONAN WAS IN THE ROOM THE WHOLE TIME!
HE SAYS THE BLOOD WAS ALREADY DRY WHEN EVERYONE HEARD THE VASE FALL.
YOU CAN'T TRUST THE BRAT'S WORD.
HE HAD A CONCUSSION!
WE DON'T EVEN KNOW THAT THUD WAS THE SOUND OF THE VASE FALLING!
AND WHY WOULD A MURDERER SET UP SUCH A FISHY SITUATION?
MOST LIKELY ...
...BECAUSE OF TWO UNEXPECTED DEVELOPMENTS.
FIRST, CONAN WAS ASLEEP IN THE ROOM.
AND SECOND, I QUICKLY PICKED THE LOCK.

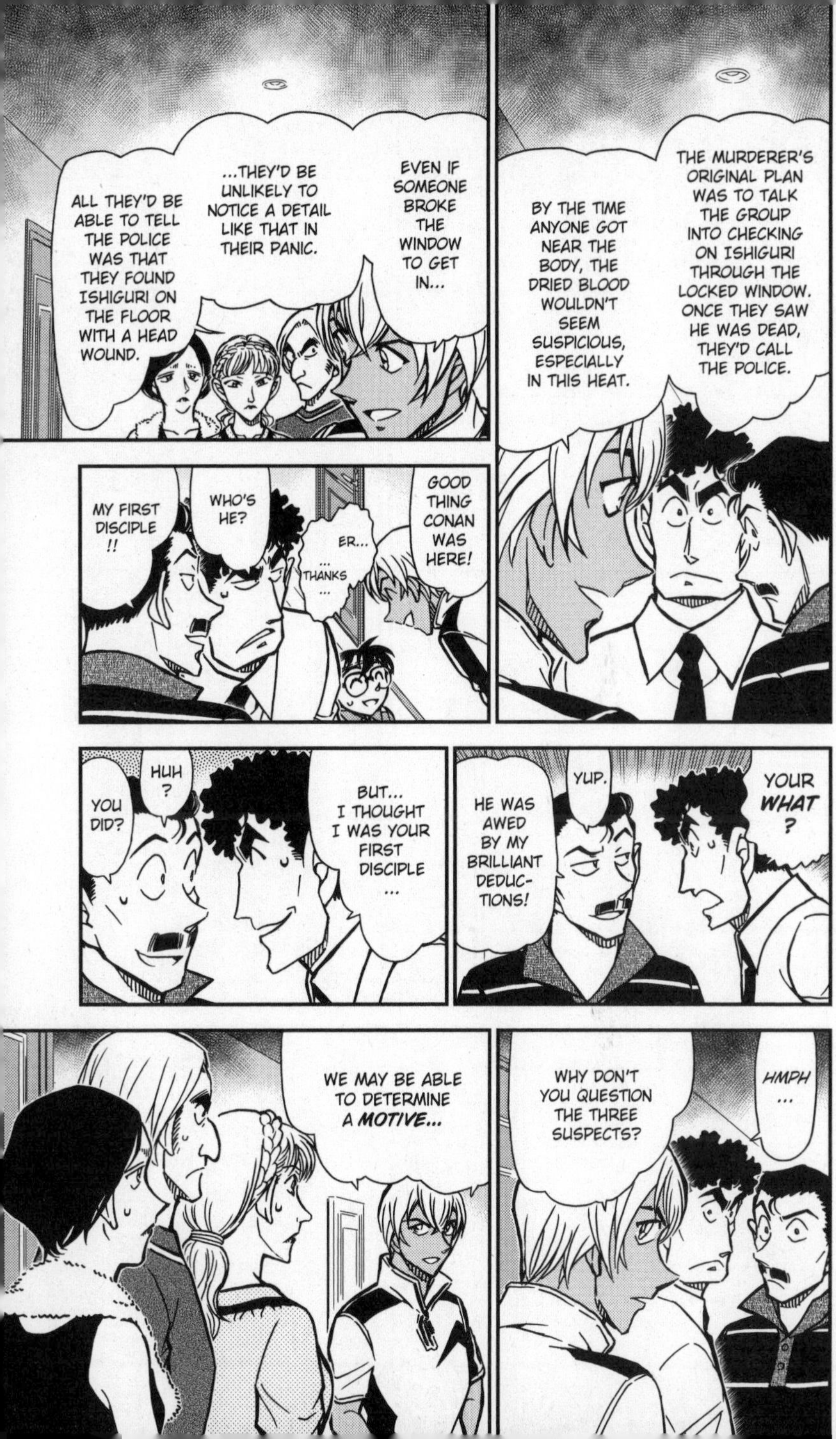
THE MURDERER'S ORIGINAL PLAN WAS TO TALK THE GROUP INTO CHECKING ON ISHIGURI THROUGH THE LOCKED WINDOW. ONCE THEY SAW HE WAS DEAD, THEY'D CALL THE POLICE.
BY THE TIME ANYONE GOT NEAR THE BODY, THE DRIED BLOOD WOULDN'T SEEM SUSPICIOUS, ESPECIALLY IN THIS HEAT.
EVEN IF SOMEONE BROKE THE WINDOW TO GET IN...
...THEY'D BE UNLIKELY TO NOTICE A DETAIL LIKE THAT IN THEIR PANIC.
ALL THEY'D BE ABLE TO TELL THE POLICE WAS THAT THEY FOUND ISHIGURI ON THE FLOOR WITH A HEAD WOUND.
GOOD THING CONAN WAS HERE!
ER... ...THANKS...
WHO'S HE?
MY FIRST DISCIPLE!!
YOUR *WHAT*?
YUP.
HE WAS AWED BY MY BRILLIANT DEDUC-TIONS!
BUT... I THOUGHT I WAS YOUR FIRST DISCIPLE...
HUH?
YOU DID?
HMPH...
WHY DON'T YOU QUESTION THE THREE SUSPECTS?
WE MAY BE ABLE TO DETERMINE A *MOTIVE*...

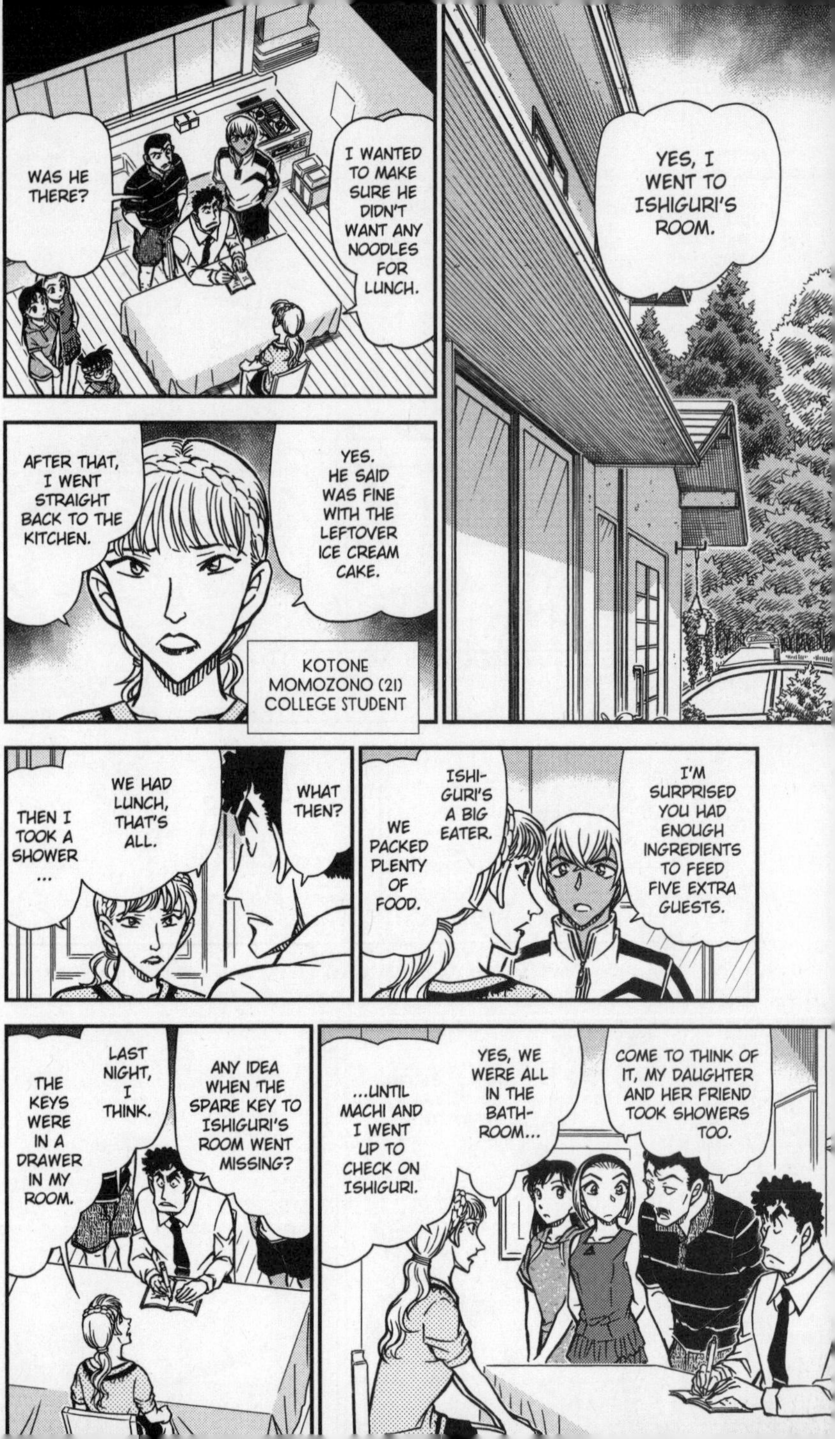
YES, I WENT TO ISHIGURI'S ROOM.
I WANTED TO MAKE SURE HE DIDN'T WANT ANY NOODLES FOR LUNCH.
WAS HE THERE?
YES. HE SAID WAS FINE WITH THE LEFTOVER ICE CREAM CAKE.
AFTER THAT, I WENT STRAIGHT BACK TO THE KITCHEN.
KOTONE MOMOZONO (21) COLLEGE STUDENT
I'M SURPRISED YOU HAD ENOUGH INGREDIENTS TO FEED FIVE EXTRA GUESTS.
ISHIGURI'S A BIG EATER.
WE PACKED PLENTY OF FOOD.
WHAT THEN?
WE HAD LUNCH, THAT'S ALL.
THEN I TOOK A SHOWER ...
COME TO THINK OF IT, MY DAUGHTER AND HER FRIEND TOOK SHOWERS TOO.
YES, WE WERE ALL IN THE BATH-ROOM...
...UNTIL MACHI AND I WENT UP TO CHECK ON ISHIGURI.
ANY IDEA WHEN THE SPARE KEY TO ISHIGURI'S ROOM WENT MISSING?
LAST NIGHT, I THINK.
THE KEYS WERE IN A DRAWER IN MY ROOM.

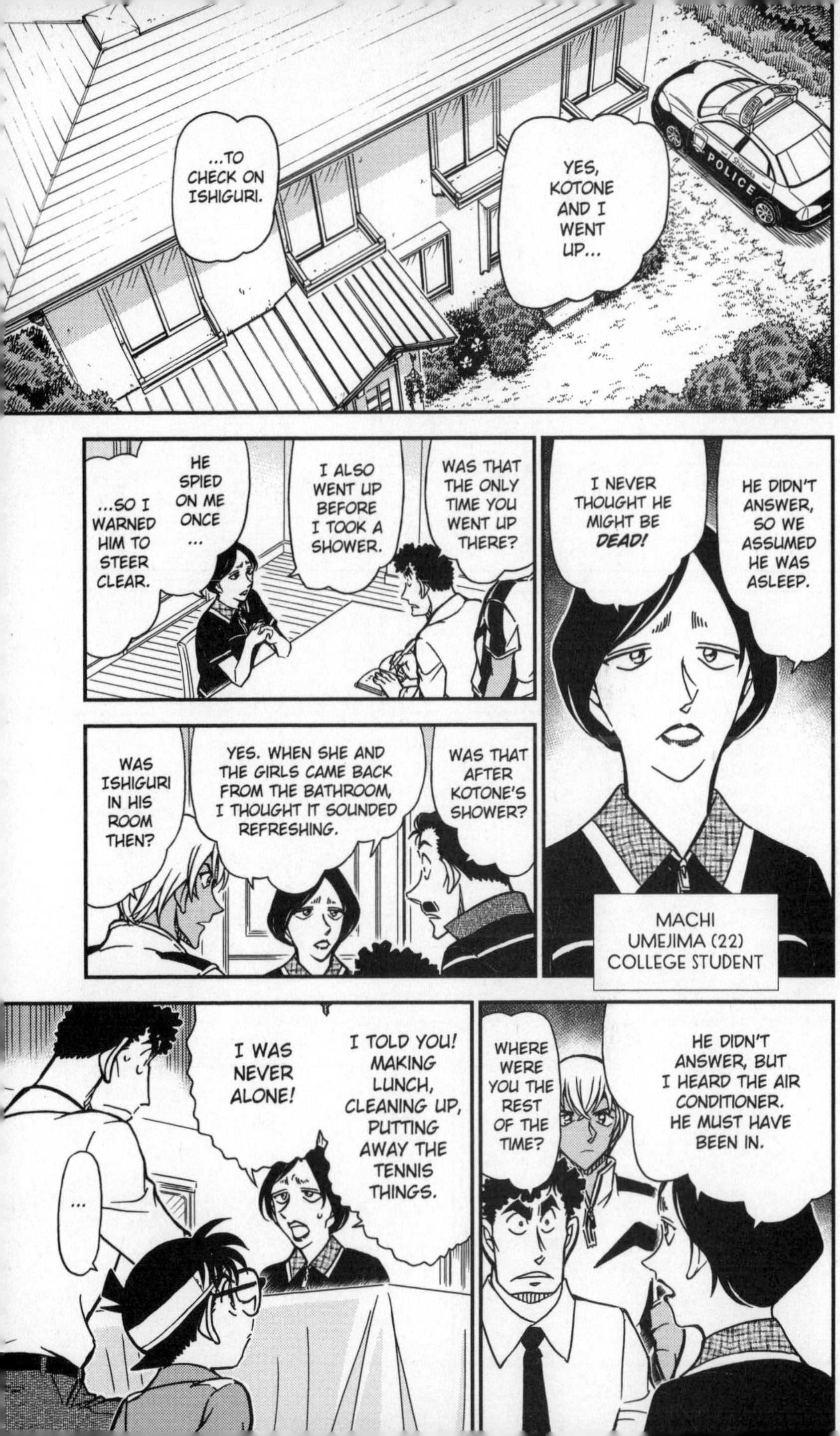
YES, KOTONE AND I WENT UP...
...TO CHECK ON ISHIGURI.
HE DIDN'T ANSWER, SO WE ASSUMED HE WAS ASLEEP.
I NEVER THOUGHT HE MIGHT BE *DEAD!*
MACHI UMEJIMA (22) COLLEGE STUDENT
WAS THAT THE ONLY TIME YOU WENT UP THERE?
I ALSO WENT UP BEFORE I TOOK A SHOWER.
HE SPIED ON ME ONCE...
...SO I WARNED HIM TO STEER CLEAR.
WAS THAT AFTER KOTONE'S SHOWER?
YES. WHEN SHE AND THE GIRLS CAME BACK FROM THE BATHROOM, I THOUGHT IT SOUNDED REFRESHING.
WAS ISHIGURI IN HIS ROOM THEN?
HE DIDN'T ANSWER, BUT I HEARD THE AIR CONDITIONER. HE MUST HAVE BEEN IN.
WHERE WERE YOU THE REST OF THE TIME?
I TOLD YOU! MAKING LUNCH, CLEANING UP, PUTTING AWAY THE TENNIS THINGS.
I WAS NEVER ALONE!
...

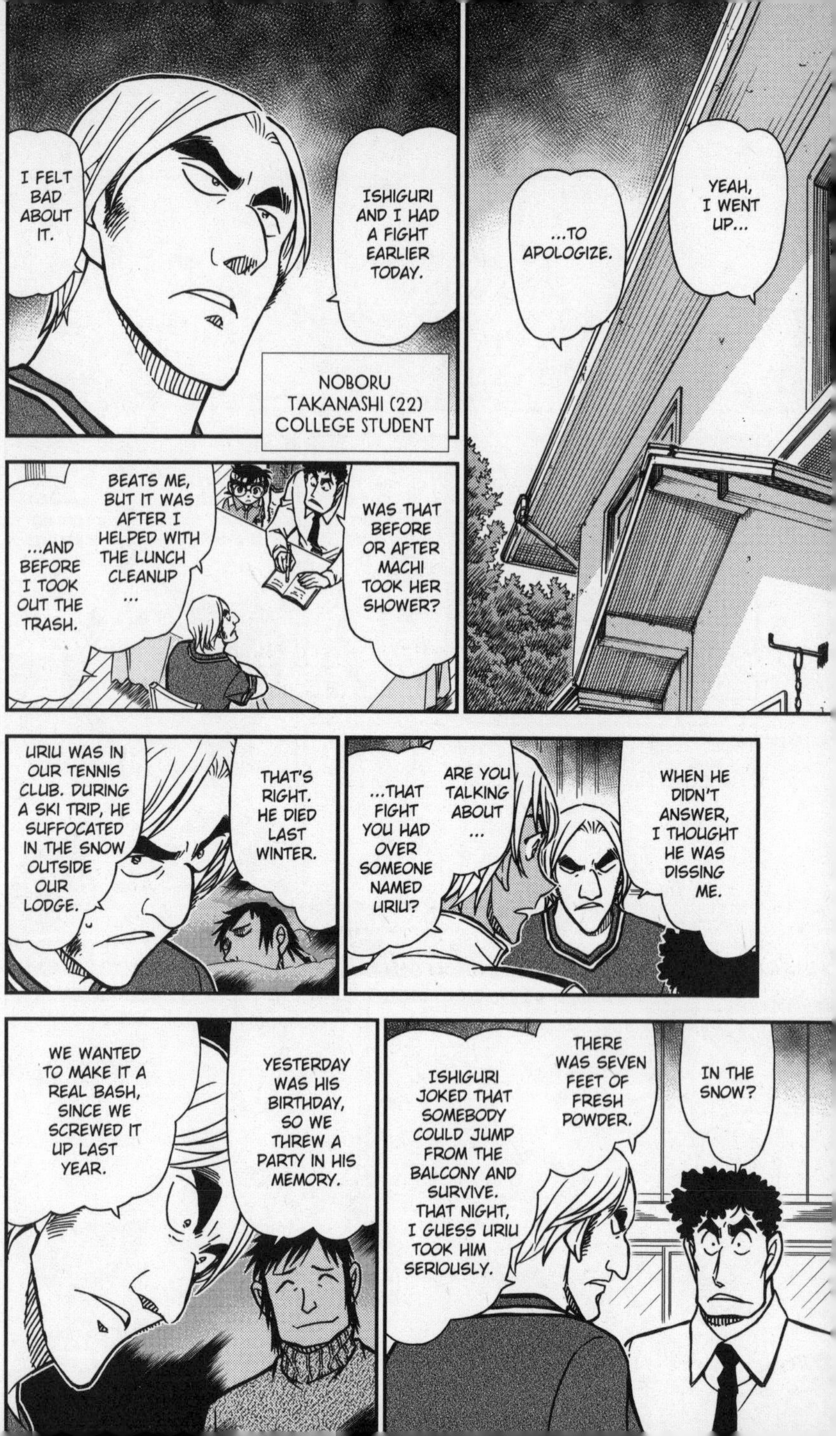
YEAH, I WENT UP...
...TO APOLOGIZE.
ISHIGURI AND I HAD A FIGHT EARLIER TODAY.
I FELT BAD ABOUT IT.
NOBORU TAKANASHI (22) COLLEGE STUDENT
WAS THAT BEFORE OR AFTER MACHI TOOK HER SHOWER?
BEATS ME, BUT IT WAS AFTER I HELPED WITH THE LUNCH CLEANUP ...
...AND BEFORE I TOOK OUT THE TRASH.
WHEN HE DIDN'T ANSWER, I THOUGHT HE WAS DISSING ME.
ARE YOU TALKING ABOUT ...
...THAT FIGHT YOU HAD OVER SOMEONE NAMED URIU?
THAT'S RIGHT. HE DIED LAST WINTER.
URIU WAS IN OUR TENNIS CLUB. DURING A SKI TRIP, HE SUFFOCATED IN THE SNOW OUTSIDE OUR LODGE.
IN THE SNOW?
THERE WAS SEVEN FEET OF FRESH POWDER.
ISHIGURI JOKED THAT SOMEBODY COULD JUMP FROM THE BALCONY AND SURVIVE. THAT NIGHT, I GUESS URIU TOOK HIM SERIOUSLY.
YESTERDAY WAS HIS BIRTHDAY, SO WE THREW A PARTY IN HIS MEMORY.
WE WANTED TO MAKE IT A REAL BASH, SINCE WE SCREWED IT UP LAST YEAR.

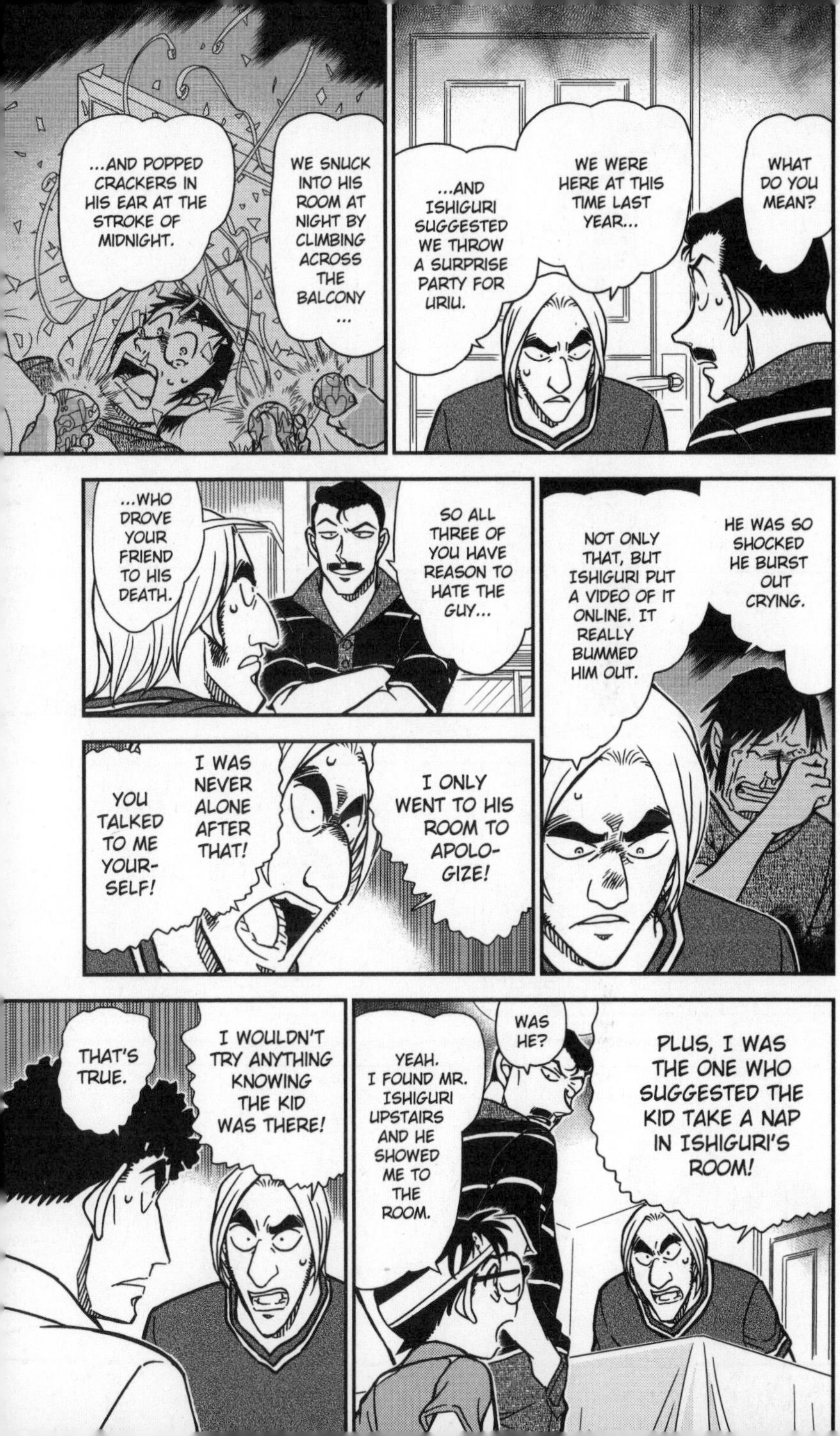
WHAT DO YOU MEAN?
WE WERE HERE AT THIS TIME LAST YEAR...
...AND ISHIGURI SUGGESTED WE THROW A SURPRISE PARTY FOR URIU.
WE SNUCK INTO HIS ROOM AT NIGHT BY CLIMBING ACROSS THE BALCONY ...
...AND POPPED CRACKERS IN HIS EAR AT THE STROKE OF MIDNIGHT.
HE WAS SO SHOCKED HE BURST OUT CRYING.
NOT ONLY THAT, BUT ISHIGURI PUT A VIDEO OF IT ONLINE. IT REALLY BUMMED HIM OUT.
SO ALL THREE OF YOU HAVE REASON TO HATE THE GUY...
...WHO DROVE YOUR FRIEND TO HIS DEATH.
I ONLY WENT TO HIS ROOM TO APOLOGIZE!
I WAS NEVER ALONE AFTER THAT!
YOU TALKED TO ME YOURSELF!
PLUS, I WAS THE ONE WHO SUGGESTED THE KID TAKE A NAP IN ISHIGURI'S ROOM!
WAS HE?
YEAH. I FOUND MR. ISHIGURI UPSTAIRS AND HE SHOWED ME TO THE ROOM.
I WOULDN'T TRY ANYTHING KNOWING THE KID WAS THERE!
THAT'S TRUE.

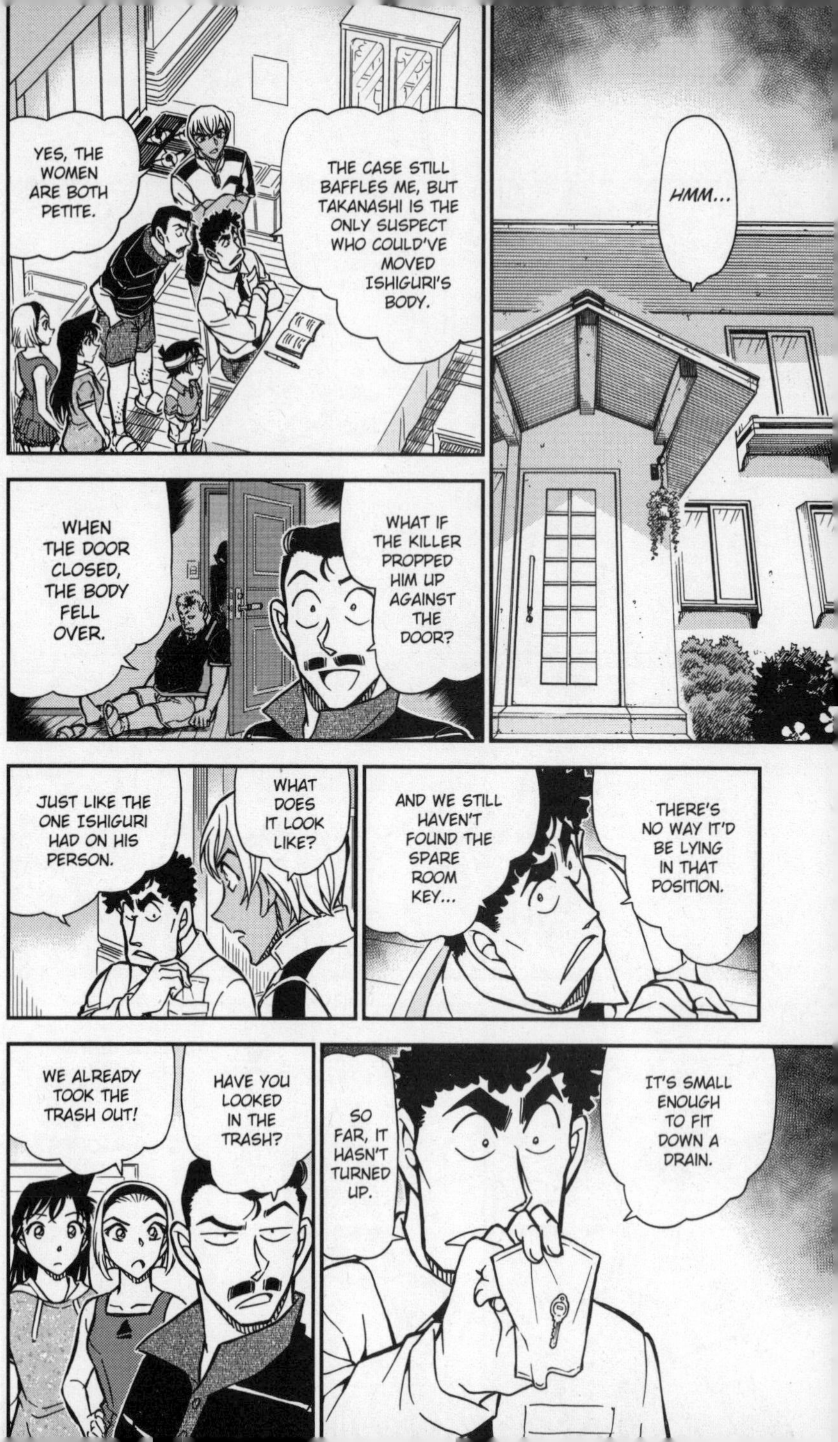
HMM...
THE CASE STILL BAFFLES ME, BUT TAKANASHI IS THE ONLY SUSPECT WHO COULD'VE MOVED ISHIGURI'S BODY.
YES, THE WOMEN ARE BOTH PETITE.
WHAT IF THE KILLER PROPPED HIM UP AGAINST THE DOOR?
WHEN THE DOOR CLOSED, THE BODY FELL OVER.
THERE'S NO WAY IT'D BE LYING IN THAT POSITION.
AND WE STILL HAVEN'T FOUND THE SPARE ROOM KEY...
WHAT DOES IT LOOK LIKE?
JUST LIKE THE ONE ISHIGURI HAD ON HIS PERSON.
IT'S SMALL ENOUGH TO FIT DOWN A DRAIN.
SO FAR, IT HASN'T TURNED UP.
HAVE YOU LOOKED IN THE TRASH?
WE ALREADY TOOK THE TRASH OUT!

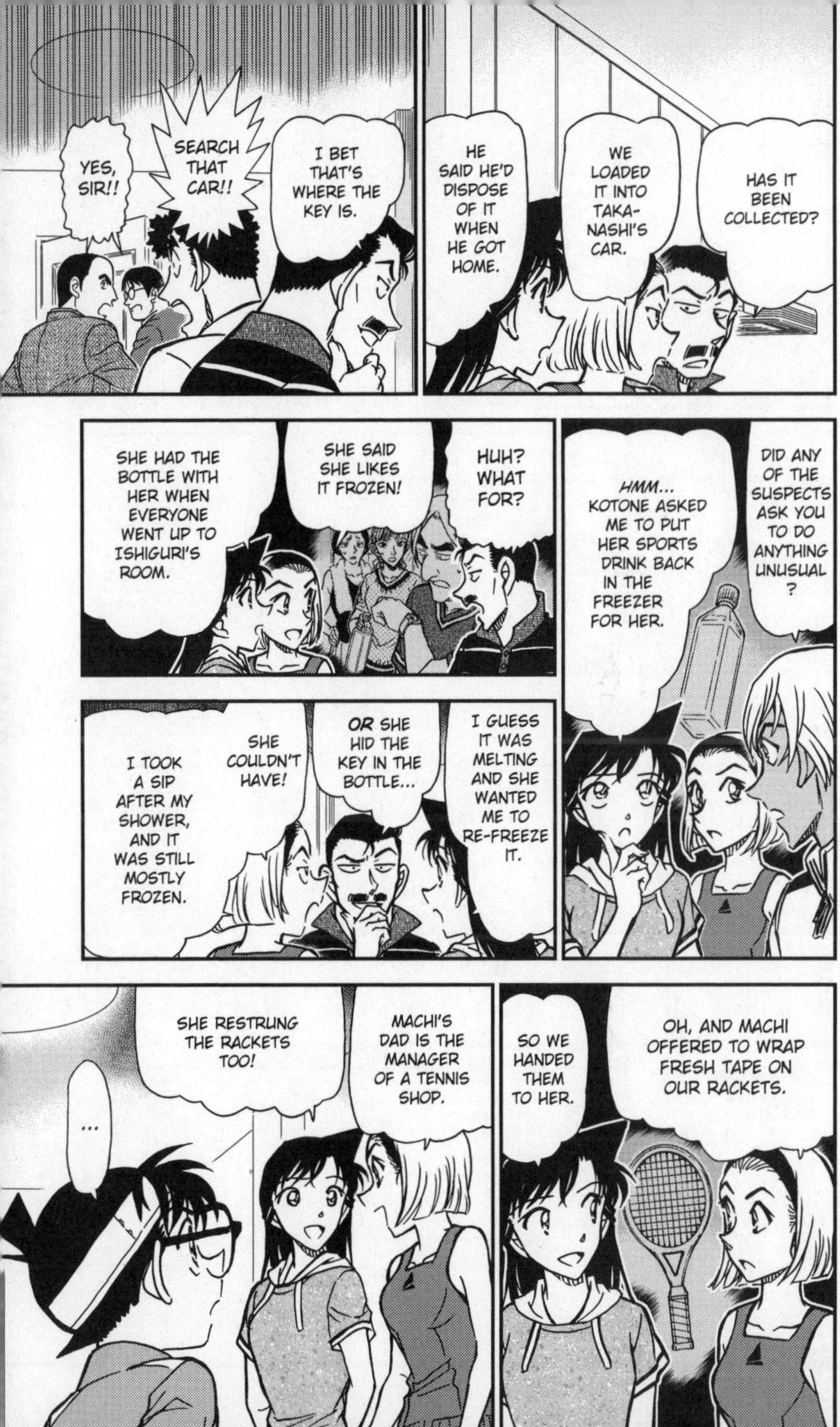
HAS IT BEEN COLLECTED?
WE LOADED IT INTO TAKA-NASHI'S CAR.
HE SAID HE'D DISPOSE OF IT WHEN HE GOT HOME.
I BET THAT'S WHERE THE KEY IS.
SEARCH THAT CAR!!
YES, SIR!!
DID ANY OF THE SUSPECTS ASK YOU TO DO ANYTHING UNUSUAL?
HMM... KOTONE ASKED ME TO PUT HER SPORTS DRINK BACK IN THE FREEZER FOR HER.
HUH? WHAT FOR?
SHE SAID SHE LIKES IT FROZEN!
SHE HAD THE BOTTLE WITH HER WHEN EVERYONE WENT UP TO ISHIGURI'S ROOM.
I GUESS IT WAS MELTING AND SHE WANTED ME TO RE-FREEZE IT.
OR SHE HID THE KEY IN THE BOTTLE...
SHE COULDN'T HAVE!
I TOOK A SIP AFTER MY SHOWER, AND IT WAS STILL MOSTLY FROZEN.
OH, AND MACHI OFFERED TO WRAP FRESH TAPE ON OUR RACKETS.
SO WE HANDED THEM TO HER.
MACHI'S DAD IS THE MANAGER OF A TENNIS SHOP.
SHE RESTRUNG THE RACKETS TOO!
...

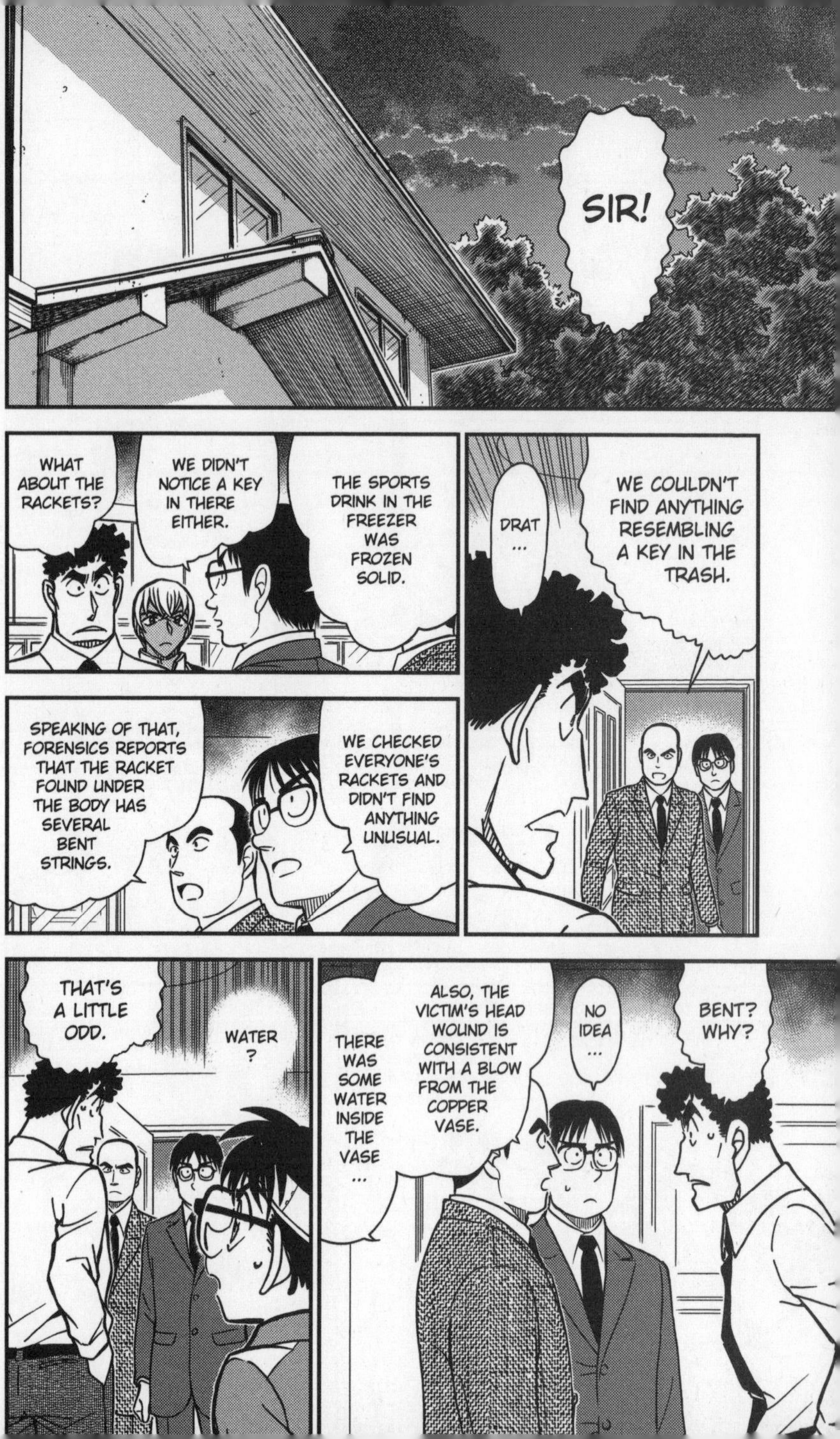
SIR!
WE COULDN'T FIND ANYTHING RESEMBLING A KEY IN THE TRASH.
DRAT ...
THE SPORTS DRINK IN THE FREEZER WAS FROZEN SOLID.
WE DIDN'T NOTICE A KEY IN THERE EITHER.
WHAT ABOUT THE RACKETS?
WE CHECKED EVERYONE'S RACKETS AND DIDN'T FIND ANYTHING UNUSUAL.
SPEAKING OF THAT, FORENSICS REPORTS THAT THE RACKET FOUND UNDER THE BODY HAS SEVERAL BENT STRINGS.
BENT? WHY?
NO IDEA ...
ALSO, THE VICTIM'S HEAD WOUND IS CONSISTENT WITH A BLOW FROM THE COPPER VASE.
THERE WAS SOME WATER INSIDE THE VASE ...
WATER ?
THAT'S A LITTLE ODD.

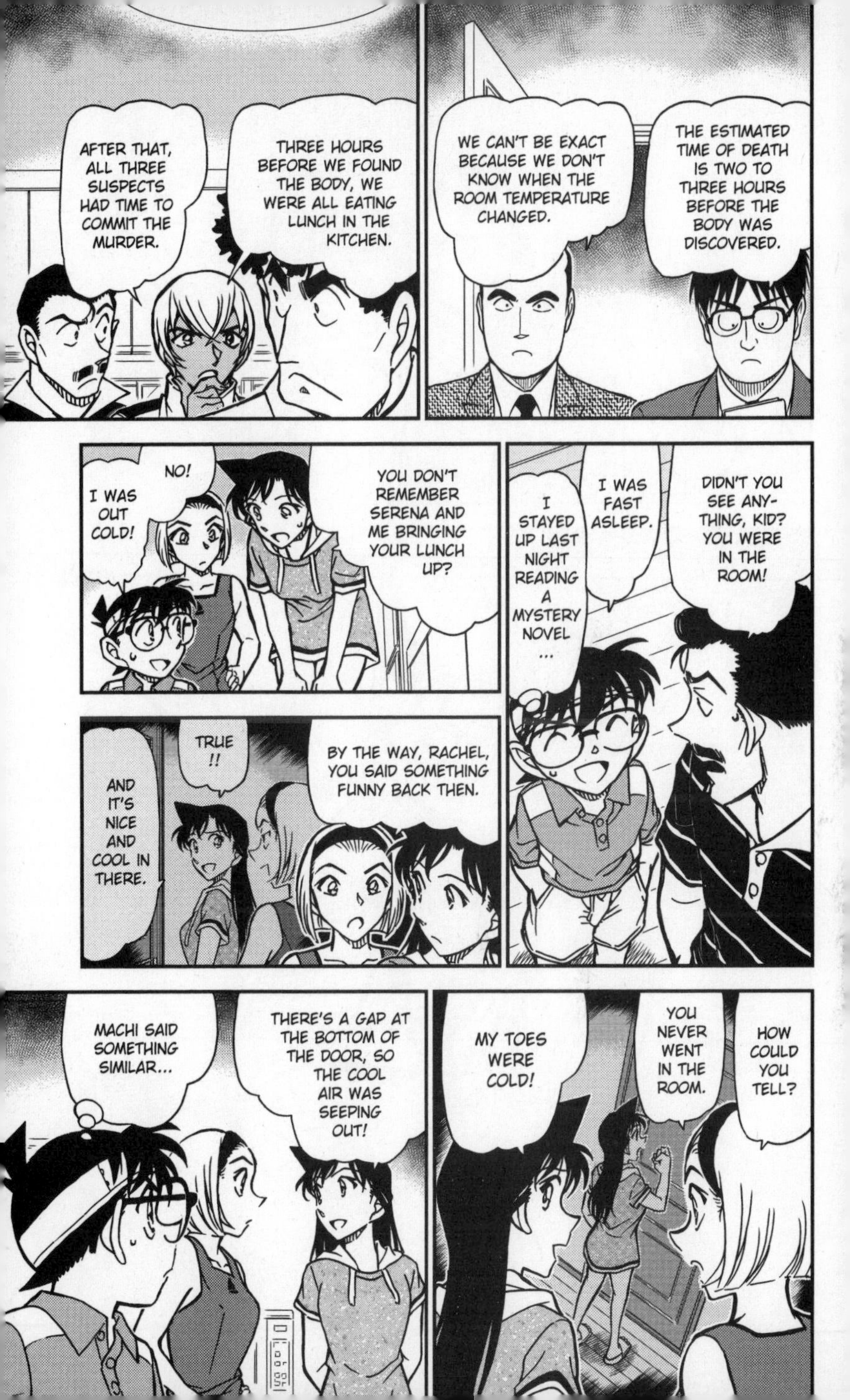
THE ESTIMATED TIME OF DEATH IS TWO TO THREE HOURS BEFORE THE BODY WAS DISCOVERED.
WE CAN'T BE EXACT BECAUSE WE DON'T KNOW WHEN THE ROOM TEMPERATURE CHANGED.
THREE HOURS BEFORE WE FOUND THE BODY, WE WERE ALL EATING LUNCH IN THE KITCHEN.
AFTER THAT, ALL THREE SUSPECTS HAD TIME TO COMMIT THE MURDER.
DIDN'T YOU SEE ANY-THING, KID? YOU WERE IN THE ROOM!
I WAS FAST ASLEEP.
I STAYED UP LAST NIGHT READING A MYSTERY NOVEL ...
YOU DON'T REMEMBER SERENA AND ME BRINGING YOUR LUNCH UP?
NO!
I WAS OUT COLD!
BY THE WAY, RACHEL, YOU SAID SOMETHING FUNNY BACK THEN.
TRUE !!
AND IT'S NICE AND COOL IN THERE.
HOW COULD YOU TELL?
YOU NEVER WENT IN THE ROOM.
MY TOES WERE COLD!
THERE'S A GAP AT THE BOTTOM OF THE DOOR, SO THE COOL AIR WAS SEEPING OUT!
MACHI SAID SOMETHING SIMILAR...

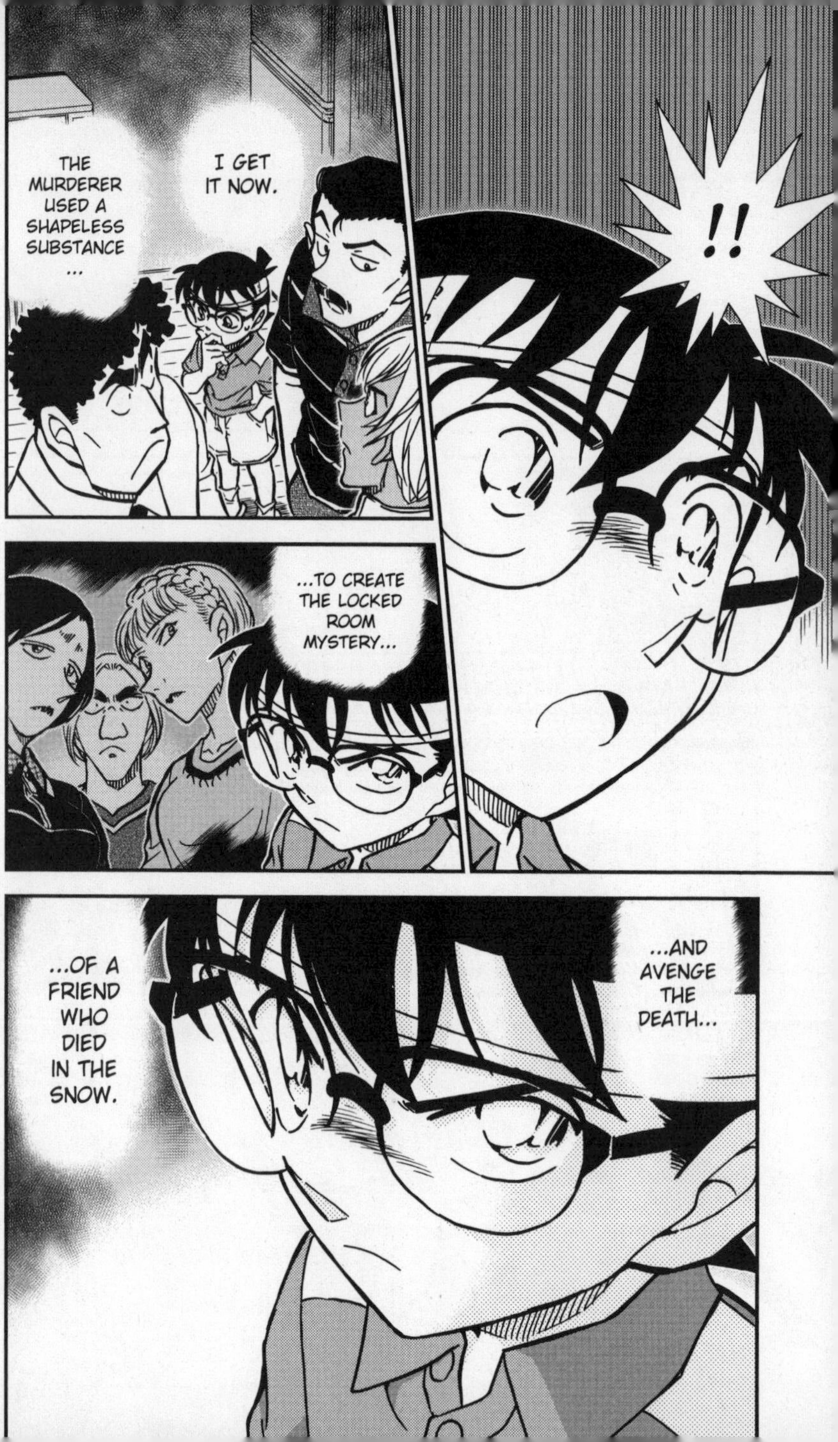
!!
I GET IT NOW.
THE MURDERER USED A SHAPELESS SUBSTANCE ...
...TO CREATE THE LOCKED ROOM MYSTERY...
...AND AVENGE THE DEATH...
...OF A FRIEND WHO DIED IN THE SNOW.

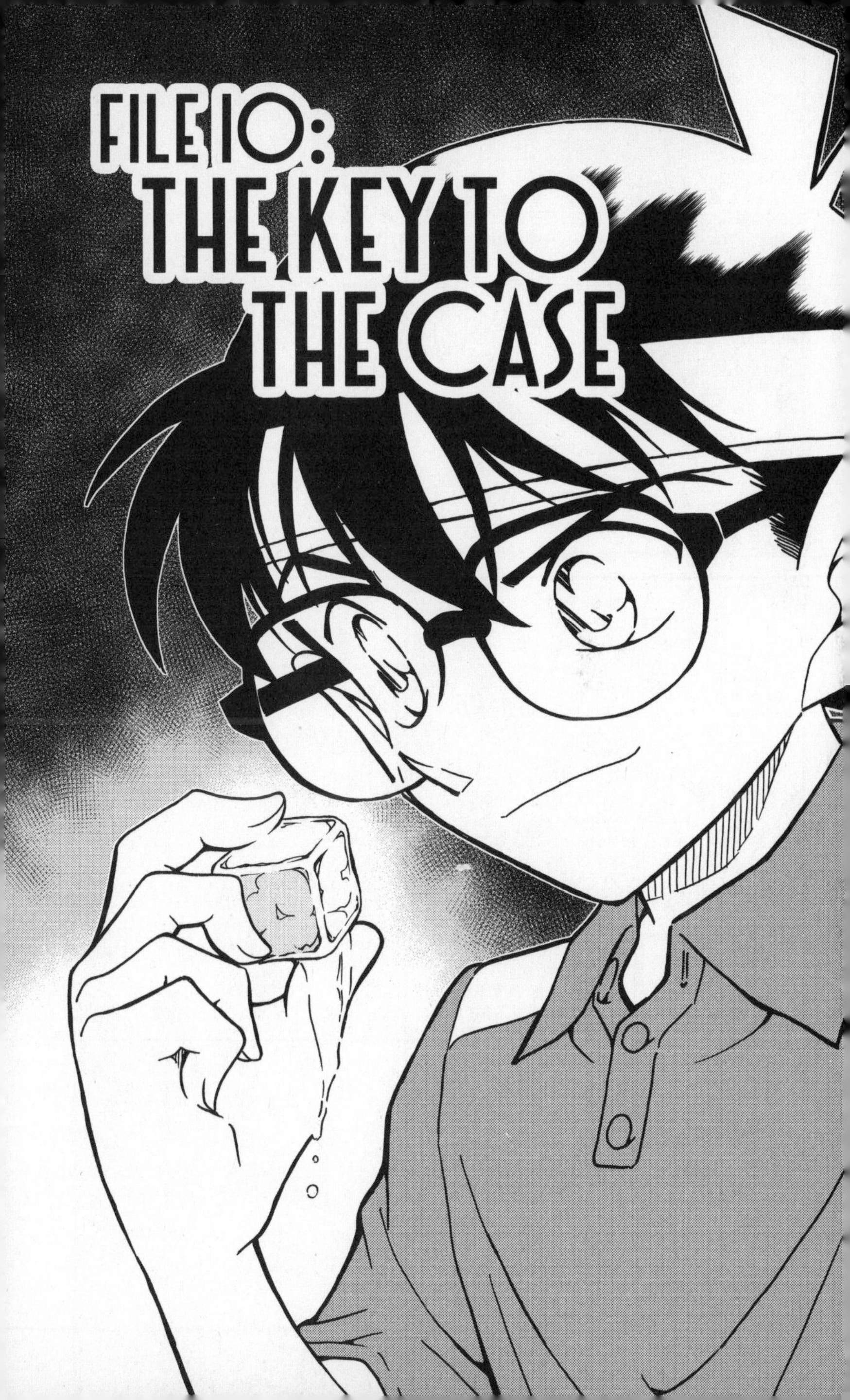
FILE 10:
THE KEY TO THE CASE

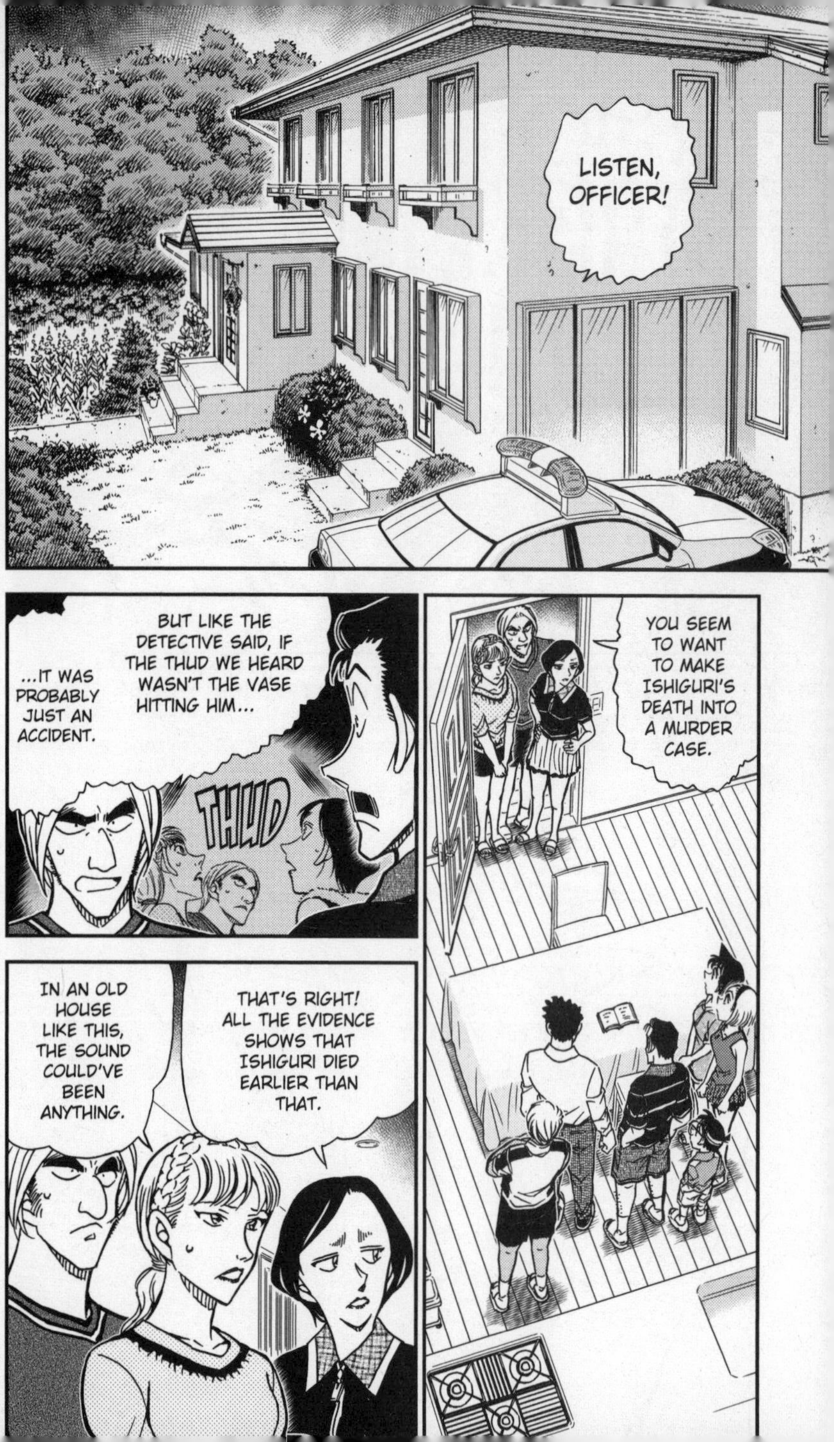
LISTEN, OFFICER!
YOU SEEM TO WANT TO MAKE ISHIGURI'S DEATH INTO A MURDER CASE.
BUT LIKE THE DETECTIVE SAID, IF THE THUD WE HEARD WASN'T THE VASE HITTING HIM...
...IT WAS PROBABLY JUST AN ACCIDENT.
THUD
THAT'S RIGHT! ALL THE EVIDENCE SHOWS THAT ISHIGURI DIED EARLIER THAN THAT.
IN AN OLD HOUSE LIKE THIS, THE SOUND COULD'VE BEEN ANYTHING.

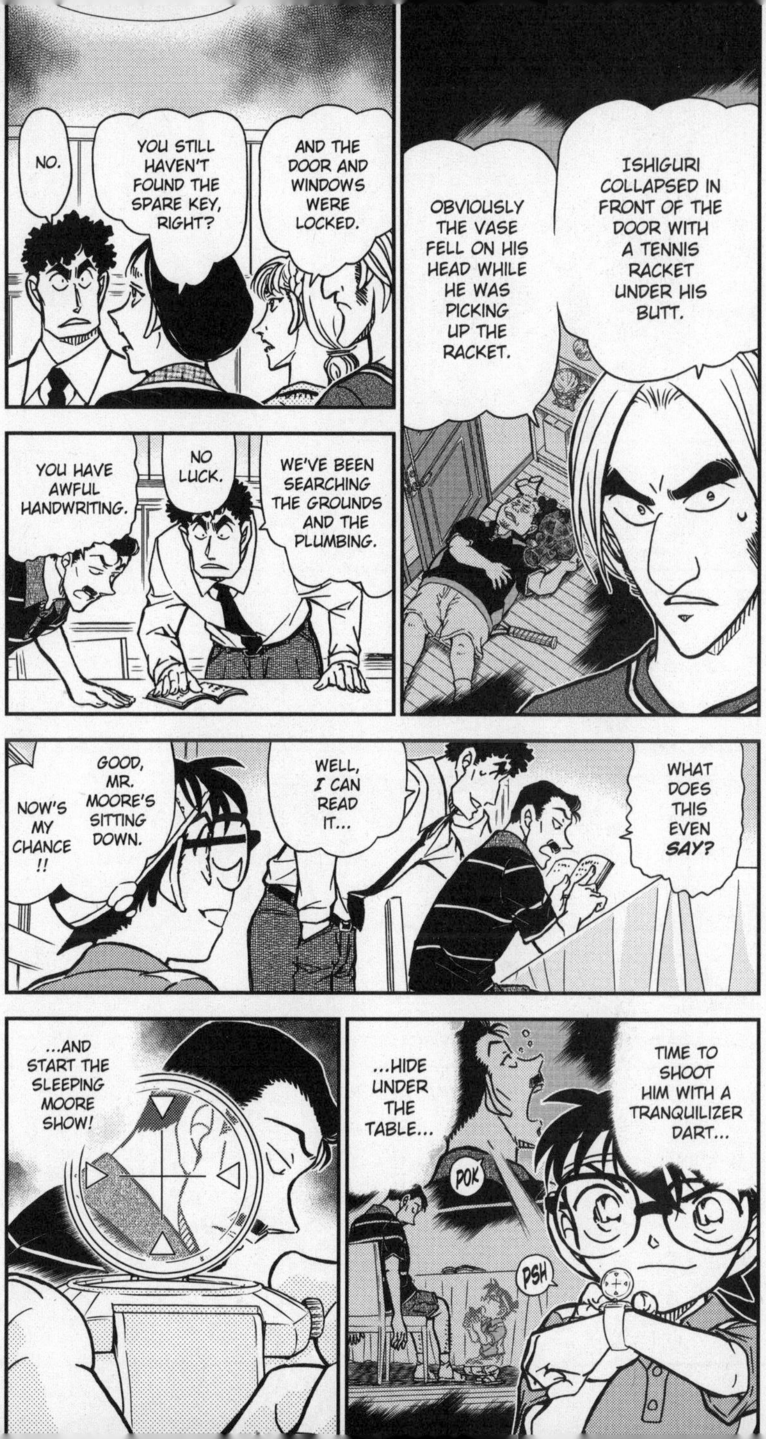
ISHIGURI COLLAPSED IN FRONT OF THE DOOR WITH A TENNIS RACKET UNDER HIS BUTT.
OBVIOUSLY THE VASE FELL ON HIS HEAD WHILE HE WAS PICKING UP THE RACKET.
AND THE DOOR AND WINDOWS WERE LOCKED.
YOU STILL HAVEN'T FOUND THE SPARE KEY, RIGHT?
NO.
WE'VE BEEN SEARCHING THE GROUNDS AND THE PLUMBING.
NO LUCK.
YOU HAVE AWFUL HANDWRITING.
WHAT DOES THIS EVEN *SAY?*
WELL, *I* CAN READ IT...
GOOD, MR. MOORE'S SITTING DOWN.
NOW'S MY CHANCE !!
TIME TO SHOOT HIM WITH A TRANQUILIZER DART...
PSH
POK
...HIDE UNDER THE TABLE...
...AND START THE SLEEPING MOORE SHOW!

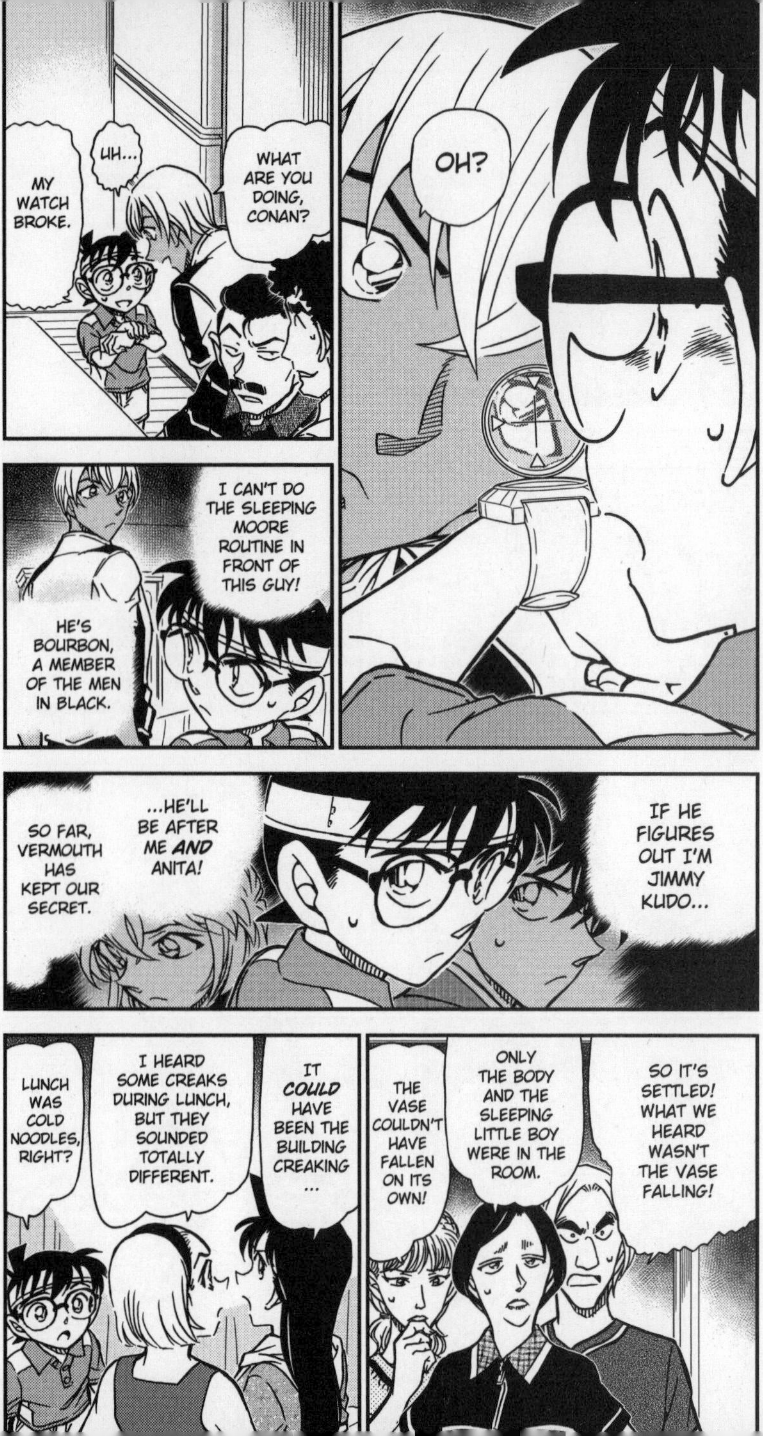
OH?
WHAT ARE YOU DOING, CONAN?
UH...
MY WATCH BROKE.
I CAN'T DO THE SLEEPING MOORE ROUTINE IN FRONT OF THIS GUY!
HE'S BOURBON, A MEMBER OF THE MEN IN BLACK.
IF HE FIGURES OUT I'M JIMMY KUDO...
...HE'LL BE AFTER ME *AND* ANITA!
SO FAR, VERMOUTH HAS KEPT OUR SECRET.
SO IT'S SETTLED! WHAT WE HEARD WASN'T THE VASE FALLING!
ONLY THE BODY AND THE SLEEPING LITTLE BOY WERE IN THE ROOM.
THE VASE COULDN'T HAVE FALLEN ON ITS OWN!
IT *COULD* HAVE BEEN THE BUILDING CREAKING...
I HEARD SOME CREAKS DURING LUNCH, BUT THEY SOUNDED TOTALLY DIFFERENT.
LUNCH WAS COLD NOODLES, RIGHT?

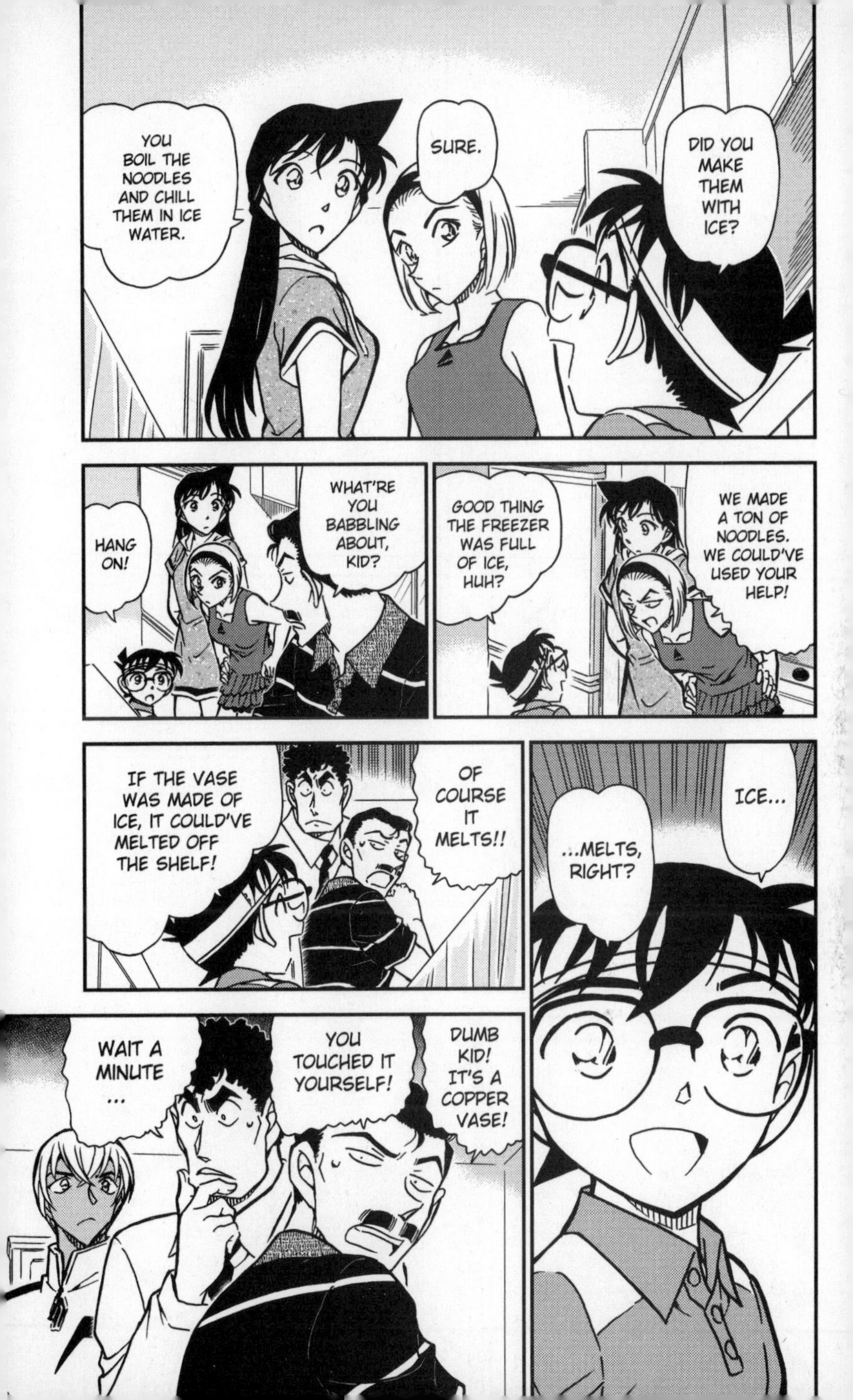
DID YOU MAKE THEM WITH ICE?
SURE.
YOU BOIL THE NOODLES AND CHILL THEM IN ICE WATER.
WE MADE A TON OF NOODLES. WE COULD'VE USED YOUR HELP!
GOOD THING THE FREEZER WAS FULL OF ICE, HUH?
WHAT'RE YOU BABBLING ABOUT, KID?
HANG ON!
ICE...
...MELTS, RIGHT?
OF COURSE IT MELTS!!
IF THE VASE WAS MADE OF ICE, IT COULD'VE MELTED OFF THE SHELF!
DUMB KID! IT'S A COPPER VASE!
YOU TOUCHED IT YOURSELF!
WAIT A MINUTE ...

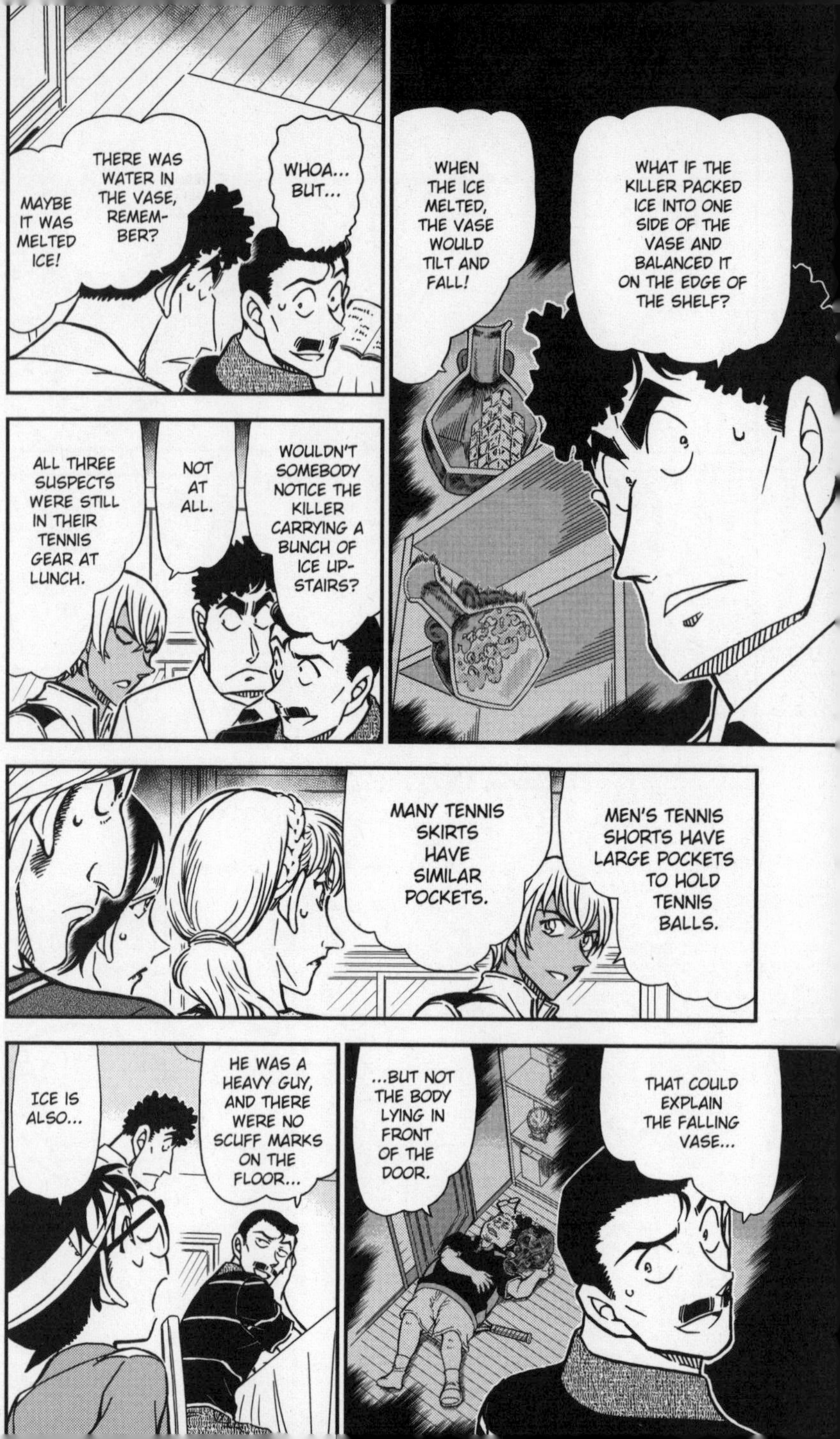
WHAT IF THE KILLER PACKED ICE INTO ONE SIDE OF THE VASE AND BALANCED IT ON THE EDGE OF THE SHELF?
WHEN THE ICE MELTED, THE VASE WOULD TILT AND FALL!
WHOA... BUT...
THERE WAS WATER IN THE VASE, REMEMBER?
MAYBE IT WAS MELTED ICE!
WOULDN'T SOMEBODY NOTICE THE KILLER CARRYING A BUNCH OF ICE UPSTAIRS?
NOT AT ALL.
ALL THREE SUSPECTS WERE STILL IN THEIR TENNIS GEAR AT LUNCH.
MEN'S TENNIS SHORTS HAVE LARGE POCKETS TO HOLD TENNIS BALLS.
MANY TENNIS SKIRTS HAVE SIMILAR POCKETS.
THAT COULD EXPLAIN THE FALLING VASE...
...BUT NOT THE BODY LYING IN FRONT OF THE DOOR.
HE WAS A HEAVY GUY, AND THERE WERE NO SCUFF MARKS ON THE FLOOR...
ICE IS ALSO...

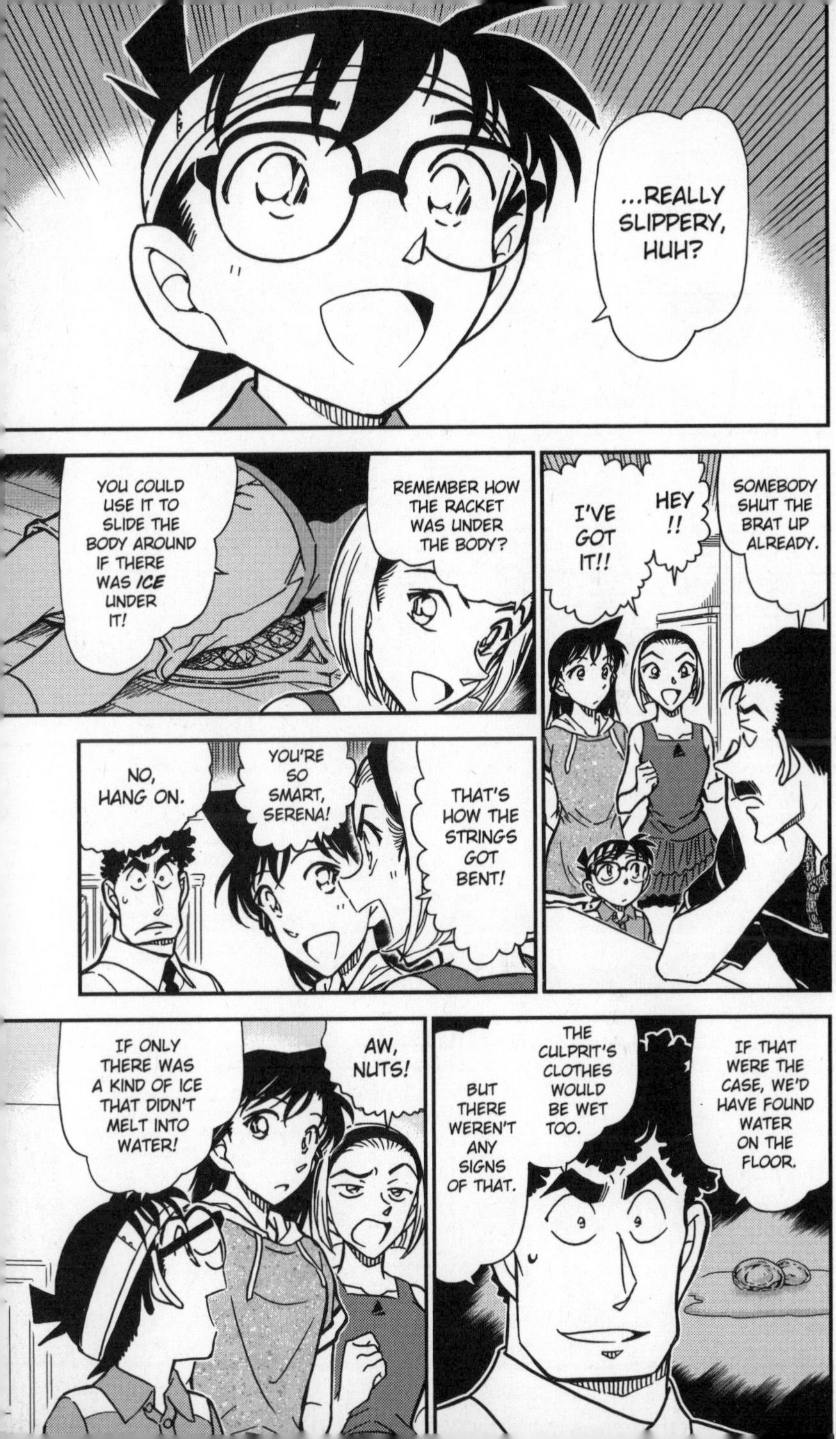
...REALLY SLIPPERY, HUH?
SOMEBODY SHUT THE BRAT UP ALREADY.
HEY!!
I'VE GOT IT!!
REMEMBER HOW THE RACKET WAS UNDER THE BODY?
YOU COULD USE IT TO SLIDE THE BODY AROUND IF THERE WAS *ICE* UNDER IT!
THAT'S HOW THE STRINGS GOT BENT!
YOU'RE SO SMART, SERENA!
NO, HANG ON.
IF THAT WERE THE CASE, WE'D HAVE FOUND WATER ON THE FLOOR.
THE CULPRIT'S CLOTHES WOULD BE WET TOO.
BUT THERE WEREN'T ANY SIGNS OF THAT.
AW, NUTS!
IF ONLY THERE WAS A KIND OF ICE THAT DIDN'T MELT INTO WATER!

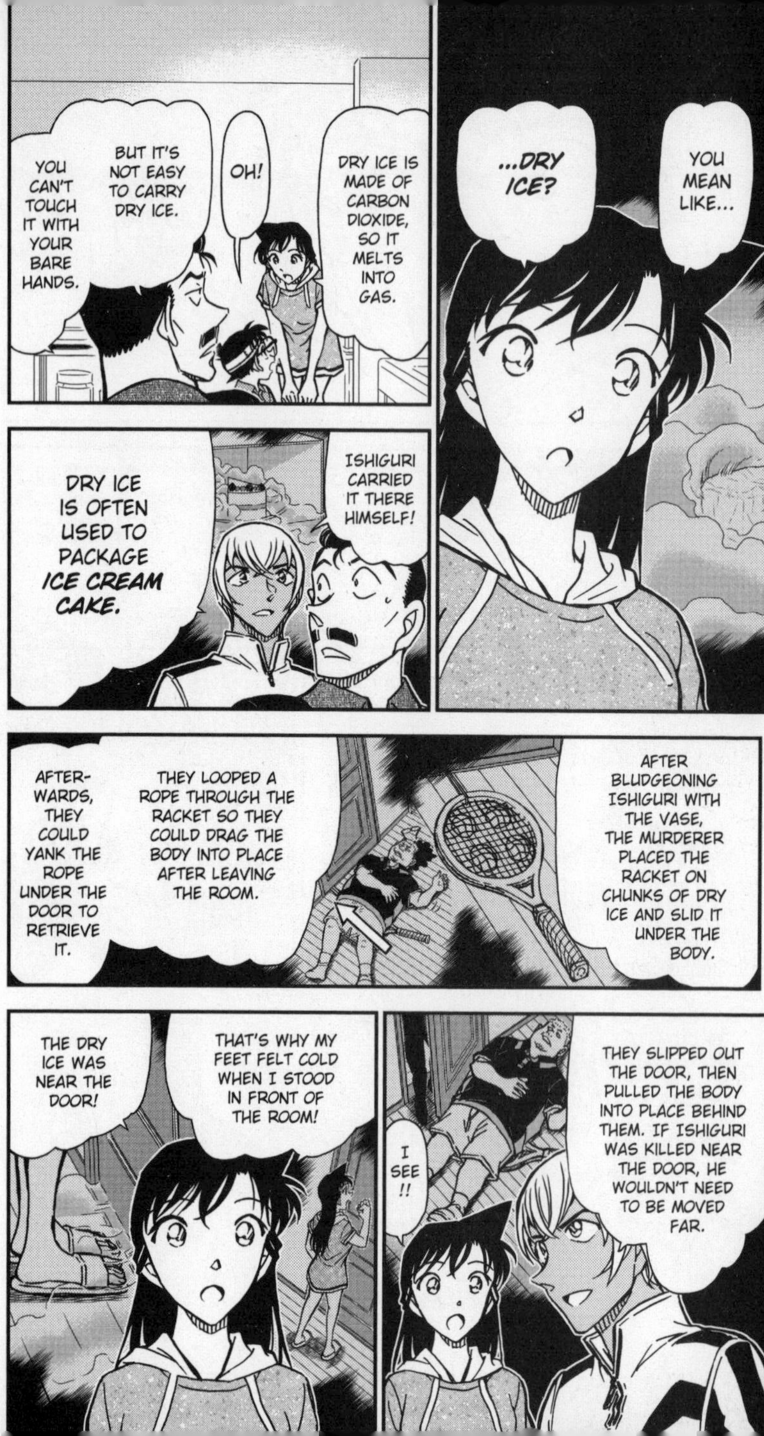
YOU MEAN LIKE...
...DRY ICE?
DRY ICE IS MADE OF CARBON DIOXIDE, SO IT MELTS INTO GAS.
OH!
BUT IT'S NOT EASY TO CARRY DRY ICE.
YOU CAN'T TOUCH IT WITH YOUR BARE HANDS.
ISHIGURI CARRIED IT THERE HIMSELF!
DRY ICE IS OFTEN USED TO PACKAGE ICE CREAM CAKE.
AFTER BLUDGEONING ISHIGURI WITH THE VASE, THE MURDERER PLACED THE RACKET ON CHUNKS OF DRY ICE AND SLID IT UNDER THE BODY.
THEY LOOPED A ROPE THROUGH THE RACKET SO THEY COULD DRAG THE BODY INTO PLACE AFTER LEAVING THE ROOM.
AFTER-WARDS, THEY COULD YANK THE ROPE UNDER THE DOOR TO RETRIEVE IT.
THEY SLIPPED OUT THE DOOR, THEN PULLED THE BODY INTO PLACE BEHIND THEM. IF ISHIGURI WAS KILLED NEAR THE DOOR, HE WOULDN'T NEED TO BE MOVED FAR.
I SEE!!
THAT'S WHY MY FEET FELT COLD WHEN I STOOD IN FRONT OF THE ROOM!
THE DRY ICE WAS NEAR THE DOOR!

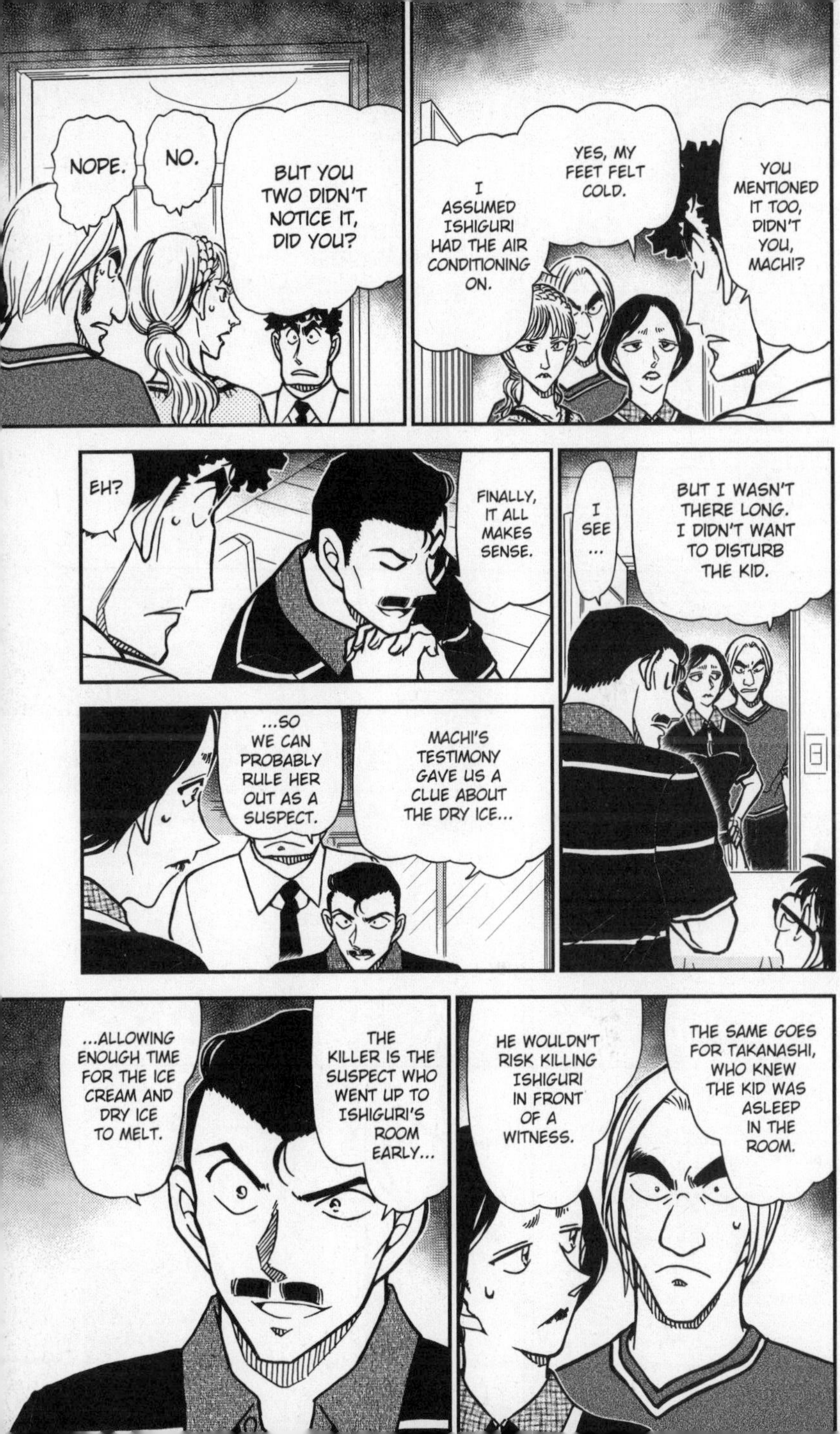
YOU MENTIONED IT TOO, DIDN'T YOU, MACHI?
YES, MY FEET FELT COLD.
I ASSUMED ISHIGURI HAD THE AIR CONDITIONING ON.
BUT YOU TWO DIDN'T NOTICE IT, DID YOU?
NO.
NOPE.
BUT I WASN'T THERE LONG. I DIDN'T WANT TO DISTURB THE KID.
I SEE...
FINALLY, IT ALL MAKES SENSE.
EH?
MACHI'S TESTIMONY GAVE US A CLUE ABOUT THE DRY ICE...
...SO WE CAN PROBABLY RULE HER OUT AS A SUSPECT.
THE SAME GOES FOR TAKANASHI, WHO KNEW THE KID WAS ASLEEP IN THE ROOM.
HE WOULDN'T RISK KILLING ISHIGURI IN FRONT OF A WITNESS.
THE KILLER IS THE SUSPECT WHO WENT UP TO ISHIGURI'S ROOM EARLY...
...ALLOWING ENOUGH TIME FOR THE ICE CREAM AND DRY ICE TO MELT.

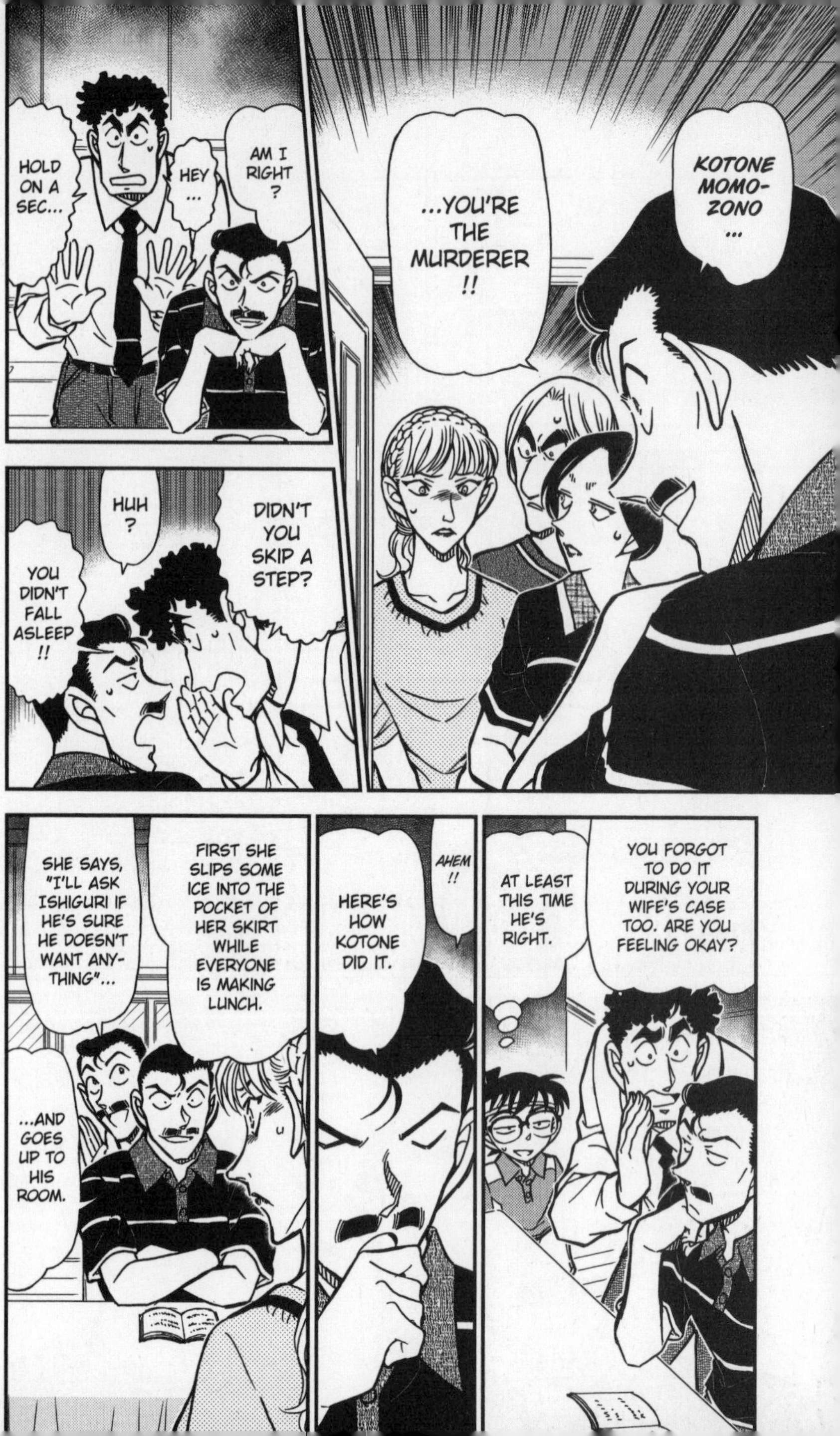
KOTONE MOMO-ZONO ...
...YOU'RE THE MURDERER !!
AM I RIGHT ?
HEY ...
HOLD ON A SEC...
DIDN'T YOU SKIP A STEP?
HUH ?
YOU DIDN'T FALL ASLEEP !!
YOU FORGOT TO DO IT DURING YOUR WIFE'S CASE TOO. ARE YOU FEELING OKAY?
AT LEAST THIS TIME HE'S RIGHT.
AHEM !!
HERE'S HOW KOTONE DID IT.
FIRST SHE SLIPS SOME ICE INTO THE POCKET OF HER SKIRT WHILE EVERYONE IS MAKING LUNCH.
SHE SAYS, "I'LL ASK ISHIGURI IF HE'S SURE HE DOESN'T WANT ANY-THING"...
...AND GOES UP TO HIS ROOM.

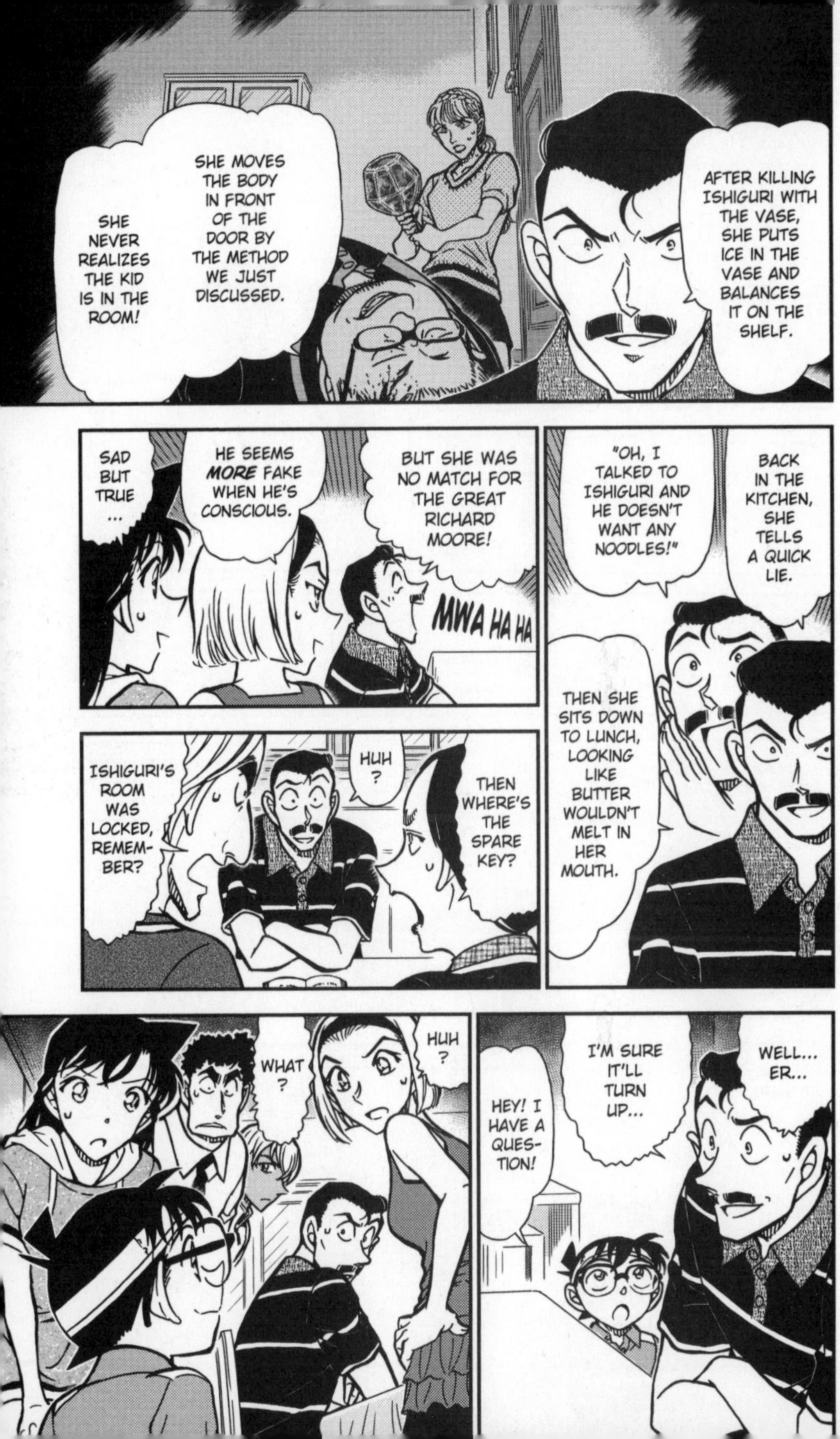
AFTER KILLING ISHIGURI WITH THE VASE, SHE PUTS ICE IN THE VASE AND BALANCES IT ON THE SHELF.
SHE MOVES THE BODY IN FRONT OF THE DOOR BY THE METHOD WE JUST DISCUSSED.
SHE NEVER REALIZES THE KID IS IN THE ROOM!
BACK IN THE KITCHEN, SHE TELLS A QUICK LIE.
"OH, I TALKED TO ISHIGURI AND HE DOESN'T WANT ANY NOODLES!"
THEN SHE SITS DOWN TO LUNCH, LOOKING LIKE BUTTER WOULDN'T MELT IN HER MOUTH.
BUT SHE WAS NO MATCH FOR THE GREAT RICHARD MOORE!
MWA HA HA
HE SEEMS *MORE* FAKE WHEN HE'S CONSCIOUS.
SAD BUT TRUE ...
THEN WHERE'S THE SPARE KEY?
HUH ?
ISHIGURI'S ROOM WAS LOCKED, REMEMBER?
WELL... ER...
I'M SURE IT'LL TURN UP...
HEY! I HAVE A QUESTION!
HUH ?
WHAT ?

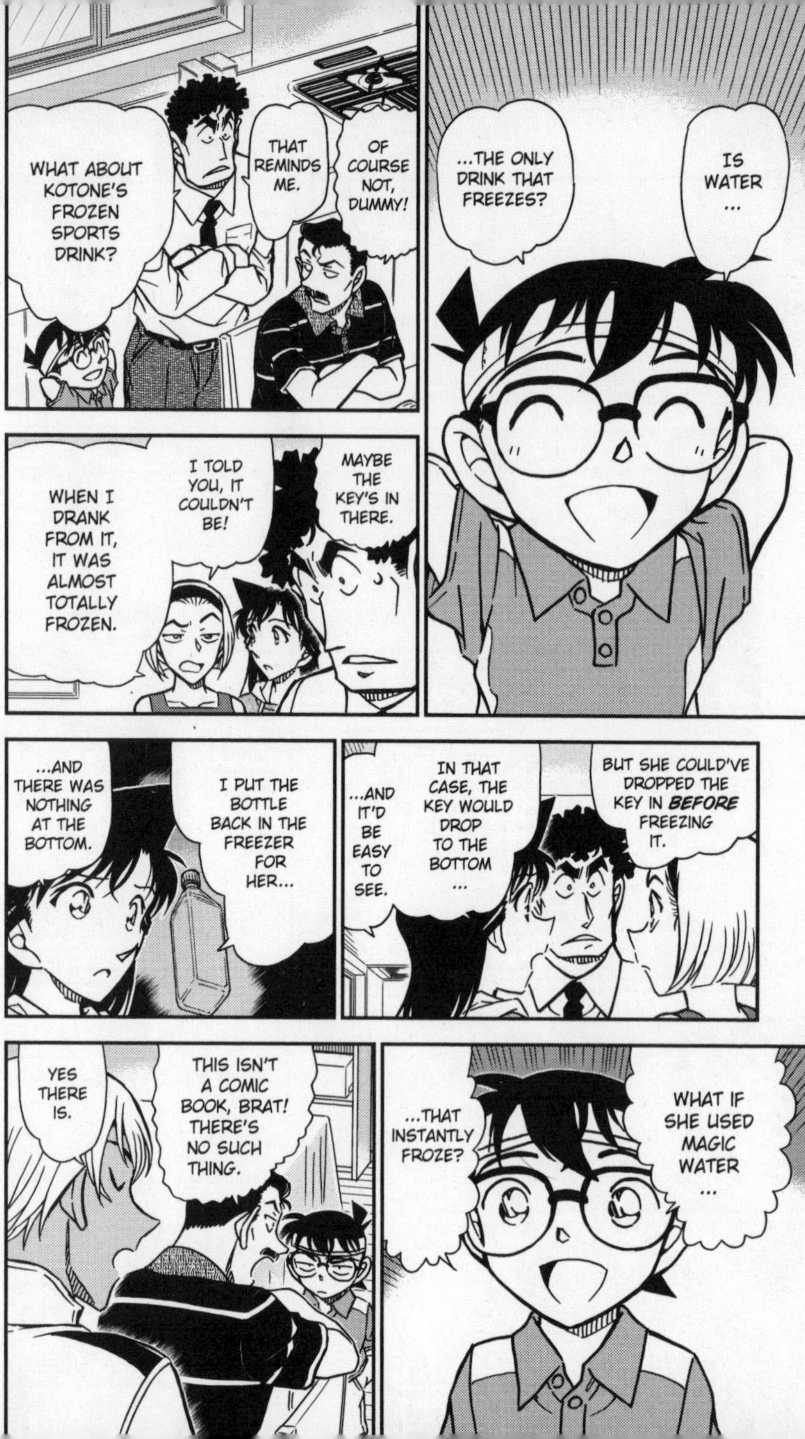
IS WATER ...
...THE ONLY DRINK THAT FREEZES?
OF COURSE NOT, DUMMY!
THAT REMINDS ME.
WHAT ABOUT KOTONE'S FROZEN SPORTS DRINK?
MAYBE THE KEY'S IN THERE.
I TOLD YOU, IT COULDN'T BE!
WHEN I DRANK FROM IT, IT WAS ALMOST TOTALLY FROZEN.
BUT SHE COULD'VE DROPPED THE KEY IN *BEFORE* FREEZING IT.
IN THAT CASE, THE KEY WOULD DROP TO THE BOTTOM ...
...AND IT'D BE EASY TO SEE.
I PUT THE BOTTLE BACK IN THE FREEZER FOR HER...
...AND THERE WAS NOTHING AT THE BOTTOM.
WHAT IF SHE USED MAGIC WATER ...
...THAT INSTANTLY FROZE?
THIS ISN'T A COMIC BOOK, BRAT! THERE'S NO SUCH THING.
YES THERE IS.

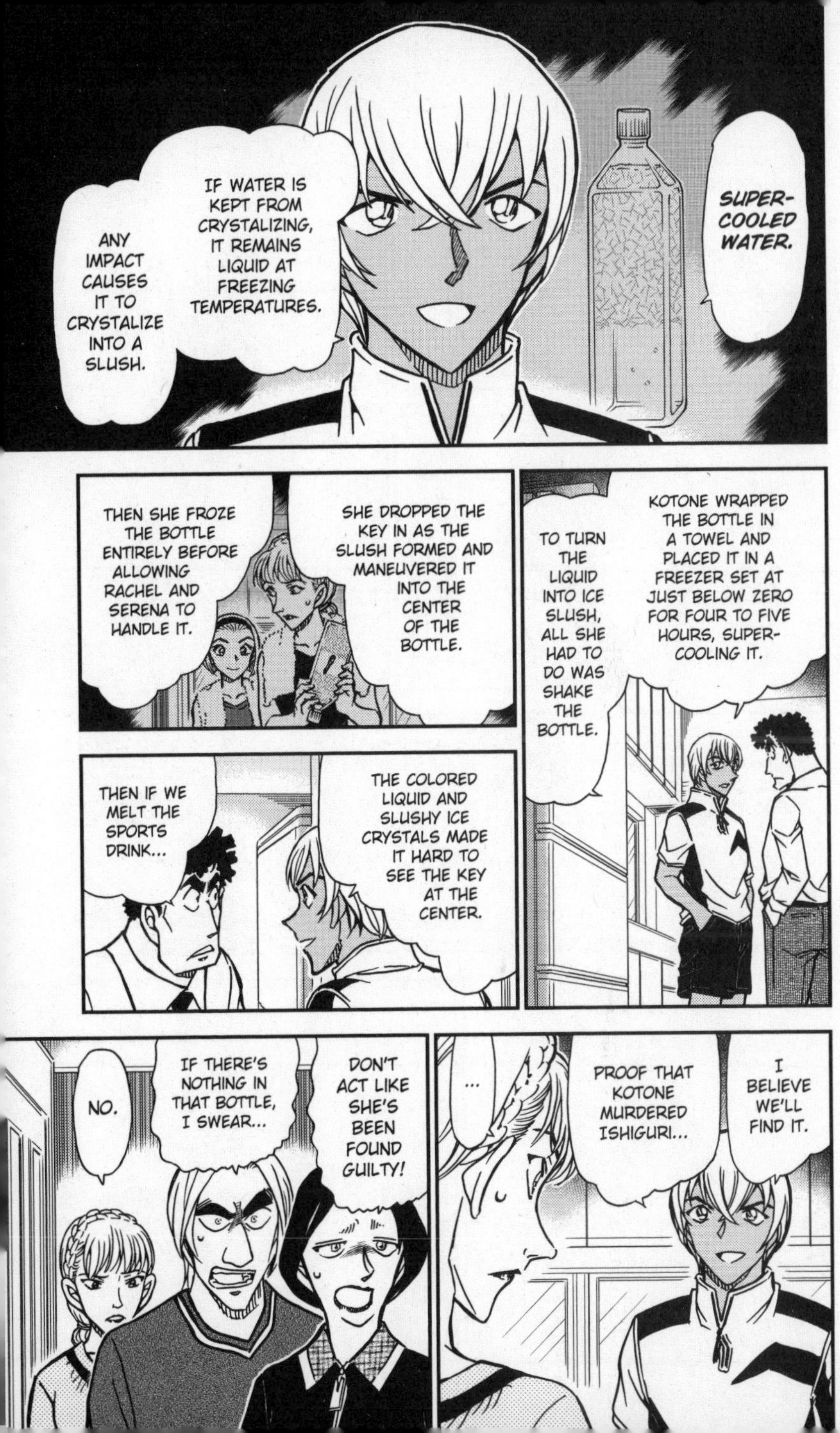
SUPER-COOLED WATER.
IF WATER IS KEPT FROM CRYSTALIZING, IT REMAINS LIQUID AT FREEZING TEMPERATURES.
ANY IMPACT CAUSES IT TO CRYSTALIZE INTO A SLUSH.
KOTONE WRAPPED THE BOTTLE IN A TOWEL AND PLACED IT IN A FREEZER SET AT JUST BELOW ZERO FOR FOUR TO FIVE HOURS, SUPER-COOLING IT.
TO TURN THE LIQUID INTO ICE SLUSH, ALL SHE HAD TO DO WAS SHAKE THE BOTTLE.
SHE DROPPED THE KEY IN AS THE SLUSH FORMED AND MANEUVERED IT INTO THE CENTER OF THE BOTTLE.
THEN SHE FROZE THE BOTTLE ENTIRELY BEFORE ALLOWING RACHEL AND SERENA TO HANDLE IT.
THE COLORED LIQUID AND SLUSHY ICE CRYSTALS MADE IT HARD TO SEE THE KEY AT THE CENTER.
THEN IF WE MELT THE SPORTS DRINK...
I BELIEVE WE'LL FIND IT.
PROOF THAT KOTONE MURDERED ISHIGURI...
...
DON'T ACT LIKE SHE'S BEEN FOUND GUILTY!
IF THERE'S NOTHING IN THAT BOTTLE, I SWEAR...
NO.

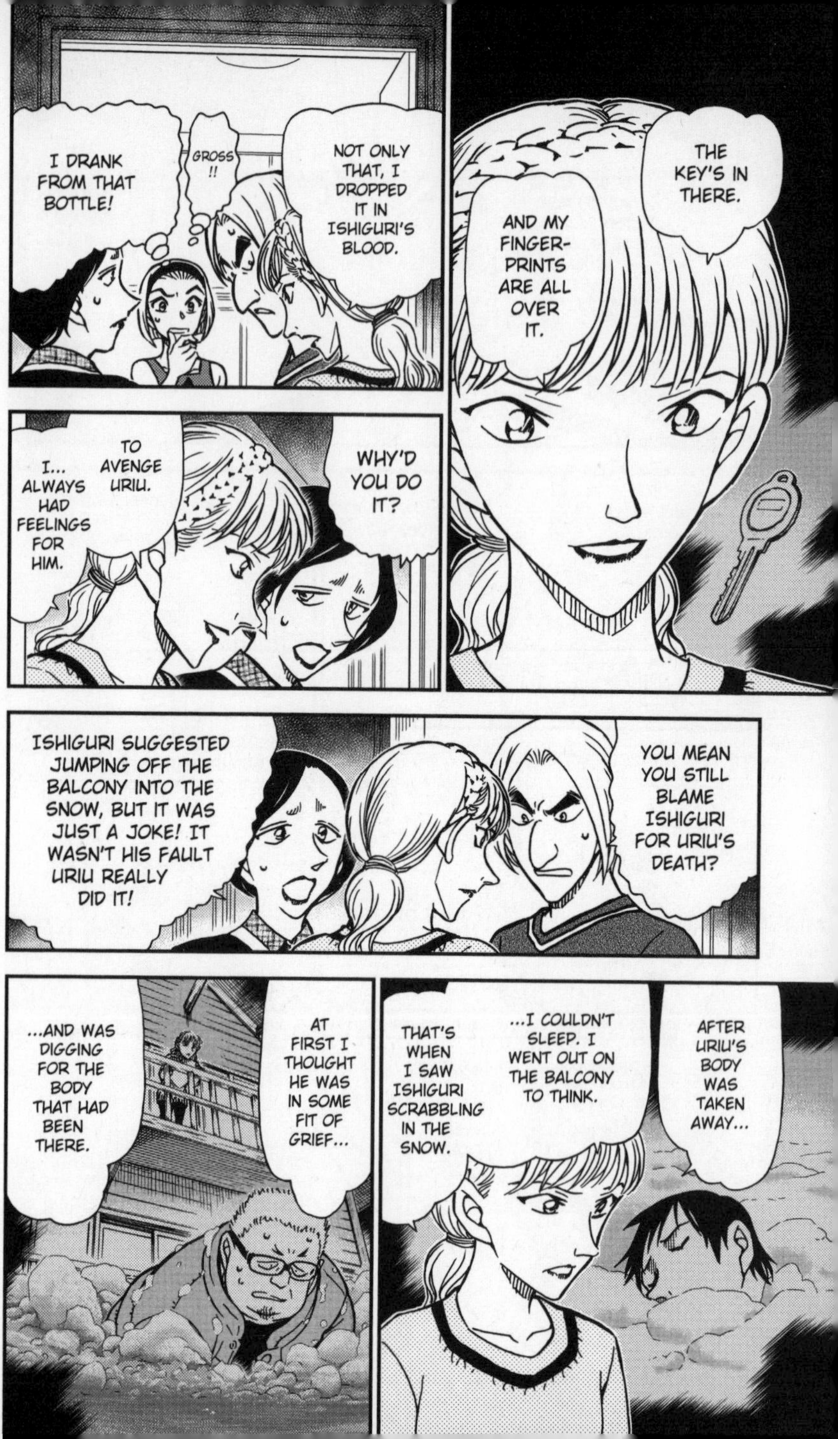
THE KEY'S IN THERE.
AND MY FINGER-PRINTS ARE ALL OVER IT.
NOT ONLY THAT, I DROPPED IT IN ISHIGURI'S BLOOD.
GROSS !!
I DRANK FROM THAT BOTTLE!
WHY'D YOU DO IT?
TO AVENGE URIU.
I... ALWAYS HAD FEELINGS FOR HIM.
YOU MEAN YOU STILL BLAME ISHIGURI FOR URIU'S DEATH?
ISHIGURI SUGGESTED JUMPING OFF THE BALCONY INTO THE SNOW, BUT IT WAS JUST A JOKE! IT WASN'T HIS FAULT URIU REALLY DID IT!
AFTER URIU'S BODY WAS TAKEN AWAY...
...I COULDN'T SLEEP. I WENT OUT ON THE BALCONY TO THINK.
THAT'S WHEN I SAW ISHIGURI SCRABBLING IN THE SNOW.
AT FIRST I THOUGHT HE WAS IN SOME FIT OF GRIEF...
...AND WAS DIGGING FOR THE BODY THAT HAD BEEN THERE.

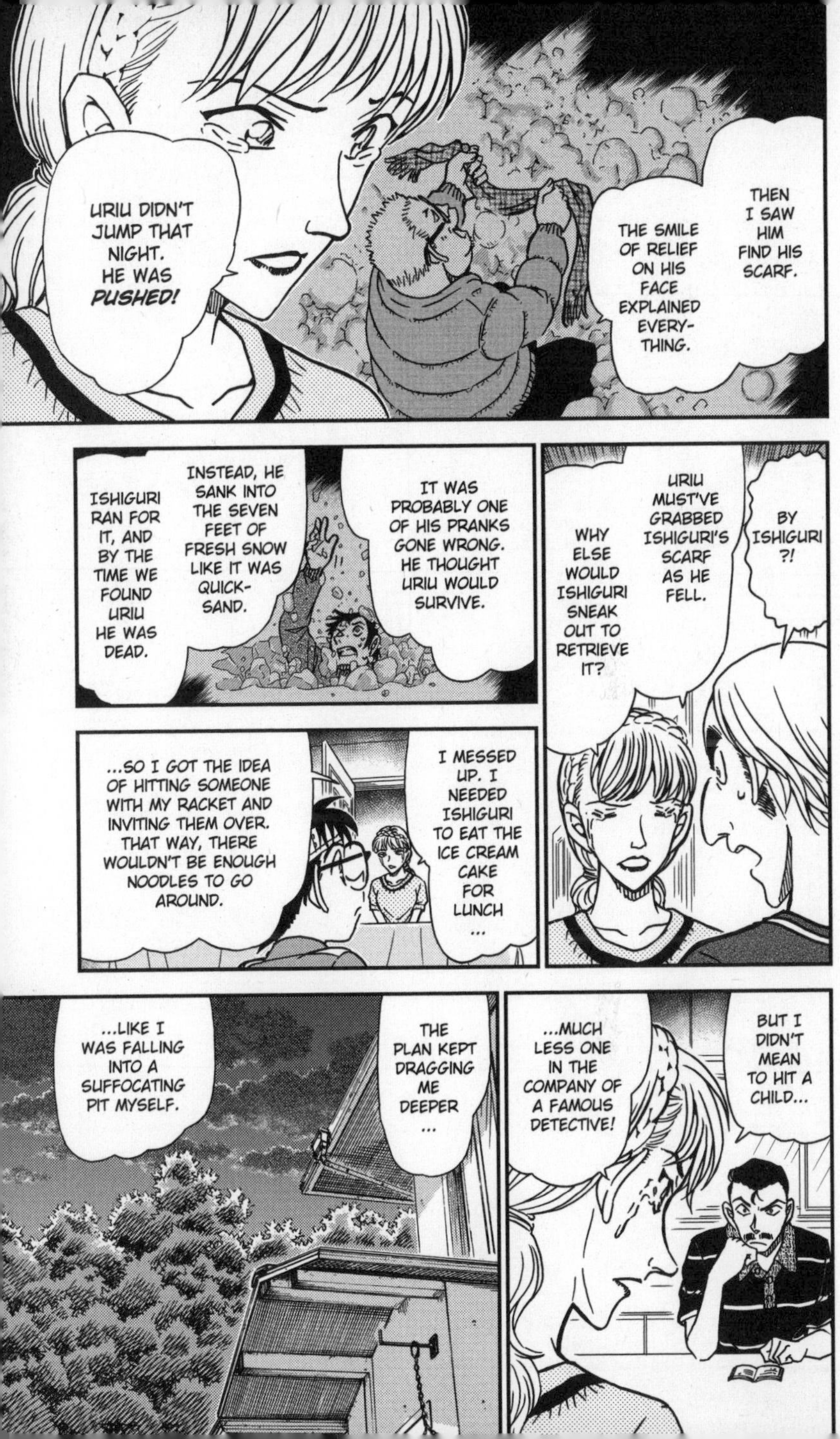
THEN I SAW HIM FIND HIS SCARF.
THE SMILE OF RELIEF ON HIS FACE EXPLAINED EVERYTHING.
URIU DIDN'T JUMP THAT NIGHT. HE WAS *PUSHED!*
BY ISHIGURI ?!
URIU MUST'VE GRABBED ISHIGURI'S SCARF AS HE FELL.
WHY ELSE WOULD ISHIGURI SNEAK OUT TO RETRIEVE IT?
IT WAS PROBABLY ONE OF HIS PRANKS GONE WRONG. HE THOUGHT URIU WOULD SURVIVE.
INSTEAD, HE SANK INTO THE SEVEN FEET OF FRESH SNOW LIKE IT WAS QUICK-SAND.
ISHIGURI RAN FOR IT, AND BY THE TIME WE FOUND URIU HE WAS DEAD.
I MESSED UP. I NEEDED ISHIGURI TO EAT THE ICE CREAM CAKE FOR LUNCH ...
...SO I GOT THE IDEA OF HITTING SOMEONE WITH MY RACKET AND INVITING THEM OVER. THAT WAY, THERE WOULDN'T BE ENOUGH NOODLES TO GO AROUND.
BUT I DIDN'T MEAN TO HIT A CHILD...
...MUCH LESS ONE IN THE COMPANY OF A FAMOUS DETECTIVE!
THE PLAN KEPT DRAGGING ME DEEPER ...
...LIKE I WAS FALLING INTO A SUFFOCATING PIT MYSELF.

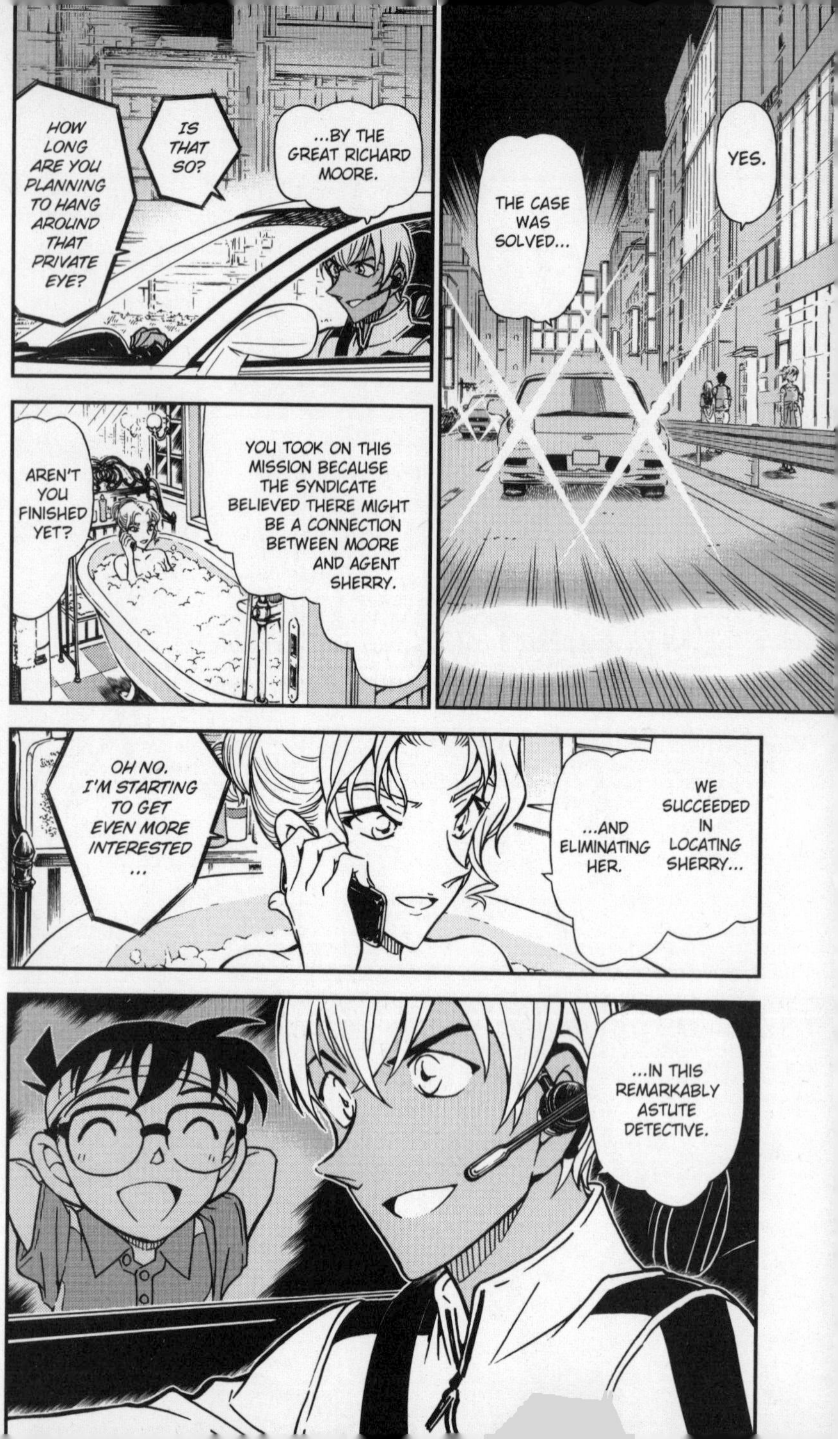
YES.
THE CASE WAS SOLVED...
...BY THE GREAT RICHARD MOORE.
IS THAT SO?
HOW LONG ARE YOU PLANNING TO HANG AROUND THAT PRIVATE EYE?
YOU TOOK ON THIS MISSION BECAUSE THE SYNDICATE BELIEVED THERE MIGHT BE A CONNECTION BETWEEN MOORE AND AGENT SHERRY.
AREN'T YOU FINISHED YET?
WE SUCCEEDED IN LOCATING SHERRY...
...AND ELIMINATING HER.
OH NO. I'M STARTING TO GET EVEN MORE INTERESTED ...
...IN THIS REMARKABLY ASTUTE DETECTIVE.

FILE 11: FOAM

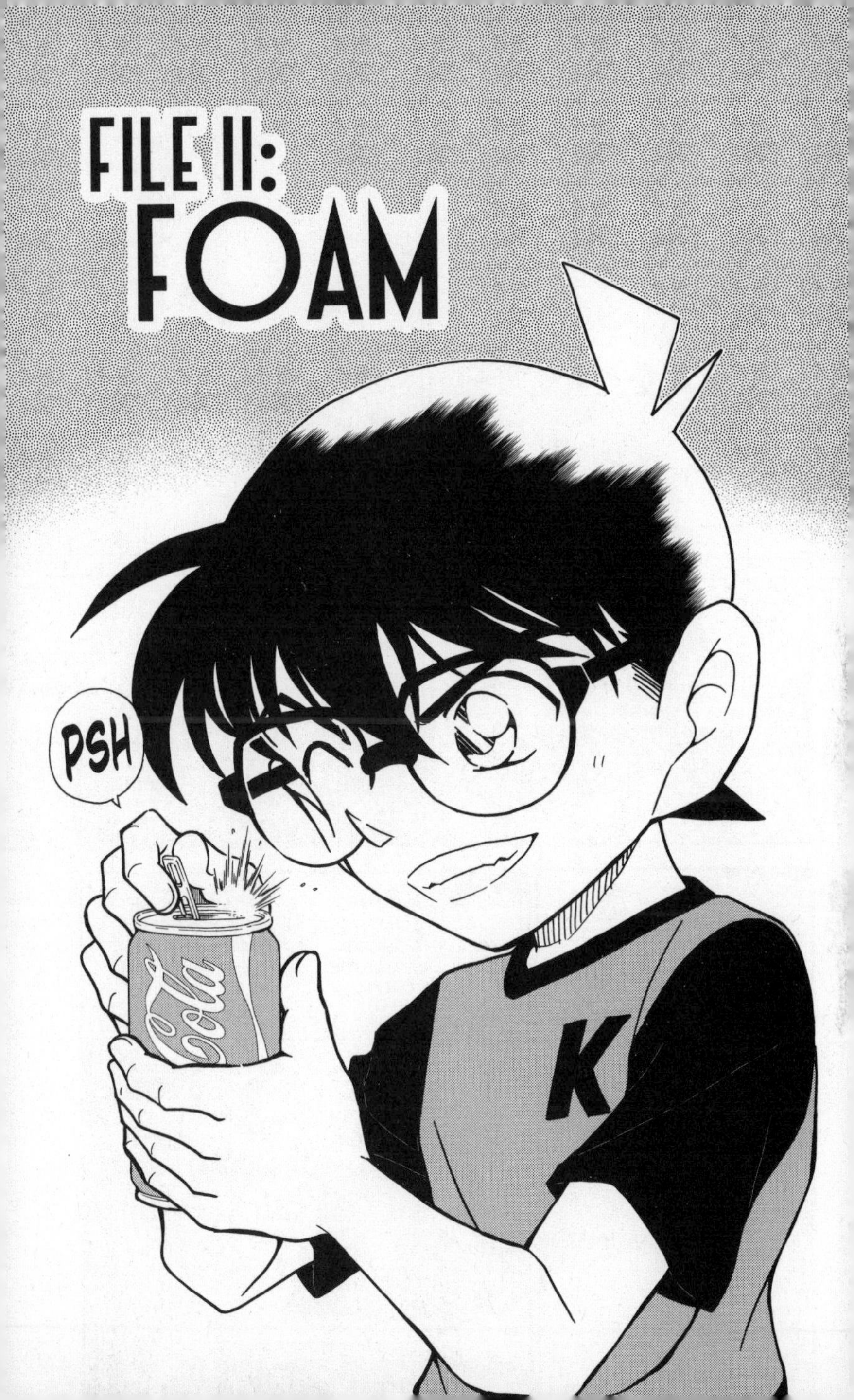

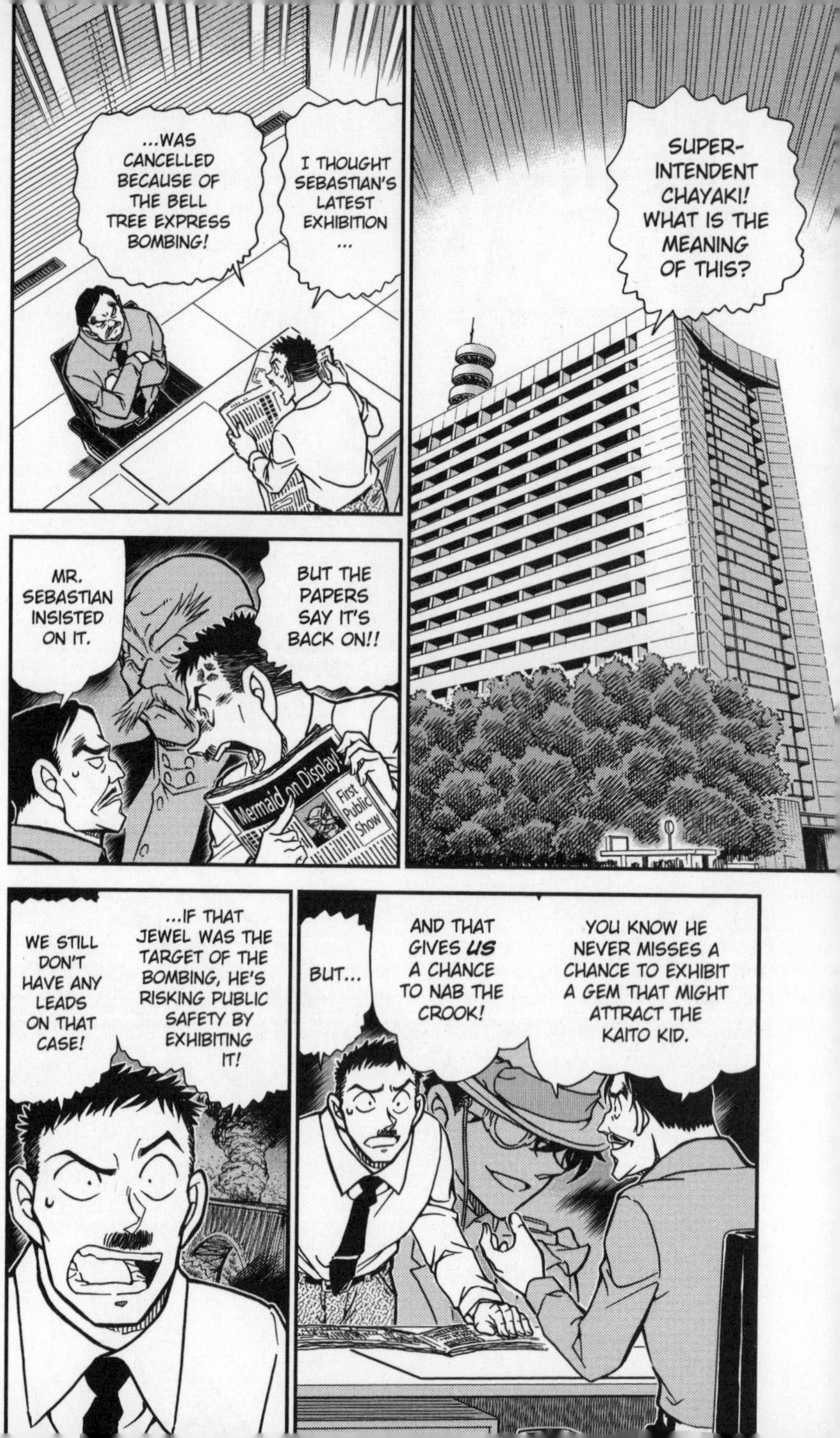
SUPER-INTENDENT CHAYAKI! WHAT IS THE MEANING OF THIS?
I THOUGHT SEBASTIAN'S LATEST EXHIBITION ...
...WAS CANCELLED BECAUSE OF THE BELL TREE EXPRESS BOMBING!
BUT THE PAPERS SAY IT'S BACK ON!!
MR. SEBASTIAN INSISTED ON IT.
Mermaid on Display!
First Public Show
YOU KNOW HE NEVER MISSES A CHANCE TO EXHIBIT A GEM THAT MIGHT ATTRACT THE KAITO KID.
AND THAT GIVES *US* A CHANCE TO NAB THE CROOK!
BUT...
...IF THAT JEWEL WAS THE TARGET OF THE BOMBING, HE'S RISKING PUBLIC SAFETY BY EXHIBITING IT!
WE STILL DON'T HAVE ANY LEADS ON THAT CASE!

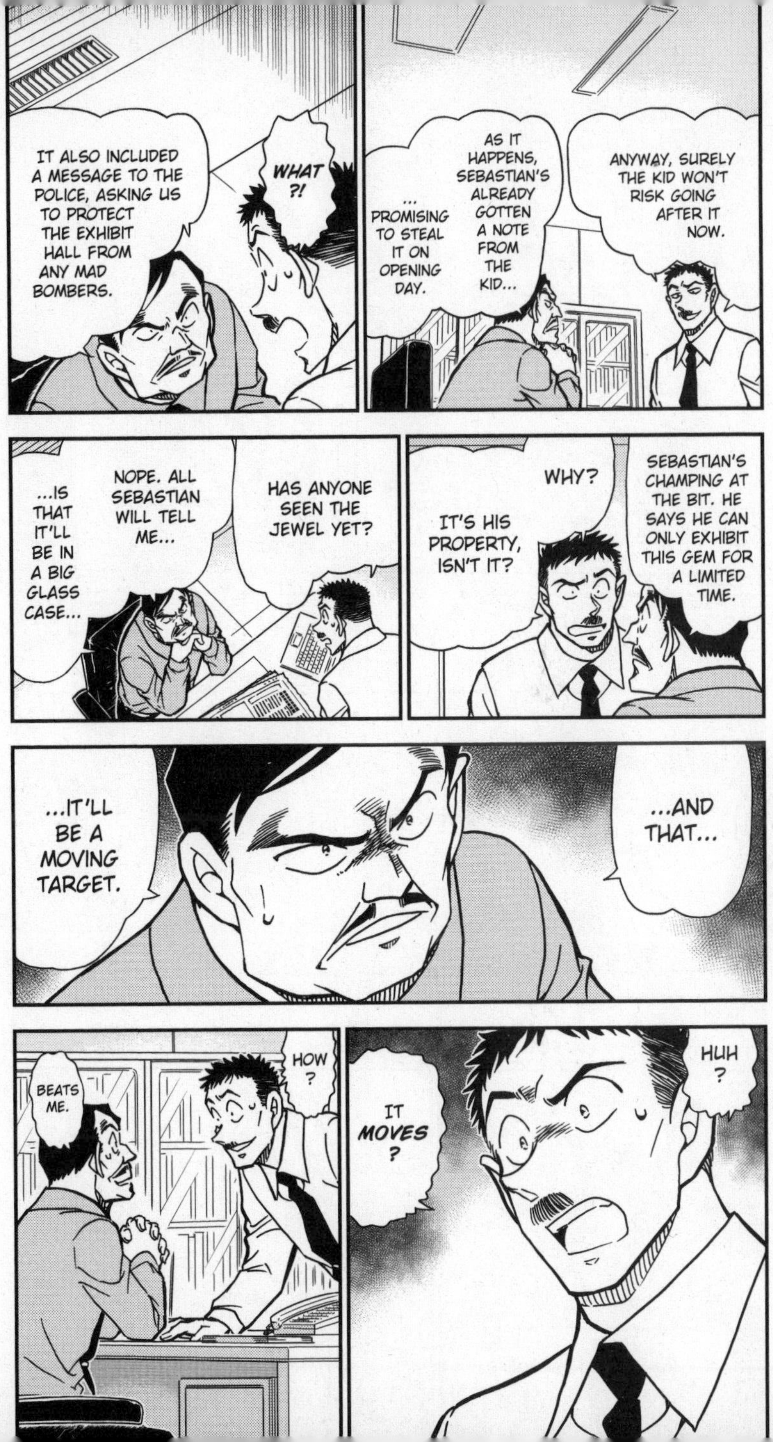
ANYWAY, SURELY THE KID WON'T RISK GOING AFTER IT NOW.
AS IT HAPPENS, SEBASTIAN'S ALREADY GOTTEN A NOTE FROM THE KID...
...PROMISING TO STEAL IT ON OPENING DAY.
WHAT ?!
IT ALSO INCLUDED A MESSAGE TO THE POLICE, ASKING US TO PROTECT THE EXHIBIT HALL FROM ANY MAD BOMBERS.
SEBASTIAN'S CHAMPING AT THE BIT. HE SAYS HE CAN ONLY EXHIBIT THIS GEM FOR A LIMITED TIME.
WHY?
IT'S HIS PROPERTY, ISN'T IT?
HAS ANYONE SEEN THE JEWEL YET?
NOPE. ALL SEBASTIAN WILL TELL ME...
...IS THAT IT'LL BE IN A BIG GLASS CASE...
...AND THAT...
...IT'LL BE A MOVING TARGET.
HUH?
IT *MOVES* ?
HOW?
BEATS ME.

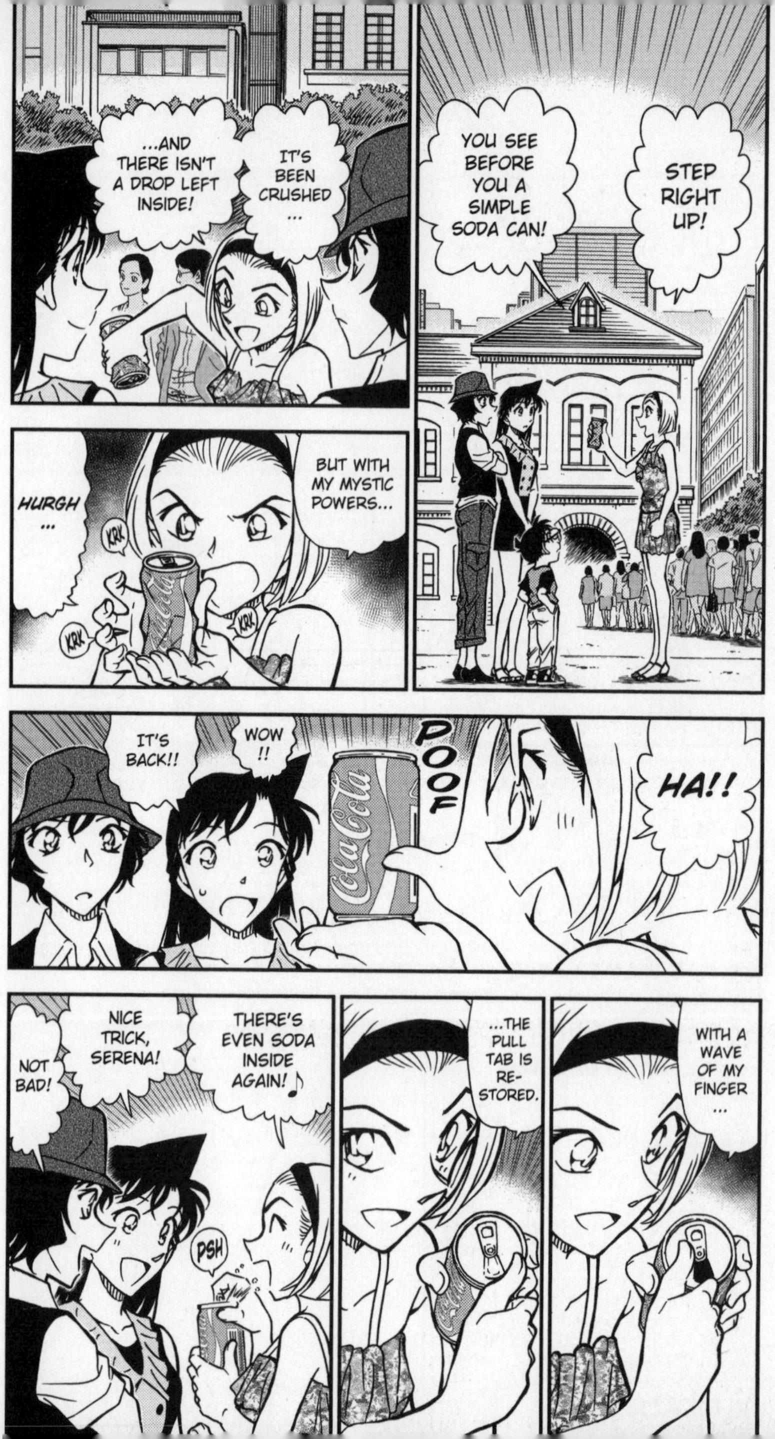
STEP RIGHT UP!
YOU SEE BEFORE YOU A SIMPLE SODA CAN!
IT'S BEEN CRUSHED...
...AND THERE ISN'T A DROP LEFT INSIDE!
BUT WITH MY MYSTIC POWERS...
KRK
KRK
KRK
HURGH...
HA!!
POOF
WOW!!
IT'S BACK!!
WITH A WAVE OF MY FINGER...
...THE PULL TAB IS RE-STORED.
THERE'S EVEN SODA INSIDE AGAIN!♪
NICE TRICK, SERENA!
NOT BAD!
PSH

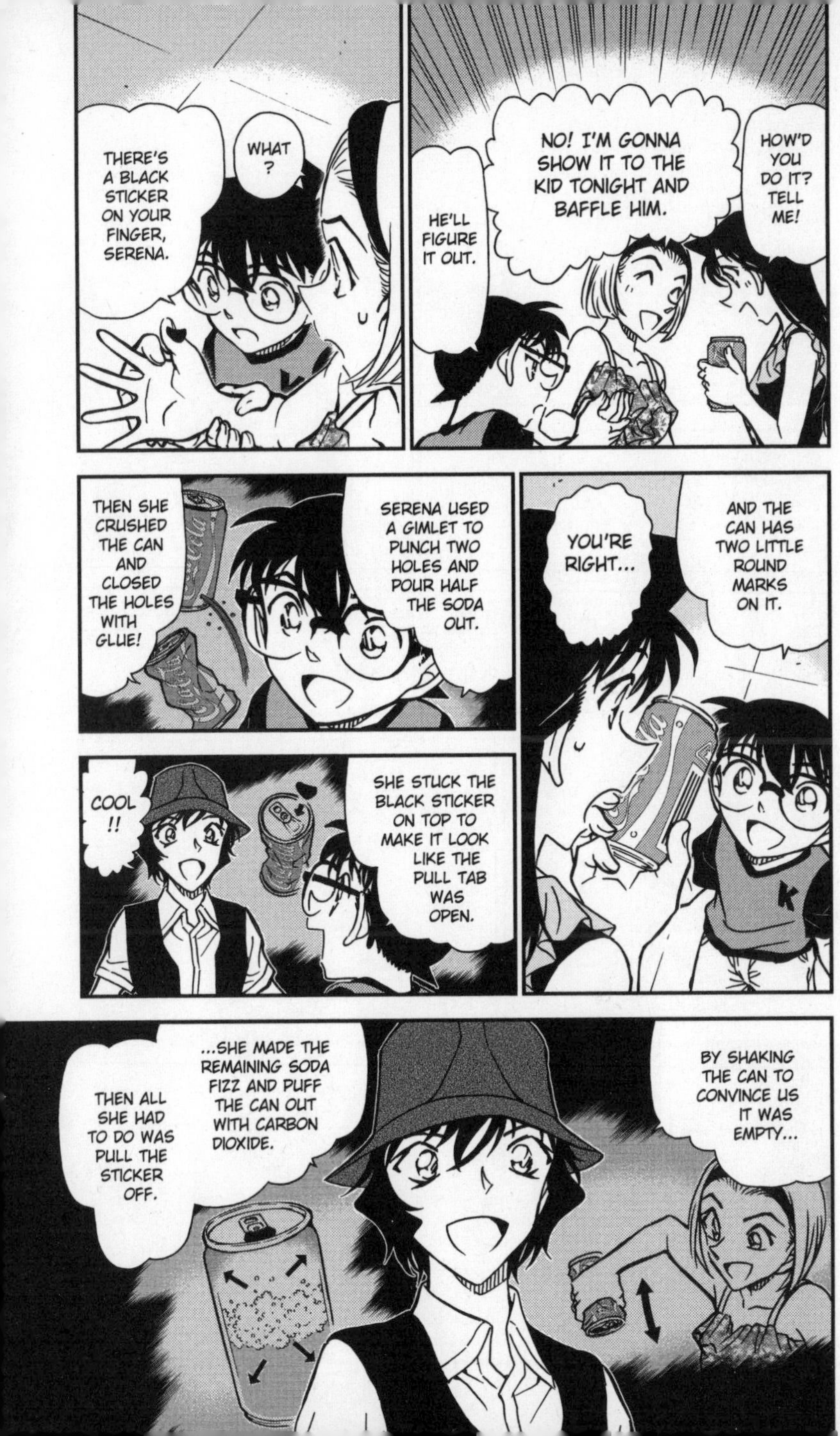
HOW'D YOU DO IT? TELL ME!
NO! I'M GONNA SHOW IT TO THE KID TONIGHT AND BAFFLE HIM.
HE'LL FIGURE IT OUT.
WHAT?
THERE'S A BLACK STICKER ON YOUR FINGER, SERENA.
AND THE CAN HAS TWO LITTLE ROUND MARKS ON IT.
YOU'RE RIGHT...
SERENA USED A GIMLET TO PUNCH TWO HOLES AND POUR HALF THE SODA OUT.
THEN SHE CRUSHED THE CAN AND CLOSED THE HOLES WITH GLUE!
SHE STUCK THE BLACK STICKER ON TOP TO MAKE IT LOOK LIKE THE PULL TAB WAS OPEN.
COOL!!
BY SHAKING THE CAN TO CONVINCE US IT WAS EMPTY...
...SHE MADE THE REMAINING SODA FIZZ AND PUFF THE CAN OUT WITH CARBON DIOXIDE.
THEN ALL SHE HAD TO DO WAS PULL THE STICKER OFF.

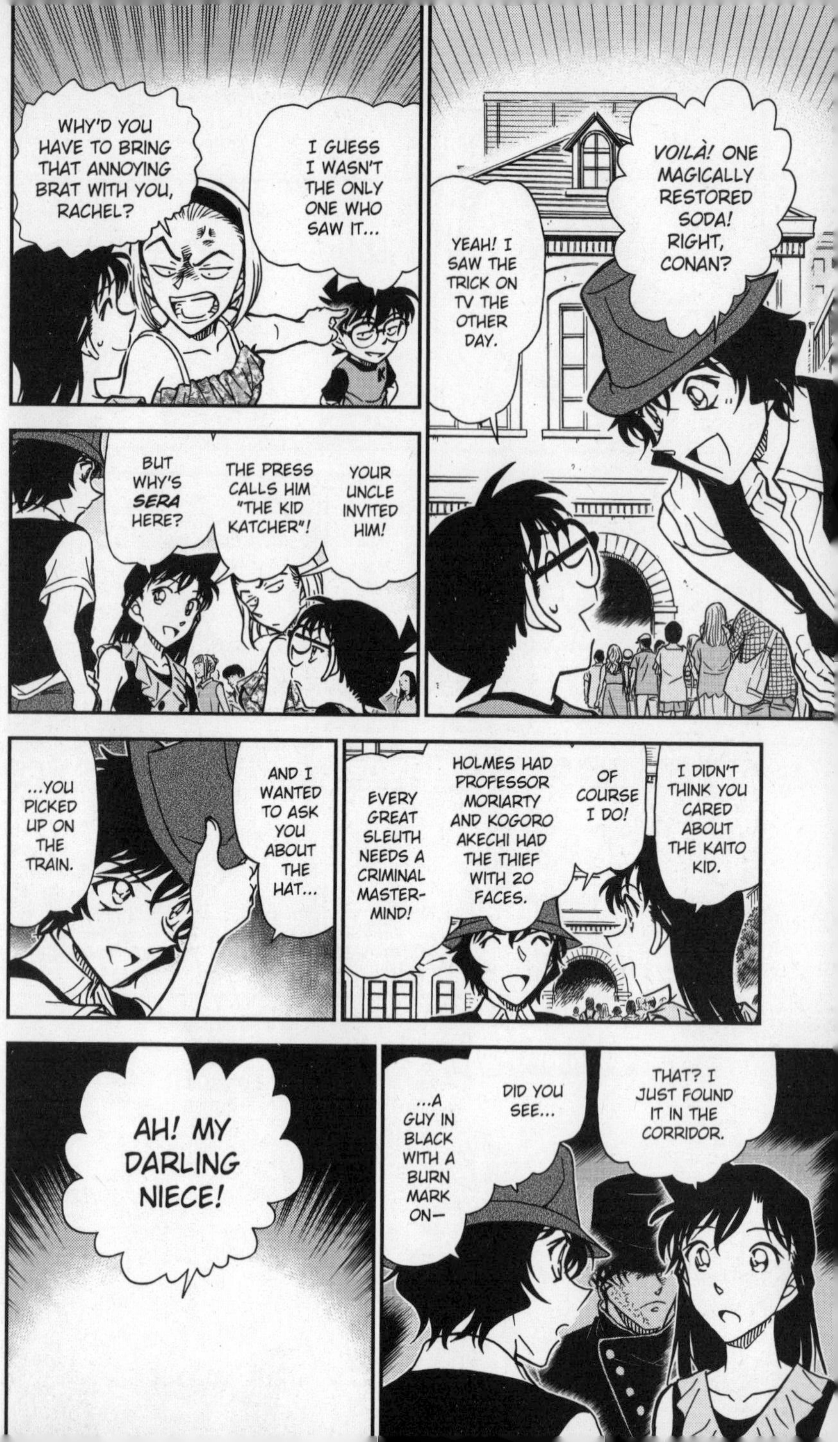
VOILÀ! ONE MAGICALLY RESTORED SODA! RIGHT, CONAN?
YEAH! I SAW THE TRICK ON TV THE OTHER DAY.
I GUESS I WASN'T THE ONLY ONE WHO SAW IT...
WHY'D YOU HAVE TO BRING THAT ANNOYING BRAT WITH YOU, RACHEL?
YOUR UNCLE INVITED HIM!
THE PRESS CALLS HIM "THE KID KATCHER"!
BUT WHY'S **SERA** HERE?
I DIDN'T THINK YOU CARED ABOUT THE KAITO KID.
OF COURSE I DO!
HOLMES HAD PROFESSOR MORIARTY AND KOGORO AKECHI HAD THE THIEF WITH 20 FACES.
EVERY GREAT SLEUTH NEEDS A CRIMINAL MASTER-MIND!
AND I WANTED TO ASK YOU ABOUT THE HAT...
...YOU PICKED UP ON THE TRAIN.
THAT? I JUST FOUND IT IN THE CORRIDOR.
DID YOU SEE...
...A GUY IN BLACK WITH A BURN MARK ON—
AH! MY DARLING NIECE!

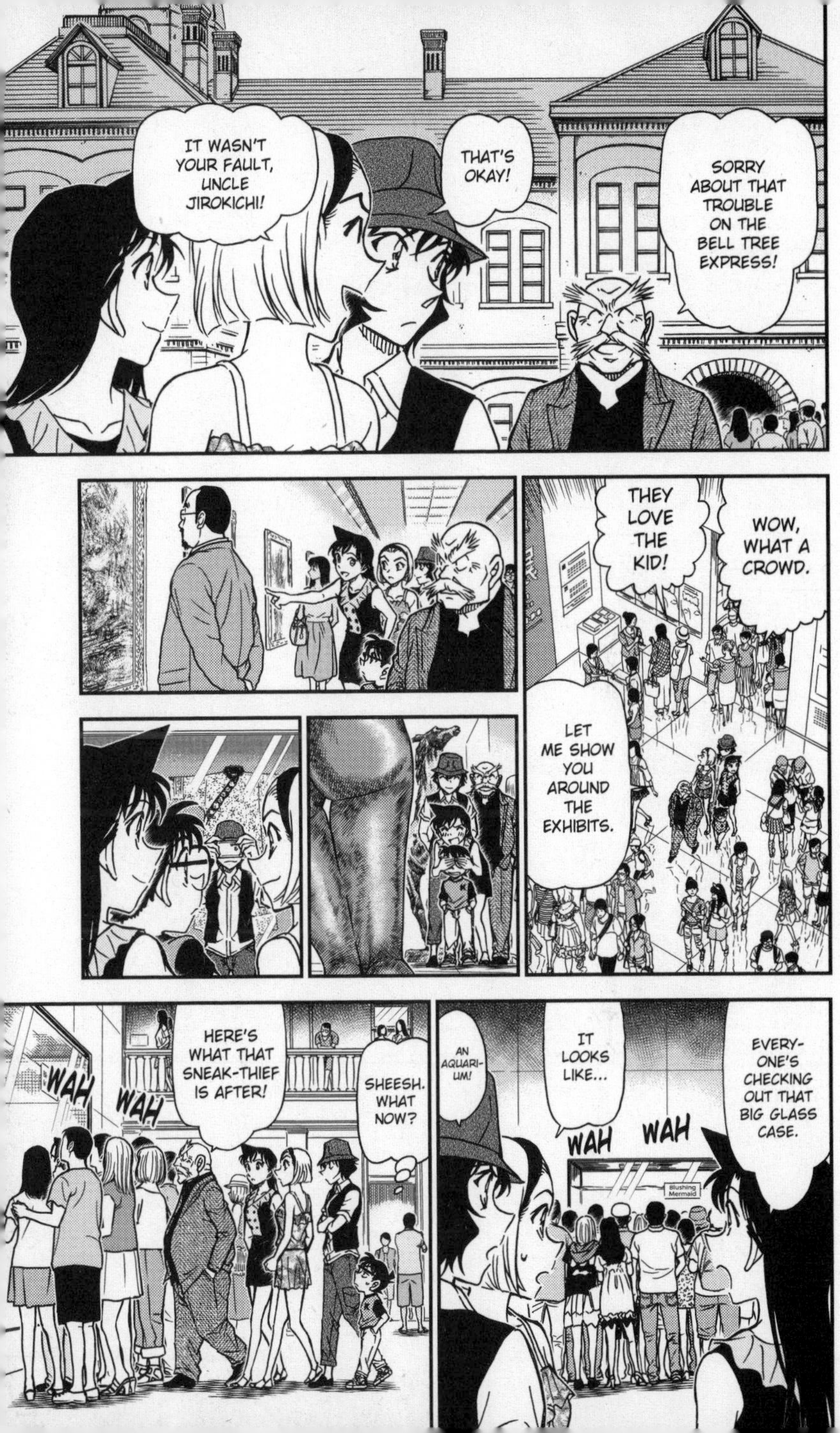
SORRY ABOUT THAT TROUBLE ON THE BELL TREE EXPRESS!
THAT'S OKAY!
IT WASN'T YOUR FAULT, UNCLE JIROKICHI!
WOW, WHAT A CROWD.
THEY LOVE THE KID!
LET ME SHOW YOU AROUND THE EXHIBITS.
EVERY-ONE'S CHECKING OUT THAT BIG GLASS CASE.
IT LOOKS LIKE...
AN AQUARI-UM!
WAH WAH
Blushing Mermaid
SHEESH. WHAT NOW?
HERE'S WHAT THAT SNEAK-THIEF IS AFTER!
WAH WAH

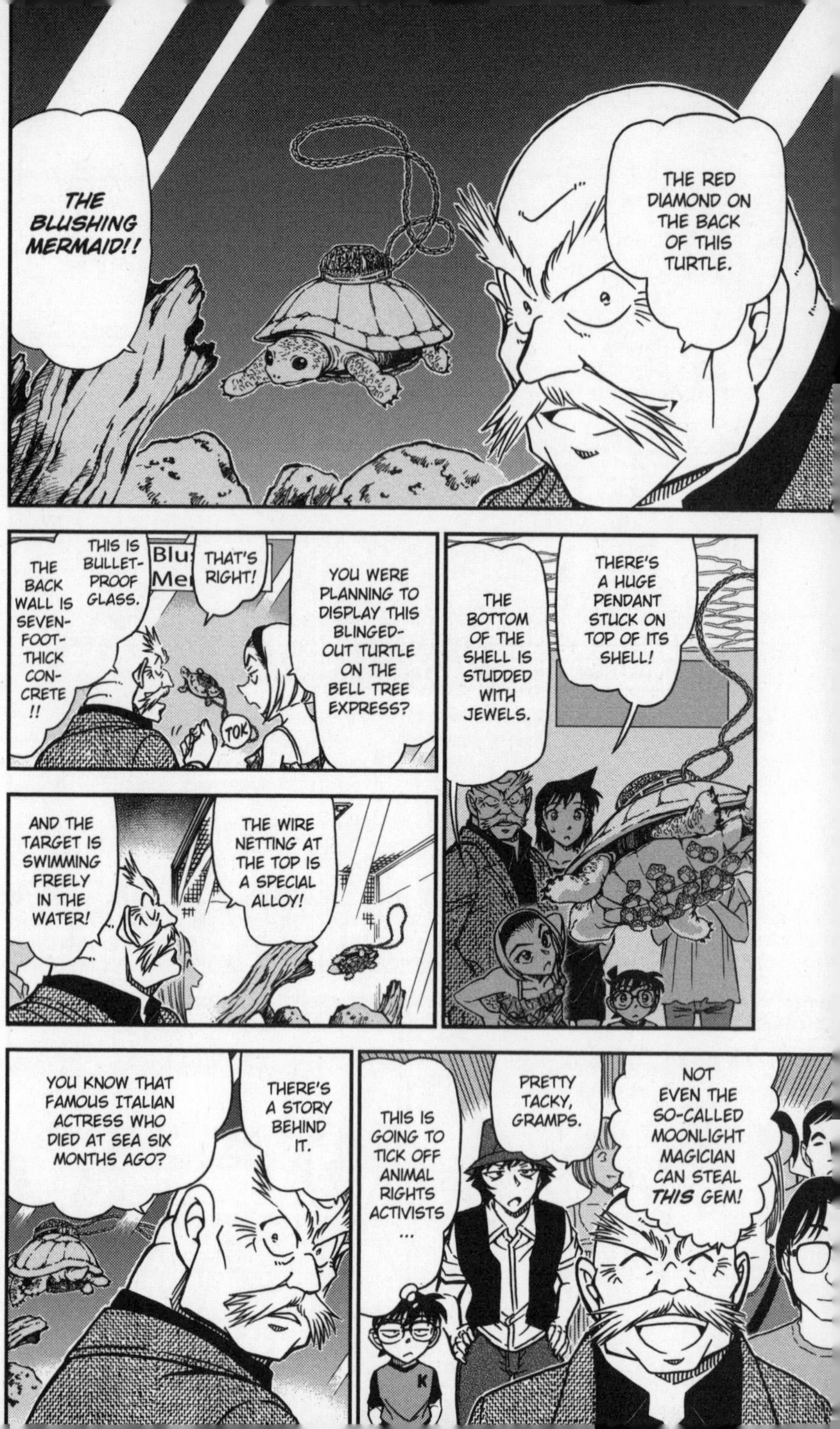
THE RED DIAMOND ON THE BACK OF THIS TURTLE.
THE BLUSHING MERMAID!!
THERE'S A HUGE PENDANT STUCK ON TOP OF ITS SHELL!
THE BOTTOM OF THE SHELL IS STUDDED WITH JEWELS.
YOU WERE PLANNING TO DISPLAY THIS BLINGED-OUT TURTLE ON THE BELL TREE EXPRESS?
THAT'S RIGHT!
THIS IS BULLET-PROOF GLASS.
THE BACK WALL IS SEVEN-FOOT-THICK CONCRETE!!
TOK
THE WIRE NETTING AT THE TOP IS A SPECIAL ALLOY!
AND THE TARGET IS SWIMMING FREELY IN THE WATER!
NOT EVEN THE SO-CALLED MOONLIGHT MAGICIAN CAN STEAL *THIS* GEM!
PRETTY TACKY, GRAMPS.
THIS IS GOING TO TICK OFF ANIMAL RIGHTS ACTIVISTS ...
THERE'S A STORY BEHIND IT.
YOU KNOW THAT FAMOUS ITALIAN ACTRESS WHO DIED AT SEA SIX MONTHS AGO?

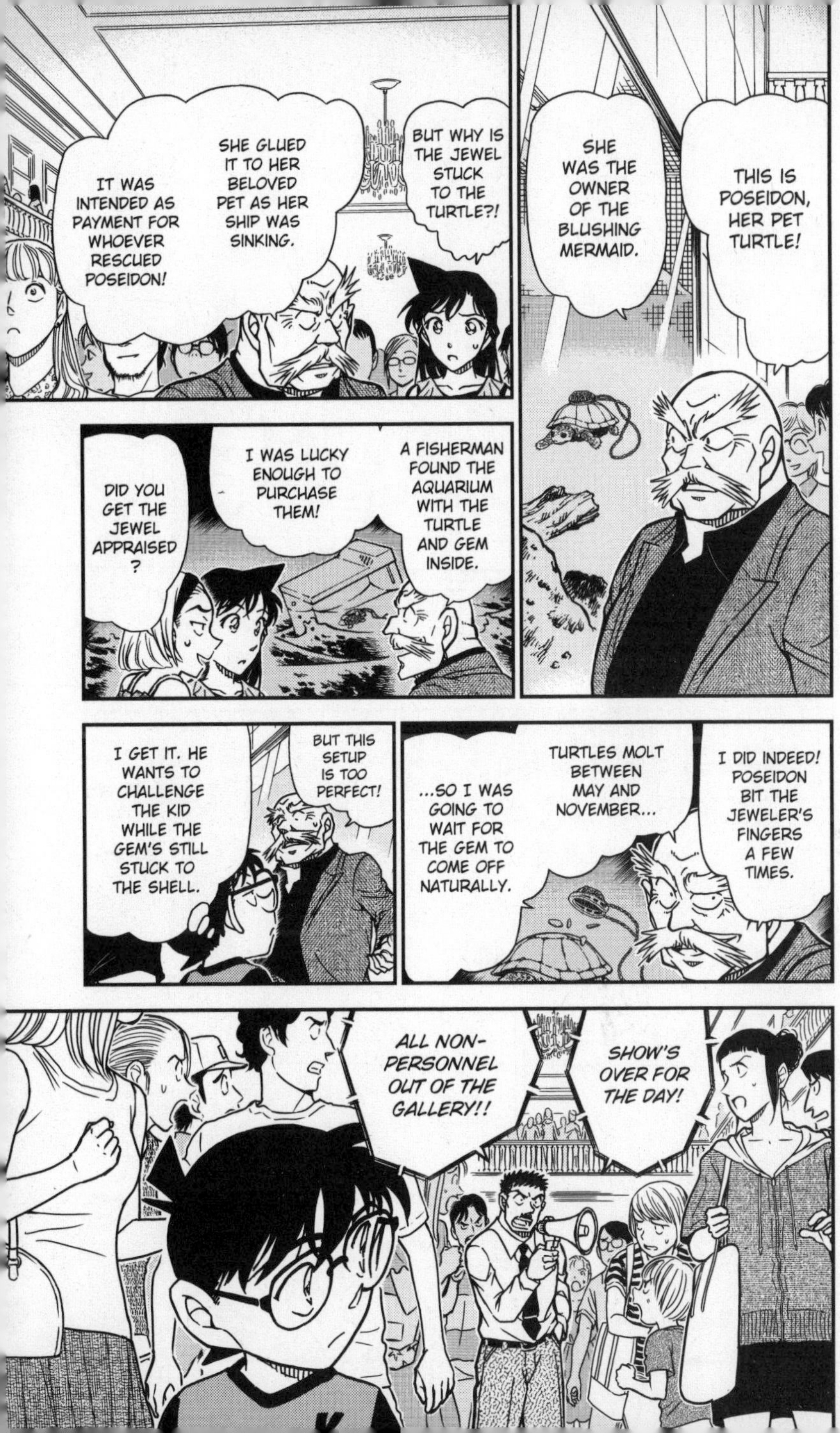
THIS IS POSEIDON, HER PET TURTLE!
SHE WAS THE OWNER OF THE BLUSHING MERMAID.
BUT WHY IS THE JEWEL STUCK TO THE TURTLE?!
SHE GLUED IT TO HER BELOVED PET AS HER SHIP WAS SINKING.
IT WAS INTENDED AS PAYMENT FOR WHOEVER RESCUED POSEIDON!
A FISHERMAN FOUND THE AQUARIUM WITH THE TURTLE AND GEM INSIDE.
I WAS LUCKY ENOUGH TO PURCHASE THEM!
DID YOU GET THE JEWEL APPRAISED?
I DID INDEED! POSEIDON BIT THE JEWELER'S FINGERS A FEW TIMES.
TURTLES MOLT BETWEEN MAY AND NOVEMBER...
...SO I WAS GOING TO WAIT FOR THE GEM TO COME OFF NATURALLY.
BUT THIS SETUP IS TOO PERFECT!
I GET IT. HE WANTS TO CHALLENGE THE KID WHILE THE GEM'S STILL STUCK TO THE SHELL.
SHOW'S OVER FOR THE DAY!
ALL NON-PERSONNEL OUT OF THE GALLERY!!

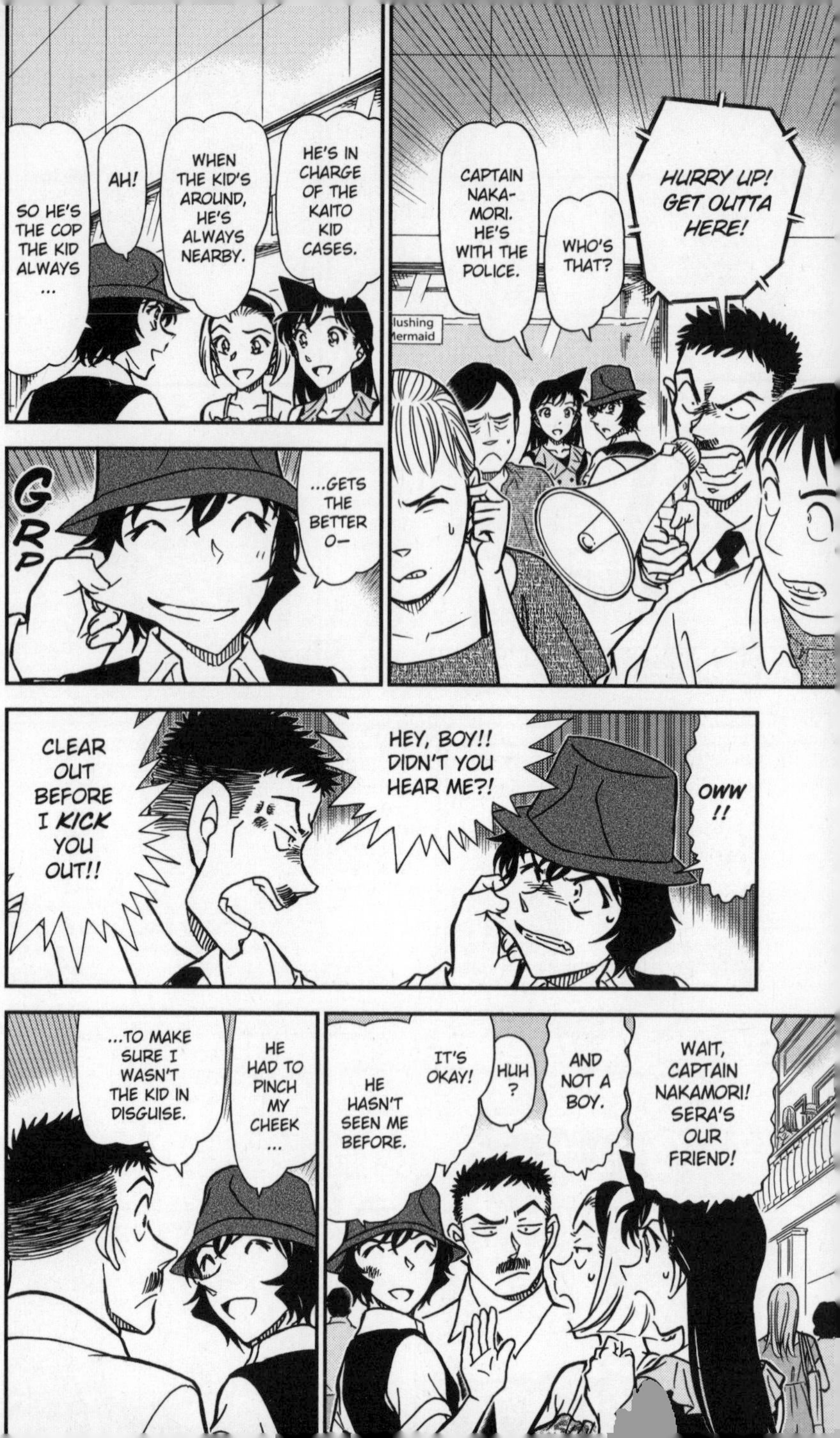
HURRY UP! GET OUTTA HERE!
WHO'S THAT?
CAPTAIN NAKA-MORI. HE'S WITH THE POLICE.
HE'S IN CHARGE OF THE KAITO KID CASES.
WHEN THE KID'S AROUND, HE'S ALWAYS NEARBY.
AH!
SO HE'S THE COP THE KID ALWAYS ...
...GETS THE BETTER O—
GRP
OWW !!
HEY, BOY!! DIDN'T YOU HEAR ME?!
CLEAR OUT BEFORE I *KICK* YOU OUT!!
WAIT, CAPTAIN NAKAMORI! SERA'S OUR FRIEND!
AND NOT A BOY.
HUH ?
IT'S OKAY!
HE HASN'T SEEN ME BEFORE.
HE HAD TO PINCH MY CHEEK ...
...TO MAKE SURE I WASN'T THE KID IN DISGUISE.

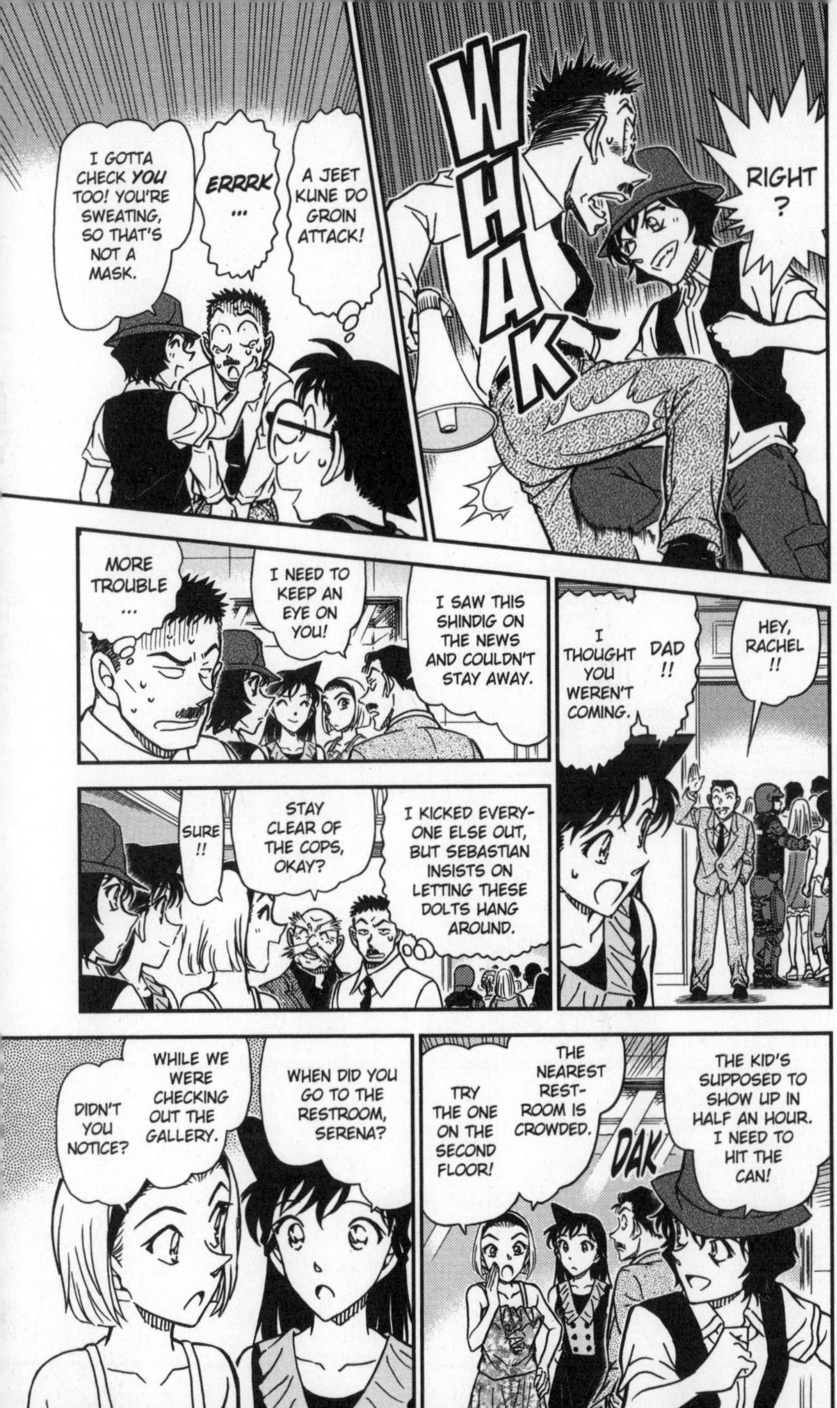
RIGHT?
WHAK
A JEET KUNE DO GROIN ATTACK!
ERRRK...
I GOTTA CHECK *YOU* TOO! YOU'RE SWEATING, SO THAT'S NOT A MASK.
HEY, RACHEL!!
DAD!!
I THOUGHT YOU WEREN'T COMING.
I SAW THIS SHINDIG ON THE NEWS AND COULDN'T STAY AWAY.
I NEED TO KEEP AN EYE ON YOU!
MORE TROUBLE...
I KICKED EVERYONE ELSE OUT, BUT SEBASTIAN INSISTS ON LETTING THESE DOLTS HANG AROUND.
STAY CLEAR OF THE COPS, OKAY?
SURE!!
THE KID'S SUPPOSED TO SHOW UP IN HALF AN HOUR. I NEED TO HIT THE CAN!
DAK
THE NEAREST REST-ROOM IS CROWDED.
TRY THE ONE ON THE SECOND FLOOR!
WHEN DID YOU GO TO THE RESTROOM, SERENA?
WHILE WE WERE CHECKING OUT THE GALLERY.
DIDN'T YOU NOTICE?

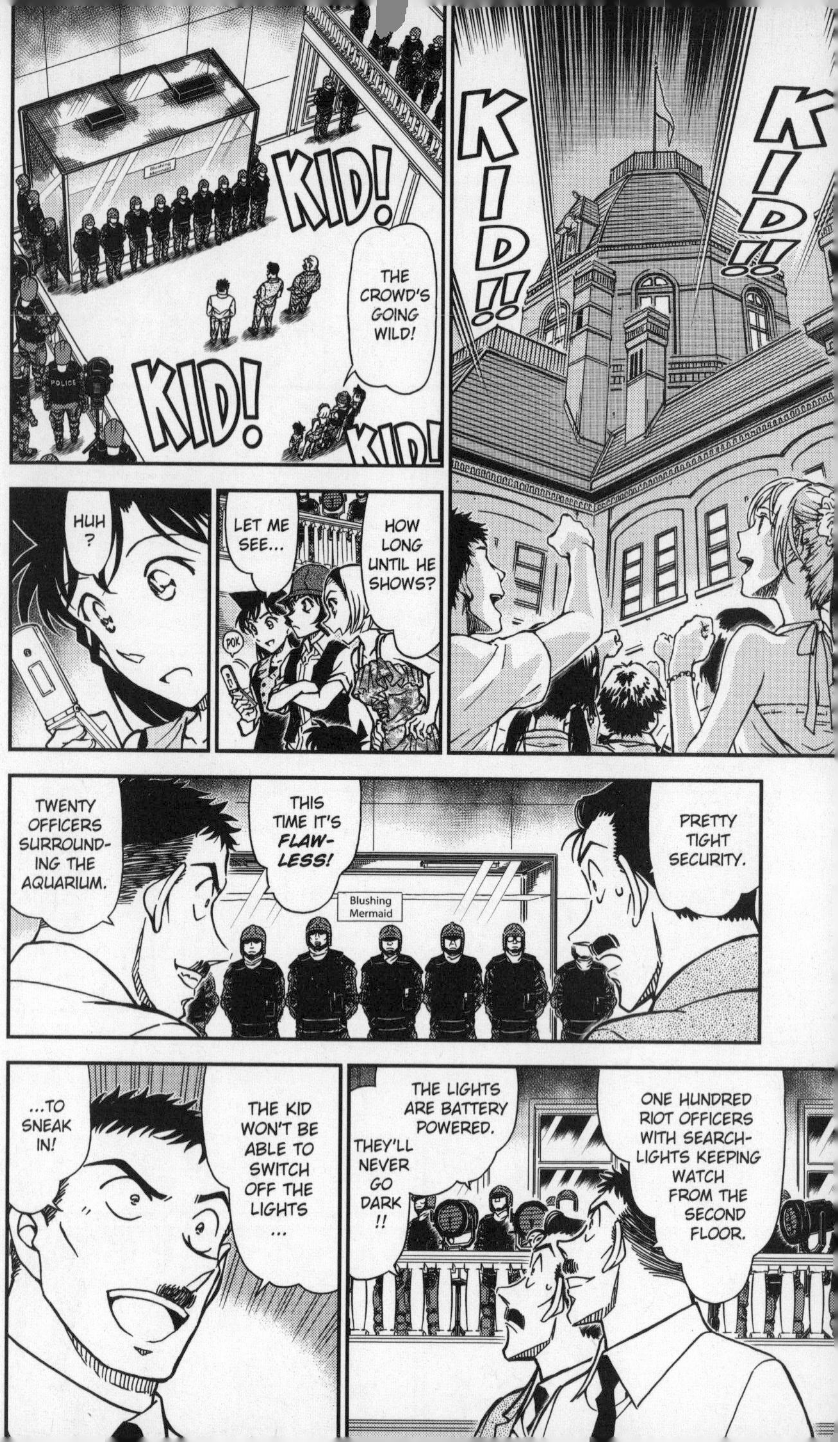
KID!!
KID!!
KID!
Blushing Mermaid
THE CROWD'S GOING WILD!
KID!
KID!
HOW LONG UNTIL HE SHOWS?
LET ME SEE...
POK
HUH?
PRETTY TIGHT SECURITY.
THIS TIME IT'S *FLAWLESS!*
Blushing Mermaid
TWENTY OFFICERS SURROUNDING THE AQUARIUM.
ONE HUNDRED RIOT OFFICERS WITH SEARCHLIGHTS KEEPING WATCH FROM THE SECOND FLOOR.
THE LIGHTS ARE BATTERY POWERED.
THEY'LL NEVER GO DARK!!
THE KID WON'T BE ABLE TO SWITCH OFF THE LIGHTS...
...TO SNEAK IN!

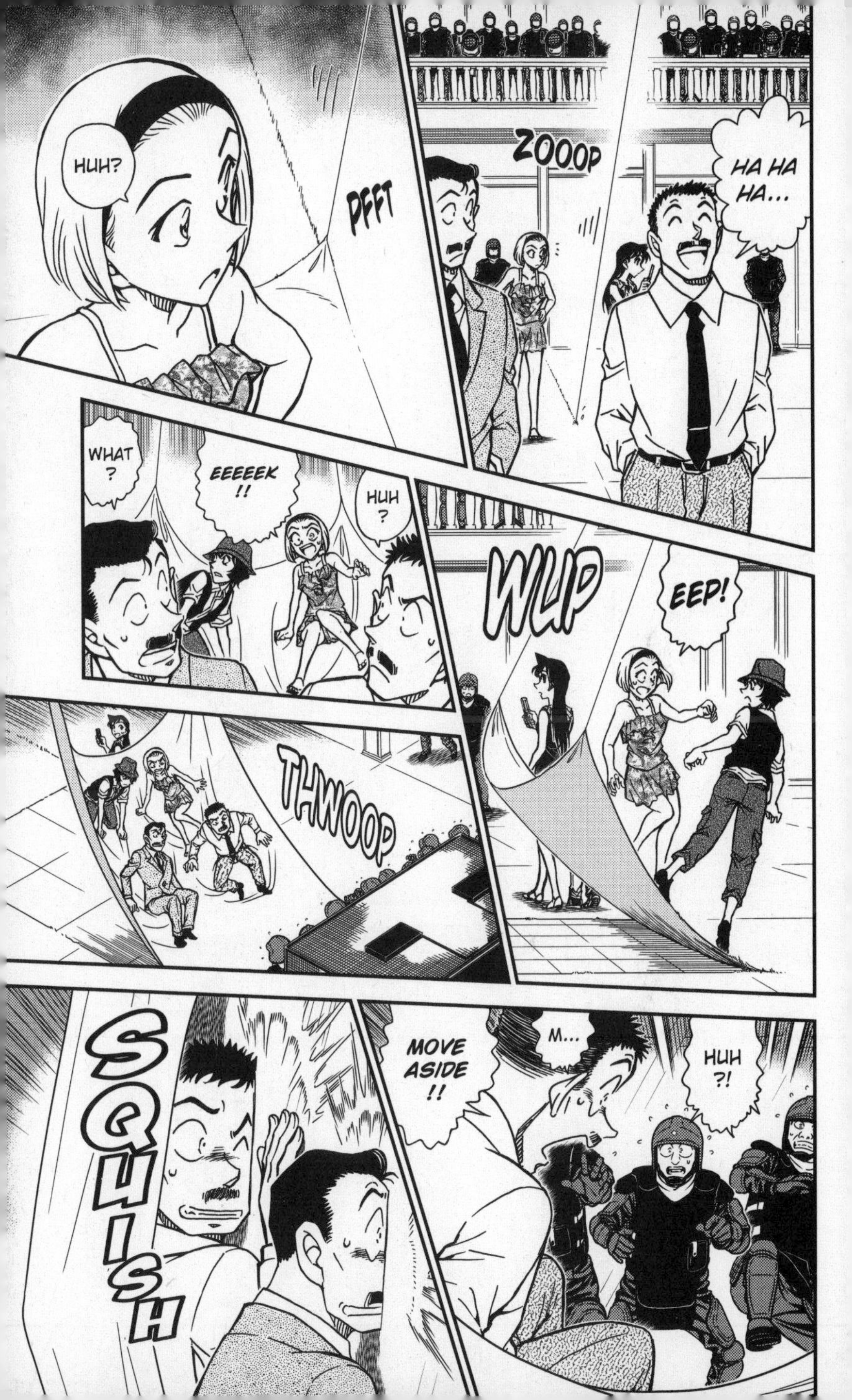

ZOOOP
HA HA HA...
HUH?
PFFT
EEP!
WLIP
HUH?
EEEEEK!!
WHAT?
THWOOP
HUH?!
M...
MOVE ASIDE!!
SQUISH

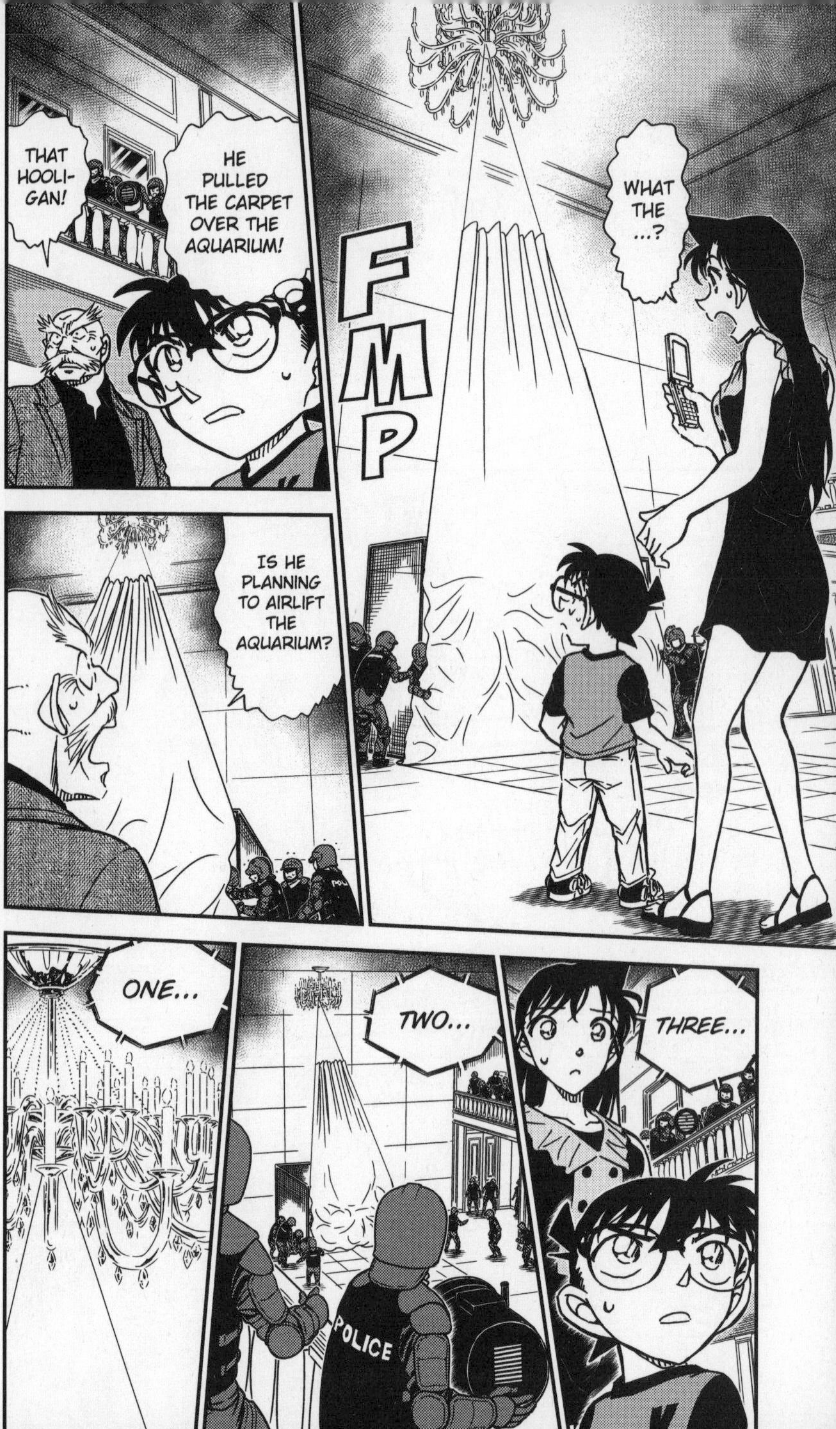
WHAT THE ...?
FMP
HE PULLED THE CARPET OVER THE AQUARIUM!
THAT HOOLI-GAN!
IS HE PLANNING TO AIRLIFT THE AQUARIUM?
ONE...
TWO...
THREE...

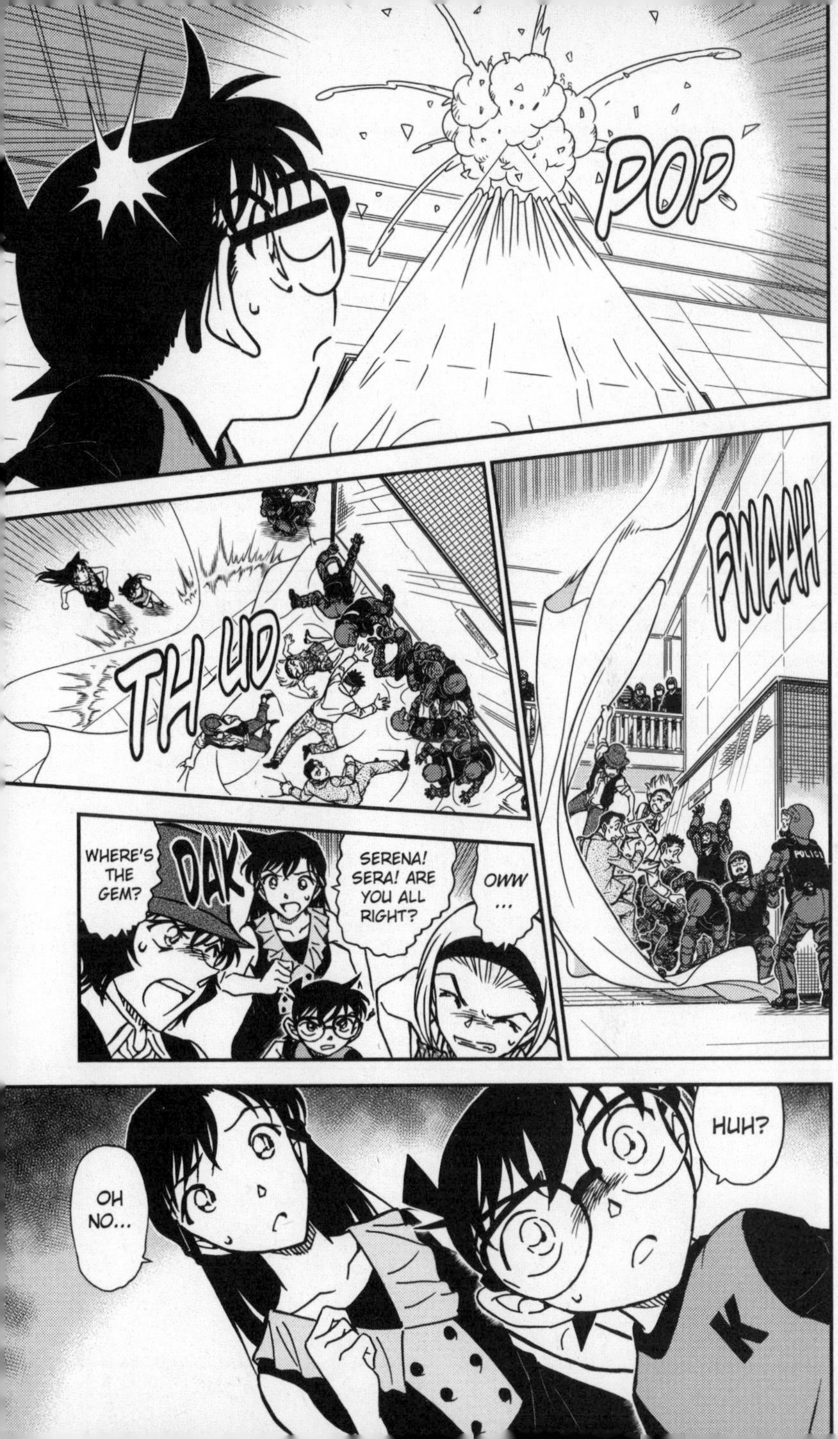
POP
FWAAH
TH UD
OWW ...
SERENA! SERA! ARE YOU ALL RIGHT?
DAK
WHERE'S THE GEM?
HUH?
OH NO...

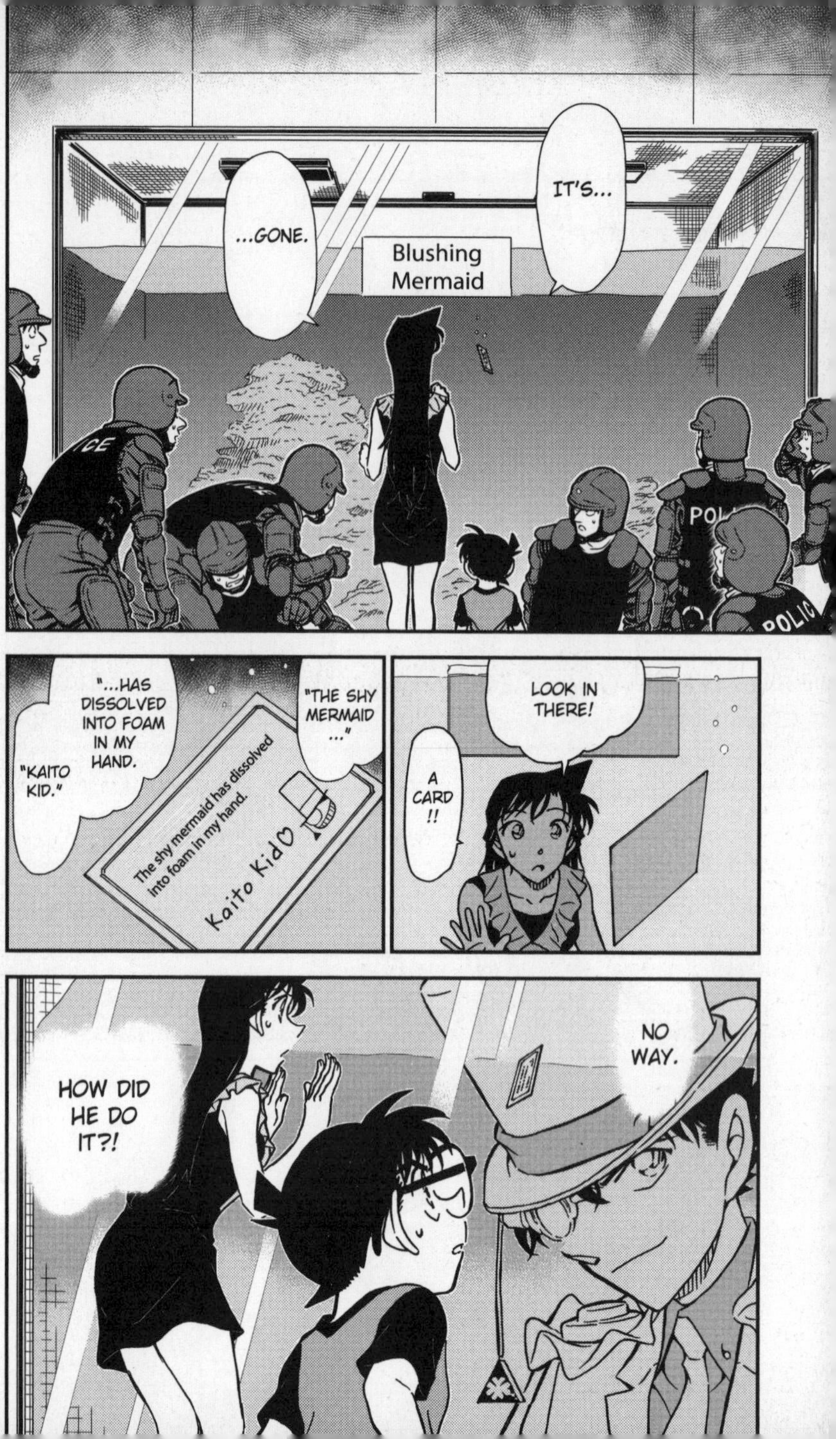
IT'S...
...GONE.
Blushing Mermaid
LOOK IN THERE!
A CARD !!
"THE SHY MERMAID ..."
"...HAS DISSOLVED INTO FOAM IN MY HAND.
"KAITO KID."
The shy mermaid has dissolved into foam in my hand.
Kaito Kid♡
NO WAY.
HOW DID HE DO IT?!

Hello, Aoyama here!

Last month, as I was flying back to my hometown in Tottori for a "Manga Summit" event, I was surprised to hear, "We will soon be arriving at Yonago Kitaro Airport!" Wow, they named an airport after Shigeru Mizuki's beloved manga character Kitaro! Someday the Tottori Airport will become the Tottori Conan Airport...or not. *Heh.*

Gosho Aoyama's
Mystery Library

78

KEISUKE SHIRATORI

Allow me to introduce Keisuke Shiratori, the sleuth who takes a scalpel to the baffling cases of the medical community! A bureaucrat in the Ministry of Health, Labor and Welfare, Shiratori is in charge of investigating deaths from medical malpractice. He's arrogant, and his methods are nothing short of outrageous. He refuses to take a hint and angers people so much with his insensitive comments that he often gets punched... but that's how he psychologically manipulates the guilty. On top of that, he's well versed in medicine, and his use of logic to unveil the truth has earned him the nickname "Logical Monster." His partner, neurologist Kohei Taguchi, who is always at his beck and call, has no choice but to recognize Shiratori's skill.

Author Takeru Kaido is a practicing doctor on top of having written numerous books. Recently I've been troubled by exhaustion, but if he examined me he'd probably just tell me to get more sleep. *Heh.*

I recommend *The Glorious Team Batista.*

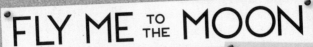

Kidnapped by the Demon King and imprisoned in his castle, Princess Syalis is...bored.

SLEEPY PRINCESS IN THE DEMON CASTLE

Story & Art by
KAGIJI KUMANOMATA

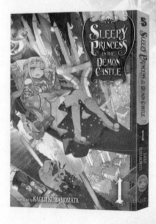

Captured princess Syalis decides to while away her hours in the Demon Castle by sleeping, but getting a good night's rest turns out to be a lot of work! She begins by fashioning a DIY pillow out of the fur of her Teddy Demon guards and an "air mattress" from the magical Shield of the Wind. Things go from bad to worse—for her captors—when some of Princess Syalis's schemes end in her untimely—if temporary—demise and she chooses the Forbidden Grimoire for her bedtime reading...

 VIZ